In recent years, collaboration has emerged as a central component of public administration and nonprofit organization management in practice as well as in theory. Yet, it is way too tempting to simply assume that when two organizations are linked within or across sectors, they will work together— collaboratively and effectively for the public good. With *Advancing Collaboration Theory*, Morris and Miller-Stevens offer us a thoughtful and interesting re-examination of the what's and how's of collaboration. This is a "must read." We are indebted to them.

J. Steven Ott, *University of Utah*

At a time when research on collaboration in the public service has significantly grown but not yet coalesced into a clear and coherent knowledge base, Morris and Miller-Stevens' *Advancing Collaboration Theory* is a welcome addition that fills a critical gap in the current study of collaboration. Deeply rooted in the scholarship, this work charts the major unanswered dilemmas in collaboration research and provides five themes that structure their understanding and exploration of collaboration in the public service. This work contains conceptual and empirical chapters that explore collaboration from multiple perspectives and in multiple settings, shining a bright light on these dilemmas and capturing perspectives on both the process of collaboration and the structures that arise from collaborative endeavors. I have little doubt this book will quickly become required reading for those interested in the study and practice of collaboration in the public service.

Jessica E. Sowa, *University of Colorado Denver*

Advancing Collaboration Theory

The term 'collaboration' is widely used but not clearly understood or operationalized. However, collaboration is playing an increasingly important role between and across public, nonprofit, and for-profit sectors. Collaboration has become a hallmark in both intragovernmental and intergovernmental relationships. As collaboration scholarship rapidly emerges, it diverges into several directions, resulting in confusion about what collaboration is and what it can be used to accomplish. This book provides much-needed insight into existing ideas and theories of collaboration, advancing a revised theoretical model and accompanying typologies that further our understanding of collaborative processes within the public sector.

Organized into three parts, each chapter presents a different theoretical approach to public problems, valuing the collective insights that result from honoring many individual perspectives. Case studies in collaboration, split across three levels of government, offer additional perspectives on unanswered questions in the literature. Contributions are made by authors from a variety of backgrounds, including an attorney, a career educator, a federal executive, a human resource administrator, a police officer, a self-employed entrepreneur, as well as scholars of public administration and public policy. Drawing upon the individual experiences offered by these perspectives, the book emphasizes the commonalities of collaboration. It is from this common ground, the shared experiences forged among seemingly disparate interactions that advances in collaboration theory arise.

Advancing Collaboration Theory offers a unique compilation of collaborative models and typologies that enhance the existing understanding of public-sector collaboration.

John C. Morris is Professor of Public Administration and Ph.D. Graduate Program Director in the School of Public Service at Old Dominion University. He has studied collaboration and public-private partnerships for more than 20 years, and has published widely in public administration and public policy.

Katrina Miller-Stevens is Assistant Professor of Public Administration in the School of Public Service at Old Dominion University. Her research interests include exploring methods of collaboration between the nonprofit and public sectors, advancing policy theory, and examining influence mechanisms of the nonprofit sector on public policy.

Routledge Research in Public Administration and Public Policy

Advancing Collaboration Theory

Models, Typologies, and Evidence

Edited by John C. Morris and
Katrina Miller-Stevens

Routledge
Taylor & Francis Group

LONDON AND NEW YORK

First published 2016 by Routledge

2 Park Square, Milton Park, Abingdon, Oxfordshire OX14 4RN
711 Third Avenue, New York, NY 10017

Routledge is an imprint of the Taylor & Francis Group, an informa business

First issued in paperback 2017

Library of Congress Cataloging-in-Publication Data
A catalog record for this book has been requested

ISBN: 978-1-138-81149-2 (hbk)
ISBN: 978-0-8153-7036-9 (pbk)

Typeset in Sabon
by Wearset Ltd, Boldon, Tyne and Wear

To Molly, Charlotte, Luis, and Laura—*John C. Morris*
To my mom and dad—*Katrina Miller-Stevens*

Contents

Figures

Tables

Contributors

Luisa Diaz-Kope holds a master's degree in Public Administration from Old Dominion University. She is a Ph.D. candidate in public policy and administration at Old Dominion University. Her research interests include collaboration, environmental policy, governance and natural resource management. Her work appears in journals such as *Politics and Policy, Public Works Management & Policy* and the *International Journal of Public Administration.*

Nathan J. Grasse is an Assistant Professor in the School of Public Policy and Administration at Carleton University. He focuses on the governance of public and nonprofit organizations, including the associations between governance and finance, collaboration, organizational behavior, and policy decisions. He has published in journals such as *Nonprofit Management and Leadership, Legislative Studies Quarterly, Public Administration Quarterly,* and *State and Local Government Review.* Dr. Grasse works with both public and nonprofit organizations on projects related to governance, finance, and human resources.

Tiffany Henley holds a master's degree in Government and a certificate in Law and Public Policy from Regent University. Prior to attending Old Dominion University Tiffany worked in the health care industry for over five years. She is presently on a dissertation fellowship and she has taught a course on ethics, governance, and accountability in public service. Her research interests include collaboration, health policy, public policy theory, and nonprofit management.

Robert Kenter holds a master's degree in Public Administration from Troy University, is a 25-year veteran of the Norfolk Police Department, and has over 10 years' experience as a private contractor providing instruction, risk management, risk mitigation, and physical security. His research interests include privatization, accountability, and collaboration. He has coauthored a chapter in *Prison Privatization: The Many Facets of a Controversial Industry.*

Deniz Zeynep Leuenberger is a Professor of Political Science/Public Administration at Bridgewater State University. She is the Coordinator of the

Master of Public Administration Program and the Faculty Director of the Institute for Policy Analysis and Regional Engagement. She is former Coordinator for the Center for Sustainability and is also the past Director of the Institute for Regional Engagement. She is coauthor of "Sustainable Development for Public Administration" and has published a number of book chapters on sustainability and public finance. She has published articles on sustainable development, strategic planning, and caring labor in *Administrative Theory and Praxis, Public Works and Management Policy, State and Local Government Review,* and *Water Policy.* Dr. Leuenberger has over 25 years of experience working with nonprofit organization and government leadership and education. She specializes in sustainable development, finance and budgeting, strategic planning, and leadership development.

Jason S. Machado has a master's degree in Public Administration and is currently a Ph.D. candidate at the University of Colorado, Denver, where he teaches graduate courses in nonprofit management, civil society, and public administration. His research interests include nonprofit advocacy, collaboration, nonprofit board governance, and election administration. He has been published in the journal *Public Administration Review.*

Brian Martinez is a retired naval officer and career civil servant working for the Department of Defense. He is pursuing a Ph.D. in Public Administration at Old Dominion University. Brian received a master's degree in Finance and Management from Webster University, Saint Louis, Missouri. Brian's research interests include interorganizational behavior, network forms of government, and the effects of information and communications technologies (ICTs) on citizenship and governance.

Martin Mayer is currently working as a graduate teaching assistant at Old Dominion University, where he is pursuing a Ph.D. in Public Administration. Prior to enrolling at Old Dominion University, Martin received a master's degree in public administration from the University of Akron. Martin's current research interests include environmental policy, resource management, public-private partnerships, and collaboration.

Amy McDowell is an Education Program Manager with the National Center for State Courts and adjunct instructor at Old Dominion University. Her research interests include policy issues within the state courts, human resources management, ethics, and administrative law. She has published in *Public Personnel Management,* coauthored a chapter in *Prison Privatization: The Many Facets of a Controversial Industry,* and coauthored the monograph *Short, Summary & Expedited: The Evolution of Civil Jury Trials.* She is Associate Editor for *Judicial Education and Training: The Journal of the International Organization for Judicial Training* and a former editor of the annual publication *Future Trends in State Courts.* Amy received a JD from the University of Richmond, T.C. Williams School of Law, and a MPA from Old Dominion University.

Madeleine W. McNamara is a Visiting Assistant Professor of Public Administration in the Department of Political Science at the University of New Orleans. Prior to her academic appointment, Dr. McNamara served as the Waterways Management Coordinator for the U.S. Coast Guard's Eighth District in New Orleans. She holds a Ph.D. and MBA from Old Dominion University in Norfolk, VA, and is a graduate of the U.S. Coast Guard Academy in New London, CT. Her research interests include collaboration, public policy, and interorganizational theory. Her work appears in journals such as *Public Works Management & Policy*, the *International Journal of Public Administration, Policy & Politics*, and the *Journal for Nonprofit Management*, among others. In addition, she authored a chapter in *Speaking Green with a Southern Accent: Environmental Management and Innovation in the South*.

Stephanie Joannou Menefee is currently working as a graduate research assistant at Old Dominion University, where she is pursuing a Ph.D. in public administration. Stephanie also obtained her master's in public administration from Old Dominion University. Stephanie's current research interests include alternative dispute resolution, collaboration, politics, and the behavior of governing bodies.

Connie Merriman is Assistant Dean and Director of the Executive Mentor Program in the Strome College of Business at Old Dominion University. Her research interests include leadership, ethics, and adjunct/contingent faculty and their role in higher education. She teaches courses in leadership, cultural competence, and communication at the graduate and undergraduate levels. Dr. Merriman holds a Ph.D. in Higher Education Administration and a Master of Public Administration, both from Old Dominion University.

Katrina Miller-Stevens is an Assistant Professor of Nonprofit Management and Public Policy in the School of Public Service at Old Dominion University. Her research interests include exploring methods of collaboration between the nonprofit and public sectors, advancing policy theory, and examining influence mechanisms of the nonprofit sector on public policy. Her work can be found in nonprofit management and public policy journals. She has served as a consultant for national, state, and local government projects researching community partnerships including the *Navy Fleet and Family Support Program's Community Capacity Study*, the *Virginia State of Early Childhood Initiative*, and the *Virginia Beach Housing Crisis Response System*.

John C. Morris is a Professor of Public Administration and Chair of the School of Public Service at Old Dominion University. He has studied collaboration and public-private partnerships for more than 20 years, and has published widely in public administration and public policy. He is the co-editor of *Speaking Green with a Southern Accent: Environmental Management and Innovation in the South* (2010, Lexington

Press) and *True Green: Executive Effectiveness in the US Environmental Protection Agency* (2012, Lexington Press). Dr. Morris is also the co-editor of *Building the Local Economy: Cases in Economic Development*, published by the Carl Vinson Institute of Government, University of Georgia, in 2008, and is the co-editor of a three-volume series (2012, Praeger) on prison privatization, titled *Prison Privatization: The Many Facets of a Controversial Industry*. His latest book is *The Case for Grassroots Collaboration: Social Capital and Ecosystem Restoration at the Local Level* (2013, Lexington Press). In addition, he has published more than 50 articles in refereed journals, and nearly 30 book chapters, reports, and other publications.

Christine Reed is a Professor in the School of Public Administration, University of Nebraska, Omaha. She earned her Ph.D. in Political Science from Brown University in 1983, and worked at the Bureau of Government Research, University of Rhode Island, National Community Development Association, and U.S. Department of Housing and Urban Development Office of Policy Development and Research before joining the UNO faculty in 1982. Dr. Reed also served for several years as Associate Vice Chancellor for Research and Dean of Graduate Studies at UNO. Her current research interests are in environmental collaborative governance, federal and local cooperation in the public management of wild horses, and animal and environmental ethics. Dr. Reed has published in all of these areas, including a forthcoming book from University of Nevada Press, titled *Saving the Pryor Mountain Mustang: A Legacy of Local and Federal Cooperation*, and a recent article in *Water Policy* titled "Social Capital in Large-Scale Environmental Collaboration: The Case of the Platte River Recovery Implementation Program," coauthored with Deniz Leuenberger and others. Research on the Platte River program is funded by the University of Nebraska Daugherty Water for Food Institute. Dr. Reed has also published in the journals *Environmental Values* and *International Journal of Public Administration* on the role of wild horses in ecological restoration, comparing public policies in the U.S. and the Netherlands.

Kevin D. Ward is an Assistant Professor in the Institute of Public Service at Seattle University where he teaches courses in public and nonprofit management, governance, and public policy. His research interests include national service programs such as AmeriCorps, nonprofit governance, motivation, and cross-sector collaboration. His work has appeared in *Public Administration Review*, *Public Personnel Management*, *Risk, Hazards, & Crisis in Public Policy* and *Journal of Nonprofit Education and Leadership*. He holds a Ph.D. from the School of Public Affairs at the University of Colorado, Denver.

Andrew P. Williams is a British national working as a policy analyst for NATO in the U.S. His research interests are in collaboration theory, program evaluation, and complexity sciences. He has recent publications in the *American Journal of Evaluation, Voluntas, International Command and Control Journal*, and *Journal of Cooperation and Conflict*. His latest book is *Advances in Measuring Progress in Conflict Environments*, published by NATO. He has conducted a variety of research studies on NATO program evaluation techniques, civil-military interaction, organizational collaboration, and relationships with private military security companies. Prior to working at NATO, he worked as an analyst for a UK defense agency. He holds a Masters of Physics from the University of Manchester, and is a Ph.D. candidate in public policy and administration at Old Dominion University.

Christopher M. Williams is program analyst for the U.S. Navy. His primary research interest is decision-making in the areas of maritime policy, port governance, and naval acquisitions. He served 21 years in the U.S. Navy as a Surface Warfare Officer and spent five years as an operational tester of naval vessel acquisitions. Chris holds a master's degree in public administration from Old Dominion University, where he is also pursuing a doctoral degree.

Acknowledgments

This project began as the result of two graduate seminars in collaboration taught at Old Dominion University in 2012 and 2013. The doctoral students in those seminars produced a set of truly outstanding papers, in which they addressed some of the more important issues in the collaboration literature. Those papers served as the genesis for this volume. Over time some of the original participants moved on to other things, and the project grew to include several people who were not part of the original group. We gratefully acknowledge the contributions of all of the seminar participants, including those whose work does not appear directly in this collection. Their contributions are inextricably woven into the ideas, approaches, and conclusions herein.

We would also like to thank a number of students who provided important assistance to bring this book to fruition. Luisa Diaz-Kope and Andy Williams, both contributors to this volume, both went above and beyond to provide critical insight, feedback, and reviews of chapters, and their efforts are gratefully acknowledged. Tiffany Henley, Somayeh Hooshmand, and Eric Schweitzer served as our Graduate Assistants, and were instrumental in preparing the final manuscript for submission. We also thank Meg Jones, Program Manager in the School of Public Service at Old Dominion University, for her support. We would also like to thank our editor at Routledge, Natalja Mortensen, and her team of highly competent colleagues, who were most helpful and supportive as we brought this manuscript to life. We also thank our copyeditor, Sarah Davies, for her significant contributions to this manuscript.

Finally, we wish to thank our families for their love and support during this project. Without their help, this book would remain just another unfulfilled promise.

Part I

Framing and Definition

1   The State of Knowledge in Collaboration

John C. Morris and Katrina Miller-Stevens

Introduction

Thirty years ago, Barbara Gray (1985) published an article entitled "Conditions Facilitating Interorganizational Collaboration" in the journal *Human Relations*. Drawing heavily from the literature on interorganizational theory, Gray (1985) argued:

> There is a growing need to promote collaborative problem solving across various sectors of society.... Organizing such collaborative efforts requires focusing on the interorganizational domain or set of interdependencies which link various stakeholders rather than on the actions of any single organization.
>
> (p. 911)

Gray's research was focused not only on an interorganizational environment, but an inter-sectoral environment as well. More traditional conceptions of the interorganizational space tended to engage either public-sector settings, in which legal authorities entrusted to organizations determined the kinds of interactions possible (see Barnard, 1938; Simon, 1997; Weber, 1968), or the private sector and market-based systems that were governed entirely by free market forces (see Buchanan & Tullock, 1962; Lawrence & Lorsch, 1978). Other scholars (e.g., Niskanen, 1994; North, 1990; Olson, 1965; E. Ostrom, 1990; V. Ostrom, 1989) argued that market values and processes should be applied to the public sector, but there was no body of literature suggesting a truly cross-sectoral approach to problem-solving. In this sense, Gray was truly an intellectual pioneer.[1]

Gray identified four ways in which her work was distinct from previous work. First, Gray (1985) focuses her analytical attention on the set of relationships present across an interorganizational domain, rather than focusing on a central (or referent) organization. For Gray, all of the relationships in the system are important, not just those involving the referent organization. Second, her work focuses on "underorganized domains" (Gray, 1985, p. 912); those that are not already engaged in highly structured networks or structures. This allows Gray to address the conditions that might allow the development of collaborative structures.

Third, Gray is concerned with settings in which "wicked problems" (Rittel & Webber, 1973) exist. In Gray's (1985) terms, these are "…domains which cannot be satisfactorily managed by a single organization or by an oligopoly" (p. 913). Wicked problems are thus problems that defy solutions (or even definitions), and that cannot be addressed satisfactorily by single organizations. Finally, Gray's work examines the set of relationships and behaviors that develop within the setting, from the premise that the set of relationships present defines the domain, rather than assuming that the type of domain present controls the behaviors and relationships present (Gray, 1985, p. 913). From the perspective of hindsight, Gray's early work arguably proved to be the foundational piece in this stream of literature. She followed the publication of her article four years later with her book *Collaborating* (1989), which more fully developed the arguments and propositions offered in the initial article, and offered a series of case study vignettes to illustrate her arguments.

Gray's work opened a floodgate of new research, as scholars began to explore more fully the theoretical and practical implications of her ideas. Early in this process, the scholarship began to move away from the explicitly interorganizational underpinnings of Gray's work, as many scholars approached collaboration as a study of institutional networks. The relatively informal nature of collaboration (when compared to more traditional authoritative interorganizational conceptualizations) lent itself well to a network approach. In this respect: relationships were not governed by an established set of rules; barriers to entry and exit were largely nonexistent; traditional public-sector accountability mechanisms, especially for both resources and outcomes, were inappropriate; and traditional conceptions of leadership were not appropriate for the setting. Personal relationships and connections were important, and power and authority were likely to be shared equally among participants. For these reasons, much of the scholarship in these early years was written by those with a strong interest in network theory.

The literature has progressed significantly in the intervening years, and scholars have brought a number of different perspectives to bear on the study of collaboration. Many articles have been written from the perspective of collaborative management (Koontz & Thomas, 2006; Leach, 2006; McNamara, 2012; Selin & Chavez, 1995; see also O'Leary & Bingham, 2009), accountability mechanisms (Bardach & Lesser, 1996; Page, 2004; Romzek, LeRoux, & Blackmar, 2012), goal-setting (Gray, 1989; Wood & Gray, 1991), collaboration as governance (Agranoff & McGuire, 1999; Ansell & Gash, 2007; Emerson, Nabatchi, & Balogh, 2011; Imperial, 2005; Provan & Kenis, 2007), and others. Throughout this period some questions about collaboration have been settled, but many more are left unanswered, and even unasked. The purpose of this volume is to examine the state of knowledge in collaboration theory and practice; we seek to provide insight into existing ideas and theories of collaboration, determine the state of knowledge in the study of collaboration, identify some of the unasked questions in the field, and offer some thoughts about questions that are at the cutting edge of collaboration research. Finally, we offer some cases to illustrate how these issues translate to help us understand collaborative processes within the public sector.

Five Themes

We begin this process by developing five overarching themes that thread their way through the chapters in this volume. Taken collectively, these chapters examine these themes in some detail, seek to identify the current state of knowledge inherent in these themes, and identify issues for future research.

Definitional Clarity is a Challenge

In the spring of 2012 we offered a graduate seminar in collaboration. As an exercise in definitional clarity, we invited students to review a group of about 30 journal articles in collaboration. The articles ranged from Gray's (1985) work to articles published in 2012, and many were chosen because they represented important contributions to the body of literature. The purpose of the exercise was to note all of the definitional elements included in each of the articles. While there were a number of elements that were included by subsets of authors, the list included more than 60 different definitional elements (many of which were included by only one author). No single element was included in more than one-third of the articles reviewed.

The wide variability noted in this vignette is endemic in the academic literature. At the same time, there are reasonable arguments both for and against definitional clarity. Definitional clarity can lead to a greater degree of both certainty and specificity in terms of the phenomenon under study. If those engaged in the discussion share a common definition, effective communication and shared knowledge are optimized. Greater definitional clarity also enhances learning, especially for students new to the literature. To the extent that academics are clear on a definition, the lessons and knowledge passed to practitioners can be more effective.

The same issue was noted by Wood and Gray (1991) more than 20 years ago. In their introduction to a journal symposium on collaboration (Wood & Gray, 1991), they wrote that:

> Definitions are crucial to theory building. A general theory of collaboration must begin with a definition of the phenomena that encompasses all observable forms and excludes irrelevant issues. We began our work on these special issues assuming that a commonly accepted definition of collaboration existed and that we could move quickly beyond this primal task. Instead, we found a welter of definitions, each

having something to offer and none being entirely satisfactory by
itself.

(p. 143)

On the other hand, one may reasonably argue that firm definitions of
complex and multifaceted human interactions suppress the ability to detect
nuances in observed behaviors that might otherwise prove to be empirically or theoretically important. A definition explains what a 'thing' is, but
it also defines what it is not. It may also be argued that the study of collaboration is still in its infancy, and that we do not yet understand the behavior well enough to arrive at a clear, useful, and relatively universal
definition. Finally, singular definitions tend to support the status quo at the
expense of creativity and scholarship outside of "normal science" (Kuhn,
1996).

Regardless of one's position on this question, the empirical evidence
suggests that we do not have a clear and widely accepted definition of the
phenomenon under study, even a quarter-century after Wood and Gray's
(1991) observation. The implications of this fact are an important theme
of this book, whether it is addressed as an issue of theoretical development,
or whether implications for practitioners are brought into focus.

Collaboration is Constantly Evolving

As noted earlier in this chapter, the study of collaboration is a relatively
young enterprise. Much like the early development of the literature in
implementation studies (see O'Toole, 1986), one may argue that collaboration research has seen steep growth in the number of studies, models, and
theories published. These efforts may seem somewhat haphazard and
undifferentiated at first, but like the implementation literature, one may
detect certain characteristics in the literature. While other chapters in this
volume will address those characteristics in more detail, our initial point is
that the steep growth in the number of collaboration studies published,
coupled with the definitional challenges noted above, indicates a field of
study in a state of constant and rapid development. As we refine our theories and models, we move collectively toward a more complete understanding of this form of interaction.

The same may be said of collaboration in practice. While the nature of
the gulf between theory and practice in public administration is beyond the
scope of this discussion, we understand intuitively that the practitioner's
view of the world (and the terms in which they describe that world) does
not always match with the views and terms found in academia. Practitioners have been employing 'collaboration' in the workplace for many years,
yet there is no more agreement among practitioners as to the definition and
operation of 'collaboration' than there is among academics. Moreover, the
term 'collaboration' may carry a different perception than 'coordination'
(for example: 'working together' vs. 'directing'), leading practitioners to

adopt different terms for the same activity, or, conversely, the same term for different activities. Still, as collaboration becomes more commonly taught in Master of Public Administration (MPA) programs and as those graduates enter the public workforce, it is more than likely that the different approaches to collaboration will find their way into both the practice and the lexicon of practitioners. The effect will be that the nature of collaboration, as practiced in the workplace, will evolve as well.

Collaboration can be Understood as Both Organizational Process and Structure

Distilled to its essence, collaboration is necessarily a group activity involving two or more people. Collaboration is an interaction that takes place between people, or organizations, or both, in a wide range of settings. In this regard, we suggest that Gray (1985, 1989) provides a useful basis for collaboration. Likewise, more recent work that treats collaboration from a distinctly network perspective is also useful. Within these arenas, one may identify literature that seeks to classify collaboration as one of several forms of organizational interaction (e.g., Imperial, 2005; McNamara, 2012). Most of these works tend to focus specifically on an interorganizational domain, much as Gray did. The underlying assumption is that collaboration takes place in an explicitly interorganizational environment, and the research questions tend to address questions of resource-sharing, goal-setting, and outputs or outcomes of the observed activity.

Other streams in the literature treat collaboration as an organizational process. Agranoff and McGuire's (1999) foundational piece on collaborative management has spawned a great deal of additional work designed to understand how collaborations are administered. Specific streams in this arena focus on goal-setting (Gray, 1989; Wood & Gray, 1991), leadership (Agranoff & McGuire, 2003; Weber & Khademian, 2008), accountability (Bardach & Lesser, 1996; Page, 2004), and decision-making (Glass, 1979; Kaner, 1996; Smith, Nell, & Prystupa, 1997), among others. Much of the empirical work in this tradition is case based and exploratory, and is often concerned with drawing comparisons between traditional public management and collaborative management.

Not all Collaboration is Equal

A relatively new stream in the literature revolves around attempts to classify different forms of collaboration, usually along a continuum of action (see Imperial, 2005; Keast, Brown, & Mandell, 2007; McNamara, 2012). Generally conceived as an ordinal scale, theorists attempt to place different forms of interaction on a scale based on a set of characteristics. The underlying idea is that these interactions can be classified in unidimensional space. More recent work has begun to suggest that, because collaboration can be thought of as a point along a continuum, there must be other similar interactions possible in proximity to 'collaboration.' This work has in turn led to the observation that not all collaboration is equal.

The work of early theorists in collaboration defined the interaction as voluntary in nature—that is, participants could choose to participate or not (Gray, 1989). However, other work (see Jennings & Krane, 1994) pointed out that public agencies may be required by higher political authority to engage in collaboration; such mandates may fundamentally alter the nature of the interaction. While mandated collaboration may have elements in common with voluntary collaboration, the presence of a mandate may be seen as somewhat closer on the continuum to coordination (see Kaiser, 2011; Mandell & Steelman, 2003).[2] Likewise, Moore and Koontz (2003) created a typology of collaboration based on the nature of the preponderance of members in the interaction—agency based, mixed, or citizen based. This typology sought to further distinguish between different types of collaboration.

Taken as a whole, these efforts lead us to conclude that, if different types of collaboration can exist, then not all collaboration can be the same. Such efforts are helpful in that they focus attention on the differences between interactions, as well as the underlying constructs employed to define the interactions at the outset. The degree to which these efforts are successful is best left to the observer, but they do offer evidence that collaboration is not a singular, monolithic interaction. Rather, collaboration may at best be construed as a highly flexible, adaptable, and fluid form of interaction.

Interdisciplinary Approaches to Collaboration are Fruitful

Like the literature in organization theory, the extant collaboration literature may be found in the journals of many disciplines and sub-fields. In addition to public administration, sociology, and education, collaboration studies may be found in journals in fields as diverse as business management, international relations, environmental management, biology, criminal justice, supply chain management, and psychology. Much like Ludwig von Bertalanffy's (1956) "general systems model," collaboration appears to be a concept that can be employed to understand observed phenomena in many settings. Unlike von Bertalanffy's intent to create a universal theory to allow scholars in different fields to communicate in the same terms, 'collaboration' is a term that not only suffers from a definitional problem in public administration; it suffers from a definitional problem in most disciplines. Collaboration between firms in the private sector often looks more akin to what public administrationists refer to as 'cooperation,' whereas collaboration as defined in the education literature may look more like 'coordination.'[3]

Nonetheless, as several chapters in this book argue, cross-disciplinary approaches to collaboration may help advance the state of knowledge in this arena. Collaboration takes place in many different settings, and understanding the behaviors, conditions, and circumstances that lead to collaborative behavior can help us better comprehend and recognize the strengths and weaknesses of our own efforts in both theory-building and testing.

Organization of This Book

As noted earlier in this chapter, the purpose of this book is to examine the state of knowledge in collaboration theory and practice. To accomplish this task, the book has been divided into three parts: Framing and Definition, Advancing Theory, and Collaboration in Action. The first part explores different interpretations of collaboration as presented in the current body of literature on this topic. The second part introduces new theories and frameworks that help explain elements and processes of collaboration. The third part presents exemplary cases that illustrate the practical application of collaboration. While much of the volume explores the current state of the literature, we also provide new models and perspectives on collaboration to advance this body of knowledge. We encourage you to keep in mind the five themes noted previously in this chapter, as each theme is woven throughout the volume.

The book begins with a section dedicated to the definitional aspects of collaboration, because we believe this issue is at the forefront of the discussion and research in this area. Andrew P. Williams (Chapter 2) starts this section by reviewing two main bodies of collaboration literature in public administration: collaboration frameworks, which emphasize input–process–outcome relationships and process dynamics; and typologies of interorganizational forms and continuums of interaction, which describe specific construct and operationalizations of collaboration and interorganizational interaction more generally. Mayer and Kenter (Chapter 3) address the definitional clarity question by exploring the prevailing elements of public-sector collaboration in three decades of extant research. The authors identify nine components most often found throughout the literature as being critical to the process and success of collaboration. In the next chapter, Madeleine W. McNamara (Chapter 4) expands our understanding of collaboration by unraveling the characteristics of mandated and voluntary collaboration along the continuum of cooperation–coordination–collaboration.

Part II of the volume focuses on the theoretical development of collaboration. Grasse and Ward (Chapter 5) apply theories from the field of biology to better understand cooperative and collaborative activities among nonprofit organizations. A typology of cooperative and collaborative organizational arrangements is developed that provides a language useful to discussing the vast array of arrangements utilized by nonprofit organizations.

In Chapter 6, McNamara suggests that the term 'collaborative entrepreneur' more accurately captures the strategic component involved in inviting participants to a collaborative arrangement. Through an intersection of the collaborative management and policy literatures, a skill set for the collaborative entrepreneur is presented.

The next three chapters propose new frameworks or models to explain specific elements of collaboration. Stephanie Joannou Menefee (Chapter 7) addresses the unexplored aspects of conflict transformation in the operation and sustainment of collaborative efforts. In this chapter, she proposes a framework to help explain conflict in the collaborative process. In Chapter 8, Miller-Stevens, Henley, and Diaz-Kope argue that collaborative federalism can be best understood as a nested system comprised of three types of governance structures including interagency governance, cross-sector governance, and grassroots governance. They offer a new model to explain the multidimensional nature of collaborative federalism.

This part concludes with a chapter that takes an organizational theory approach to collaboration. Williams, Merriman, and Morris (Chapter 9) apply an organizational life-cycle model to collaboration by examining the commonalities between collaborative arrangements and traditional organizational structures. The authors present a collaboration life cycle comprised of six phases including issue, assembly and structure, productivity, decline, rejuvenation, and dissipation.

The final part of this book is a collection of cases that illustrate collaboration in action. This section moves the reader from the definitional and theoretical aspects of collaboration to explore collaboration in specific real-world settings. In Chapter 10, Miller-Stevens, Machado, and Joannou Menefee seek to identify whether organizational characteristics impact the likelihood of a nonprofit organization to collaborate with nonprofit, private, or public-sector organizations to lobby or advocate for public policy issues, and whether this tactic is perceived as effective.

Amy McDowell (Chapter 11) explores collaboration in the judiciary setting. She argues that the judiciary's desire to be accountable to the public offers a powerful incentive for collaboration, yet the collaboration literature largely overlooks the role of the judiciary as a collaborative partner. In another setting, Leuenberger and Reed (Chapter 12) examine two case studies in which the use of social capital helps to form and sustain collaborative governance by overcoming problems of collective action. They provide evidence that collective action founded on social capital resources provides a means of managing common pool resources in complex public administration arenas. The final context exploring collaboration is offered by Brian Martinez (Chapter 13) who examines the practices of interagency collaboration in the national security domain. Martinez determines how interagency collaboration distinguishes itself as a unique form of collaboration, and how the interagency experience in the national security domain is different from interagency collaboration outside this domain.

We conclude the volume by revisiting the themes presented in Chapter 1 and addressing how they are woven throughout the book. We then present unanswered questions and streams of inquiry in the area of collaboration that can be addressed in future research endeavors.

Notes

1 Of course, Gray's work did not appear in a vacuum. Gray was heavily influenced by a series of theoretical streams, including the then-burgeoning literature on interorganizational theory. While much of the earlier literature describes both theories and empirical findings that look much like 'collaboration,' we credit Gray with explaining how collaboration is distinct from the broader interorganizational theory literature, and for using the term 'collaboration' to describe a specific form of interorganizational interaction. Gray's 1985 work can thus be reasonably viewed as the 'starting point' for the body of collaboration literature.

2 The specific differences between 'collaboration' and 'mandated collaboration' are addressed in Chapter 4. For our immediate purpose, we suggest that an important difference is that 'collaboration' is usually defined as a voluntary action, whereas 'mandated collaboration' requires participation of at least some actors (i.e., participation is not voluntary).

3 Later chapters in this volume will address the definitional questions in more detail. In terms of the present discussion, we suggest these forms of interaction are distinct, and thus may be defined as discrete arrangements.

References

Agranoff, R., & McGuire, M. (1999). Managing in network settings. *Policy Studies Review, 16*(1), 18–41.

Agranoff, R., & McGuire, M. (2003). *Collaborative public management: New strategies for local government.* Washington, DC: Georgetown University Press.

Ansell, C., & Gash, A. (2007). Collaboration governance in theory and practice. *Journal of Public Administration Research and Theory, 18*, 543–571.

Bardach, E., & Lesser, C. (1996). Accountability in human services collaboratives: For what? And To Whom? *Journal of Public Administration Research Theory, 2*, 197–224.

Barnard, C. (1938). *The functions of the executive.* Cambridge, MA: Harvard University Press.

Buchanan, J. M., & Tullock, G. (1962). *The calculus of consent.* Ann Arbor, MI: University of Michigan Press.

Emerson, K., Nabatchi, T., & Balogh, S. (2011). An integration framework for collaboration governance. *Journal of Public Administration Research and Theory, 22*, 1–19.

Glass, J. (1979). Citizen participation in planning: The relationship between objectives and techniques. *Journal of the American Planning Association, 45*(2), 180–189.

Gray, B. (1985). Conditions facilitating interorganizational collaboration. *Human Relations, 38*(10), 911–936.

Gray, B. (1989). *Collaborating: Finding common ground for multiparty problems.* San Francisco, CA: Jossey-Bass.

Imperial, M. (2005). Using collaboration as a governance strategy: Lessons from six watershed management programs. *Administration & Society, 37*(3), 281–320.

Jennings, E. T., Jr., & Krane, D. (1994). Coordination and welfare reform: The quest for the philosopher's stone. *Public Administration Review, 54*(4), 341–348.

Kaiser, F. (2011). *Interagency collaborative arrangements and activities: Types, rationales, considerations.* Washington, DC: Congressional Research Service.

Kaner, S. (1996). *Facilitator's guide to participatory decision making.* Gabriola Island, British Columbia: New Society Publishers.

Keast, R., Brown, K., & Mandell, M. (2007). Getting the right mix: Unpacking integration, meanings and strategies. *International Public Management Journal,* 10(1), 9–33.

Koontz, T., & Thomas, C. (2006). What do we know and need to know about the environmental outcomes of collaborative management? *Public Administrative Review,* 66(Special Issue), 111–121.

Kuhn, T. S. (1996). *The structure of scientific revolutions* (3rd ed.). Chicago, IL: University of Chicago Press.

Lawrence, P. R., & Lorsch, J. W. (1978). *Organization and environment: Managing differentiation and integration.* Homewood, IL: R. D. Irwin.

Leach, W. (2006). Collaborative public management and democracy: Evidence from western watershed partnerships. *Public Administrative Review,* 66(Special Issue), 100–110.

McNamara, M. (2012). Starting to untangle the web of cooperation, coordination, and collaboration: A framework for public managers. *International Journal of Public Administration,* 35, 389–401.

Mandell, M., & Steelman, T. (2003). Understanding what can be accomplished through interorganizational innovations. *Public Management Review,* 5(2), 197–224.

Moore, E., & Koontz, T. (2003). A typology of collaborative watershed groups: Citizen-based, agency-based and mixed partnerships. *Society and Natural Resources,* 16, 451–460.

Niskanen, W. A. (1994). *Bureaucracy and public economics.* Aldershot, UK: E. Elgar.

North, D. C. (1990). *Institutions, institutional change and economic performance.* New York, NY: Cambridge University Press.

O'Leary, R., & Bingham, L. B. (Eds.). (2009). *The collaborative public manager: New ideas for the twenty-first century.* Washington, DC: Georgetown University Press.

Olson, M. (1965). *The logic of collective action.* Cambridge, MA: Harvard University Press.

Ostrom, E. (1990). *Governing the commons: The evolution of institutions for collective action.* New York, NY: Cambridge University Press.

Ostrom, V. (1989). *The intellectual crisis in American public administration* (2nd ed.). Tuscaloosa, AL: University of Alabama Press.

O'Toole, L. J., Jr. (1986). Policy recommendations for multi-actor implementation: An assessment of the field. *Journal of Public Policy,* 6(2), 181–210.

Page, S. (2004). Measuring accountability for results in interagency collaboratives. *Public Administration Review,* 64(5), 591–606.

Provan, K., & Kenis, P. (2007). Modes of network governance: Structure, management, and effectiveness. *Journal of Public Administration Research,* 18(2), 229–252.

Rittel, H. W. J., & Webber, M. (1973). Dilemmas in a general theory of planning. *Policy Sciences,* 4, 155–169.

Romzek, B., LeRoux, K., & Blackmar, J. (2012). A preliminary theory of informal accountability among network organizational actors. *Public Administration Review,* 72(3), 442–453.

Selin, S., & Chavez, D. (1995). Developing a collaborative model for environmental planning and management. *Environmental Management,* 19(2), 189–195.

Simon, H. A. (1997). *Administrative behavior: A study of decision-making processes in administrative organizations* (4th ed.). New York, NY: Free Press.

Smith, G., Nell, C., & Prystupa, M. (1997). The converging dynamics of interest representation in resources management. *Environmental Management, 21*(2), 139–146.

von Bertalanffy, L. (1956). *General systems theory: Foundations, development, applications* (Revised ed.). New York, NY: George Braziller.

Weber, E., & Khademian, A. (2008). Managing collaborative processes: Common practices, uncommon circumstances. *Administration and Society, 40*(5), 431–464.

Weber, M. (1968). *Economy and society* (G. Roth & C. Wittich, Eds.). Berkeley, CA: University of California Press.

Wood, D., & Gray, B. (1991). Toward a comprehensive theory of collaboration. *Journal of Applied Behavioral Science, 27*(2), 139–162.

2 The Development of Collaboration Theory

Typologies and Systems Approaches

Andrew P. Williams

Introduction

As a fundamental aspect of human society and part of our basic paradigm and value systems, collaboration has a long history of practice and theory. Some scholars have expressed collaboration in terms of the political traditions of civic republicanism and classic liberalism in America (Perry & Thomson, 2004), whereas others identify American federalism and intergovernmental cooperation as the crucible for collaboration practice (Agranoff & McGuire, 2003; McGuire, 2006). Collaboration is a thread, although often not explicitly mentioned, which runs throughout the broader disciplines of public administration and policy implementation (Head & Alford, 2013; O'Toole, 1986).

Yet even given the pervasiveness of collaboration in public administration research, there are several challenges to its study. There is neither a unified nor distinct theory of collaboration, but rather a complex set of entangled threads of theory linking back to precursor theory in organizational science (Alter & Hage, 1993), group psychology (Fisher, 1990), conflict resolution and management (Fisher, Ury, & Patton, 1991; Kriesberg, 2007), conflict stakeholder theory (Barringer & Harrison, 2000) and institutionalism (Ostrom, 2007). Given that collaborations are complex organizational entities in their own right, theory development is often thematic, with scholars focusing on one or two particular concepts in detail such as accountability (Bardach & Lesser, 1996), trust (Mitchell, Ripley, Adams, & Raju, 2011), leadership (Getha-Taylor & Morse, 2013), or membership (Huxham & Vangen, 2000). Consequently, there is comparatively little theoretical work viewing collaboration as a total system, although the literature is growing in both collaboration and the related field of networks (Huxham & Vangen, 2005; Keast, Brown, & Mandell, 2007; Parmigiani & Rivera-Santos, 2011).

Unpacking and analyzing this theoretical literature is challenging as terminology is used inconsistently across theoretical disciplines, and, more fundamentally, scholars have emphasized different and often competing theoretical lineages to varying extents in conceptualization of collaboration. Collaboration can be studied at different levels of analysis: individual, group, organization, or society. Similarly, collaboration can occur on different scales, depending on the particular 'unit' involved (Emerson, Nabatchi, & Balogh, 2012). A large body of literature, for example, covers 'collaboration' between individuals that occurs in 'teamwork' (Bedwell et al., 2012). Collaboration may occur between groups, organizations, individuals, and various combinations of these units.

In order to consider the future of collaboration theory, we need to understand the numerous threads of thought that form the discipline's knowledge base. This chapter unravels several such threads by focusing on two important groups of literature emphasizing an organizational perspective in collaboration. The first group can be considered as the mainstay of contemporary collaboration theory in the public administration literature, which exists in the form of systems-based frameworks. These frameworks view collaboration as a dynamic organizational system set in a wider environment. The second group encompasses the literature on typologies and 'interorganizational arrays,' which specify constructs and operationalizations of collaboration and other related interaction terms, and help categorize and organize important variables.

The focus in this chapter on these two bodies of literature is important for several reasons. First, with a few notable exceptions (McNamara, 2008; Thomson, 2001), there has been little attempt at rigorous theoretical conceptualization of collaboration for the purpose of empirical research. This has led to a multitude of conceptual frameworks, typologies, definitions, and interchangeable terminology, many of which were developed in case studies. While many of these efforts have merit, cumulative empirical research has suffered in the absence of standardized conceptualization and operationalization. The intermingled usage of 'collaboration,' 'cooperation,' 'coordination', and other interaction terms, is so widespread in general organizational life that these terms are practically interchangeable for most practitioners—and even many scholars. This results in a loss of appreciation of the conceptual richness inherent in these constructs, and the potential for unknown and unintentional confusion, or intentional political distortion. A key role for academic research should be to establish rigorous and empirically grounded conceptual frameworks and accompanying terminologies, which can prevent miscommunications or distortions in practice.

The second—and more practice-related reason—concerns the way in which the concept of collaboration is used by actual organizations. The idea that governance is now more important than government is commonplace in recent policy and administration literature, thus increasing the emphasis on studying how organizations work together rather than solely how individual organizations work (O'Leary & Bingham, 2009). Both practitioners and scholars of public administration need to ask important questions about performance, effectiveness, and outcomes in this new landscape. Collaboration is often a formal requirement for organizations, and a developing stream of research looks at how to evaluate joint efforts

(Cross, Dickmann, Newman-Gonchar, & Fagan, 2009; Woodland & Hutton, 2012). It is imperative for future empirical research and evaluation that suitable tools exist to study the various forms of collaboration and its antecedents, processes, and outcomes.

The first section of this book considers how collaboration is framed and defined, and part of this endeavor must begin with considering the broader theoretical base from which definitions are derived. Thus this chapter proceeds as follows. First, we review systems-based collaboration frameworks primarily from public administration scholarship and organizational, behavioral, and political science works that have significantly informed public administration literature. Second, we examine literature on typologies and 'interorganizational arrays,' which specify constructs and operationalizations of collaboration and other related interaction terms. Finally, we compare and contrast these two bodies of knowledge and draw further recommendations for study. A chapter of this length cannot do justice to the entire body of literature, thus this review is limited in scope to works found mainly in the public administration field covering public- and third-sector organizations, rather than similar works from business and management scholars focusing on private organizations. We also must omit the strong body of scholarship on networks, which overlaps considerably with the collaboration literature.

Collaboration Frameworks and Theory

Given that collaborations occur as dynamic processes in complex organizational and institutional settings, there are many variables to consider (Emerson et al., 2012). Scholars have made a variety of attempts to describe these variables and their interactions. Most attempts are examples of "frameworks," as Ostrom (2005) termed them, which strive to organize, order, and prioritize key variables for further theoretical refinement. Much of the collaboration framework literature stems from work of early system theorists, who recognized that social systems could be represented in the form of input-process-output frameworks. Easton's (1957) political system framework, for example, describes a general political system as one that converts inputs into outputs, with a feedback loop connecting back to the inputs, all nested within a wider contextual environment. While this approach was critiqued as overly general, it laid the foundation for a way of thinking about and ordering research on complex organizational systems; the vast majority of collaboration framework literature adopts this basic systems approach. This section reviews key collaboration frameworks from the past two decades.

Early Systems-Based Frameworks

Frameworks vary in their level of detail and specificity. Some simply organize important variables in the categories of inputs, processes, and outcomes, and suggest basic associations between them at the level of category (e.g., that processes affect outcomes). Some propose hypotheses that a variable in one category affects another category overall (e.g., continuous trust building (a variable in the 'process' category) leads to greater collaboration outcomes (Bryson, Crosby, & Stone, 2006)). Others specify causal paths directly between variables in different categories, causally linking, for example, a specific antecedent variable to a specific process variable (e.g., interdependence between stakeholders (antecedent variable) leads to greater interorganizational communications (process variable) (Gray, 1985)). Furthermore, frameworks operate at varying levels of analysis, although most tend to be multilevel. While all frameworks employ the basic systems template categories of inputs-processes-outputs, some frameworks emphasize the process aspect more so than others.

One of the early and influential frameworks, developed by Gray (1985, 1989), shows associations between antecedent factors, collaborative forms, and outcomes. For example, if the antecedent driver of collaboration is conflict and the expected outcome is a joint agreement, then the collaborative process will likely take the form of a negotiated settlement. Gray (1989) also elaborates "collaborative forms" to specify a sequential process conducted during collaboration: problem setting, direction setting, then implementation. Each of these stages are described by specific activities performed by collaborative groups such as stakeholder or resource identification, establishing ground rules, and searching for information jointly (Gray, 1989).

Gray is explicit about the boundary of application of her framework. Its level of analysis is the interorganizational domain, where a domain is the "set of actors that become joined by a common problem or interest" (Gray, 1985, p. 921) and the problem is one that cannot be dealt with unilaterally by any single organization. The framework applies only to "underorganized systems," meaning that domains are characterized by loosely connected networks, rather than well-established collaborations. The three stage process of collaboration conveys moving from a state of low intensity to higher intensity interorganizational interaction, thus capturing the full development process from initial conditions to collaboration.

Gray and Wood (1991) emphasize the process aspect of collaboration, which was recognized to be under-theorized. In another similar framework that emphasizes process but omits inputs and outputs, Ring and Van de Ven (1994) analyze how interorganizational relationships develop and dissolve over time. In a work that is foundational to much of the collaboration literature, they describe an iterative and cyclical process of negotiation, developing commitment, and implementation, with assessments of each stage. If organizations negotiate and then develop certain expectations about necessary collaborative action, they will then commit to certain steps of implementation. If organizations assess that commitments are met, then they will increase their mutual commitments to further implementation. If commitments are not met, then corrective measures will be taken to potentially de-escalate their commitment or the implementation overall (Thomson & Perry, 2006).

Ring and Van de Ven's (1994) framework is multilevel. The overall framework explains, at the interorganizational domain level, how organizations develop interorganizational relationships involving mutual commitments and trust at the organizational level; however, the explanatory variables are all individual or group-level phenomena such as trust, sensemaking, and motivation. Ring and Van de Ven hypothesize that as interorganizational relationships become more "institutionalized," informal relationships become initially more important than formalized organizational structures and rules, but eventually formal agreements such as rules, policies, and contracts then start to mirror the informal relationships. Thus organizational-level characteristics are driven partially by individual-level variables.

There is broad consensus that the process aspect of collaboration is intrinsic to the very nature of the phenomenon; indeed, as Weick (1985) considered "organizing" a more appropriate way to discuss "organization," the literature on 'collaboration' could be better described by 'collaborating.' Many of the key frameworks in the collaboration literature emphasize this dynamic and self-reinforcing process aspect and specify causal pathways involving individual-level variables in a manner similar to Ring and Van de Ven (1994).

Collaboration Frameworks in the Public Administration Literature

In the context of public administration, the process of governance is an important consideration. Like its collaboration cousin, governance itself is a slippery concept, however, broadly speaking it refers to the manner by which collective impacts are produced in a social system (Hill & Hupe, 2009). From a major review of the collaboration literature, Ansel and Gash (2007) derive a "collaborative governance" framework that describes "a governing arrangement where one or more public agencies directly engage nonstate stakeholders in a collective decision-making process that is formal, consensus-orientated, and deliberative and that aims to make or implement public policy or manage public programs or assets" (p. 544). This differentiation between state and nonstate actors implies that multi-organizational collaboration between only state agencies is somehow different from when nonstate organizations are included. While Ansel and Gash (2007) do not elaborate on the extent to which actor type affects the nature of collaboration, other scholars have explored this question in typologies, described in the next section (Diaz-Kope & Miller-Stevens, 2014; Margerum, 2008; Moore & Koontz, 2003; Morris, Gibson, Leavitt, & Jones, 2013), and in research on the mechanisms of collective action in networks (Herranz, 2008).

Ansel and Gash's (2007) collaborative governance framework incorporates multiple levels of analysis. At the individual and group levels of analysis, they describe a cyclical positive feedback process very similar to the Ring and Van de Ven (1994) framework. Face-to-face dialogue leads to trust building, which in turn enhances participants' commitment to the process. Commitment is characterized by mutual recognition of interdependence, shared ownership of processes, and understanding of mutual gains. Trust and commitment allows shared understanding to develop. Depending on the context and the activity undertaken by the interorganizational form, partners may work on problem definition, mission planning, and identification of mindsets and values. These intermediate outcomes reinforce further face-to-face dialogue and further trust building, and a positive feedback loop is created.

Ansel and Gash (2007) recognize that the interorganizational collaborative process is highly dynamic and cyclical, but is affected by broader institutional factors such as the formal or informal governance and administrative structures created by interacting organizations. Part of the collaborative process involves creating such organizational level structures, which then in turn interact with the individual level variables. Positive feedback loops at the individual levels then reinforce the development and subsequent stability of organizational or institutional-level structures and rules.

Emerson et al. (2012) refine the Ansel and Gash (2007) framework by removing the emphasis on government as the convener of collaboration. They describe a "collaborative governance regime" as the:

> processes and structures of public policy decision making and management that engage people constructively across the boundaries of public agencies, levels of government, and/or the public, private and civic spheres in order to carry out a public purpose that could not otherwise be accomplished.
>
> (p. 2)

Emerson et al.'s (2012) framework is in the form of input–process–output, but with some key differences to many other frameworks of this form. First, they distinguish between two types of inputs/antecedents to collaboration: the general system context, which describes situational aspects often present in collaborations such as turbulence and complexity; and specific drivers of collaboration, which are necessary conditions to collaboration forming (leadership, consequential incentives, interdependence, and uncertainty). Second, they distinguish between the immediate outputs of collaboration (e.g., getting resources, enacting policy) and the longer term impacts that are described in reference to the system context. Finally, they specify adaptation as a separate outcome of collaboration, in that collaborations that adapt to system contexts and changes in rule structures are more likely to be sustainable and self-reinforcing. In a manner similar to Ansel and Gash (2007), they identify positive feedback between individual-level factors such as motivation and engagement, with the creation and sustainment of more formalized institutional rules and processes.

While the Emerson et al. (2012) and Ansel and Gash (2007) frameworks are widely cited in recent collaboration literature, a closer look reveals some potential issues. First, both frameworks clearly focus on the 'governance' level of organizations and thus are more applicable to organizational leadership responsible for negotiating and authorizing collaborations; it is not clear if these frameworks apply at all levels of the organization including at the 'street level' where much actual collaborative implementation happens. Second, the frameworks do not elaborate on important organizational factors such as authority to commit resources, organizational size, goals, and structure. As the following review of interorganizational arrays and typologies reveals, hierarchical structure and the distribution of authority within an organization are of key importance to determining the intensity of interorganizational interaction. While the Emerson et al. (2012) and Ansel and Gash (2007) frameworks are clearly multilevel, it is not clear how to overlay the frameworks on the standard levels of analysis of individual, structural-organizational, interorganizational domain, and ecological (Scott, 2003). This reflects the challenging nature of identifying levels of analysis at which conceptual or statistical inferences are made in networks and collaboration research.

The frameworks covered so far have placed great emphasis on the process of collaboration, but lesser focus on the surrounding context, antecedent conditions, and outcomes. A framework developed by Bryson et al. (2006) expands more on these other dimensions[1] in addition to the process. The framework links antecedents—which they call "starting conditions"—to outcomes, via two related dimensions: process, and structure and governance. The process dimension identifies both formal and informal mechanisms for developing interorganizational agreements, leadership, legitimacy, and trust. They identify that managing interorganizational conflict (e.g., disagreement over goals, strategy, or use of resources) and planning are key elements of any interorganizational interaction (Bryson et al., 2006; Lai, 2012).

In contrast to other frameworks covered, they separate out the structure/governance dimension from the process dimension, although a bidirectional arrow between the two dimensions conveys a close relationship. The structure dimension considers how partnering organizations are structurally arranged in their collective work, such as the linkages between levels of organization, or whether their interdependence is sequential or pooled (O'Toole, 1986). While other frameworks emphasize the self-reinforcing relationship between individual motivation and trust, and institutional governance structures created in the collaboration, Bryson et al. (2006) point out the connection between antecedents and context. The governance structure in a collaboration could take one of a number of forms: hierarchically flat inclusive deliberative panels; via a powerful lead agency such as a government agency or major nonprofit; or via a 'network organization' created especially for the collaboration. Bryson et al. (2006) contend that the matching between antecedent factors (such as stability of the policy context, turbulence of situation, and participants) and the particular governance structure has a major effect on collaborative outcomes.

In a modification to the Bryson et al. (2006) framework, Simo and Bies (2007) look at the particular nature of cross-sector collaborations as an explanatory dimension for collaborative outcomes. Simo and Bies (2007) identify the importance of "informal sector involvement," in which out of a sense of community spirit individuals and local groups spontaneously organize. This localized emergent collaboration often becomes formalized, or strengthens the collaborative initiatives of formal organizations including government agencies and established nonprofits. Morris et al. (2013) pick up on this theme by introducing the dimension of social capital to the input-process-output framework. In the context of local grassroots collaborations, social capital is considered as an antecedent, process, and output and thus is a key explanatory factor in the self-reinforcing nature of the collaborative process (Wagner & Fernandez-Gimenez, 2008).

The concept of social capital is fundamental to Thomson's (2001) framework, which seeks to conceptualize and operationalize collaboration, rather than describe the dynamics of collaboration as other frameworks do. Thomson (2001) describes two competing views of collaboration in the literature: aggregative, in which collaboration translates private preferences into collective choices via a mechanism of rational utility maximization (Ostrom, 1990); and integrative, in which collaboration creates new shared understandings and consensus over compromise (March & Olsen, 2010). Underlying these collaboration mechanisms are two perspectives of social capital, described by Morris et al. (2013). One views social capital as a transactional mechanism between actors that requires mutual exchange to establish norms of trust and reciprocity. Another views social capital as generated in a generalized way from social interactions across a network (Putnam, 2000).

Linking Back to Foundations—Ostrom's Institutional Framework

Social capital as the basis of collective action is also at the heart of Ostrom's (2005, 2007) institutionalist framework, which is one of the most refined and general frameworks derived from a systems approach. Institutional approaches to political science analyze how a wide variety of social interactions found in hierarchies, markets, political systems, and societies can be described by a set of underlying components universal to all situations. One such component is that of the institution—formal and informal rules, prescriptions, and structures that individuals use to organize a variety of structured interactions. Institutions affect the behavior of individuals by affecting the various incentives and constraints confronting an individual (Ostrom, 2005, 2007), and the development of reciprocity, reputation, and trust, which are the drivers of collective action (Ostrom, 1998). By adopting the basic assumptions of institutionalism and systems theory, Ostrom led a research effort to develop multilevel frameworks and conceptual language to describe the fundamental components of social interactions, whether market or hierarchy.

The basic conceptual template is a systems framework that describes a process of social interaction affected by inputs and contexts, and leading to certain outcomes, which then become part of the inputs in a cyclical fashion (Figure 2.1). In true systems fashion, this template is 'nested' at different levels depending on the scale of the participants (e.g., from individual to nation-state) and the type of rules governing the situation (from 'operational rules' to 'constitutional rules'). The most important part of the framework is arguably the basic process unit of social interaction called an 'action arena,' which refers to the social space in which individuals interact, exchange resources, and enact or resolve conflicts. Using a rational actor assumption and game-theoretic reasoning where actors rationally evaluate costs and benefits of their actions and expected outcomes, Ostrom (2005) surmised that any collective interaction situation could be generalized by looking at seven core variables: the involved participants; their positions; their potential outcomes; the link between their actions and outcomes; the various controls that participants exercise; the types of information generated; and the costs and benefits assigned to actions and outcomes (Ostrom, 2007).

New institutionalism is a foundation of Ostrom's (2007) collective action framework. This theory presumes that actors are rational and self-interested, but that their perception of what is optimal is affected by a surrounding institutional context. Moreover, in situations where no external authority is present to resolve problems or coordinate action, actors create new institutions in the form of rules, sanctions, and monitoring systems in order to govern self-organized collective action (Ostrom, 2007). A problem with previous rational theories and economically focused game theoretical

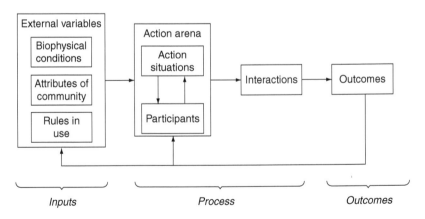

Figure 2.1 Ostrom's Institutional Development Framework in Input–Process–Outcome Form (source: Ostrom, 2007).

models of collective action, was that they failed to explain why rational actors create self-governing systems in the first place, when in many cases a better option would be to "defect" and act purely in their own self-interest (Olsen, 1965; Ostrom, 1990).

Ostrom (1990) showed that this "institutional supply" problem, coupled with the interrelated problems of developing mutual monitoring and credible commitments, could be solved by face-to-face communications involving discussion about the governance system of rules and monitoring. Face-to-face communication builds trust, which increases the propensity of actors to commit to a governance system. Once the governance system of joint decision-making, mutual monitoring, and administrative implementation is established and continued, participants experience joint benefits. Successful governance systems continue, while others are either discarded or adapted. This evolutionary adaptation of governance systems, in effect, increases trust between participants. Ostrom (1990) found that, providing a minimal amount of face-to-face communication occurred, governance systems transform into trusted institutions. This explains why, in general, stronger governance and administrative systems in collaboration would be associated with great norms of trust and reciprocity.

Likewise, whereas an antecedent to collaboration is known to be "problem" interdependence (Emerson et al., 2012; Gray, 1985; Trist, 1977), once participants jointly develop governance and administration arrangements a new form of interdependence emerges. First, as a governance system is created, participants face increasing psychological sanctions for defection from a collective action, where breaking commitments is viewed very negatively in a group setting (Ostrom, 2007). Second, entering into a shared governance and administration system involves transaction costs, which represent a deterrent to leaving the system especially when significant time and resources have been committed. Finally, increasing development of joint decision-making and administrative processes enables participants to better identify opportunities where resources can be shared. Thus collaboration is stimulated by resource dependence, but this dependence requires collective governance processes rather than purely economic considerations to be activated.

These basic theoretical mechanisms explained by Ostrom (1990, 2005) underpin much of the more recent work on collaboration frameworks. Emerson et al. (2012), for example, describe a "collaborative governance regime," meaning the implicit and explicit principles, rules, norms, and decision-making procedures that govern actors' behaviors. The collaborative governance regime is bolstered by an iterative collaborative process in which "principled engagement" (communication), "shared motivation" (trust, commitment, and mutuality), and "capacity for joint action" (administrative procedures) reinforce each other in a positive feedback loop to strengthen the institutional regime of collaboration. Based on this logic, Emerson et al. (2012) hypothesize that "the quality and extent of collaborative dynamics depends on the productive and self-reinforcing interactions among principled engagement, shared motivation, and the capacity for joint action" (p. 17).

Ostrom's (2005) framework works well for common pool resource problems where the costs of not participating are often greater than participation. The framework relies upon the assumption that the above list of core variables such as costs and benefits are explicitly known, and that the boundaries of the collective interaction situation can be defined; indeed, a core prediction of the game-theoretic logic behind the framework is that collective action is more effective when costs are known, information is available, and participants can expect repeated and routinized interactions thus increasing incentive to cooperate (Axelrod, 1984; Ostrom, 1990). Much of the collaboration literature, however, takes different starting assumptions due to the 'wickedness' of public problems where costs and benefits are much harder to calculate and the constituent factors and participants of the problem situation are rarely stable and identified.

While there are collaboration cases where Ostrom's (2005) framework likely can be applied, public domain problems require different incentives to participate in collaboration such as high levels of interdependence (Emery & Trist, 1965; Logsdon, 1991; Trist, 1977), turbulence (Bryson et al., 2006; Gray, 1989) and a favorable social and political climate (Mattessich, Murray-Close, & Monsay, 2001). Furthermore, collaborative mechanisms, which mirror "action situations" in Ostrom's (2005) framework, can be described in different ways by variables derived from other bodies of literature such as conflict resolution, leadership, management, and stakeholder theory. This does not mean that the list of core variables of action situations identified by Ostrom are incorrect or do not apply, but that given the wicked problem situations encountered in collaboration research, the core variables rarely can be objectively identified in a useful manner.

Thematic Frameworks of Collaboration

Other scholars do not use a systems-based approach to develop collaboration theory. The final framework covered, developed by Huxham (1996, 2003) and Huxham and Vangen (2000, 2005), is a "theme-based" framework. The core of the framework is a collection of "practitioner-generated" themes created from extensive grounded theory case study work of participants in collaborations. They subsequently identify "cross-cutting" themes that are part of all the practitioner themes, "policy-maker" themes identified by policy researchers and policymakers not necessarily directly involved in the collaborations, and "researcher-generated" themes such as social capital, which academic researchers identify as important but are not necessarily identified by practitioners (Huxham & Vangen, 2005, p. 38). The work by Huxham and Vangen (2000, 2005) does not specify detailed collaborative dynamic processes nor suggest causal linkages, but in identifying and describing key variables of interest in collaboration it is more intuitive and useful to practitioners, who are provided with a conceptual landscape of all things important in collaboration.

One particular variable of interest with respect to the present study and defining collaboration is that of *membership structure* in the collaboration; Huxham and Vangen (2005) identify three issues of ambiguity, complexity, and dynamics. They note that collaborations are often characterized by ambiguity in membership and status, meaning that participants' perceptions about the extent to which other participants are involved may vary. Furthermore, participants exhibit ambiguity over the extent to which an individual participant is acting individually or representing an organization. While many other collaboration frameworks and typologies define collaboration, in part, by membership structure and type (Keast et al., 2007), Huxham and Vangen (2005) present evidence to suggest otherwise. This raises an important scoping issue in respect to the present study. As collaboration may be intrinsically different depending on the extent to which individual citizens are involved versus individuals acting on behalf of organizations, or citizen groups, it is important to sample only one kind; in this case, collaboration between organizations.

Another key observation is the complexity of collaboration structures, especially within a single policy domain. Huxham and Vangen (2005) show that often multiple collaborations exist within any policy domain, and most have overlapping goals, structures, and participants. Often, collaborations evolve complex hierarchies of structure such as working groups, committees, and network organizations—a fact identified in other collaboration frameworks. Different departments within an organization may participate independently in the same collaboration, or are involved in many different collaborations. This creates difficult sampling issues in terms of whether individuals, departments, organizations, or collaborative groupings are the unit of analysis.

Finally, Huxham and Vangen (2005) note the dynamic nature of membership. Many scholars identify increasing membership stability as a feature of increasing interorganizational interaction and thus collaboration (Keast et al., 2007; McNamara, 2012), or assume stable membership in the cyclical trust-commitment feedback loops (Ansel & Gash, 2007; Ring & Van de Ven, 1994). Huxham and Vangen point out that inevitably, people change jobs, organizations send different staff to the collaboration on different days, and organizations face other pressures that affect their involvement. They contend that dynamic variation in membership affects the collaboration *purpose* and creates a situation of continual negotiation and renegotiation of aims and goals. While collaborations with stable memberships can be found, care is needed in research as application of many of the systems frameworks requires an assumption of stable membership.

Conclusions—Collaboration Frameworks and Theories

Several conclusions can be drawn from this review of collaboration frameworks. First, they reflect a fundamental point about the complexity of collective action. Most frameworks are constructed in input-process-output form with multiple possible hypotheses linking variables and feedback loops between dimensions, demonstrating that collective action situations are *complex adaptive systems*. Various scholars have considered the implications of this in organizational terms (Anderson, 1999; Bovaird, 2008; Innes & Booher, 2010; Thietart & Forgues, 1995). Multiorganizational systems tend to exhibit chaotic—unpredictable but not random—behavior as a result of counteracting forces such as the autonomy tension between individual or organizational goals and those of the collaboration (Thietart & Forgues, 1995). Positive feedback loops between collaboration dimensions and variables creates nonlinear relationships, meaning caution must be applied when attempting to test hypotheses (Aydinoglu, 2010). Stable equilibrium states such as regular stakeholder meetings may develop but are highly sensitive to contextual conditions (Bryson et al., 2006; Van Buuren & Gerrits, 2008).

Consequently, as a result of the multiplicity of variables and their potential combinations and dynamic iteration, organizations and derivative collaborative groupings exhibit *action irreversibility* such that encountering the same situation and combination of factors more than once is unlikely (Thietart & Forgues, 1995). This emphasizes the importance of rigorous case study research, however, as was realized in earlier strands of policy implementation research (Goggin, 1986; O'Toole, 2000), complexity and an abundance of variables does not make cumulative and generalized collaboration research a hopeless endeavor as the various frameworks show broadly similar findings and prioritize important factors.

Second, in conceptual terms all frameworks suggest relationships between levels of analysis. In many cases, positive feedback loops generate emergent characteristics in which aggregate, higher-level characteristics are generated from complex interactions of individual-level factors such as links between individual trust and organizational-level structures created during collaborations. However, this is also an indication of institutionalism. Apart from the special case of conflicts over common pool resources, which have particular dynamics and outcomes (Ostrom, 1990), in situations where stakeholders are interdependent and face a common and individually unresolvable problem, certain collaborations tend to develop features of organization (regular meetings, aspects of hierarchy, division of labor) reflecting the pervasive institutional norm of organization as a way to achieve collective goals in unstable or unordered situations (Thacher, 2004).

Third, inherent in the basic systems structure of most frameworks is adaptation and iteration, allowing for changes in processes, participants, and governance structures as a situation changes. While the frameworks specify little about how this adaptation might unfold, other scholars have described a series of first, second, and third order effects that result from collaborative activities. Innes and Booher (1999), for example, describe first order effects as *collaborative outputs* as per many of the frameworks: creation of social capital, robust agreements, innovative solutions, or stable collaborative organizations. Second order effects are similar to the *collaborative impacts* described by Emerson et al. (2012): changes in original contexts, offshoot partnerships arising as a result of increasing network density, or changes in practices and perceptions (Bryson et al., 2006). Finally, third order effects may emerge after some time and include new cultural or societal norms about conflict resolution and deliberative planning. This suggests that second and third order effects may be an 'indicator' of collaboration, an observation that is missing from the typology literature reviewed in the next section.

Fourth, the frameworks have little utility in defining collaboration or other related terms, with the exception of Thomson (2001). Frameworks reflect the general features of collaboration (e.g., trust, common goals, interdependence, mutual benefit, etc.), but as the next section of this chapter illustrates, the use of the term 'collaboration' in the framework literature is not consistent. All the frameworks could apply at different levels of interorganizational interaction, and some are explicitly intended to capture the whole life cycle of collaboration from birth to dissolution. The basic self-reinforcing feedback loops show how these collective action situations form with limited levels of interaction (i.e., 'deconfliction' or 'cooperation') and then ratchet up all the way to full collaboration—a much higher intensity of interaction. While this is not necessarily a problem in terms of the frameworks, there is an inconsistency with the body of work on typologies and arrays, which ascribes specific operationalizations to common terms such as 'coordination,' 'cooperation' or 'collaboration.' In some cases, a more appropriate and general name for 'collaboration' framework may be 'interorganizational interaction' framework.

Fifth, while most frameworks intend to be general, the dynamic of collaboration is affected by context, specifically the nature and organizational level of participants, the scale of the policy problem, and the size of the collaboration. For collaborations involving organizations rather than individual citizens, the organizational hierarchical level at which a framework applies is not specified. In the typology literature, for example, lower levels of interaction (cooperation) are distinguished from higher levels (collaboration) by the involvement of more senior staff or denser interactions from working level up to leadership level. Some frameworks may apply only to leadership (Ansel & Gash, 2007), but then other frameworks explicitly spell out roles for all participants (Gray, 1989). While there is no conclusive evidence from the literature and further research is needed, the case may be that regardless of level in the hierarchy, drivers and mechanisms of collaboration are similar, with the exception that higher-up levels tend to have greater authority to commit resources.

Another issue affecting collaboration dynamics is the importance of the *scale* of the policy problem and the way participants 'interface' with the problem. Morris et al. (2013), for example, point out that the failures of collaborative efforts in Chesapeake Bay restoration projects may stem from the large number of organizations involved, the large geographic area over which the problem exists, and the very broad policy problem. This is in contrast to successful efforts to restore the rivers in the Hampton Roads, Virginia area, which involved locally based groups, smaller numbers of organizations and individuals, and thus allowed social capital to be a 'gluing' mechanism of collaboration. While some of the typology literature has attempted to include characteristics of the policy problem into a definition of collaboration, it is unclear the extent to which the collaboration frameworks apply across varying geographic, financial, or impact scales of policy problems.

The final conclusion concerns the challenge of developing theory in collaboration literature. Several scholars note that the particular type of collaboration (Gray, 1989) or the particular organizational forms that emerge from the process (Bryson et al., 2006) depend strongly on the localized context such as the nature of the participants or the stability of the policy domain. The domain of applicability for collaboration frameworks requires clarification by understanding how differing combinations of participants, situation type, policy domain, and other contextual factors, affect the process. This conclusion points toward the tension between creating generalized mechanisms of collaboration versus highly specific cases that enumerate all possible combinations of inputs, processes, and outputs. This may explain why many scholars either develop high-level frameworks, or pick out specific variables for study and create highly specific 'models,' which look at one or two particular relationships from a framework under particular cases. In sum, developing theory of collaboration is very challenging.

Another related 'theoretical' aspect concerns the paradigmatic basis of the frameworks. With the exception of Huxham's and Vangen's (2005), all are generally functionalist—they assume objective reality and tangible variables. Huxham and Vangen (2005), however, open the door for a social constructivist perspective, noting that collaboration dynamics depend largely on the perceptions of participants. Furthermore, while all frameworks treat collaboration as an open system, they emphasize natural and rational aspects to varying extents. Thomson (2001), for example, specifies explicit operationalizations of governance and administration structures as intrinsic to the collaborative process, whereas Gray (1989) emphasizes human relations aspects such as the legitimacy and power balance of participants, and the importance of the convener and mediator roles in collaboration.

Lawrence and Lorsch (1967) postulate that the reasons for such diversity of theory lie in the different backgrounds and experiences of the theoreticians: rational theorists typically have managerial or engineering backgrounds, whereas natural theorists tend to be academics. Scott (2003) notes that the type of organization that theorists study is important. Rational theorists typically study business firms or government bureaucracies, whereas natural theorists study voluntary, service, or community organizations. Continuing the example above, Thomson, who trained at a mainstream public administration school, developed her framework by studying a major nationwide nonprofit organization; Gray, who was an organizational behavior theorist, developed her work from studying conflict situations in local community problems.

While these observations may be unsurprising, they highlight an important point with regard to the collaboration frameworks. Rational paradigms are intuitively applicable to stable organizations or collaborative groups, whereas natural paradigms fit with dynamically varying or less-structured organizations or groups. The collaboration frameworks do not specify their limits of applicability in terms of the various actors constituting the collaboration, the stability of participation, or the dynamic variation in system context. The case may be that collaborations between government bureaucracies, with all other things equal, are more likely to recreate signatures of hierarchy during the collaboration as observed by Bardach (1998), in comparison to collaborations between local community groups and individuals. This is not about the definition or conceptualization of collaboration, but highlights the limits of generalized frameworks, as the dynamic unfolding of a collaboration over time may vary quite considerably depending on the history, experiences, and identities of the participants.

Interorganizational Arrays and Typologies

Organizations are intricate systems composed of multiple social structures, participants, goals, and technologies, interacting with the external environment and exhibiting complex individual and group behaviors. From this initial description, scholars have identified many distinct 'dimensions' of organizations that merit study and often form the basis of entire disciplines. Rainey (2003), for example, identifies key dimensions as: goals, values, leadership, strategy, culture, organization type, hierarchical structure, processes, tasks, technologies, performance, incentives, individuals, and groups.

While this list of dimensions describes a single organization, the interorganizational literature recognized that when organizations interact and form interorganizational relationships and structures, these dimensions are generally affected by the interaction and can be used to describe the emergent interorganizational form resulting from the interaction (Whetten, 1981). Efforts to define collaboration and related terms can be considered part of this broader body of interorganizational literature, which attempts to create typologies of interorganizational forms using the organizational dimensions—with some additions particular to interorganizational structures—as discriminating characteristics. An important subset of this literature—and the focus of this next section—develops *interorganizational arrays*, which describe discrete interorganizational forms placed on a scale or continuum of interaction.

From the literature reviewed, interorganizational arrays generally have two axes as illustrated in Table 2.1. The first (horizontal) axis defines names for a particular interorganizational interaction, form, or relationship, for example: collaboration, cooperation, or partnership. The second (vertical) axis contains the discriminating characteristics or 'dimension,' for example: information, structure, resource, or decision-making. Each cell of the array then describes what that particular dimension looks like for each interorganizational form.

Gray (1989), in her influential book on interorganizational relationships, which she terms as "collaborations," emphasizes that the characteristics of interorganizational forms vary depending on context, and that the form eventually affects outcomes. She defines four interorganizational forms first by the function that they perform, and second by the possible outcomes that may result from the collaboration. An "exploratory" collaboration may occur as one of the first activities between organizations in order to acknowledge interdependence between actors, establish trust, and conduct initial problem scoping. "Advisory" collaborations extend these functions and identify solutions. "Confederative" collaborations consider implementation of solutions, and may start to exchange resources to do so and develop increasingly formalized agreements. Finally, "contractual" collaborations see a high level of formalized solution implementation with legally binding contracts. A research and development consortia of industry and academic organizations is an example of a contractual collaborative, in which participants develop legal contracts about profits and copyright, but also complex formal and informal rules about how participating organizations interact.

Employing the function or purpose to discriminate interorganizational forms such as in the Gray (1989) typology is useful to allow a researcher

Table 2.1 Generic Construct of Interorganizational Arrays

Dimensions (distinguishing characteristics)	Interorganizational Form		
	Form Type A	Form Type B	Form Type C...
Dimension 1	Indicator of Dimension 1 for Form Type A	Indicator of Dimension 1 for Form Type B.	Etc.
Dimension 2	Indicator of Dimension 2 for Form Type A	Etc.	
Dimension 3	Etc.		

to relate interorganizational interaction directly to the context of the situation or environment, and this approach has been employed in many typologies and interorganizational arrays. From a review of 36 environmental management case studies, Margerum (2008) constructs a typology of three interorganizational forms: action, organizational, and policy "collaboratives," according to whether the main reason for interaction between organizations is to act directly, change organizations' policies about a collective problem, or attempt to change government policy concerning the problem. In a similar vein, Alter and Hage (1993) identify different "coordination methods" depending on whether the interaction is for policy-making, administration, or operations. More recently, Donahue and Zeckhauser (2011) organize their analysis on whether collaboration is for the purpose of improving productivity, gaining information, increasing legitimacy, or sharing resources. As will be discussed later, however, while this approach is useful in some respects, attempting to define interaction terms using dimensions of function, purpose, or outcomes introduces logical errors.

Gray (1989) and Margerum (2008) do not elaborate further on the discriminating dimensions of interorganizational forms, making it challenging to use their typologies other than for initial theory development. Gray (1989), however, introduces the notion that interorganizational interactions become "progressively more institutionalized" (p. 240) proceeding from exploratory to contractual forms. That different interorganizational forms exhibit different "intensities" of interaction is the foundation for another influential early work on interorganizational theory: *Organizations Working Together* by Alter and Hage (1993).

Alter and Hage (1993) start with a "form of interdependence" dimension with two values of competitive and symbiotic—the justification being that organizations in symbiotic relationships have much different logics and more opportunity for interaction compared to competitive relationships. They add another dimension with two categories based on the number of partnering organizations (dyadic/triadic interactions, or multisectoral/networks), given strong findings from interorganizational relations literature noting that collectivities with few members exhibit much greater tendency for self-interested behaviors. They use these four basic combinations to define the nature of three types of interorganizational forms: limited, moderate, and broad 'cooperation.' Alter and Hage's (1993) work, which established the idea that interorganizational interaction occurred on a scale of "intensity" or magnitude, led to subsequent efforts to classify interorganizational forms based on level of interaction.

Empirical research on interorganizational interaction is challenging because interorganizational forms evolve considerably with time and many organizational behaviors are affected by social constructions (Ansel & Gash, 2007; Lincoln, 1985). Many of the typologies and arrays reviewed attempt to classify interorganizational forms into categories based on simple characteristics with qualitative values (e.g., network strength as 'high' or 'low'), yet network strength may vary considerably over time, or may be measured in different ways by different observers. Such inconsistencies diminish the empirical utility of the early typological approaches. Later examples of interorganizational arrays by McNamara (2012), Williams (2010), and Keast et al. (2007), for example, include mixes of objective organizational characteristics in addition to more general qualitative dimensions. These arrays, in effect, provide 'snapshots' of complex and dynamic interaction processes and give reasonable indicators about the level of interaction, without overly specifying structural details. In reality, the particular choice of name for an interorganizational form— whether 'cooperation' or 'collaboration'—is largely arbitrary; what is important is how the dimensions change for that particular form, and what this signifies for an organization. While the arrays do not spell out these implications in detail, they provide a starting point.

The most developed array to date is McNamara (2008, 2012), which built on prior work by Fagan (1997), Mattessich et al. (2001), and Thatcher (2007). McNamara (2012) defines three levels of interaction— cooperation, coordination, and collaboration—and 10 dimensions: design of administrative structures supporting the collective efforts; formality of the agreement determining roles and responsibilities; organizational autonomy; key personnel who have responsibility for implementing the partnership; information-sharing; decision-making; the extent to which there is a process for resolution of turf issues; resource allocation; systems thinking; and trust.

Some scholars use characteristics of the context or situation in which interorganizational interaction takes place to define the extent of interaction. For example, the McNamara (2008) array has additional dimensions over her later 2012 version, including: duration of interaction (time); difficulty of task; and impetus for collective action. Moore and Koontz (2003) create a typology based on the type of participant to the collaboration: agency, citizen, or mixed. While these dimensions have descriptive utility, using them to define the interorganizational form is a logical fallacy—equivalent to defining a river by the presence of a valley: this works in some cases, but not all. Similarly, those typologies that incorporate antecedents and outcomes of interorganizational interaction suffer from the same logic error. For example, the Margerum (2008) typology discriminates interorganizational forms on the basis of whether the goal of participating organizations is to act directly, change organizations' policies about a collective problem, or change government policy concerning the problem area. It stands to reason that any collective effort could have all three or none of these goals; thus, defining interorganizational forms in these terms is not rigorous. A more rigorous approach to definition involves those dimensions relating to the interorganizational form itself, and those relating to the organizations involved in the partnership.

Comparing the typologies and arrays reviewed, it is possible to classify the various dimensions used into three categories, as shown in Table 2.2:

Table 2.2 Summary of Typology and Interorganizational Array Dimensions Arranged in Three Categories

Dimensions Relating to Context, Situation, Antecedents, or Outcomes	Dimensions Relating to Structural and Behavioral Aspects of Participating Organizations[1]	Dimensions Relating to Interorganizational Interaction (II)[2]
Time required for problem solution	Level of staff participating in II (e.g., leadership, junior, working level)	Time duration of II
Length of time problem has existed	Type of interdependence between organizations (e.g., organizations could achieve goals without II, or require II to achieve goals)	Frequency of II
Complexity of problem domain		Differential of level of staff engaged in interaction (e.g., manager–manager, CEO–manager, CEO–CEO)
Antecedents to collective action (e.g., extent of history of prior work together; extent to which an organization is well known in problem domain)	Organizational autonomy	Formality of interorganizational agreement
Function of II (e.g., information exchange, production, resolving conflict, planning, analysis, evaluation)	Authority over goals, resources	Extent of information-sharing
	Key personnel	*Decision-making*
	Decision-making[3]	*Resource allocation*
Type of goods produced by II (public, private, common-pool)	*Resource allocation*	Resolution of turf issues
	Systems thinking	*Culture*
Intended outcomes of II (e.g., policy change, rule change, direct action)	Incentives	
	Commitment	
Type of organization involved (e.g., government, nonprofit, private company, coalition, charity)[4]	Willingness to change	
	Trust	
	Risk-taking behavior	
Number of organizations or other participants involved	Level of risk assumed by participants, financial or otherwise	
Geographic distribution of participants	*Culture*	
Whether participants interact voluntarily or mandated		

Notes

1 Organization is understood in a conventional 'rational' perspective with boundaries defined by the hierarchical structure (i.e., org chart).
2 The dimensions belonging under the II column are those that *emerge* out of the interaction, and are not something that can be measured meaningfully in the participating organizations.
3 Italic text denotes that the dimension can be categorized under two columns, depending on how it is defined.
4 This dimension is not placed in the 'organization' column as it is not a structural or behavioral characteristic. That is, while different types of organization will vary in structural forms, the impact of organization type on II is minimal or random.

dimensions relating to the context or environment in which the interorganizational interaction occurs; dimensions relating to the interacting organizations; and dimensions relating to the actual interorganizational form
itself. For example, the dimensions of 'organizational autonomy' and 'key
personnel' are clearly from the perspective of the organization, whereas
'formalized agreements' relates only to the interorganizational form. In
effect, Table 2.2 lays out all the various parameters (i.e., dimensions) by
which collaboration and other interorganizational forms *could be* defined.

Conclusions—Interorganizational Arrays and Typologies

Several conclusions can be drawn from this review of arrays and typologies. First, the terms chosen for various interorganizational forms are arbitrary and their acceptance is a matter of convention. This explains, for
example, how Himmelman (2002) considers "networking" as the most
informal and limited interorganizational interaction, whereas Mandell and
Steelman (2003) define it almost oppositely as the most intense and comprehensive interaction. Apart from the recent exceptions of McNamara
(2008), Thatcher (2007) and Thomson, Perry, and Miller (2009), definitions created by many scholars are generally conceptually constructed by
thinking, rather than taxonomically generated from categorization based
on empirical observations (Bailey, 1994; Smith, 2002). What is more
important is understanding how the various dimensions pair together in
certain combinations and what effects these have on outcomes. It is useful
for future research, however, to create standardization in the usage of
terms.

Second, the interorganizational arrays specify that interorganizational
interactions exist on a 'continuum' characterized by both increasing magnitude of implications for partnering organizations and increasing formalization and interdependence of the emergent interorganizational form. In
most cases, however, this continuum is 'quantized' as most dimensions
have only a discrete number of values. While some arrays use the term
'maturity' to describe the increasing interorganizational interactions that
occur from cooperation to collaboration (Alberts & Hayes, 2007), 'maturity' suggests both elements of quality and superiority and implies that
moving up the scale of interaction is preferable. Many studies suggest,
however, that operating at the highest level is not appropriate for all situations (Chisholm, 1992; Mattessich et al., 2001). Although the term 'magnitude' can be misconstrued to imply quantity, this is not the intent.
Interaction magnitude is meant to convey that the magnitude of the *impact*
on partnering organizations will be greater at higher levels of interaction.

Third, an observation unexamined in the literature is that these typologies and arrays represent a 'morphological field,' that is, a way of display-
ing all the possible combinations of dimensions that *could* occur (Ritchey,
2011). The arrays lead to the conclusion that 'cooperation' is defined by
the occurrence of *all* the dimensional indicators at that level, yet this may

not be the case. Many situations could occur where dimensions A and B indicate a *high* level of interaction (i.e., collaboration), but dimensions C and D indicate a *low* level of interaction (i.e., coordination). Interorganizational arrays do not tell us how to define this state. Furthermore, the evolution of an interorganizational interaction through time may see ebbs and flows of interaction intensity, a fact not captured by the arrays.

While typologies and arrays represent a useful abstraction or conceptual tool, they mask the complex reality of interorganizational interaction, as hinted at by the collaboration framework literature. Other research has suggested that cross-level combinations are indeed possible. In research using a network perspective, Herranz (2008) defines a typology of "network coordination." He shows that depending on the "strategic orientation" of network actors (the extent to which actors prefer collective action to be conducted bureaucratically, entrepreneurially, or community focused), the form of 'coordination' displays differing combinations of dimension, which do not correspond with the levels of interaction reviewed thus far. This indicates that further research is needed about the possible combinations that could occur in reality, versus those that are theoretically or logically excluded.

The final conclusion concerns the paradigm of typologies and arrays. Given their basic purpose is to classify concepts and generate rigorous definitions for terms, all the typologies and arrays assume an objective functionalist paradigm. They aim to give descriptive indicators or 'snapshots' of how various levels or forms of interorganizational interaction are operationalized in terms of key organizational dimensions, in addition to some emergent characters of the interorganizational form. Neither typologies nor arrays can be considered as 'theory' per se, as they say little about explanatory relationships. They provide a starting point, however, for the organization of key variables and suggest some important hypotheses, when examined with the collaboration framework literature in mind.

Conclusions

As the mainstay of contemporary collaboration research relies either on frameworks or typologies and interorganizational arrays, a comparison between the two is pertinent. This comparison, which is summarized in Table 2.3, highlights the strengths and limitations of each approach. It is not intended to be a normative evaluation as both the framework and typological/array (henceforth just 'typological') approaches have theoretical and practical utility depending on the circumstances and particular research questions.

First, as a basic consequence of systems-based construction with feedback loops and adaptation, collaboration frameworks emphasize the complexity of collective action. While certain patterns in collaboration processes can be observed and predicted, emergent behavior and the fact that each case of collaboration process is slightly different makes theoretical generalizability

Table 2.3 Comparison of Conclusions From Framework and Typology/Array Analysis

Collaboration Frameworks	Interorganizational Arrays and Typologies
Illustrate the complexity of collective action: chaotic, nonlinear processes, with action irreversibility	Portray linear steps between stages or levels of interaction; assumes collaboration or other levels are repeatable or standard forms of interaction
Postulate causal relationships between levels of analysis, and between multiple variables	Causality is not directly specified Dimension indicators for each stage of interaction are correlated as a result of the typology structure
Collaboration processes adapt to context and lead to broader impacts	Adaptation is not considered
Definition of collaboration, in contrast to other interaction terms, remains ambiguous	Very specific about definitions of interaction terms, though the choice of term is ultimately arbitrary Present a 'quantized' continuum of interaction, but in reality represent a morphological field with multiple possible combinations
Ambiguous about the extent to which frameworks can be applied at different organizational levels (e.g., leadership level or street level), or in different contexts (e.g., for policy change, implementation, temporary emergencies)	Very specific, in certain cases, about applicability to different organizational levels and contexts

and conceptual operationalization challenging. In contrast, many typologies assume that stable—and thus presumably repeatable—characteristics of 'collaboration' exist. Furthermore, while collaboration frameworks stress the dynamic, iterative, and adaptive nature of collaboration, typologies say little about adaptation, nor the conditions under which a shift from one level of interaction to another would occur. This does not intend to imply that developers of typologies fail to recognize this important point, but simply that typologies are limited by their structure in what can be represented.

Second, frameworks and typologies differ in the extent to which they capture relationships between collaboration input, process, and output variables. Typologies suggest relationships between variables in the sense that 'collaboration' or other interaction terms are defined by the simultaneous presence of disparate indicators of variables (i.e., dimensions) at the same level of interaction. In contrast, frameworks hypothesize specific relationships between variables, often at different levels of analysis. Frameworks offer descriptions of process, whereas, in general, typologies cannot capture the process aspect of collaboration particularly well.

Third, frameworks are ambiguous about the extent of their applicability to different organizational levels (from the leadership level where collaboration is governed, to collaboration on the 'street level' where implementation actually happens), or in different contexts such as situation type or the purpose of collaboration (e.g., for policy change, implementation, temporary emergencies). In contrast, typologies clearly specify the level of applicability in organizational terms, and often build context into the construction of the typology—even though this creates situations of non-mutually exclusive distinctions between different levels of interaction.

Finally, while typologies offer definitional operationalizations of interaction terms as a result of their intrinsic purpose, frameworks have less utility in this area. Many of the frameworks specify processes that span multiple levels of interaction, meaning they apply equally to coordination and collaboration. Furthermore, some frameworks imply dynamically varying combinations of dimensions across interaction terms that are undefined by the typologies, such as a combination of several dimensions of cooperation with several of collaboration.

A View for Future Theory?

This chapter has covered the mainstay of contemporary collaboration theory research in public administration and finds that the two main ways in which collaboration is conceptualized are complementary in some ways and contradictory in others. The literature is complementary because similar variables are emphasized in importance and provide some 'triangulation' and consistency with other important theories in political and economic science—namely institutionalism. Research is contradictory in that the typological and interorganizational array literature reveals the lack of generalizability of collaboration frameworks. Typologies and arrays demonstrate that while 'pure' or 'general' forms of interorganizational interaction can be described, they are rarely meaningful outside a given context and environment. Either scholars must specify in detail the domain applicability of their frameworks, or they must develop a suite of different frameworks for each contextual variable specified in the interorganizational array and typology literature.

Future theoretical work will first require greater empirical research. Much of the typology, array, and framework literature described originated from purely conceptual work, or from case study research. The interorganizational arrays represent fertile ground for easy empirical testing—can the interorganizational forms described by the arrays be observed in reality? Furthermore, the framework literature in the past few years has generated a long list of testable propositions that deserve further research. Finally, theorists and empirical scholars must be very mindful that as beauty is in the eye of the beholder, so collaboration is always seen through a lens of context.

Note

1 Up to this point, *category* was used to refer to a collection of variables organized in input, process, or output *categories*. As subsequent frameworks create separate groupings of variables within categories, they are referred to as *dimensions*.

References

Agranoff, R., & McGuire, M. (2003). *Collaborative public management: New strategies for local governments.* Washington, DC: Georgetown University Press.
Alberts, D., & Hayes, R. (2007). *Planning for complex endeavors.* Washington, DC: Command and Control Research Program.
Alter, C., & Hage, J. (1993). *Organizations working together.* Newbury Park, CA: Sage.
Anderson, P. (1999). Complexity theory and organizational science. *Organization Science, 10*(3), 216–232.
Ansel, C., & Gash, A. (2007). Collaborative governance in theory and in practice. *Journal of Public Administration, Research and Theory, 18*(4), 543–571.
Axelrod, R. (1984). *The evolution of cooperation.* New York, NY: Basic Books.
Aydinoglu, A. U. (2010). Scientific collaborations as complex adaptive systems. *Emergence: Complexity & Organization, 12*(4), 15–29.
Bailey, K. D. (1994). *Typologies and taxonomies: An introduction to classification techniques.* Thousand Oaks, CA: Sage.
Bardach, E. (1998). *Getting agencies to work together.* Washington, DC: Brookings Institute.
Bardach, E., & Lesser, C. (1996). Accountability in human services collaboratives: For what? And to whom? *Journal of Public Administration Research and Theory, 6*(2), 197–224.
Barringer, B. R., & Harrison, J. S. (2000). Walking a tightrope: Creating value through interorganizational relationships. *Journal of Management, 26*(3), 367–403.
Bedwell, W. L., Wildman, J. L., DiazGranados, D., Salazar, M., Kramer, W. S., & Salas, E. (2012). Collaboration at work: An integrative multilevel conceptualization. *Human Resource Management Review, 22*(2), 128–145.
Bovaird, T. (2008). Emergent strategic management and planning mechanisms in complex adaptive systems. *Public Management Review, 10*(3), 319–340.
Bryson, J., Crosby, B., & Stone, M. (2006). The design and implementation of cross-sector collaborations: Propositions from the literature. *Public Administration Review, 66*(s1), 44–55.
Chisholm, D. (1992). *Coordination without hierarchy: Informal structures in multiorganizational systems.* Berkeley, CA: University of California Press.
Cross, J. E., Dickmann, E., Newman-Gonchar, R., & Fagan, J. M. (2009). Using mixed-method design and network analysis to measure development of interagency collaboration. *American Journal of Evaluation, 30*(3), 310–329.
Diaz-Kope, L., & Miller-Stevens, K. (2014). Rethinking a typology of watershed partnerships: A governance perspective. *Public Works Management & Policy.* doi: 10.1177/1087724x14524733.
Donahue, J. D., & Zeckhauser, R. J. (2011). *Collaborative governance: Private roles for public goals in turbulent times.* Princeton, NJ: Princeton University.
Easton, D. (1957). An approach to the analysis of political systems. *World Politics, 9*(3), 383–400.

Emerson, K., Nabatchi, T., & Balogh, S. (2012). An integrative framework for collaborative governance. *Journal of Public Administration Research and Theory*, 22(1), 1–29.

Emery, F. E., & Trist, E. (1965). The causal texture of organizational environments. *Human Relations*, 18(1), 21–32.

Fagan, P. (1997). *Collective efficiency and collaboration: A case study of a comunity-based partnership* (Doctoral dissertation, Texas A&M University, College Station, TX, 1997).

Fisher, R. J. (1990). *The social psychology of intergroup and international conflict resolution*. New York, NY: Springer-Verlag Publishing.

Fisher, R., Ury, W., & Patton, B. (1991). *Getting to yes: Negotiating agreement without giving in*. New York, NY: Penguin Books.

Getha-Taylor, H., & Morse, R. S. (2013). Collaborative leadership development for local government officials: Exploring competencies and program impact. *Public Administration Quarterly*, 37(1), 72–103.

Goggin, M. L. (1986). The "too few cases/too many variables" problem in implementation research. *Political Research Quarterly*, 39(2), 328–347.

Gray, B. (1985). Conditions facilitating interorganizational collaboration. *Human Relations*, 38(10), 911–936.

Gray, B. (1989). *Collaborating: Finding common ground for multiparty problems*. San Francisco, CA: Jossey-Bass.

Gray, B., & Wood, D. J. (1991). Collaborative alliances: Moving from practice to theory. *The Journal of Applied Behavioral Science*, 27(1), 3–22.

Head, B. W., & Alford, J. (2013). Wicked problems: Implications for public policy and management. *Administration & Society*. doi: 10.1177/0095399713481601.

Herranz, J., Jr. (2008). The multisectoral trilemma of network management. *Journal of Public Administration Research and Theory*, 18(1), 1–31.

Hill, M., & Hupe, P. (2009). *Implementing public policy* (2nd ed.). Thousand Oaks, CA: Sage.

Himmelman, A. (2002). *Collaboration for a change: Definitions, decision-making models, roles, and collaboration process guide*. Minneapolis, MN: Himmelman Consulting.

Huxham, C. (Ed.). (1996). *Creating collaborative advantage*. Thousand Oaks, CA: Sage.

Huxham, C. (2003). Theorizing collaboration practice. *Public Management Review*, 5(3), 401–423.

Huxham, C., & Vangen, S. (2000). Ambiguity, complexity and dynamics in the membership of collaboration. *Human Relations*, 53(6), 771–806.

Huxham, C., & Vangen, S. (2005). *Managing to collaborate: The theory and practice of collaborative advantage*. Abingdon, England: Routledge.

Innes, J. E., & Booher, D. E. (1999). Consensus building and complex adaptive systems. *Journal of the American Planning Association*, 65(4), 412–423.

Innes, J. E., & Booher, D. E. (2010). *Planning with complexity: An introduction to collaborative rationality for public policy*. New York, NY: Routledge.

Keast, R., Brown, K., & Mandell, M. P. (2007). Getting the right mix: Unpacking integration meanings and strategies. *International Public Management Journal*, 10(1), 9–33.

Kriesberg, L. (2007). *Constructive conflicts: From escalation to resolution*. Lanham, MD: Rowman and Littlefield.

40   A. P. Williams

Lai, A. Y.-H. (2012). Towards a collaborative cross-border disaster management: A comparative analysis of voluntary organizations in Taiwan and Singapore. *Journal of Comparative Policy Analysis, 14*(3), 217.

Lawrence, P. R., & Lorsch, J. W. (1967). *Organization and environment: Managing differentiation and integration.* Boston, MA: Harvard University Press.

Lincoln, Y. S. (Ed.). (1985). *Organizational theory and inquiry: The paradigm revolution.* Newbury Park, CA: Sage.

Logsdon, J. M. (1991). Interests and interdependence in the formation of social problem-solving collaborations. *The Journal of Applied Behavioral Science, 27*(1), 23–37.

McGuire, M. (2006). Collaborative public management: Assessing what we know and how we know it. *Public Administration Review, 66*(s1), 33–43.

McNamara, M. (2008). Exploring interactions during multiorganizational policy implementation: A case study of the Virginia Coastal Zone Management program (Doctoral dissertation, Old Dominion University, Norfolk, VA, 2008).

McNamara, M. (2012). Starting to untangle the web of cooperation, coordination, and collaboration: A framework for public managers. *International Journal of Public Administration, 35*(6), 389–401.

Mandell, M. P., & Steelman, T. A. (2003). Understanding what can be accomplished through interorganizational innovations. *Public Management Review, 5*(2), 197–224.

March, J. G., & Olsen, J. P. (2010). *Rediscovering institutions: The organizational basis of politics.* New York, NY: The Free Press.

Margerum, R. D. (2008). A typology of collaboration efforts in environment management. *Environmental Management, 41*(4), 487–500.

Mattessich, P. W., Murray-Close, M., & Monsay, B. R. (2001). *Collaboration: What makes it work* (2nd ed.). St. Paul, MN: Fieldstone Alliance.

Mitchell, R. M., Ripley, J., Adams, C., & Raju, D. (2011). Trust an essential ingredient in collaborative decision making. *Journal of School Public Relations, 32*(2), 145–170.

Moore, E. A., & Koontz, T. M. (2003). Research note a typology of collaborative watershed groups: Citizen-based, agency-based, and mixed partnerships. *Society & Natural Resources, 16*(5), 451–460.

Morris, J. C., Gibson, W. A., Leavitt, W. M., & Jones, S. C. (2013). *The case for grassroots collaboration: Social capital and ecosystem restoration at the local level.* Lanham, MD: Lexington.

O'Leary, R., & Bingham, L. B. (Eds.). (2009). *The collaborative public manager.* Washington, DC: Georgetown University Press.

O'Toole, L. J. (1986). Policy recommendations for multi-actor implementation: An assessment from the field. *Journal of Public Policy, 6*(2), 181–210.

O'Toole, L. J. (2000). Research on policy implementation: Assessment and prospects. *Journal of Public Administration Research and Theory, 10*(2), 263–288.

Olsen, M. (1965). *The logic of collective action: Public goods and the theory of groups.* Cambridge, MA: Harvard.

Ostrom, E. (1990). *Governing the commons: The evolution of institutions for collective action.* New York, NY: Cambridge.

Ostrom, E. (1998). A behavioral approach to the rational choice theory of collective action. *American Political Science Review, 92*(1), 1–22.

Ostrom, E. (2005). *Understanding institutional diversity.* Princeton, NJ: Princeton University.

Ostrom, E. (2007). Instituitional rational choice: An assessment of the institutional analysis and development framework. In P. A. Sabatier (Ed.), *Theories of the policy process* (2nd ed., pp. 21–64). Boulder, CO: Westview.

Parmigiani, A., & Rivera-Santos, M. (2011). Clearing a path through the forest: A meta-review of interorganizational relationships. *Journal of Management, 37*(4), 1108–1136.

Perry, J. L., & Thomson, A. M. (2004). *Civic service: What difference does it make?* Armonk, NY: M. E. Sharpe.

Putnam, R. (2000). *Bowling alone: The collapse and revival of American community.* New York, NY: Simon and Schuster.

Rainey, H. G. (2003). *Understanding and managing public organizations* (3rd ed.). San Francisco, CA: Jossey-Bass.

Ring, P. S., & Van de Ven, A. H. (1994). Development processes of cooperative interorganizational relationships. *Academy of Management Review, 19*(1), 90–118.

Ritchey, T. (2011). *Wicked problems – social messes: Decision support modelling with morphological analysis.* Berlin: Springer.

Scott, W. R. (2003). *Organizations: Rational, natural, and open systems* (5th ed.). Upper Saddle River, NJ: Prentice Hall.

Simo, G., & Bies, A. L. (2007). The role of non-profits in disaster response: An expanded model of cross-sector collaboration. *Public Administration Review, 67*(s1), 126–142.

Smith, K. B. (2002). Typologies, taxonomies, and the benefits of policy classification. *Policy Studies Journal, 30*(3), 379–395.

Thacher, D. (2004). Interorganizational partnerships as inchoate hierarchies: A case study of the community security initiative. *Administration & Society, 36*(1), 91–127.

Thatcher, C. (2007). A study of an interorganizational arrangement among three regional campuses of a large land-grant university (Doctoral dissertation, University of Hartford, Hartford, CT, 2007).

Thietart, R.-A., & Forgues, B. (1995). Chaos theory and organization. *Organization Science, 6*(1), 19–31.

Thomson, A. M. (2001). *Collaboration: Meaning and measurement* (Doctoral dissertation, Indiana University, Bloomington, IN, 1995).

Thomson, A. M., & Perry, J. L. (2006). Collaboration processes: Inside the black box. *Public Administration Review, 66*(s1), 20–32.

Thomson, A. M., Perry, J. L., & Miller, T. K. (2009). Conceptualizing and measuring collaboration. *Journal of Public Administration Research and Theory, 19*(1), 23–56.

Trist, E. (1977). A concept of organizational ecology. *Australian Journal of Management, 2*(2), 161–175.

Van Buuren, A., & Gerrits, L. (2008). Decisions as dynamic equilibriums in erratic policy processes. *Public Management Review, 10*(3), 381–399.

Wagner, C. L., & Fernandez-Gimenez, M. (2008). Does community-based collaborative resource management increase social capital? *Society and Natural Resources, 21*(4), 324–344.

Weick, K. E. (1985). Sources of order in underorganized systems: Themes in recent organizational theory. In Y. S. Lincoln (Ed.), *Organizational theory and inquiry: The paradigm revolution* (pp. 106–136). Newbury Park, CA: Sage.

Whetten, D. A. (1981). Interorganizational relations: A review of the field. *The Journal of Higher Education, 52*(1), 1–28.

Williams, A. P. (2010). Implications of operationalizing a comprehensive approach: Defining what interagency interoperability really means. *The International C2 Journal, 4*(1), 1–30.

Woodland, R. H., & Hutton, M. S. (2012). Evaluating organizational collaborations: Suggested entry points and strategies. *American Journal of Evaluation, 33*(3), 366–383.

3 The Prevailing Elements of Public-Sector Collaboration

Martin Mayer and Robert Kenter

Introduction

As the world has become increasingly connected over the last few decades, government and public managers have had to adapt from traditional unitary, hierarchical organizations to networked, collaborative, multi-organizational arrangements (O'Leary & Vij, 2012). This changing environment and the continued growth of third-party governance have led to an abundance of collaborative public management scholarship (O'Leary & Vij, 2012; Thomson, Perry, & Miller, 2009). Much of this literature is by its nature multidisciplinary, vast, and highly fragmented. While the varying conceptualizations add perspective and depth to the field, this richness also makes it difficult to compare results and communicate across disciplines (Thomson et al., 2009).

What this variation produces is not a simple agreed upon definition of the study of collaboration, but an array of wide-ranging theoretical perspectives, definitions, and understandings of collaborative public management (Thomson et al., 2009). Disagreements abound, from process and structure, to distinctions of organizational relationships, all of which have only served to add to the confusion and ambiguity shrouding the field (Morse & Stephens, 2012). To move forward and to build a common language across the multidisciplinary field of study, it is imperative that we heed the advice of prior work in an effort to identify and discuss the core values comprising interorganizational collaboration. This will allow us not only to better understand collaborative elements and processes, but also to gain additional insight into the critical components that help collaboratives to successfully achieve their program goals.

The purpose of this chapter is twofold; first, to identify the components critical to collaboration through the literature, and second, to examine the progress made in collaboration theory-building since the Wood and Gray (1991) symposium to see if we are any closer to reaching agreement on what collaboration is. This work, through the review of the Wood and Gray (1991) symposium, and synthesis of the subsequent literature, attempts to bring some clarity to the definitional issue by exploring the prevailing elements of public-sector collaboration. It is only through definitional clarity that a theory of collaboration will emerge.

The chapter begins by reviewing the definitional conundrum plaguing the theoretical development of collaboration scholarship. After discussing wicked problems and the state of the literature, we will then examine the findings of the 1991 symposium article by Wood and Gray before setting out to replicate and expand on their work. We will delineate prevailing elements of collaboration from the multidisciplinary literature, both to gain a better understanding of what makes up collaboration and also to further examine the progress made over the nearly quarter-century since Wood and Gray (1991) first set out to synthesize the literature toward a definition of collaboration. This is followed by the results of our analysis of the collaboration literature, and what amounts to the prevailing elements that make up public-sector collaboration. A summary conclusion will be offered in which the results of our analysis are contrasted with the findings of Wood and Gray (1991) in an effort to examine the progress made over the last few decades in defining and understanding collaboration. Finally, implications of the findings, particularly the framing and definitional concerns for both scholars and practitioners will be discussed as well as a call for future research.

Overview: The Definitional Conundrum

Wicked Problems

Policy problems by nature are difficult to define, and rarely are clear-cut solutions found for the exceedingly complex problems. Rittel and Webber (1973) were among the first to raise the idea that planning problems are, in and of themselves, wicked problems. Rittel and Webber (1973) point out that wicked problems are termed as such not due to ethical concerns, but due to the difficult nature of the problems, which are often both hard to define and to solve. Ackoff (1973) refers to such issues as "messes," and "systems of problematic situations" (p. 156). Mayer and Harmon (1982) take Ackoff's definition a step further, stating that wicked problems are "ambiguous, value-laden, political, constantly changing, and not amenable to clear definition, much less 'solution' in any sense this word is commonly used" (p. 221). In the past, wicked problems were typically approached in an analytic manner, focusing on scientific management (Ackoff, 1973; Mayer & Harmon, 1982). Such a manner of addressing wicked problems not only fails to fully address the root of the concern, but it also often exacerbates the initial problem (Ackoff, 1973). The divergences and disagreements over how to define such difficult public-sector problems has led to even greater disagreement over how to address these 'wicked problems' when many of the systems presently in place lack the interdependencies necessary to produce the desired outcomes. In situations where wicked problems are prevalent, collaboration has often been sought as a means to address them. By bringing together multiple stakeholders sharing resources and working toward a common goal, collaborations are able to work outside of typical structural constraints in an effort to better address and respond to wicked problems that may otherwise prove too difficult for any one entity to address on its own.

State of the Field

Gray's 1985 article, "Conditions Facilitating Interorganizational Collaboration" in *Human Relations*, widely recognized as the seminal work on collaboration, offers collaboration as a prescription to these wicked problems. Gray (1985) defines collaboration as "the pooling of appreciations and/or tangible resources, e.g. information, money, labor etc., by two or more stakeholders, to solve a set of problems which neither can solve individually" (p. 912). She argues that when stakeholders pool resources and perceptions through collaboration, solutions to these wicked problems can become clearer. Gray (1985) argues a pluralistic view of the problem from a diverse group of stakeholders will result in solutions that go well beyond the capacity of any one organization.

Gray (1989) expounded on these views in her follow-up book, *Collaborating: Finding Common Ground for Multiparty Problems*, in which she characterizes the confluence of wicked problems as an environmental turbulence. Gray (1989) describes collaboration as a process in which the inherent environmental turbulence can be constructively explored from multiple visions and approaches. Gray (1989) further defines collaboration as something that "transforms adversarial interaction into a mutual search for information and for solutions that allow all those participating to insure that their interests are represented" (p. 7).

In an effort to craft a general theory of collaboration, Wood and Gray (1991) facilitated a two-part symposium in the *Journal of Applied Behavioral Science*. At the onset they assumed the definitional aspect was already mutually agreed upon and the majority of the work would center on building a general theory of collaboration. What the authors quickly discovered was their definitional assumption was flawed. Each article had a different perspective and a different definition of collaboration. In the six years since Gray's 1985 article, the concept had quickly diverged in several unrelated directions.

In the nearly quarter-century since the symposium, and as collaborative arrangements have grown significantly, this disagreement has only grown wider. Context and scope have played a significant role in how one defines collaboration. Some have defined it as a shared process (Gray, 1989; Thomson & Perry, 2006; Wood & Gray, 1991), whereas others view collaboration as simply a "temporary social arrangement" (Roberts & Bradley, 1991, p. 212). Some definitions are broader, encompassing any organizations that work together toward the creation of public value (Imperial, 2005; Muller, 2010), whereas others are more specific, examining negotiation strategies and rule structuring (Thomson et al., 2009). As different as the definitions may be, many of them still build on the same concepts.

Toward a Comprehensive Theory of Collaboration

In their 1991 symposium, Wood and Gray examined nine articles in an attempt to move forward with a general definition of collaboration critical to further theory-building. As noted previously, what the authors found was that there was very little agreement from study to study. Some of the work highlighted the importance of particular components over others, while some overlapped. Ultimately, noting this disparity Wood and Gray (1991) set out to highlight the common elements of the varying definitions. What they identified were six prevailing elements of collaboration that emerged from their two-part, nine-article symposium.

The first element they identify is "stakeholders of a problem domain" (p. 146). In identifying this element, they noted that the stakeholders may begin the process with different interests, but this may morph into common interests over time as the collaborative effort unfolds. They are clear in their assertion that all stakeholders need not be represented, but a cross section of stakeholders is vital. The second fundamental element of collaboration is autonomy. Stakeholders may have varying levels of autonomy, but maintaining a degree of autonomy is a foundation to collaboration that makes it unique from a merger or a corporatist model. The authors identify a third element of collaboration as an interactive process that facilitates organizational change. This is a process in which all stakeholders must be involved.

Wood and Gray's (1991) conceptualization of collaboration must also include shared rules, norms, and structures. These elements may be implied or the stakeholders may mindfully negotiate their terms. Wood and Gray (1991) intentionally omit the term limit of a collaboration, as the structures can and often do evolve over time. That said, however, duration of the effort does not define an effort as being collaborative; it is simply used to classify the effort.

Intentional action is another foundational element the authors posit. Stakeholders must move beyond merely discussing solutions to a wicked policy issue. For an effort to be considered collaboration the stakeholders must act to address that issue. The authors are clear that reaching a desired outcome is not a defining element but the effort itself is the foundational element. The final foundational element is the effort must be focused on a specific domain. The domain can be as localized as small watershed protection efforts or involve international policy issues. The size of the domain is irrelevant; but the policy issue addressed must be in an effort to affect the domain's future appearance.

After reviewing the literature, Wood and Gray realized just how disparate the definitions were and how far the field still had to come in order to move beyond the preliminary task of defining the concept to advance toward collaboration theory-building. The six elements described above are the result of Wood and Gray's (1991) attempt to build a generalizable theory of collaboration. By replicating and expanding on the process Wood and Gray (1991) went through, we hope to both provide additional insight into collaborative processes while also examining the progress made in the field since Wood and Gray's symposium.

Methodology

In an attempt to better understand the collaboration literature at a broad, macro-level, this chapter employs and expands on an approach first utilized by Wood and Gray in 1991. By reviewing the collaboration literature for key processes and definitional differences of collaborative structures we are able to better understand both how collaboration is defined and the elements critical to its existence. Furthermore we can chart and examine the progress made by the field in the nearly 25 years that have passed from the Wood and Gray (1991) symposium.

This chapter began by discussing wicked problems and the definitional issues that have plagued collaboration theory-building from the beginning. In order to gauge both where the literature stands and the progress, or lack thereof, since the Wood and Gray (1991) article, we reviewed multiple databases and collected well over 100 articles in the processes and components of public-sector collaboration. The field was then narrowed down through the application of a few specific criteria: that the articles attempt to define collaboration; that they discuss components and/or processes of collaboration; and that they focus primarily on public-sector collaboration. After applying this set of criteria, the number of initial studies was pared down to 60 to be used in the final analysis. Of the 60 selected studies, each was carefully reviewed for key terms, processes, and components of public-sector collaboration. In the manner of Wood and Gray (1991) and Mattessich, Murray-Close, and Monsey (2001), these terms were then tallied and compared, in order to delineate the common elements of collaboration across the literature.

The initial review provided a large list of terms, components, and processes of collaboration. Redundant items were then collapsed and what emerged were the nine most common elements of collaboration from the reviewed literature. The nine components of collaboration examined are: communication, consensus decision-making, diverse stakeholders, goals, leadership, shared resources, shared vision, social capital, and trust. These nine components provide insight into collaborative structure in an attempt to begin to address the definitional issue through synthesis of the literature, while also allowing for a comparison between the Wood and Gray (1991) study to see how much or how little the field has changed. These components are not meant to be exhaustive or mutually exclusive; in fact, many of them are mutually reinforcing, often contingent upon, or building on, one trait or another. Table 3.1 presents the summary definitions of each of the nine components.

After discussing each of the nine components, a summary conclusion is offered that includes a discussion of the progress, or lack thereof, since the Wood and Gray (1991) article, and, finally, a brief discussion of the implications of our findings for both scholars and practitioners is offered while also highlighting the potential for future research.

Table 3.1 Key Components of Collaboration Defined

Component	Description
Communication	Frequent and open lines of communication help to promote healthy dialogue, information-sharing, and increased social capital
Consensus Decision-Making	Requires well-defined and mutually agreed upon goals. Encourages cooperation, reduces risk, and promotes an inclusive collaborative process
Diverse Stakeholders	Must be actively sought and can be integral to effective decision-making. Diverse stakeholders bring a variety of intellectual and tangible resources to a collaborative
Goals	Must be clearly articulated and attainable to provide an effective evaluative criterion. Also must balance individual and group goals to ensure an effective working environment
Leadership	Often shared, within both formal and informal structures. Strong leadership adds legitimacy and credibility to a collaborative
Shared Resources	The pooling of resources is one of the primary reasons people agree to collaborate. Shared resources lead to the creation of something greater than any one individual could produce on their own
Shared Vision	Can be the initial bond that brings stakeholders together. Shared vision leads to greater buy-in, fit, and incentive for stakeholders to work together for the greater good
Social Capital	Critical in advancing collaboration beyond the formative stages. Social capital eases the process and has the ability to grow networks to increase organizational problem-solving
Trust	Based on mutual understanding and developed through significant dialogue, trust is critical to bringing in stakeholders willing to share resources

Prevailing Elements of Collaboration

Communication

There are a number of important aspects critical to the success of collaboration; perhaps none more so than the need for frequent and open lines of communication (Borden & Perkins, 1999; Johnson, Zorn, Yung Tam, Lamontagne, & Johnson, 2003). Frequent and open lines of communication and a well-thought out communication strategy can promote dialogue and information-sharing (McNamara, 2012), which can lead to more effective stakeholder interaction (Lasker, Weiss, & Miller, 2001) and increased social capital. A communication strategy is particularly important when stakeholders come from different backgrounds and organizational cultures (Ferreyra & Beard, 2007). By creating and promoting both formal and informal channels of communication, information-sharing, mutual understanding, and group learning are promoted within the collaborative (Keast, Brown, & Mandell, 2007). This can have a ripple effect encouraging and promoting diverse organizational partnerships, which leads to greater organizational buy-in that can be critical in breaking down walls and effectively solving problems (Ferreyra & Beard, 2007). In high-functioning organizations, communication and dialogue are vital to articulating and achieving shared goals and collective objectives (Gajda & Koliba, 2007); both quantity and quality matter (Emerson, Nabatchi, & Balogh, 2012). Quantity is particularly important in the early stages of a collaborative when attempting to build interest and attract stakeholders (Emerson et al., 2012). Over time, quality takes precedence to ensure that the right people are brought to the decision-making table (Emerson et al., 2012). By balancing quantity and quality, collaborative managers are able to have lasting and effective impacts on collaborative processes (Heikkila & Gerlak, 2014).

Collaborative arrangements characterized by poor communication can suffer from a number of inter- and intraorganizational challenges that can adversely affect the collaboration and the relations of the stakeholders within it (Ferreyra & Beard, 2007). One challenge in particular that collaborations struggle with is the need to centralize a communication strategy amongst decentralized partners (Thomson & Perry, 2006; Thomson et al., 2009); this can be exacerbated in organizations with low social capital, where organization and trust may be lacking. Without taking sufficient time to build the necessary channels, implementing and successfully carrying out a communication strategy can become a significant challenge. Another challenge, common in low-functioning organizations, is that dialogue and communication can take on a confirmatory tone, one in which congeniality is confused with professional discourse; this can foster an unhealthy and ineffective collaborative environment (Gajda & Koliba, 2007). In addition, in collaboration plagued by poor communication, it becomes exceedingly difficult to promote and carry out consensus decision-making (Noonan, McCall, Zheng, & Gaumer-Erickson, 2012), because stakeholders tend to feel alienated and ultimately participation and effectiveness decreases (Ansell & Gash, 2007).

Consensus Decision-Making

Consensus decision-making is seen throughout the literature as both a necessary and vital component of group decision-making in collaborative structures. Consensus decision-making promotes representation (Margerum, 2002), encourages cooperation (Ansell & Gash, 2007), and reduces risk (Innes & Booher, 1999); however, it does not come without its difficulties. As with any organizational arrangement, structure plays a critical role in building the necessary channels to achieve consensus. In collaboration, this means fashioning organizational structure in a manner to dissipate authority equally to all stakeholders, which in turn promotes consensus building and makes mutual goal recognition more achievable (Innes & Booher, 1999). When creating organizational structures aimed at consensus building, it is imperative that relations promote group ownership rather than a subordinate-to-superior relationship; this helps to promote an inclusive and collaborative process while mitigating potential stakeholder unrest (Innes & Booher, 1999).

As difficult as it is to build consensus decision-making structures, parties still have a significant amount of additional work to be done when consensus decision-making structures are in place. First, there must be well-defined, mutually agreed upon goals supported by effective leadership (Ansell & Gash, 2007; Strieter & Blalock, 2006). Leaders must be able to relate to all stakeholders, as they play a major part in this formative step (Margerum, 2002). Consensus building is an inclusive process; a process that brings together stakeholders through both internal and external communication strategies. When done effectively, which does not necessarily mean reaching consensus as much as it does going through the process (Ansell & Gash, 2007), consensus building can promote greater cohesion within the collaboration (Noonan et al., 2012). The process has the ability to overcome barriers between stakeholders, while at the same time fostering a dialogue that is critical in identifying conditions for mutual benefit (Ansell & Gash, 2007). Although consensus is not always sought or achieved (Leach, Pelkey, & Sabatier, 2002), some degree of consensus is often required to move collaborations forward.

Ultimately, consensus building is an ideal to be strived for (Emerson et al., 2012); one that to achieve can often be both costly and time-consuming (Berner & Bronson, 2005; Leach et al., 2002). In addition to operational constraints, a number of additional contextual and ideological obstacles exist that can inhibit consensus building in collaboration (Gray, 1989; Margerum, 2002). Once again, effective leadership is highly important in mitigating these concerns and successfully moving collaboration forward (Margerum, 2002).

Diverse Stakeholders

The inclusion of diverse stakeholders in collaboration helps to mitigate against factions forming amongst stakeholders, which can be integral to effective decision-making. The presence of diversity among stakeholders creates "a richer, more comprehensive appreciation of the problem" (Gray, 1989, p. 5). Diverse stakeholders bring a variety of resources and perceptions to the table, which allow for a true collective, collaborative process in which organizational capacity is increased (Lasker et al., 2001). A primary benefit of having a diverse membership base is the stakeholders' individual abilities and existing ties to the community. This preexisting level of trust and resources helps to build social capital for collaboration faster than would otherwise be possible without stakeholder diversity (Majumdar, Moynihan, & Pierce, 2009).

Diversity and participation of stakeholders is not something that is "simply tolerated but must be actively sought" (Ansell & Gash, 2007, p. 556). High levels of diversity amongst stakeholders can lessen disagreement by bringing a number of valuable and diverse perspectives to the table (Gray, 1989). As was the case with consensus decision-making, high levels of social capital, along with effective leadership, are critical to bringing diverse stakeholders into a collaborative agreement (Ferreyra & Beard, 2007). Collaborations with diverse stakeholders who are engaged and present throughout the decision-making process tend to "produce more robust and legitimate strategies" than collaboratives made up of a more homogenous group (Innes & Booher, 2003, p. 17).

One way in which to foster stakeholder presence and engagement is to attempt to include individuals from a number of different levels within member organizations (Provan & Lemaire, 2012). When both top administrators and street-level administrators converge and mutually work toward a common goal, Provan and Lemaire (2012) suggest the result will be increased efficacy of the collaboration that will carry over to increased efficacy of the parent organization as well. This level of inclusion can help to promote greater working environments, both within and outside of the collaborative, and is a necessary component of collaborative organizations attempting to address wicked and often boundaryless problems (Lasker et al., 2001).

While the inclusion of diverse stakeholders brings many valuable traits to collaboration, some potential causes for concern are present. A primary obstacle to overcome is one of trust. In partnerships comprised of individuals from a number of different personal and professional backgrounds, trust commonly has to be earned in order to overcome skepticism and misgivings about shared power (Lasker et al., 2001). To build high levels of trust, it often takes time and sacrifice, especially in collaboration that does not benefit from high social capital upon inception (Lasker et al., 2001). Leadership is often instrumental in properly incorporating diverse stakeholders into an organization and navigating the time-consuming challenges inherent before realizing the potential that each stakeholder brings to the collaborative.

Goals

The need for attainable, clearly articulated and agreed upon goals forms the basic foundation of the work of collaboration (Conley & Moote, 2003). In a collaborative, goal congruence and consensus decision-making set the agenda for collaboration, while also playing an important role as the primary benchmark for establishing evaluative criteria (Conley & Moote, 2003). Easily measured goals allow for a baseline to measure progress, as well as offering a deliverable objective that stakeholders can take back to their parent organization as a sign of development (Woodland & Hutton, 2012). Goal-setting can be an instructive process that can enhance social capital, trust, and relationship building (Lasker et al., 2001; Strieter & Blalock, 2006). When properly carried out, this process can create the buy-in and cohesion necessary to ensure stakeholders place the goals of the collaborative over their own individual or organizational goals (Johnston, Hicks, Nan, & Auer, 2011). Collaborative leaders must be mindful of this because individual goals and motivations, especially when divergent from the goals of the collaborative, can impact the effectiveness and work environment of all involved parties (Bryson, Crosby, & Stone, 2006). Generally, the greater the social capital of the collaborative, the more legitimacy stakeholders attribute to it, the more collective goal congruence is possible (Bryson et al., 2006; O' Leary & Vij, 2012).

Although goal congruence is imperative for collaboration, often a delicate balance exists that must be nurtured and maintained during the goal-setting process. While collective goals are the objective, the importance and motivating factors of individual or stakeholder goals should not be overlooked (Logsdon, 1991; O' Leary & Vij, 2012; Thomson & Perry, 2006; Thomson et al., 2009). Failure to acknowledge or incorporate individual goals into the collective effort can result in a tension that requires collaborative managers to deal with many challenging and conflicting situations that can be exacerbated by the personalities of the individuals involved (O'Leary & Vij, 2012). This can be further compounded by the voluntary nature of, and the nontraditional accountability mechanisms inherent in, collaborative arrangements (Huxham, 1996). While addressing these challenges, the leadership can often use the challenges as means to address concerns through honest and transparent dialogue (Connelly, Zhang, & Faerman, 2008), which may have the potential to provide creative solutions to complex problems (Innes & Booher, 1999; McKinney & Field, 2008).

Leadership

The role of leadership in collaboration is equivalent to that of traditional hierarchical structured organizations, with the primary difference being the emphasis on a number of different management attributes (O'Leary, Choi, & Gerard, 2012). In collaboration, leadership is much more likely to be shared and transferred, as well as both formal and informal (Bryson et al., 2006). "Desired behaviors are identifying stakeholders, assessing stakeholders, framing strategic issues, convening working groups, facilitating mutual learning processes, inducing commitment, and facilitating trusting relationships among partners" (O'Leary et al., 2012, p. S74).

Effective leadership often necessitates a strong convener, an individual or individuals responsible for initiating the collaboration and early process-oriented tasks, such as bringing in stakeholders, goal-setting and guiding the process through inevitable challenges inherent to group activity (Bryson et al., 2006; Gray, 1989). The presence of strong leadership and an effective convener (one with high social capital) can add legitimacy and credibility, while also providing "essential mediation and facilitation for the collaborative process" (Ansell & Gash, 2007, p. 550). Effective leadership can also transcend organizational boundaries, making other stakeholders aware of the macro-importance of the outcomes of their efforts, and summoning them to infuse the goals of the collaboration into the goals of their parent organization (Denhardt & Campbell, 2006; Miner, 2005).

Effective leadership is perhaps the most critical element of a collaborative being able to achieve its goals. Effective leadership not only guides the collaboration, but also impacts and influences all of the additional components that influence the work of a collaborative. Leadership can be a great challenge for any collaborative arrangement at both an organizational and individual level. First, a leader must be designated or emerge from the group of stakeholders already involved in the collaborative process. In cases when there is no willing or able leadership, a 'binding agent' is often tasked with keeping the organization on task while social capital increases and additional leadership options emerge (Ansell & Gash, 2007; Morse, 2010).

This difficult process of identifying a leader within collaboration carries with it a number of potentially high transaction costs associated with convening collaboration (Emerson et al., 2012). One of the primary tasks of collaboration leadership is to attract key stakeholders who have the resources and wherewithal to address need in shared power arrangements, while also bringing a number of varying and complementary resources in to the fold (Crosby & Bryson, 2005). In order for leadership to effectively bring in such stakeholders, the focus must be on the process of creating a shared vision and achieving common good as opposed to organizational goals (Morse, 2010). Dealing with inevitable conflicts that arise from bringing together a large pool of diverse stakeholders can be quite challenging, often hinging on interpersonal skills and social capital. By successfully sustaining organizational commitment, leaders are likely to have greater long-term and sustaining success as additional social capital is built throughout the process (Morse, 2010). Those who have a background in public management may find this task especially daunting. Public managers have traditionally relied on hierarchical relations within the bureaucracy and legal rational authority to legitimize their leadership. When confronted with leading from within a collaborative, these individuals find themselves challenged with the demands of leading across traditional boundaries (Getha-Taylor & Morse, 2013). Due to the growth of the information age, this collaborative horizontal approach to management is increasingly common (Agranoff & McGuire, 2003) and supported by younger, highly educated managers at a higher rate than their less-educated, older counterparts (Esteve, Boyne, Sierra, & Ysa, 2014). The authors argue these types of leaders perceive collaboration as a more useful tool than their older counterparts, which results in a more adaptive leadership style that collaboratives find conducive to success. This mindset is especially critical in the early phases of collaboration, when fledgling organizations often lack social capital and organizational trust, and must look to an individual for leadership and direction.

Shared Resources

Shared resources is another critical element to the overall success of collaboration in achieving its organizational goals, but like many of the components examined earlier in this chapter, shared resources are predicated on a number of additional factors. Leadership must be able to span boundaries and foster an environment in which stakeholders are comfortable and willing to expose themselves to risk for the collective good (Margerum & Robinson, 2015).

One of the primary reasons collaborators pledge resources is to address a particular interest more efficiently than they may otherwise be able to on their own (Logsdon, 1991). Collaboratives align stakeholders and resources, bringing both to the table to effect change; this is not done effectively without a significant amount of trust because individual stakeholders can open themselves to substantial risk by pledging resources (Innes & Booher, 2003). In order for a collaborative to attract diverse stakeholders willing to share resources, a high level of social capital and sense of legitimacy within the collaborative must be present (Bryson et al., 2006; Logsdon, 1991; McNamara, 2012). This can be achieved in part by fostering an environment of reciprocity in which leadership is able to encourage diverse stakeholders to participate and contribute resources equally for the mutual benefit of all involved parties (Logsdon, 1991). Shared resources may refer to more than just capital; technical expertise and nontangible aspects, such as shared legitimacy, are among the many items that can be viewed as a shared resource (Agranoff, 2006). Collaboration, "by combining the individual perspectives, resources, and skills of the partners ... creates something new and valuable together, a whole that is greater than the sum of its individual parts" (Lasker et al., 2001, p. 184).

As critical as shared resources are to collaborations being able to reach their goals, they also have the ability to create conflict between stakeholders in collaboration. Power imbalances may form when there are a majority of resources being contributed from a minority of the stakeholders; this is not simply limited to collaboratives with low social capital either (O' Leary & Vij, 2012). The difficulty in quantifying different types of resources further contributes to the problem, as "the most costly resources of collaboration are not money but time and energy...." (Thomson & Perry, 2006, p. 28). In addition to resource definition, free-riders can also be a problem. Leaders must be cognizant of the potential that shared resources can have empowering free-riders, and in turn must design organizational processes to combat such potential pitfalls. One of the primary mechanisms often employed to combat free-riders is the introduction of coercion or incentives by leadership, and another is to keep groups small and in turn more manageable from which to promote a shared vision (Olson, 2009). Collaboratives with high social capital and inclusive transparent processes are more likely to foster an environment where stakeholders hold each other accountable and free-riders are less of an issue (Ansell & Gash, 2007).

Shared Vision

Shared vision and common interest play an important role throughout all phases of collaboration success. Common interest is often the first link that brings stakeholders together; allowing a bond to form and facilitating a sense of group ownership of an issue (Gajda & Koliba, 2007). At this point dialogue is critical in transforming a common interest into a shared vision; "stakeholder values, perspectives, and expectations" must be considered in order to define and negotiate goals as well as articulate vision and strategy (Ferreyra & Beard, 2007, p. 290). When a collaborative effort achieves synergy early on, the chances of improved outcomes are increased (Bardach & Lesser, 1996). An articulated shared vision and the buy-in that comes from a "cultural fit" allows for participants from a variety of backgrounds to quickly get up to speed and adapt to the collaborative structure (Shaw, 2003, p. 110). Stakeholders can then work together in a more efficient manner, pooling resources, minimizing service duplication, and achieving "a vision that would not otherwise be possible to obtain as separate actors working independently" (Gajda, 2004, p. 68).

A broadly shared vision both attracts and provides incentive for stakeholders to contribute resources and work together to overcome difficulties (Ansell & Gash, 2007; Gajda & Koliba, 2007). Shared vision promotes trust and the building of social capital through mutual respect and a sense of group ownership (Gray, 1989). In a collaborative environment, a shared vision is essential to the goal-setting and formulation phases, while also serving as a barometer of the overall health of the collaboration (Ansell & Gash, 2007). Shared vision requires a dedication to project goals, general agreement on scope of the collaborative, and a certain level of sacrifice for the greater good of the group; without this agreement collaboration has little chance of being successful (Gajda, 2004).

Agreeing on a shared vision and especially the strategy to achieve it can be especially difficult in collaboratives that have leadership conflicts or a number of strong personalities that differ on how to best move forward (Morse, 2010). In such organizations, it then becomes important for leadership to articulate the significance of the interdependence between stakeholders that is necessary in order to achieve the greater good (Gray, 1989). "Heightening parties' awareness of their interdependence often kindles renewed willingness to search for trade-offs that could produce a mutually beneficial solution" (Gray, 1989, p. 11). This ability to bring stakeholders to the table, especially in times of conflict, highlights the importance of social capital as it relates to the success of collaboration and the articulation of a shared vision.

Social Capital

Social capital, the presence of existing and trusting relationships and their value, is a major component in advancing collaboration from a formative stage to a functioning outcome-oriented one. The presence of social capital, built through prior working relationships, can substantially cut down the amount of time required for dialogue, deliberation, and trust building during the formation stage of the collaboration (Gerlak & Heikkila, 2007; Mandarano, 2008; O'Leary & Vij, 2012). In a collaborative lacking social capital, it is often a lengthy, time-consuming process to build strong working relationships (Innes & Booher, 2003).

The presence of social capital is not static; it can fluctuate over time, mirroring the health of the collaborative itself (Genskow & Born, 2006; Leach et al., 2002). Periodic evaluations are key to building and maintaining social capital (Leach et al., 2002; Majumdar et al., 2009). Evaluations offer the collaborative and its stakeholders a critical analysis of the progress toward shared goals, and highlight areas where improvement is needed. Social capital can be both a critical component to the start-up of collaboration, an input that leads to collective action as well as an output, the result of the newly formed synergy between participants (Morris, Gibson, Leavitt, & Jones, 2013). High social capital has the ability to broaden the participants' existing network and allows them to increase organizational problem-solving capacity as necessary through their network without additional outside resources (Morris et al., 2013).

In organizations with little or no social capital, much more work needs to be focused early on in terms of relationship building and networking that could otherwise be devoted to addressing a problem issue (Innes & Booher, 2003). Collaborations lacking social capital will have a more difficult time exchanging information, which may in turn lead to a competitive environment where stakeholders leverage resources for individual rather than mutual benefit (Thomson & Perry, 2006). Trustworthiness ultimately proves critical to building social capital and maintaining a healthy collaborative organizational environment geared toward collective action and mutual benefit (Ostrom, 1998).

Trust

Trust is often cited as one of the most vital components necessary to build and sustain collaboration (Gray, 1985; Huxham, 1996; Mattessich & Monsey, 1992; Morris et al., 2013; O'Leary & Vij, 2012; Thomson & Perry, 2006). Trust can be defined as "a willingness to take risk" through the vulnerability that one party has to another in a relationship (Mayer, Davis, & Schoorman, 1995, p. 712). "Trust between partners in interorganizational arrangements is based on mutual understanding and confidence that all partners are working toward collective action" (McNamara, 2012, p. 397). Stakeholder face-to-face dialogue, what Ansell and Gash (2007) term "thick communication" (p. 588), is imperative to develop trust and, in turn, the social capital necessary to perpetuate a process of encouragement and goodwill (Morris et al., 2013).

Trust building is time-consuming, challenging, and frequently the most critical part of an early collaborative (Ansell & Gash, 2007; Bryson et al., 2006; McNamara, 2012; Thomson & Perry, 2006; Thomson et al., 2009). Trust, shared responsibility, and social capital are strongly correlated, and with the absence of one, the likelihood of a collaborative working well and being successful decreases significantly (Lasker et al., 2001).

While trust is frequently a strong factor in collaborations, Ansell and Gash (2007) "note that strong trust and interdependence among subsets of stakeholders may actually discourage collaborative strategies among a wider set of actors" (p. 554). This is often the case when stakeholders view fellow stakeholders as competitors instead of collaborators, and can result in factions forming within the larger group (Sharfman, Gray, & Yan, 1991). Lack of trust can also result in ineffective and varied levels of organizational commitment (Gray, 1989). In order to mitigate these concerns, trust building must been seen as an ongoing process and a necessary element throughout all phases of collaboration (Ring & Van de Ven, 1994).

Conclusions

Simply put, collaboration is a challenge. The multidisciplinary literature, the disagreements over how to articulate and address wicked problems, and the ambiguity that characterizes attempts to define and delineate collaboration from other multiorganizational arrangements highlight some of the inherent difficulties faced by those attempting to describe the process, structure, and relationships in this form of public-sector governance. While this multidisciplinary approach contributes to the disagreement and ambiguity exemplified by the difficulty defining collaboration conceptually, it also adds richness and complexity to the variety of approaches in the literature.

This chapter set out to provide insight and clarity into the elements critical to a collaborative's ability to achieve its goals and objectives despite the disagreements present in the literature. Through a review of the multidisciplinary literature we have identified nine components that help to explain the structure inherent to such public-sector organizational arrangements; these components include: (1) communication; (2) consensus decision-making; (3) diverse stakeholders; (4) goals; (5) leadership; (6) shared resources; (7) shared vision; (8) social capital; and (9) trust.

Each of the nine discussed components forms a critical aspect of collaborative arrangements. They are not mutually exclusive, can exist in various arrangements at various levels, and can and frequently do overlap. The nine key components discussed herein offer a broad set of criteria as identified by the literature of what is required for collaboration to successfully achieve its goals and objectives. By further understanding how each of the nine elements works within collaboration, we are better able to identify and understand collaborative processes, as well as how collaboratives operate and why some are able to achieve their goals in the face of wicked problems whereas others are not.

Progress

Our analysis resulted in the identification of nine elements of collaboration that have been consistently represented in the literature as foundations. When contrasted with the results achieved by Wood and Gray (1991) after a similar exercise more than 20 years ago, it becomes apparent that the concept of collaboration has evolved considerably. Of the six elements that Wood and Gray argue are vital to collaboration, our analysis resulted in just two related elements: the importance in the diversity of stakeholders, and the domain orientation which could potentially fall into either goals or shared vision.

Part of the reason for this could be due to the fact that Wood and Gray (1991) only reviewed nine articles, but the small sample aside, this exercise, especially when compared with their results from more than 20 years ago, produces some interesting findings. First, it becomes evident that the fragmentary nature that plagued collaboration theory development at the time of their study has not dissipated, and if anything it has become more widespread and accepted over time. The difference between the results of the two studies points toward an evolution in thinking when it comes to the critical components of collaboration, but it could just as likely be the result of examining just a sliver of a greatly expanding body of literature. While the results have evolved from one study to the next, whether that constitutes progress is left to debate.

Implications

This work is valuable to both academics and practitioners alike that are interested in collaboration, especially how and why it works. Furthermore, this work should be of particular interest to those initiating, engaging in, and wanting to enhance public-sector collaborative arrangements as the nine components provide a checklist of the elements influencing and comprising public-sector collaborative arrangements.

This work builds on prior research through the examination of key elements necessary in high-performing public-sector collaboration. The nine identified elements provide a framework for understanding and implementing critical collaborative processes.

Future Research

While we have set forth a basic framework for understanding collaborative processes, for future research it would be interesting to operationalize these components and pose them to collaborative organizations as a way to gain additional insights into how prevalent and necessary they truly are from a practitioner's point of view. Not only would this provide empirical insight into the prevailing elements of collaboration and how the literature aligns with results from the field, it would also raise a number of additional avenues for future research, such as examining how different level organizations utilize particular components and how this varies across a number of additional factors.

Appendix: Table 3.A.1

Table 3.A.1 Key Components of Collaboration in the Literature

Component	Work Cited
Communication	Ansell & Gash, 2007; Borden & Perkins, 1999; Emerson et al., 2012; Ferreyra & Beard, 2007; Frey et al., 2006; Gajda, 2004; Gajda & Koliba, 2007; Heikkila & Gerlak, 2014; Imperial, 2005; Innes & Booher, 2003; Johnson et al., 2003; Keast et al., 2007; Lasker et al., 2001; McKinney & Field, 2008; McNamara, 2012; Mattessich et al., 2001; Noonan et al., 2012; O'Leary & Vij, 2012; Sharfman et al., 1991; Thomson & Perry, 2006; Thomson et al., 2009; Woodland & Hutton, 2012
Consensus Decision-Making	Ansell & Gash, 2007; Berner & Bronson, 2005; Conley & Moote, 2003; Emerson et al., 2012; Frey et al., 2006; Gajda, 2004; Gray, 1989; Innes & Booher, 1999; Leach et al., 2002; McNamara, 2012; Margerum, 2002; Muller, 2010; Noonan et al., 2012; Strieter & Blalock, 2006; Thomson et al., 2009; Woodland & Hutton, 2012
Diverse Stakeholders	Ansell & Gash, 2007; Bryson et al., 2006; Conley & Moote, 2003; Ferreyra & Beard, 2007; Gray, 1989; Imperial, 2005; Innes & Booher, 2003; Lasker et al., 2001; Leach et al., 2002; Logsdon, 1991; Majumdar et al., 2009; Mandarano, 2008; Mattessich et al., 2001; Muller, 2010; Noonan et al., 2012; O'Leary & Vij, 2012; Provan & Lemaire, 2012; Strieter & Blalock, 2006; Thomson et al., 2009; Wood & Gray, 1991

continued

60   M. Mayer and R. Kenter

Table 3.A.1 Continued

Component	Work Cited
Goals	Ansell & Gash, 2007; Borden & Perkins, 1999; Bryson et al., 2006; Conley & Moote, 2003; Connelly et al., 2008; Ferreyra & Beard, 2007; Gajda, 2004; Genskow & Born, 2006; Huxham, 1996; Innes & Booher, 1999; Innes & Booher, 2003; Johnston et al., 2011; Lasker et al., 2001; Leach et al., 2002; Logsdon, 1991; McKinney & Field, 2008; McNamara, 2012; Mattessich et al., 2001; O'Leary & Vij, 2012; Strieter & Blalock, 2006; Thomson & Perry, 2006; Thomson et al., 2009; Wood & Gray, 1991; Woodland & Hutton, 2012
Leadership	Agranoff & McGuire, 2003; Ansell & Gash, 2007; Borden & Perkins, 1999; Bryson et al., 2006; Crosby & Bryson, 2005; Denhardt & Campbell, 2006; Emerson et al., 2012; Esteve et al., 2014; Ferreyra & Beard, 2007; Gajda, 2004; Genskow & Born, 2006; Gerlak & Heikkila, 2007; Getha-Taylor & Morse, 2013; Gray, 1989; Innes & Booher, 2003; Lasker et al., 2001; Logsdon, 1991; Mandarano, 2008; Mattessich et al., 2001; Miner, 2005; Morse, 2010; Muller, 2010; Noonan et al., 2012; O'Leary et al., 2012; Thomson & Perry, 2006; Thomson et al., 2009; Wood & Gray, 1991; Woodland & Hutton, 2012
Shared Resources	Agranoff, 2006; Ansell & Gash, 2007; Bryson et al., 2006; Ferreyra & Beard, 2007; Frey et al., 2006; Gerlak & Heikkila, 2007; Imperial, 2005; Innes & Booher, 2003; Lasker et al., 2001; Logsdon, 1991; McNamara, 2012; Majumdar et al., 2009; Margerum, 2002; Margerum & Robinson, 2015; Noonan et al., 2012; O'Leary & Vij, 2012; Olson, 2009; Sharfman et al., 1991; Thomson & Perry, 2006; Thomson et al., 2009; Wood & Gray, 1991
Shared Vision	Ansell & Gash, 2007; Bardach & Lesser, 1996; Conley & Moote, 2003; Ferreyra & Beard, 2007; Gajda, 2004; Gajda & Koliba, 2007; Gray, 1989; Imperial, 2005; McKinney & Field, 2008; Mattessich et al., 2001; Morse, 2010; Noonan et al., 2012; O'Leary & Vij, 2012; Shaw, 2003; Strieter & Blalock, 2006; Thomson & Perry, 2006; Thomson et al., 2009; Woodland & Hutton, 2012
Social Capital	Berner & Bronson, 2005; Bryson et al., 2006; Conley & Moote, 2003; Ferreyra & Beard, 2007; Frey et al., 2006; Genskow & Born, 2006; Gerlak & Heikkila, 2007; Innes & Booher, 2003; Leach et al., 2002; Majumdar et al., 2009; Mandarano, 2008; Morris et al., 2013; Muller, 2010; O'Leary & Vij, 2012; Ostrom, 1998; Thomson & Perry, 2006

Table 3.A.1 Continued

Component	Work Cited
Trust	Ansell & Gash, 2007; Bryson et al., 2006; Conley & Moote, 2003; Frey et al., 2006; Gerlak & Heikkila, 2007; Gray, 1985; Gray, 1989; Huxham, 1996; Innes & Booher, 2003; Lasker et al., 2001; McKinney & Field, 2008; McNamara, 2012; Mandarano, 2008; Mattessich & Monsey, 1992; Mattessich et al., 2001; Mayer et al., 1995; Morris et al., 2013; Noonan et al., 2012; O'Leary & Vij, 2012; Ring & Van de Ven, 1994; Sharfman et al., 1991; Thomson & Perry, 2006; Thomson et al., 2009; Woodland & Hutton, 2012

References

Ackoff, R. (1973). Planning in the systems age. *Indian Journal of Statistics: Series B (1960–2002), 35*(2), 149–164.

Agranoff, R. (2006). Inside collaborative networks: Ten lessons for public managers. *Public Administration Review, 66,* 56–65.

Agranoff, R., & McGuire, M. (2003). Inside the matrix: Integrating the paradigms of intergovernmental and network management. *International Journal of Public Administration, 26*(12), 1401–1422.

Ansell, C., & Gash, A. (2007). Collaborative governance in theory and practice. *Journal of Public Administration Research and Theory, 18,* 543–571.

Bardach, E., & Lesser, C. (1996). Accountability in human services collaboratives: For what? And to whom? *Journal of Public Administration Research and Theory, 6*(2), 197–224.

Berner, M., & Bronson, M. (2005). A case study of program evaluation in local government: Building consensus through collaboration. *Public Performance & Management Review, 28*(3), 309–325.

Borden, L., & Perkins, D. (1999). Assessing your collaboration: A self evaluation tool. *Journal of Extension, 37*(2).

Bryson, J., Crosby, B., & Stone, M. (2006). The design and implementation of cross-sector collaborations: Propositions from the literature. *Public Administration Review, 66*(Special Issue), 44–53.

Conley, A., & Moote, M. (2003). Evaluating collaborative natural resource management. *Society and Natural Resources, 16,* 371–386.

Connelly, D., Zhang, J., & Faerman, S. (2008). The paradoxical nature of collaboration. In L. B. Bingham & R. O'Leary (Eds.), *Big ideas in collaborative public management* (pp. 17–35). New York, NY: M. E. Sharpe.

Crosby, B. C., & Bryson, J. M. (2005). A leadership framework for cross-sector collaboration. *Public Management Review, 7*(2), 177–201.

Denhardt, J., & Campbell, K. (2006). The role of democratic values in transformational leadership. *Administration & Society, 38*(5), 556–572.

Emerson, K., Nabatchi, T., & Balogh, S. (2012). An integrative framework for collaborative governance. *Journal of Public Administration Research and Theory, 22*(1), 1–29.

Esteve, M., Boyne, G., Sierra, V., & Ysa, T. (2014). Organization collaboration in the public sector: Do chief executives make a difference. *Journal of Public Administration Research and Theory, 23*, 927–952.

Ferreyra, C., & Beard, P. (2007). Participatory evaluation of collaborative and integrated water management: Insights from the field. *Journal of Environmental Planning and Management, 50*(2), 271–296.

Frey, B., Lohmeier, J., Lee, S., & Tollefson, N. (2006). Measuring collaboration among grant partners. *American Journal of Evaluation, 27*(383), 383–393.

Gajda, R. (2004). Utilizing collaboration theory to evaluate strategic alliances. *American Journal of Evaluation, 25*(65), 65–77.

Gajda, R., & Koliba, C. (2007). Evaluating the imperative of intraorganizational collaboration: A school improvement perspective. *American Journal of Evaluation, 28*(26), 25–44.

Genskow, K., & Born, S. (2006). Organizational dynamics of watershed partnerships: A key to integrated watershed management. *Journal of Contemporary Water Research & Education, 135*, 56–64.

Gerlak, A., & Heikkila, T. (2007). Collaboration and institutional endurance in U.S. water policy. *PS: Political Science and Politics, 40*(1), 55–60.

Getha-Taylor, H., & Morse, R. S. (2013). Collaborative leadership development for local government officials: Exploring competencies and program impact. *Public Administration Quarterly, 37*(1), 71–102.

Gray, B. (1985). Conditions facilitating interorganizational collaboration. *Human Relations, 38*(10), 911–936.

Gray, B. (1989). *Collaborating: Finding common ground for multiparty problems.* San Francisco, CA: Jossey-Bass.

Heikkila, T., & Gerlak, A. K. (2014). Investigating collaborative processes over time A 10-year study of the South Florida Ecosystem Restoration Task Force. *The American Review of Public Administration*, 1–21. doi: 0275074014544196

Huxham, C. (Ed.). (1996). *Creating collaborative advantage.* London: Sage Publications.

Imperial, M. (2005). Using collaboration as a governance strategy: Lessons from six watershed management programs. *Administration & Society, 37*, 281–320.

Innes, J. E., & Booher, D. E. (1999). Consensus building and complex adaptive systems: A framework for evaluating collaborative planning. *Journal of The American Planning Association, 65*(4), 412.

Innes, J. E., & Booher, D. E. (2003). The impact of collaborative planning on governance capacity. *IURD Working Paper Series*, 1–32.

Johnson, L. J., Zorn, D., Yung Tam, B. K., Lamontagne, M., & Johnson, S. A. (2003). Stakeholders' views of factors that impact successful interagency collaboration. *Exceptional Children, 69*, 195–209.

Johnston, E. W., Hicks, D., Nan, N., & Auer, J. C. (2011). Managing the inclusion process in collaborative governance. *Journal of Public Administration Research and Theory: J-PART, 21*(4), 699–721. doi: 10.2307/41342601

Keast, R., Brown, K., & Mandell, M. (2007). Getting the right mix: Unpacking integration meanings and strategies. *International Public Management Journal, 10*(1), 9–33.

Lasker, R., Weiss, E., & Miller, R. (2001). Partnership synergy: A practical framework for studying and strengthening the collaborative advantage. *The Milbank Quarterly, 79*(2), 179–205.

Leach, W. D., Pelkey, N. W., & Sabatier, P. (2002). Stakeholder partnerships as collaborative policymaking: Evaluation criteria applied to watershed management in

California and Washington. *Journal of Policy Analysis and Management, 21*(4), 645–670.

Logsdon, J. (1991). Interest and interdependence in the formation of social problem-solving collaborations. *Journal of Applied Behavioral Science, 27,* 23–37.

McKinney, M., & Field, P. (2008). Evaluating community-based collaborations on federal lands and resources. *Society and Natural Resources, 21,* 419–429.

McNamara, M. (2012). Starting to untangle the web of cooperation, coordination, and collaboration: A framework for public managers. *International Journal of Public Administration, 35,* 389–401.

Majumdar, S., Moynihan, C., & Pierce, J. (2009). Public collaboration in transportation: A case study. *Public Works Management & Policy, 14,* 55–80.

Mandarano, L. A. (2008). Evaluating collaborative environmental planning outputs and outcomes: Restoring and protecting habitat and the New York-New Jersey Harbor Estuary Program. *Journal of Planning Education and Research, 27,* 456–468.

Margerum, R. D. (2002). Collaborative planning: Building consensus, and building a distinct model for collaboration. *Journal of Planning Education and Research, 21,* 237–253.

Margerum, R. D., & Robinson, C. J. (2015). Collaborative partnerships and the challenges for sustainable water management. *Current Opinion in Environmental Sustainability, 12,* 53–58.

Mattessich, P. W., & Monsey, B. R. (1992). *Collaboration: What makes it work. A review of research literature on factors influencing successful collaboration.* Saint Paul, MN: Amherst H. Wilder Foundation.

Mattessich, P. W., Murray-Close, M., & Monsey, B. R. (2001). *Collaboration: What makes it work [a review of research literature on factors influencing successful collaboration]* (2nd edn.). Saint Paul, MN: Amherst H. Wilder Foundation.

Mayer, R. C., Davis, J. H., & Schoorman, F. D. (1995). An integrative model of organizational trust. *Academy of Management Review, 20*(3), 709–734.

Mayer, R. C., & Harmon, M. (1982). Teaching moral education in public administration. *Southern Review of Public Administration, 6*(2), 217–226.

Miner, J. B. (2005). *Organizational behavior 1: Essential theories of motivation and leadership.* Armonk, NY: M.E. Sharpe.

Morris, J. C., Gibson, W. A., Leavitt, W. M., & Jones, S. C. (2013). *The case for grassroots collaboration: Social capital and ecosystem restoration at the local level.* Lanham, MD: Lexington Books.

Morse, R. S. (2010). Integrative public leadership: Catalyzing collaboration to create public value. *The Leadership Quarterly, 21*(2), 231–245.

Morse, R. S., & Stephens, J. B. (2012). Teaching collaborative governance: Phases, competencies, and case-based learning. *Journal of Public Affairs Education, 18*(3), 565–583. doi: 10.2307/23272656

Muller, K. (2010). Creating public value through collaborative environmental governance. *Administratio Publica, 18*(4), 141–152.

Noonan, P., McCall, Z., Zheng, C., & Gaumer-Erickson, A. (2012). An analysis of collaboration in a state-level interagency transition team. *Career Development and Transition for Exceptional Individuals, 35,* 144–153.

O'Leary, R., Choi, Y., & Gerard, C. M. (2012). The skill set of the successful collaborator. *Public Administration Review, 72*(s1), S70–S83.

64   *M. Mayer and R. Kenter*

O'Leary, R., & Vij, N. (2012). Collaborative public management: Where have we been and where are we going. *The American Review of Public Administration*, 42(5), 507–522.

Olson, M. (2009). *The logic of collective action: Public goods and the theory of groups* (Vol. 124). Harvard University Press.

Ostrom, E. (1998). A behavioral approach to the rational choice theory of collective action: Presidential address, American Political Science Association, 1997. *American Political Science Review*, 1–22.

Provan, K. G., & Lemaire, R. H. (2012). Core concepts and key ideas for understanding public sector organizational networks: Using research to inform. *Public Administration Review*, 72(5), 638–648.

Ring, P. S., & Van de Ven, A. H. (1994). Developmental processes of cooperative interorganizational relationships. *Academy of Management Review*, 19(1), 90–118.

Rittel, H., & Webber, M. (1973). Dilemmas in a general theory of planning. *Policy Sciences*, 4(2), 155–169.

Roberts, N. C., & Bradley, R. T. (1991). Stakeholder collaboration and innovation: A study of public policy initiation at the state level. *The Journal of Applied Behavioral Science*, 27(2), 209–227.

Sharfman, M., Gray, B., & Yan, A. (1991). The Context of interorganizational collaboration in the garment industry: An institutional perspective. *The Journal of Applied Behavioral Science*, 27, 181–208.

Shaw, M. M. (2003). Successful collaboration between the nonprofit and public sectors. *Nonprofit Management & Leadership*, 14(1), 107–120.

Strieter, L., & Blalock, L. (2006). Journey to successful collaborations. *Journal of Extension*, 44(1). Retrieved from www.joe.org/joe/2006february/tt4p.shtml.

Thomson, A. M., & Perry, J. (2006). Collaboration processes: Inside the black box. *Public Administration Review*, 66, 20–32.

Thomson, A. M., Perry, J., & Miller, T. (2009). Conceptualizing and measuring collaboration. *Journal of Public Administration Research and Theory: J-PART*, 19(1), 23–56.

Wood, D., & Gray, B. (1991). Toward a comprehensive theory of collaboration. *Journal of Applied Behavioral Science*, 27, 139–162.

Woodland, R., & Hutton, M. (2012). Evaluating organizational collaborations: Suggested entry points and strategies. *American Journal of Evaluation*, 33(3), 366–383.

4 Unraveling the Characteristics of Mandated Collaboration

Madeleine W. McNamara

Introduction

Networks are linked to implementation in today's complex policy environment. As fiscal stresses and resource shortages challenge the boundaries of unitary organizations, public administrators often rely on a myriad of partnerships to achieve policy and program goals. According to O'Toole (1997), "networks are structures of interdependence involving multiple organizations or parts thereof, where one unit is not merely the formal subordinate of the others in some larger hierarchical arrangement" (p. 45). Through these horizontal linkages, diversification of resources and expertise allow public organizations to increase their capacity for addressing complex problems that cannot be resolved by an individual organization (Agranoff, 2006; Chisholm, 1989; McGuire, 2006; Mandell & Steelman, 2003; Provan & Milward, 2001). Therefore, it is important to expand our understanding of the interactions that take place within multiorganizational arrangements.

'Cooperation,' 'coordination,' and 'collaboration' are terms used to describe interactions among partners (see, for example, Jennings & Ewalt, 1998; Agranoff, 2006; Caruson & MacManus, 2006; Robinson, 2006; Lundin, 2007). This chapter focuses on collaboration—an interaction between participants who work together to pursue complex goals based on shared interests and a collective responsibility for interconnected tasks which cannot be accomplished individually (McNamara, 2012). Collaboration differs from cooperation and coordination in that it "require[s] much closer relationships, connections, and resources and even a blurring of the boundaries between organizations" (Keast, Brown, & Mandell, 2007, p. 19).

There are many examples drawing from empirical research in the literature that highlight the use of collaboration to address complex social and environmental problems. For example, Regional Health Boards in Canada convened neighborhood health and social service agencies to integrate health care delivery services (Rodriguez, Langley, Beland, & Denis, 2007). A holistic approach for addressing the protection of coastal resources on the Eastern Shore of Virginia was developed through a collaborative network of 15 organizations (McNamara, 2008). County and city officials in Florida indicated that federal and state mandates concerning emergency preparedness post-9/11 foster intergovernmental collaboration to ensure preparedness and standardization within the homeland security mission (Caruson & MacManus, 2006). Commonalities among these cases are the presence of a policy mandate creating an impetus for participation and the involvement of government representatives within the collaborative arrangement. As these cases highlight, participation in a collaborative arrangement can be based on formal mandates written into legislation (Agranoff, 2006; Imperial, 2005) even though the literature often presumes voluntary action. Collaboration may be mandated for reasons such as creating standardization among multiple levels of government (Caruson & MacManus, 2006), integrating service delivery (Rodriguez et al., 2007), organizing overlapping jurisdictional boundaries (Taylor & Sweitzer, 2005), or to create opportunities for interaction that might not otherwise occur.

While some research focuses on empirical distinctions between the interactions of cooperation, coordination, and collaboration (see, for example, Keast et al., 2004; McNamara, 2012; Mandell, Brown, & Woolcock, 2004; Mattessich, Murray-Close, & Monsey, 2001), little attention is placed on distinctions between voluntary and mandated collaborative interactions. How do mandated collaborations differ from voluntary collaborations? More specifically, what procedural, structural, or managerial differences exist? This chapter focuses on theoretical development and addresses these questions by extending a previously developed framework to incorporate distinctions based on the ways collaborative interactions are initiated. Through the use of the expanded Multiorganizational Interaction Model, theorists and practitioners may capture a more detailed picture of collaborative interactions. The purpose of this chapter is not to provide an empirical test, but to introduce a framework that can be tested separately.

This research is important for three reasons which all support this book's theme pertaining to definitional clarity. First, there is a need to distinguish between different types of interactions because a specific type of interaction will not be effective in all settings (Imperial, 2005; Keast et al., 2007; McNamara, 2012; O'Toole, 1993). The current body of collaboration literature often ignores the nuances that distinguish various multiorganizational relationships (McNamara, 2012). Without acknowledging differences between relationships, such as mandated and voluntary collaboration, researchers use terms arbitrarily and cannot properly consider the range of interactions potentially useful in multiorganizational settings. Interactions form in various ways (Robinson, 2006); there are procedural, structural, and managerial differences between mandated and voluntary collaboration.

Second, now more than ever, public administrators must find ways to nurture horizontal relationships within hierarchical operating systems. The number of mandates used to control government activities has increased in recent years in addition to a broadened scope of those mandates (Lovell, 1981). "In fact, evidence is beginning to accumulate that mandates serve as the most important determinant of local government expenditures and as the single most important influence on local government policy making" (Lovell & Tobin, 1981, p. 318). As the presence of government contracting and multiorganizational partnerships continue to increase in the delivery of goods and services, it is imperative for today's public administrators to understand how to work within and across boundaries. Nylen (2007) refers to some types of mandated relationships as "professionals' collaboration" (p. 145).

Third, today's public administrators can be placed frequently in difficult situations where values, such as bureaucratic authority and discretion, are in constant competition. Therefore, administrators must be able to develop relationships based on a mandate to do so but absent of the accountability mechanisms that would traditionally be used when control is placed with a single actor. Likewise, mandates that require participation from more than one agency rely on relationships that may not develop organically. In these situations, a better understanding of the elements that foster collaborative characteristics within mandated relationships may help administrators create a context more conducive to collective action that would not develop otherwise.

The chapter's first section introduces mandated collaboration within the context of a continuum of interaction. The placement of mandated collaboration on this continuum is addressed. Second, an expansion of the Multiorganizational Interaction Model is presented through a series of elements that introduce variations between voluntary and mandated collaboration. Operationalizations are based on linkages with the interorganizational theory and policy literatures. The chapter concludes with suggestions regarding the potential impacts the framework may make on broadening the scope of current theory and practice.

A Continuum of Interaction

Administrators and theorists use terms such as 'cooperation,' 'coordination,' or 'collaboration' to describe a continuum of increased interactions (Keast et al., 2007; Mattessich et al., 2001; McNamara, 2012; Thomson & Perry, 2006). No type of interaction is better than another as certain conditions lend themselves to the use of a particular relationship (McNamara, 2008). "At one end of the continuum, cooperation is defined as an interaction between participants with capabilities to accomplish organizational goals but chose to work together, within existing structures and policies, to serve individual interests" (McNamara, 2012, p. 391). Practitioners describe cooperation as "getting along with others so that you c[an] both achieve your own goals" (Keast et al., 2007, p. 17). Little interaction is needed from an organizational perspective regarding changes to mission, structure, or planning efforts as the focus is on individuals communicating informally to help one another. This type of interaction typically occurs across the lowest levels of an organization and does not require the involvement of organizational leaders (McNamara, 2008).

"Coordination is placed in the middle of the continuum and is an interaction between participants in which formal linkages are mobilized because some assistance from others is needed to achieve organizational goals" (McNamara, 2012, p. 391). This type of interaction can be described as an "instrumental process" (Keast et al., 2007, p. 18) as it focuses on linking organizations in specific areas where assistance is needed to accomplish individual missions (Jennings, 1994; Jennings & Ewalt, 1998; Keast et al., 2007). Traditional government models rely typically on coordinative interactions due to the utilization of legal-rational authority and hierarchical controls to link organizational infrastructure. Much emphasis is placed on identifying means to attain organizational ends for all participants.

Collaboration is located at the opposite end of the continuum and is defined as "an interaction between participants who work together to pursue complex goals based on shared interests and a collective responsibility for interconnected tasks which cannot be accomplished individually" (McNamara, 2012, p. 391). Trust and long-standing relationships are considered typical elements of collaboration based on repeated connections between individuals (Keast et al., 2007; McNamara, 2012). Collaboration differs from cooperation and coordination in that it "require[s] much closer relationships, connections, and resources and even a blurring of the boundaries between organizations" (Keast et al., 2007, p. 19).

By and large, the collaboration literature assumes participants come together on a voluntary basis with the more formalized process associated with coordination. However, in her case study of human service networks in Sweden, Nylen (2007) acknowledges that collaboration can be "arranged in different ways" (p. 144) and describes a more structured form of collaboration based on "formalized partnerships or new organizational units" (p. 144). When we look at collaborative arrangements that include public organizations, it becomes conceivable that those organizations may be required to participate based on legislative mandate. Mandated collaboration "could take the shape of, for instance, a permanent, multi-disciplinary team with representatives from several agencies" (Nylen, 2007, p. 146). What the literature does not address, and this chapter sheds light on, is how a mandate impacts other elements that have long been associated with a voluntary form of collaboration.

A mandate is defined "as any responsibility, procedure or other activity that is imposed on one government by another by constitutional, legislative, administrative, executive, or judicial action as a direct order, or as a condition of aid" (Lovell, 1981, p. 60). A mandate may require organizations to work together during program or policy implementation (see, for example, Caruson & MacManus, 2006; Kuska, 2005; O'Toole & Montjoy, 1984; Raelin, 1982). Mandated collaboration occurs when bureaucratic or hierarchical mechanisms are used by a third party to bring separate organizations together to pursue complex objectives (Rodriguez et al., 2007). It can be helpful in situations where participants do not see the benefits in working together (Rodriguez et al., 2007), trust is low, multi-jurisdictional boundaries are involved, participants are unable to develop mutual interaction on their own, or physical, professional, or cultural barriers occur (Nylen, 2007). Although the literature often applies mandated collaboration to situations where higher levels of government create policy mandates for lower levels (see, for example, Brummel, Nelson, & Jakes, 2012; May, 1995) mandated collaboration can also apply to a situation where Congress requires federal or state agencies to collaborate on certain policy issues.

On the continuum of interaction, mandated collaboration occupies an area between coordination and collaboration. This area is identified as an appropriate location for mandated collaboration because this type of interaction seems to take on coordinative properties in elements pertaining to structure and process while collaborative properties pertain to managerial and other personal elements. May (1995), Rodriguez et al. (2007), and Lurie (2009) explain this distinction in similar ways. All three researchers offer that the process and planning for interaction can be prescribed through mandate while the interaction among participants emerges based on contextual factors in the environment. May (1995) describes this mandated approach as "collaborative planning" where government entities are empowered to develop the capacity to achieve policy goals through financial and technical assistance (p. 90). Nylen (2007) refers to this interaction as "formalized strategic alliances among agencies" (p. 145) or a "finalized team building strategy" (p. 162).

The Multiorganizational Interaction Model

An organizational framework was developed through an intersection of the public administration and health education literatures to distinguish between cooperation, coordination, and collaboration (see McNamara, 2012). This model uses 10 elements to make distinctions: design, formality of the agreement, organizational autonomy, key personnel, information-sharing, decision-making, resolution of turf issues, resource allocation, systems thinking, and trust. While this model provides a significant start in distinguishing between interactions, it does not account for the different ways collaboration is initiated and the resulting impacts of that initiation on other elements.

The following section uses these same elements to add mandated and voluntary collaboration to the existing framework. Operationalizations for mandated collaboration come from the policy implementation and interorganizational theory literatures. A description for each element linked to mandated collaboration is summarized in Table 4.1 as part of its integration into the extended framework. Discrete categories are used to identify areas for each interaction on the continuum; this chapter focuses on distinguishing mandated collaboration from other forms of interaction. While

Table 4.1 The Multiorganizational Interaction Model: Distinctions on the Continuum

Element	Cooperation	Coordination	Mandated Collaboration	Voluntary Collaboration
Design	Work within existing organizational structures	Centralized control through hierarchical structures	Hierarchical arrangement with convening authority oversight	Shared power arrangements
Formality of the Agreement	Informal agreement	Formalized agreements	Mandate formalizes structural elements of planning process	Informal and formal agreements
Organizational Autonomy	Fully autonomous; policies to govern the collective arrangement are not developed	Semiautonomous; policies to govern the collective arrangement may be developed by higher authorities	Pseudo-autonomous; policies to govern the collective arrangement are developed jointly by participants within the confines of the mandate	Not autonomous; policies to govern the collective arrangement are developed jointly by participants
Key Personnel	Implementation of the partnership occurs at the lowest levels; leaders are not involved	Implementation of the partnership is based on a higher authority; a boundary spanner may be used to foster linkages	Implementation of the partnership is based on the convening authority; a referent organization and the mandate may be used to foster linkages	Implementation of the partnership is based on the participants; a convener may help bring participants together
Information-Sharing	Basic information shared through informal channels	Information is exchanged through more formal channels	Convening authority pulls specialized information through formal channels established by mandate	Open and frequent communications through formal and informal channels

	Independent decision-making	Centralized decision-making	Clan-based decision-making	Participative decision-making
Decision-Making				
Resolution of Turf Issues	Conflicts avoided through independence	A neutral facilitator may help resolve conflicts	Convening authority establishes status differences to minimize conflicts via mandate specificity	Participants work together to resolve conflicts
Resource Allocation	Information is exchanged	Physical and nonphysical resources are exchanged to achieve individual goals	Physical and nonphysical resources are leveraged by convening authority around stable resource stream to achieve mandated goals	Physical and nonphysical resources are pooled by participants in support of collective goals
Systems Thinking	System integration does not occur	System integration may occur to better achieve individual goals	System integration does occur through the convening authority to better achieve mandated goals	System integration does occur to better achieve collective goals
Trust	Trust relationships are not necessary	Trust relationships focus on intraorganizational domain to solidify collective commitment	Trust relationships may become an output from continued work through convening authority	Trust relationships at all organizational levels are needed as an input to sustain relationships

the 10 elements are treated independently for the purpose of extending the framework, relationships between elements are likely to exist.

Implications exist regarding potential relationships among elements. For example, some elements may impact interactions more than others. In addition, elements of greater impact may change depending on the type of interaction. It is important for theorists and practitioners to be aware of these relationships as some elements may be more powerful predictors of successful interaction. In other words, it may be more important for practitioners to focus on the development of certain elements if they seem to have greater influence on a particular type of interaction. McNamara (2012) suggests the unlikelihood that relationships operate entirely in one area of the continuum across all elements. Therefore, practitioners may focus limited time and resources on the elements found to be most important for the desired interaction. Likewise, elements of greatest influence on particular interactions may focus theoretical developments which could further inform practice.

Design

The design element is defined as the administrative structure supporting multiorganizational efforts (McNamara, 2012). It focuses on the presence of linkages between organizational structures participating in the collective arrangement. In cooperation, an informal structure is based on loose linkages among existing organizational structures. As this type of relationship generally focuses on simpler tasks, there is no need for organizations to link their independent structures. Autonomous operations are maintained (McNamara, 2012). In coordination, an emphasis on hierarchical structures enhances specialized roles and responsibilities among participants. While organizations retain separate entities, centralized control is used to manage specializations (McNamara, 2012). In voluntary collaboration, participants develop a new structure of shared power to address a common problem. The new structure is developed jointly by participants. Focus is placed on developing a holistic approach to address the goals of the collective arrangement (McNamara, 2012).

In mandated collaboration, participants become part of a new structure that places the convening entity in a position of authority over other partnering organizations. There may be a decision-making board whose creation is required by mandate and organized by a designated convening entity. "The design of policy mandates is important in signaling cooperative desires and structuring implementation to foster appropriate agency implementation styles" (May, 1995, p. 113). It is through "organizational rearrangements" that policy is managed, a lead agency is formalized, and grant money is distributed (Caruson & MacManus, 2006, p. 523). A formalized planning structure is typical in a mandated collaborative to ensure all participants are organized in a way that is congruent with achieving policy goals. Relationships within the structure may be specified in policy or supplemental directives. In a case study of multiple organizations implementing coastal resource policies on Virginia's Eastern Shore, organizational rearrangement occurred in alignment with an executive order that explained the program's mission, specified policy goals, identified a lead agency, and required the involvement of specific participants in program implementation.

While both mandated and voluntary collaboration are based on the development of new arrangements, there are some important distinctions between the two types of interaction. In a voluntary collaboration, participants develop jointly a structure of shared power (McNamara, 2012). On the other hand, the operating structure for mandated collaboration is specified through the mandate with the convening entity playing a prominent role in monitoring program or policy implementation. As a result, the convening entity maintains a position of authority within the arrangement instead of the participatory approach typical of voluntary arrangements.

Formality of the Agreement

The formality of the agreement element focuses on the determination of roles and responsibilities of participants in the multiorganizational arrangement (McNamara, 2012). In cooperation, informal agreements are used to discuss short-term roles and responsibilities that are mutually beneficial to participants. A decision to work together is based on a short-term need to share information or build capacity (McNamara, 2012). In coordination, formalized agreements, developed by organizational leaders, identify clear roles and responsibilities for participants that align with organizational interests. Higher levels of commitment are generated through formalized agreements and processes (McNamara, 2012). In voluntary collaboration, formal and informal agreements are developed jointly by participants to create roles and responsibilities that contribute to the collective effort. Informal agreements help the arrangement make necessary changes as the group evolves while social norms may be formalized over time to generate stability (McNamara, 2012).

In mandated collaboration, formalized agreements are prescribed by the convening authority to determine roles and responsibilities for participants most central to implementation. The mandate may specify the organization that will take on the role of the convener or which organizations will provide a funding stream to support the effort. In this element, the mandate plays an important role in establishing formal authority to support governance mechanisms—like a hierarchically tiered arrangement within a multiorganizational governing body (Brummel et al., 2012). Policy objectives are established by the mandate in addition to prescribing processes to support those objectives (Brummel et al., 2012).

For this element, mandated collaboration most closely resembles formalized agreements in coordination. The distinction between the two types of interaction has to do with where emphasis is placed within the agreement. In coordination, formalized agreements emphasize regulatory prescription, detailed standards, strong sanctions, and hierarchical monitoring (May, 1995). In mandated collaboration, the emphasis is placed on empowering those responsible for implementation to achieve policy outcomes. Even though a collaborative mandate may prescribe structural elements of the planning process, the means used to achieve policy outcomes are left to the discretion of participants involved in implementation. May (1995) describes this type of mandate as "co-production" or "collaborative planning" (p. 90). A facilitative style is embraced to carry out the goals set in the formalized agreement. Implementation may include informal discussions amongst participants and flexible interpretations of the guidance to attain policy goals (May, 1995). This type of policy mandate would be described by Montjoy and O'Toole (1979) as a vague mandate that allows for some discretion during implementation.

Mandated collaboration differs from voluntary collaboration in terms of the organizational authority for policy development. In a mandated context, the policy agreement is developed by an entity with the authority to prescribe processes for participations and goals to be reached. Outside entities use formal authority to guide the arrangement, and participants are responsible to these authorities for outcomes. In a voluntary context, the authority for policy development lies with the participants themselves and not with another entity. Without an emphasis on formal authority by outside entities, participants have more opportunities to exercise discretion. Therefore, there is latitude to develop jointly multiorganizational agreements and processes to guide the arrangement.

Organizational Autonomy

Organizational autonomy refers to the independence in organizational operations and the adaptation of operational procedures and policies to align with the interorganizational arrangement (McNamara, 2012). The term "interconnectivity" is used to describe this concept (DeLeon & Varda, 2009, p. 68). Organizations are fully autonomous in cooperative interactions, and independent decision-making processes for respective organizations remain intact. Therefore, multiorganizational policies and procedures are not developed (McNamara, 2012). Organizations are semi-autonomous in coordinative interactions as policies to govern the collective arrangement may be developed by higher authorities if there is a perception that a joint protocol is needed to couple independent decision-making processes to accomplish specific organizational goals. It is possible for organizational goals to be achieved by individual organizations but a decision to work together is viewed as beneficial to accomplishing organizational goals (McNamara, 2012). Organizations are not autonomous in voluntary collaboration as participants relinquish some autonomy to the collective arrangement to establish policies and procedures for the entire group. Therefore, integrated policies and procedures occur as participants develop a collective identity (McNamara, 2012).

In mandated collaboration, organizations are pseudo-autonomous as operating procedures and policies to govern the collective arrangement can be developed by participants within the boundaries prescribed by the planning process within the mandate. As in voluntary collaboration, it is important for shared rules, a collective purpose, and a joint course of action to be developed. While both types of collaboration relinquish some autonomy to the collective unit, the amount and type of autonomy relinquished in mandated collaboration is prescribed by the mandate and occurs in a more formal way. This presumption takes into account the notion of legal authority that McNamara (2012) linked to the participation of public organizations in multiorganizational arrangements. Because mandated collaboration involves public organizations, changes to organizational policies and procedures are more likely to occur at the programmatic level and within the boundaries of an organization's legal authorities.

Key Personnel

Key personnel refers to the participants' implementation responsibilities within the multiorganizational arrangement (McNamara, 2012). Key personnel may be identified by looking at the stakeholders who control resources or have formal authority within the group (McNamara, 2012). In cooperation, connections occur between people at the lowest levels of the organization. Therefore, this type of relationship is typically established without involvement from higher authorities. In coordination, personnel in supervisory roles have great responsibility for implementing the partnership. Boundary spanners or interdepartmental liaisons may help facilitate communications across organizational boundaries (McNamara, 2012). In voluntary collaboration, an emphasis on group deliberation places participants in an important role throughout implementation. Conveners help identify and invite participants with niche expertise to the table. High levels of expertise and credibility help conveners establish legitimacy within the group (McNamara, 2012).

In mandated collaboration, a convening authority plays an important role to "integrate the work of several organizations" (Nylen, 2007, p. 146). As in voluntary collaboration, specialization is paramount. However, the distinction between the two types of collaboration has to do with the way in which key personnel come to the table for implementation. In voluntary collaboration, a convener invites personnel to join the arrangement based on the presence of particular resources or expertise needed to achieve the collective effort. Mandated collaboration relies on the convening authority and the strength of the mandate to establish a referent organization and require organizational personnel to participate in the arrangement. As conveyed in the broader interorganizational theory literature (see Bryson, Crosby, & Stone, 2006; McNamara, 2008; Morris & Burns, 1997; Wood & Gray, 1991), a referent organization facilitates interactions between organizations and generates stability within the organizational environment through resource and information exchange. The primary distinction between mandated and voluntary collaboration is that mandated collaboration relies on formal authority whereas voluntary collaboration utilizes informal influence generated through expertise and credibility (McNamara, 2012).

In both situations, legitimacy is important but placed upon different entities. In voluntary collaboration, participants must perceive the convener to have legitimate knowledge and relationships to organize the arrangement (Gray, 1985). In mandated collaboration, participants must perceive the mandate to be legitimate and the convening authority a proper vehicle for carrying out the mandate. Therefore, the mandate legitimizes the arrangement by identifying a problem and identifying participants with needed specializations to address the problem. The mandate may also identify a boundary spanner that can help supervisors make connections across organizational boundaries. As a result, organizational supervisors hold an important position within the arrangement as they have authority through the policy mandate and a formal structure to ensure assistance, resources, and time are utilized in a way that aligns with the mandate (May, 1995). Organizational leaders make decisions regarding the implementation of the mandate.

> If the leadership has a coherent goal and/or world view, we would expect the policy to be interpreted in that light. In the absence of a clear purpose on the part of leadership, it is possible that the opportunity to direct agency activity would be passed on to other actors.
>
> (May, 1995, p. 466)

In his research on floodplain management, May (1995) introduces the idea of a facilitative implementation style to foster increased agency commitment and capacity, increased government commitment to the policy goal, and increased citizen involvement.

Information-Sharing

Information-sharing refers to the methods for producing and communicating information between organizations in pursuit of shared objectives (McNamara, 2012). In cooperative arrangements, dialogue is maintained through informal communication channels to share basic information among participants. Through repeated communications, additional topics may be discussed (McNamara, 2012). More formal communication channels are used in coordination to exchange information within and across organizational boundaries while facilitating increased communication. Working partnerships, regular meetings between staff, and interdepartmental liaisons may be considered formal channels of communication (Jennings, 1994). A level of joint planning is needed to carry out the exchange of information which distinguishes coordination from cooperation (McNamara, 2012). Open and frequent communications in voluntary collaboration promote understanding among participants to build relationships and develop trust. Sharing information can reduce information asymmetries provided that organizations clearly state what they can and cannot offer the multiorganizational arrangement (McNamara, 2012). A convener in a voluntary collaboration will broker relationships among participants to enhance communication and build a common vision.

For mandated collaboration, the convening authority pulls specialized information through formal channels established by the mandate. Much like a voluntary collaboration, there is an emphasis on "repeated opportunities for communication [to] allow for conflict management" (Brummel et al., 2012, p. 527). However, communications in mandated collaboration focus less on promoting understanding among participants and more on identifying the specialized skills and resources needed to achieve policy goals. Committees and interorganizational task forces are several vehicles that may be used to develop communication channels that acknowledge "respective domains of activity and modes of intervention" (Rodriguez et al., 2007, p. 157). The prominent role of the convening authority can also be used to distinguish between mandated and voluntary collaboration. Where the convener facilitates discussion among participants in voluntary collaboration, the convening authority gathers information from participants in mandated collaboration.

Decision-Making

Decision-making refers to the way in which organizations reach consensus within the arrangement (McNamara, 2012). An independent decision-making process is emphasized in cooperative arrangements as organizational autonomy is maintained along with a focus on continuing to meet individual needs. In coordinative arrangements, a centralized approach is taken in decision-making as a dominant organization tends to emerge. The dominant organization orchestrates the process (McNamara, 2012). A collective effort and participative approach are typical of voluntary collaboration as consensus and compromise bridge differences among participants. Transparency develops through the creation of shared norms, rules, and processes (McNamara, 2012).

In mandated collaboration, "clan-based governance mechanisms" provide the basis for implementing goals set by a convening authority (Rodriguez et al., 2007, p. 157). "Clan governance implies by definition the existence of shared values and beliefs to enhance coordination" (Rodriguez et al., 2007, p. 157). The mandate prescribed by the convening authority is intended to unite participants around desired goals. Much discretion is given to participants to determine the best way to implement policies hierarchically imposed to achieve mandated goals. In this sense, participants behave as "regulatory trustees" while identifying the means to achieve performance standards (May, 1995, p. 91). This type of interaction moves beyond coordination in the sense that guidelines are provided for consideration into the planning process rather than prescribed regulation. With a focus on developing "sustainable management" (May, 1995, p. 93), participants have the discretion to determine the best course of action based on environmental and economic factors. Decision-making in mandated collaboration is participative in terms of developing the means to the goals prescribed by the convening authority (May, 1995).

Mandated collaboration carves out a niche between coordination and voluntary collaboration. It works within a hierarchical process similar to coordination, although participants have the discretion more often associated with voluntary collaboration based on the presence of a strong voice in determining how to implement the prescribed goals. Because mandated collaboration is built on the strength of organizational specializations (Caruson & MacManus, 2006; Nylen, 2007), this path to decision-making ensures that specialized strengths are factored into the implementation process. Final decisions are made by the entity given the formal authority to do so by mandate. One potential benefit to this decision-making process is that the formal authority rests with an entity that is familiar with the operations of the entire arrangement while understanding the specializations of each participant (Rodriguez et al., 2007).

Resolution of Turf Issues

Resolution of turf issues refers to the problem-solving process used by participants to work through conflicts (McNamara, 2012). Turf issues typically do not occur in cooperative relationships as there is no expected change to existing operations while participants establish win–win solutions. Turf issues arise in coordinative scenarios when organizations have competing goals to fulfill; a neutral facilitator can help resolve conflicts. Turf issues also arise in voluntary collaborative situations when organizational and collective demands placed on participants are conflicting; a process for solving conflicts is prevalent as participants typically work with one another to make adjustments to reduce conflict (McNamara, 2012).

As in coordination and voluntary collaboration, the potential for turf issues also exists in mandated collaboration if participants perceive "unequal distribution of costs versus benefits" among the collective group (Nylen, 2007, p. 164). However, mandated collaboration differs from other types of interaction in that the mandate itself can be used to minimize these issues. For example, public funds between agencies can be reallocated (Nylen, 2007), a more specific mandate can be developed at the beginning of the partnership (Montjoy & O'Toole, 1979), or sufficient resources can be attached to the mandate (Montjoy & O'Toole, 1979). According to Gray (1985), high mandate specificity can reduce "power negotiations" within the group by establishing status differences from the beginning of the partnership (p. 929). In New Zealand, local government personnel perceived a facilitative approach in dealing with national government agencies which created opportunities for discussion within existing pathways of hierarchical structure (May, 1995). Through these pathways, higher level government officials facilitated a sense of trust among subordinates while ensuring movement in the intended direction.

Resource Allocation

Resource allocation refers to the independent contributions organizations allocate to the multiorganizational arrangement (McNamara, 2012). In cooperative interactions, physical or financial resources may be exchanged based on mutual benefits to participating organizations. In voluntary collaboration, resources are pooled willingly to leverage personnel, expertise, and funding to support collective goals (McNamara, 2012). Participants determine how resources are utilized in achieving collective goals. In leveraging these resources, the collective arrangement is better positioned to accomplish priorities determined jointly (McNamara, 2012).

In mandated collaboration, resources are also pooled but this is done by the convening authority around a stable financial stream prescribed by the mandate. Funding made available through the mandate can be a powerful incentive to bring organizations to the table (McNamara, 2008). Instead of participants determining how resources are leveraged and utilized for particular goals, these decisions are made by the convening authority. Through the structure of the mandate and the convening authority, the pooling of resources is not only expected but also aligned with desired goals. Nylen (2007) uses the term "reciprocal interdependence" to describe how the pooling of resources and provision of services is "continuously intertwined" (p. 145).

Based on the research of Van de Ven and Walker (1984), interdependencies generated through financial resources create a more structured approach to interaction as conditions are placed in contractual agreements. It is also common for the mandate to require certain conditions be met prior to receiving aid. For example, a flood management policy in Australia mandated a planning process be in place as a condition to receiving planning grants at the local and regional levels of government (May, 1995). Nylen (2007) points out that it can be challenging when an agency bears additional costs associated with resource provision but does not experience maximum benefits. In this situation, it is up to the convening authority to reallocate financial resources between organizations (Nylen, 2007).

Systems Thinking

Systems thinking refers to the organizational systems used to assist in decision-making within the collective arrangement (McNamara, 2012). In cooperative interactions, organizational systems for individual organizations are maintained as independent decision-making processes do not necessitate integration. In coordinative interactions, some integration may occur if it helps organizations achieve individual goals. Compatibility among existing systems may be explored (McNamara, 2012). In voluntary collaboration, an emphasis is placed on integrating systems to enhance linkages between personnel. New systems may be developed to support these linkages and ensure important information is passed throughout the collective arrangement (McNamara, 2012).

Much like its voluntary counterpart, May (1995) recognizes that overlap in organizational systems is needed to help facilitate mandated collaboration. For this element, a distinction between voluntary and mandated collaboration is more difficult to determine based on discussion in the extant literature. As with voluntary collaboration, it seems that the complexity of issues would demand an integrated communication approach. The distinction between the two has to do with mandate specificity versus the building of relationships. Specificity within a mandate can be utilized to outline linkages for organizational systems with potential benefits to the collective arrangement. For example, an interagency database can be supported through a mandate to help make information widely accessible to all participants. To ensure participation, requirements for information can be attached to grant contracts. With a formal approach to integrating systems, mandated collaboration places less emphasis on relationships between personnel.

Trust

Trust refers to vulnerability and mutual understanding among participants working toward collective action (McNamara, 2012). In cooperation, maintaining individual roles does not require the development of trusting relationships. In coordination, trust may develop intraorganizationally as leaders identify a benefit in working across hierarchical boundaries and communicate its importance to subordinates. In voluntary collaboration, trust is required among participants at all organizational levels to sustain relationships and develop a common purpose (McNamara, 2012).

In mandated collaboration, trust may be generated as an output of working together rather than it being a necessary input to voluntary collaboration. The model developed by Morris, Gibson, Leavitt, and Jones (2013) suggests that some level of social capital is a necessary precondition to voluntary collaboration. After a long history of involvement developed among different levels of government implementing environmental management policy in Australia, a culture of support and facilitation developed (May, 1995). Frequent interactions enhanced communications and helped facilitate a strong record for working together (May, 1995). However, this record is established over the term of the relationship rather than being intact at the outset. However, relationships that lack social capital and trust are potential opportunities for the use of mandated collaboration. A lack of trust is one of several conditions where mandated collaboration may be most applicable (Nylen, 2007). The role of a convening authority, use of formalized agreements, and emphasis on bureaucratic control make the development of trust less necessary in mandated collaboration as centralized authority is used to direct goals.

Discussion

A fuller understanding of multiorganizational interactions must acknowledge that collaboration can be initiated in formal and informal ways. Although most of the collaboration literature focuses on voluntary collaboration, mandated interactions are frequently initiated by policy mandates, agency rulemaking, organizational procedures, and grant contracts. The extended framework proposed in this chapter further solidifies a conceptual foundation for continued exploration into better understanding vocabulary for interaction. With cross-pollination of the policy implementation literature, the framework begins to carve a distinction between mandated and voluntary collaboration. While the exact points along the continuum in which one interaction crosses the threshold to another interaction are still unclear, it is through continued application and empirical testing in future research that the exact placement of mandated collaboration along the continuum may be clarified.

Future application of the framework may benefit the interorganizational literature in two ways. First, exploring the initiation of collaboration may improve our conceptual understanding of accountability within multiorganizational settings. Because the accountability mechanisms typically found in bureaucratic organizations do not appear in most multiorganizational settings, formally initiated collaborative interactions fill an important gap. It is suggested in the literature that voluntary collaboration may be particularly difficult for public administrators to sustain as conventional bureaucratic systems emphasizing stovepipe specializations, hierarchical structures, and formal governance mechanisms do not inherently accommodate shared power and joint decision-making (Keast et al., 2007). Discretionary judgment is seemingly at odds with command and control authority. Perhaps it is easier for public administrators to sustain mandated collaboration as the relationships are balanced by bureaucratic mechanisms—this is an empirical question worthy of additional research.

Second, mandated collaboration highlights the importance in balancing the relationships between politics and administration. In a mandated context, the technicalities and specificity of the mandate become an important aspect of the multiorganizational relationship itself as the mandate can be used to create pathways for communication, resource distribution, and governance mechanisms. Mandated collaboration challenges the politics-administration dichotomy (Wilson, 1887) and the implementation paradox (Pressman & Wildavsky, 1973), as a strong connection between the politicians crafting the mandate and the bureaucrats implementing it is imperative. Without understanding the dynamic context of the multiorganizational arrangement, politicians may focus the technicalities of the mandate in a direction that will not achieve the intended goals. The elements of the mandate may help administrators facilitate legitimate relationships, generate interdependency, and reach policy outcomes. On the other hand, participants must have some level of discretion to make organizational decisions based on the evolution of group deliberation (Mattessich et al., 2001). A focus on mandate specificity further supports the notion that collaborative success is predetermined (see McNamara, 2008).

Application of this framework may also benefit the practice of public management in two ways. First, a distinction between mandated and voluntary collaboration supports Kettl's (2006) call for today's public administrators to be able to work comfortably within horizontal and vertical linkages. The governance structure for mandated collaboration is hierarchically connected to the convening authority while participation at the operational level will rely on informal relationships growing from the prescribed linkages. As in the broader public administration context, there is an inherent emphasis on competing values for participants of mandated collaboration. For example, there is a strong presence of bureaucratic authority through the mandate but some flexibility is needed to allow for operational discretion and leveraging connections among participants. "Policy-mandated collaborations may produce more consistent social network outcomes and may be more adaptable in the face of environmental change by creating a structure flexible enough to accommodate the local, political, social, and ecological context" (Brummel et al., 2012, p. 526). Especially in the beginning of a mandated collaboration relationship, it is likely that there will be fragile legitimacy for administrators in positions of authority (Rodriguez et al., 2007). Successful collaboration will require administrators to develop relationships that go beyond the structure prescribed in the mandate. "It's likely that mandates erect a formal structure within which collaboration can occur, but structure without other facilitative conditions is insufficient to promote collaboration" (Gray, 1985, p. 929).

Second, this chapter introduces elements for operationalizing mandated collaboration which may help administrators and politicians better understand the conditions that facilitate this type of interaction. Mandated collaboration may occur in situations where legislation requires it, ambiguous lines of authority and jurisdictions overlap (Taylor & Sweitzer, 2005), or standardization is needed among multiple levels of government (Caruson & MacManus, 2006). It may be best to embrace mandated collaboration in situations where operating procedures and planning processes are prescribed in policy mandate, lower levels of trust prevent the natural development of long-standing relationships, resources are leveraged around financial assistance, or policy goals cut across various departments, programs, or functions (Lovell & Tobin, 1981). A major benefit of mandated collaboration is that it can create opportunity for interaction that might not otherwise occur (Brummel et al., 2012).

Conclusion

This chapter introduces an extension of the Multiorganizational Interaction Model that highlights distinctions between mandated and voluntary collaboration. Participation in collaborative arrangements can be based on a mandate requiring interaction. Elements within the framework are defined to operationalize mandated collaboration as it is placed on the continuum of interaction between coordination and collaboration. This position on the continuum seems most appropriate as elements associated with multiorganizational processes and planning can be prescribed through a mandate and are more aligned with coordinative properties. Elements associated with relationships among participants are based on contextual factors and are more aligned with collaborative properties.

The proposed framework is important from a theoretical standpoint because it explores different types of interactions in multiorganizational settings. In addition, this framework provides a strong foundation for future exploration into alternate types of interactions also deserving of a spot on the continuum. For example, contingent coordination is used in the literature to describe coordinative relationships that have flexibility to respond to emergent conditions (Kettl, 2003; McNamara, Morris, & Mayer, 2014). As the framework continues to develop, the easier it will be for theorists to place different types of interactions on the continuum.

The proposed framework is also important from a practical standpoint because it helps clarify the meaning behind different types of interactions. To date, terms are often used arbitrarily and interchangeably within the literature without regard for nuanced differences between them (McNamara, 2008). Because different types of interactions are comprised of different elements, it is important for practitioners to understand what elements need to be in place for a particular type of interaction to be viable. In addition, it is important for practitioners to explore the identity of elements that contribute to the success of a particular interaction so the development of those elements can be the focus of limited resources and time.

While both types of collaboration focus on addressing problems that cannot be resolved individually, it remains to be seen whether the way in which collaboration is initiated impacts relationship outcomes. Empirical testing in future research will help determine the framework's usefulness for exploring a full range of multiorganizational interactions. A qualitative methodology suits this research because it allows for in-depth exploration of the elements within each type of interaction. In addition, textual data may help researchers understand the importance of some elements over others in determining the success or failure of an arrangement.

References

Agranoff, R. (2006). Inside collaborative networks: Ten lessons for public managers. *Public Administration Review*, 66(supplement), 56–65.

Brummel, R., Nelson, K., & Jakes, P. (2012). Burning through organizational boundaries? Examining inter-organizational communication networks in policy-mandated collaborative bushfire planning groups. *Global Environmental Change, 22,* 516–528.

Bryson, J., Crosby, B., & Stone, M. (2006). The design and implementation of cross-sector collaborations: Propositions from the literature. *Public Administration Review, 66,* 44–55.

Caruson, K., & MacManus, S. (2006). Mandates and management challenges in the trenches: An intergovernmental perspective on Homeland Security. *Public Administration Review, 66*(4), 522–536.

Chisholm, D. (1989). *Coordination without hierarchy: Informal structures in multiorganizational systems.* Berkeley, CA: University of California Press.

DeLeon, P., & Varda, D. (2009). Toward a theory of collaborative policy networks: Identifying structural tendencies. *Policy Studies Journal, 37*(1), 59–74.

Gray, B. (1985). Conditions facilitating interorganizational collaboration. *Human Relations, 38*(10), 911–936.

Imperial, M. (2005). Using collaboration as a governance strategy: Lessons from six watershed management programs. *Administration & Society, 37*(3), 281–320.

Jennings, E. (1994). Building bridges in the intergovernmental arena: Coordinating employment and training programs in the American states. *Public Administration Review, 54*(1), 52–60.

Jennings, E., & Ewalt, J. (1998). Interorganizational coordination, administrative consolidation, and policy performance. *Public Administration Review, 58*(5), 417–428.

Keast, R., Brown, K., & Mandell, M. (2007). Getting the right mix: Unpacking integration meanings and strategies. *International Public Management Journal, 10*(1), 9–33.

Keast, R., Mandell, M., Brown, K., & Woolcock, G. (2004). Network structures: Working differently and changing expectations. *Public Administration Review, 64*(3), 363–371.

Kettl, D. (2003). Contingent coordination: Practical and theoretical puzzles for homeland security. *American Review of Public Administration, 33*(3), 253–277.

Kettl, D. (2006). Managing boundaries in American administration: The collaborative imperative. *Public Administration Review, 66*(Special Issue), 10–19.

Kuska, G. (2005). Collaboration toward a more integrated national ocean policy: Assessment of several U.S. Federal interagency coordination groups. *Dissertations & Thesis Full Text, 66*(12), (UMI No. 3200549).

Lovell, C. (1981). American federalism and prefectorial administration. *Publius, 11*(2), 59–78.

Lovell, C., & Tobin, C. (1981). The mandate issue. *Public Administration Review, 41*(3), 318–331.

Lundin, M. (2007). Explaining cooperation: How resource interdependence, goal congruence, and trust affect joint actions in policy implementation. *Journal of Public Administration Research and Theory, 17*(4), 651–672.

Lurie, S. (2009). Getting to integration: Command and control or emergent process. *The Innovation Journal: The Public Sector Innovation Journal, 14*(1), 1–25.

McGuire, M. (2006). Collaborative public management: Assessing what we know and how we know it. *Public Administration Review, 66,* 33–43.

McNamara, M. (2008). Exploring interactions during multiorganizational policy implementation: A case study of the Virginia Coastal Zone Management Program. *Dissertations and Thesis Full Text, 69*(11), (UMI No. 3338107).

McNamara, M. (2012). Struggling to untangle the web of cooperation, coordination, and collaboration: A framework for public managers. *International Journal of Public Administration, 35*(6), 389–401.

McNamara, M. W., Morris, J. C., & Mayer, M. (2014). Expanding the universe of multiorganizational arrangements: Contingent coordination and the Deepwater Horizon transportation challenges. *Policy & Politics, 42*(3), 345–367.

Mandell, M., & Steelman, T. (2003). Understanding what can be accomplished through interorganizational innovations: The importance of typologies, context, and management strategies. *Public Management Review, 5*(2), 197–224.

Mattessich, P., Murray-Close, M., & Monsey, B. (2001). *Collaboration: What makes it work*. Saint Paul, MN: Amherst H. Wilder Foundation.

May, P. (1995). Can cooperation be mandated? Implementing intergovernmental environmental management in New South Wales and New Zealand. *Publius, 25*(1), 89–113.

Montjoy, R., & O'Toole, L. (1979). Toward a theory of policy implementation. *Public Administration Review, 39*(5), 465–476.

Morris, J., & Burns, M. (1997). Rethinking the interorganizational environments of public organizations. *Southern Political Review, 25*(1), 3–25.

Morris, J. C., Gibson, W. A., Leavitt, W. M., & Jones, S. C. (2013). *The case for grassroots collaboration: Social capital and ecosystem restoration at the local level*. Lanham, MD: Lexington Books.

Nylen, U. (2007). Interagency collaboration in human services: Impact of formalization and intensity on effectiveness. *Public Administration, 85*(1), 143–166.

O'Toole, L. (1993). Interorganizational policy studies: Lessons drawn from implementation research. *Journal of Public Administration Research and Theory, 3*(2), 232–251.

O'Toole, L. (1997). Treating networks seriously: Practical and research-based agendas in public administration. *Public Administration Review, 57*(1), 45–52.

O'Toole, L., & Montjoy, R. (1984). Interorganizational policy implementation: A theoretical perspective. *Public Administration Review, 44*(6), 491–503.

Pressman, J., & Wildavsky, A. (1973). *Implementation* (3rd ed.). Berkeley, CA: University of California Press.

Provan, K., & Milward, H. (2001). Do networks really work? A framework for evaluating public sector organizational networks. *Public Administration Review, 61*(4), 414–423.

Raelin, J. A. (1982). A policy output model of interorganizational relations. *Organization Studies, 3*(3), 243–267.

Robinson, S. (2006). A decade of treating networks seriously. *The Policy Studies Journal, 34*(4), 589–598.

Rodriguez, C., Langley, A., Beland, F., & Denis, J. (2007). Governance, power, and mandated collaboration in an interorganizational network. *Administration & Society, 39*(2), 150–193.

Taylor, B., & Sweitzer, L. (2005). Assessing the experience of mandated collaborative inter-jurisdictional transport planning in the United States. *Transport Policy, 6*, 500–511.

Thomson, A., & Perry, J. (2006). Collaboration processes: Inside the black box. *Public Administration Review, 66*(supplement), 20–32.

Van de Ven, A., & Walker, G. (1984). The dynamics of interorganizational coordination. *Administration Science Quarterly, 29*(4), 598–621.

Wilson, W. (1887). The study of administration. *Political Science Quarterly, 2*(2), 197–222.

Wood, D., & Gray, B. (1991). Toward a comprehensive theory of collaboration. *Journal of Applied Behavioral Science, 27*(2), 139–162.

Part II

Advancing Theory

5 Applying Cooperative Biological Theory to Nonprofit Collaboration

Nathan J. Grasse and Kevin D. Ward

For centuries, designers and engineers have looked to the natural world for inspiration in an effort innovate their products and services. The Wright brothers drew inspiration for their early gliders and later the 'Wright Flyer' while watching and analyzing the flight of birds. More recently, bioengineers at Boston Dynamics have created biped and quadruped balancing robots that emulate animals and their movements in the natural world (e.g., the Atlas, Cheetah, and Wildcat robots). Engineers at the University of Pennsylvania are developing low-cost flying micro robots that work in swarms, similar to bees or birds, in an effort to improve emergency response operations. Similarly, social scientists have borrowed from biological or ecological theory for new insights on how policies might change or how humans might socialize with one another. Frank Baumgartner and Bryan Jones's (1993) punctuated equilibrium theory borrows from evolutionary biology to describe long stagnations in policy arenas punctuated by periods of rapid policy change. Similarly, John M. Gaus (1947) borrowed from the ecology literature to explain how environment and context matter to public administration and management. To better explain the structure and motives of collaborative relationships, this paper examines the parallels between nonprofit networks and cooperative behavior found in nature. Eusociality is considered an advanced organizational arrangement that reflects the development of integrated behaviors, signified by: a clear division of labor, commonly relating to reproduction; cooperative care of young; and overlapping generations, whereby more capable generations help less capable, either taking care of offspring or elderly members.

Eusocial behavior in nature is relevant to collaboration among charitable organizations, as it relies on an understanding of the relatedness of the organisms participating in cooperative activities. While in nature this shared purpose is most easily understood by examining genetic similarity, in charitable organizations it can be understood by the similarity of organizations' missions. This chapter proposes a new theoretic lens for thinking about the ways in which organizational similarity acts as an antecedent to decisions to cooperate, conditioning each organization's assessments of costs and benefits. Further, this chapter posits that collaboration among nonprofit organizations cannot be understood without accounting for the relatedness of nonprofit organizations. Unlike for-profit firms, nonprofits can have primary purposes or missions that they share with other non-profit organizations. These shared missions can serve as critical anteced-ents to collaboration and condition organizations' perceptions of potential collaborative endeavors.

To develop this proposed lens, we first briefly examine the literature on nonprofit collaboration. Particular attention is paid to the role of hierarchy and structure in nonprofit collaboration. The benefits and costs of collabora-tion are also considered. Next, the biological concept of eusociality is exam-ined in order to relate this biological understanding to cooperative decisions by charitable organizations, followed by propositions and a typology of hier-archy within nonprofit organizations. Finally, implications are discussed.

Review of Collaboration Literature

Over the past 20 years, rapid advancements in technology and declining budgets have accelerated the rate at which nonprofit organizations and public agencies coordinate action. While literature on networks has largely kept pace with this expansion of networks in practice, the public and non-profit network literature is often criticized for lacking theoretic founda-tions and clear concepts (see Klijn & Koppenjan, 2000; Isett, LeRoux, Mergel, Mischen, & Rethemeyer, 2011). To better understand how and why nonprofit organizations coordinate action, this section examines the literature on collaborative structure, rationale for participation, and pro-posed frameworks for studying collaborative processes.

Defining Collaboration

Within the public and nonprofit management literatures, increased atten-tion is being paid to the modes and methods by which organizations work together to address public and social problems. While these arrangements have been called by many names, the term 'collaboration' is frequently used to describe basic patterns of mutual dependence and coordination between organizations. Sink (1998) defines collaboration as the "process by which organizations with a stake in a problem seek a mutually deter-mined solution [by pursuing] objectives they could not achieve working alone" (p. 1188). In a similar spirit, Gazley (2008a) suggests that "collabo-rations require voluntary, autonomous membership (partners retain their independent decision-making powers even when they agree to some common rules), and they have some transformational purpose or desire to increase systemic capacity by tapping shared resources" (p. 142).

Structures of Collaboration

While these definitions demonstrate convergence around the concept of collaboration, collaborations take many shapes and forms. Numerous scholars have attempted to develop typologies to better describe different types of collaborative arrangements (Agranoff, 2007; Agranoff & McGuire, 2003; Pisano & Verganti, 2008). While these typologies of cooperation and collaborative arrangements have made useful contributions to the literature, one dimension is of particular interest in this chapter: hierarchy.

While networks and hierarchy are often conceptualized as opposites on a spectrum of formality/rigidity, many collaboratives and nonprofit networks operate under a hybrid structure. The role of hierarchy in collaboration has been qualitatively described by Agranoff (2007) as "collaborarchy." Agranoff (2007) examines the role that authority and power play in determining whether hierarchy develops. Formally chartered public management networks often have clear roles, responsibilities, and agreements that can result in the perception of more hierarchical arrangement (Agranoff, 2007). While much of the collaboration literature suggests that individual actors/organizations are autonomous and participate in networks at will, power dynamics appear to inject an element of hierarchy into many collaborative arrangements. Burt (2004) suggests that certain organizations hold greater power due to their ability to span structural holes, which results in greater leverage among peer organizations, and Rhodes (1997) describes the impact that resource dependency has on the allocation of power within networks.

Similarly, in describing the importance of understanding the role that hierarchy plays in networks, Kadushin (2012) describes the importance of position in networks:

> Positions are a key idea in whole networks. Positions can be socially defined statuses, such as father, son, president, or positions can be defined by the observer through network analysis.... Positions are sometimes arranged in a hierarchy or a tree. The rules for these hierarchies are generally created by the social system in which they are embedded, though further informal interaction can alter the hierarchies and the rules.
>
> (p. 43)

In creating new and more comprehensive typologies, units of analysis are important to consider for improving theory development (Provan, Fish, & Sydow, 2007; Isett et al., 2011). Hierarchy is perhaps more important in organizational networks than individual or social networks. Thus, there appears to be an intermediate level of analysis in these organizational networks. While networks are often thought of as 'flat,' where all nodes are of equal weight or voice, networks at the organizational level of analysis often contain intermediate-level networks that are not observed. Here, it is common for organizations to band together in coalitions to improve economies of scale, but also to improve legitimacy when competing for resources. Thus, hierarchy is created in these networked arrangements not through formal hierarchy, but through advocacy coalitions (DeLeon & Varda, 2009; Sabatier & Jenkins-Smith, 1993).

Despite the apparent importance of hierarchy in networks or collaborative governance, the existing literature on hierarchy or rigidity in structure in public and nonprofit management networks describes four major types of collaboration, ranging from the most formal or hierarchical to the least. These include: mergers, partnerships, coordinated coalitions, and ad hoc networks. Nonprofit mergers, acquisitions, or consolidations occur when one organization's resources, processes, personnel, and market share or access to target populations are fully integrated into the operations of another organization (Singer & Yankey, 1991; McLaughlin, 2010).

Mergers

Mergers often initially result in redundancy or duplication of services and personnel, but aim to achieve long-term economies of scale and increased access to resources.

Partnership

Partnerships may occur between nonprofit and private entities, particularly around corporate social responsibility campaigns, but the term more frequently refers to the relationships developed between nonprofit and governmental entities to address public problems. Partnerships were initially examined as an outgrowth of the privatization movement (Brinkerhoff, 2002; Gazley, 2008b) in which contracts, grants, and memoranda of understanding were common, but have since evolved into a separate field of study. These transactional arrangements often rely on principal-agent type relationships with heavy emphasis on contract drafting, contract management, and monitoring or oversight. Within this literature, exchange and transaction theories are often employed.

While the term 'partnership' is commonplace in management literature, the definition and application of the term is often inconsistent (Gazley, 2008b). Brinkerhoff (2002) offers one such definition of a partnership as:

> A dynamic relationship among diverse actors, based on mutually agreed objectives, pursued through a shared understanding of the most rational division of labour based on the respective comparative advantages of each partner. Partnership encompasses mutual influence, with a careful balance between synergy and respective autonomy, which incorporates mutual respect, equal participation in decision making, mutual accountability and transparency.
>
> (p. 22)

In examining the local government-nonprofit partnerships that were not governed by formal contracts, Gazley and Brudney (2007) find that several important motivations distinguish these arrangements from public–private partnerships. In public-nonprofit partnerships, "the motivation to partner is driven by a desire to secure those resources most scarce for the respective sector; expertise and capacity for government, funding for nonprofits" (Gazley & Brudney, 2007, p. 389).

Finally, partnerships are occasionally described as a more formal approach to collaboration (Goldenkoff, 2001; Kamensky & Burlin, 2004), although this criterion has been disputed (Gazley, 2008b).

Coordinated Coalitions

Coalitions or alliances tend to signify a public policy or community-organizing focus. Here, advocacy groups coalesce around deep-seated core beliefs, and organize to affect community-level policy change (Stone & Sandfort, 2009; Scott, Deschenes, Hopkins, Newman, & McLaughlin, 2006). Research relating to the antecedents of nonprofit advocacy have found organizational mission, coalition governance structures, and organizational structures may affect advocacy decisions in coalition-type arrangements (Miller-Stevens & Gable, 2012). Additional research has suggested that policy networks, often supported by philanthropic foundations and large coalitions such as the United Way, are playing an increasingly important role in policy change, particularly at the local and state levels (Stone & Sandfort, 2009; Klijn & Koppenjan, 2000).

The term 'collaboration,' while commonly used as a blanket term to cover all interorganizational structures, is used to signify a relationship between two or more organizations defined by norms of reciprocity and shared norms or beliefs. Perhaps the most common form of collaboration is coordinated action among autonomous organizations.

Whereas networks are nonhierarchical and largely self-organizing (Weiner, 1990), the process of structuring and operating does not automatically happen. The absence of clear lines of authority and mutual tasking does not mean that a sequence of actions and managerial actions do not ensue (Agranoff & McGuire, 2001; Kickert & Koppenjan, 1997). Someone must guide the process, the work needs to be divided, courses of action need to be agreed to, agreements are carried out. Do these sound like management processes? Indeed they do. Just how different is network management from traditional management? If the processes are similar in name are they similar or different in substance? In the information era Drucker and Wilson (2001) say that contrary to Frederick W. Taylor 100 years ago, "One does not 'manage' people. The task is to lead people" (p. 81). The task here is to find out when, if and how such leadership is different or similar (Agranoff, 2007, p. 4).

These coordinated activities, however, often develop governance structures with varying degrees of hierarchy (Agranoff, 2007). In lead organization-governed networks, there is often one strong central organization. In this arrangement, "all major network-level activities and key decisions are coordinated through and by a single participating member. This results in highly centralized and brokered network governance with asymmetrical power" (Provan & Kenis, 2008, p. 235). This organization often manages the network and assists organizations in achieving their individual goals. These centralized organizations often serve as a hub and tend to have greater power or influence within the collaborative (Provan et al., 2007).

An alternative to the lead organization structure is a network administration organization structure, where members of networks develop a separate administrative entity to facilitate fair and dedicated governance (Agranoff, 2007; Provan et al., 2007). This governance structure often includes a board which consists of network members. The board is responsible for the formal decision-making and strategic planning of the networks. Formal and informal negotiating among actors frequently occurs through the board.

Networks

Networks are structures of interdependence with multiple actors seeking to gain mutual advantage to advance their independent causes, as well as causes pursued by the whole network. Agranoff (2007) defines public networks as "collaborative structures that bring together representatives from public agencies and NGOs to address problems of common concern that accrue value to the manager/specialist, their participating organizations, and their networks" (p. 2). Recently, advancements have been made in the measurement and description of public and nonprofit networks (Varda, 2011; Varda, Shoup, & Miller, 2012; Rethemeyer, 2009; Isett et al., 2011; Agranoff & McGuire, 2003; Provan, 1984; Provan & Milward, 1995).

Network structures are often governed by participant organizations, or participant-governed networks (Agranoff, 2007). These are the most common and simplest form of network governance. They are arguably the 'flattest' and least hierarchical arrangements that engage in collective governance. All organizations hold the same power, despite the age or size of the organization. Provan et al. (2007) suggest that these structures are informal and are commonly denoted by flat structures.

Existing Frameworks

Relatively few predictive models of collaboration exist within the public and nonprofit literature. However, several process models stand out. Thomson and Perry (2006) develop a process framework of collaboration creating hypotheses relating to the antecedent condition of collaboration, which include high levels of interdependence, need for resources and risk-sharing, resource scarcity, history of collaboration, possibility of resource exchange, and complex issues. They then identify the processes involved in collaboration, particularly relating to governance, administration, organization autonomy, mutuality, and norms of trust and reciprocity. Finally, they identify several collaborative outcomes, including achievement of goals, instrumental transactions that transform into embedded social relationships, the better identification of and ability to leverage resources, and self-governing collective action to solve problems. Additional network processes include negotiation, trust, mutual dependency, knowledge management, and network performance (Agranoff, 2007). While these process frameworks may be useful in explaining the processes and relationships between attributes and dimensions of collaboration, little is understood about the role or effect of hierarchy/rigidity in collaboration on outcomes. Thomson and Perry (2006) suggest that "a more systematic attention to understanding the process of collaboration will further the public value of this emerging field of study" (p. 30).

Relatedness

Within the social network literature, the theory of homophily suggests that individuals tend to associate with other individuals with whom they share similar attributes, beliefs, or behaviors. Because individuals share common characteristics, they are more likely to initially make connections and once they connect, they are more likely to have sustained relationships. These similarities also encourage convergence within the group and often lead to "social contagion" whereby social networks influence individuals (Christakis & Fowler, 2013). Here, we apply this opportunity-based antecedent at the organizational level to suggest that organizations are likely to partner with other organizations that share common characteristics, including mission, target populations, geographic location, and core beliefs. Hannan and Feeman (1977) suggest that these organizational groupings are result of "competitive isomorphism," whereby organizations that might work to differentiate themselves from other similar, potentially competing organizations, more commonly adopt the qualities of these similar organizations.

Another important determinant of engaging in collaboration relates to the potential perceived benefits of deciding to partner. There are many proposed drivers of the rise in popularity of engaging in networks, as well as studying networks. Some scholars cite the shift in U.S. labor markets from labor oriented to knowledge oriented (Agranoff, 2007). Other scholars suggest that public management reforms relating to reinventing government and contracting increased coordination between the public and nonprofit sectors (Agranoff & McGuire, 2003; O'Toole, 1997). As the public and nonprofit sectors grow to address increasingly complex problems, organizations have engaged in boundary-spanning behavior or horizontal integration (as well as vertical integration) to address public problems (Mandell & Steelman, 2003).

These shifts have prompted rational responses, particularly among nonprofit organizations to improve network success and curb failure. There are a multitude of motives for nonprofit organizations choosing to participate in networked arrangements, including, but not limited to: complexity of problems, seeking specialized expertise, improved access to new information, improved identification of scarce resources, increased legitimacy around a specific policy issue, better organized advocacy for programs/resources, seeking emotional support, and achieving economies of scale.

Complexity of Problems

As governments grow to tackle more complex issues, while budgets also tighten, nonprofit organizations are being more heavily relied upon to deliver public goods and services (Provan & Milward, 1995). The increasing complexity of public problems and continued skepticism around public-sector spending suggested a sustained reliance on the nonprofit sector in addressing public problems. These new demands may strain individual actors or organizations so responsibilities are broadcast among stakeholder organizations.

Seeking Specialized Expertise

Related to compartmentalizing functions, organizations often seek partnerships or participation in networks to gain access to technical skills or expertise that they require. Organizational functional needs such as accounting, legal, and marketing may be shored up in networks. More commonly, organizations seek expertise relating to target populations, knowledge of governmental institutions, and experience adhering to legal procedural protocols from these arrangements.

Improved Access to New Information

Networks often develop out of informal relationships in which actors share information to improve their organizational effectiveness. Organizations also elect to partner to reduce uncertainty (Galaskiewicz, 1985). Information exchange spurs innovation and other synergies as actors learn and synthesize information collectively.

Resource Exchange

Social exchange theory posits that organizations coordinate action to share resources (Cropanzano & Mitchell, 2005). Organizations engaging in social exchanges benefit from resource abundance or capability available in partnering organizations. Similarly, resource dependence has developed as a theoretic framework to explain collaboration (Pfeffer & Salancik, 1978).

In addition to better identifying resources, networks occasionally provide an opportunity to achieve greater efficiencies for network members. However, networks require time and resources to establish infrastructure, maintain relationships, and communicate information. Transaction cost approaches to estimating efficiency would suggest that networks are likely inefficient organizational arrangements that would benefit from more formal integration, greater division of labor, and elimination of redundancies.

Improved Identification of Scarce Resources

In scarce funding environments, nonprofit organizations often share information relating to revenue streams that seek to fund larger causes. Similar to private businesses, nonprofits can also provide referrals to other partnering organizations (Varda & Talmi, 2013).

Increased Legitimacy Around a Specific Policy Issue

As more or larger nonprofit organizations and public agencies engage in a particular network, legitimacy around the common mission or goals of the network may increase (Galaskiewicz, 1985). Additionally, these large coordinated efforts have the ability to crowd in additional resources by prospective funders interested in higher returns on investments. This 'bandwagon effect' may also generate additional media attention.

Better Organized Advocacy for Programs/Resources

The policy advocacy literature has demonstrated a propensity of organizations with similar belief systems and core policy beliefs to develop coalitions to lobby for policy changes (Sabatier & Weible, 2007; Miller-Stevens & Gable, 2012; Child & Grønbjerg 2007). State-level nonprofit associations, as well as industry trade associations, advocate for change on the behalf of their member organizations.

Seeking Emotional Support and Advancing the Cause

The theory of homophily is frequently cited as a motivating force for organizations to engage in network arrangements, which suggests that 'birds of feather flock together,' i.e., organizations that share similar traits are naturally attracted to work with each other (McPherson, Smith-Lovin, & Cook, 2001). Often in the nonprofit sector, however, organizations that are similar on many dimensions are often directly competing with one another for scarce resources. But, occasionally, these organizations enter into networks not to seek new information or learn, but to commiserate with other organizations experiencing similar struggles. Alternatively, organizations may choose to work together with their competitors to advance their overarching mission and values, even at the potential detriment of the individual organization.

Safety

Safety is the motivation to derive support from one's social environment and corresponds to dense, cohesive networks. It is also a common motive in social or herding animals seeking to minimize risk of threats. In networks that emphasize safety, trust is an important attribute (Kadushin, 2012).

Effectance

Effectance is the motivation to reach out beyond one's current situation and comfort zone (Kadushin, 2012) and corresponds to networks with structural holes. Making connections, or acting as a broker to new networks that otherwise would not be connected, is a priority.

In addition to the perceived benefits of collaboration, participants must also consider the costs. While often initially overlooked, transaction (or process) costs associated with cultivating and maintaining relationships can be steep. Williamson (1981) and other transaction cost researchers argue that transactions are the most basic unit of analysis for determining organizational efficiency. When organizations decide to engage other entities outside of their organizational boundaries, additional costs and inefficiencies will be incurred. As such, local governments are increasingly incorporating these costs into budget estimations when choosing between internal production, joint production with another government, or private or nonprofit production of services (Carr, LeRoux, & Shrestha, 2009). Within the nonprofit sector, transaction costs have been conceptualized as information-gathering costs, information-processing costs, and communication costs, as well as monitoring for opportunistic behavior (Valenetinov, 2007).

Once organizations have elected to engage in collaborative processes, reliability and trust are additional factors that contribute to the success or failure of these arrangements. The social capital literature emphasizes the importance of trust and shared norms of reciprocity (Putnam, 1993). To facilitate collaborative effectiveness, managers often reflect on their credibility and reliability, which Weiner, Alexander, and Zuckerman (2000) argue they should work to build and maintain. Trust is also linked to expectancy theory. Organizational partners prefer to be better able to anticipate actions and contributions by other partners. In particular, Lane and Bachman (1998) argue that trust assumes interdependence between actors, that it provides a mechanism for dealing with uncertainty, and that it assumes that opportunistic organizations will not exploit vulnerabilities of other partners. Organizations that are reliable and cultivate high levels of trust are likely to be seen as strong collaborators. This chapter aims to explain mutually reliant behavior by organizations by examining the fundamental mechanisms that facilitate mutual reliance, as well as creating a classification system differentiating between various structural manifestations of this behavior in organizations. We hope this will help to connect the literatures on nonprofit organizational networks, alliances, partnerships, affiliations, and mergers. While these literatures have done much to further our understanding of the network and/or cooperative behavior of organizations, they have primarily done so focused on a behavior within a relatively narrow range or through a particular perspective. We posit that this may lead to missed opportunities for integrating knowledge around key concepts, and that attempting to do so may reveal more about interorganizational relations, suggesting the origins of particular structural forms and how they might transition from one to another.

To explain organizational cooperation, this paper postulates that a hierarchy of mutual reliance exists and that organizations' decisions on how to work with others are a function of their perception of cost and benefit, as well as organizational learning. This learning concerns their organization's mission achievement, environments, information on potential cooperative partners, and the past success of mutually reliant endeavors. Feedback conditions organizations' disposition toward mutual reliance and, all things being equal, we expect that the interaction of learning behavior and environmental conditions may generate trends toward the increased scope and formality of mutually reliant behavior among organizations.

Theory

The fundamental rationale for this chapter is borrowed from the literature on biology. Biology has examined cooperative behavior from the perspective of the organism, noting that some organisms function predominantly as solitary actors, whereas others participate in highly rigid and coordinated societies. This literature has the potential to inform the literature on organizations due to the past utility of biological theory to explicate the adaptive behaviors of organizations through the lens of biology, creating the field of systems theory.

Systems theory taught us a great deal about the process by which organizations attempted to achieve negative entropy, avoiding the dysfunction that characterizes closed systems. This trend toward disorder invariably plagues static organizations, which fail to adapt to changing environments by utilizing resources to generate adaptive change. In short, these organizations utilize feedback from their environment to condition their operations, creating more effective outcomes through effective organizational change and avoiding maladaptive operations (Kast & Rosenzweig, 1972; Senge, 2000; Barnard, 1968; Churchman, 1968; Schein, 1970). This body of literature grew out of the work of von Bertalanffy (1956, 1959), who realized that both organisms and organizations utilized their environments to facilitate growth and avoid death. This theory has been applied to operations management, policy studies, change management, and strategic planning, as well as many other disciplines (Mintzberg, 1979; Senge, 2000; Kast & Rosenzweig, 1972).

Just as systems theory borrowed from biology to explain the mechanisms by which organizations modify behavior to suit their environments, we believe theories of cooperative social behavior focused on organisms can help to explain organizations' behavior in the area of mutual reliance. Our premise holds that organizations that hope to adapt to their environment can make choices beyond just their own operations, including choices of attempting to achieve their goals with the help of others.

The similarity of organizations and organisms in this regard will pertain to the structures and outcomes of these structured behaviors, despite the fundamentally different mechanism by which these changes arrive. While mutual reliance in organisms is predominantly an outcome of biological processes rather than conscious choice, we do not believe this undermines the utility of the theory's application. This is due to the nature of human social behavior, which has been partially untethered from genetic change, facilitating the creation and adaptation of social technology (such as organizations) at speeds far beyond what biological evolution might allow (Wilson, 1975, 1978).

Mechanisms of Nonprofit Cooperation

In order to understand how nonprofit organizations engage in collective endeavors, this work relies heavily on literature originating in other disciplines to offer potential explanations for cooperative phenomena. We believe this is necessary due to a fundamental difference between nonprofit organizations and the other types of organizations that have been subjected to study in the area of interorganizational cooperation. This difference is the potential for organizational action to be conditioned by 'relatedness.' In the context of this paper, relatedness can be defined as a shared mission or purpose, something going far beyond the potential for mutual benefit that would result from cooperation between other types of organizations. For example, much literature on cooperation at both the organizational and individual levels focuses on the tension between cooperation and competition (see Chen & Miller, 2012; Dyer & Singh, 1998; Gulati & Westphal, 1999; Das & Teng, 1998), which results from the tension between costs and benefits that result from collaboration.

Biological Theory—Eusociality

We posit that biological theory may help to explain cooperation among organizations, utilizing the study of the evolution of this 'truly social' behavior, or 'eusociality' toward this end. Eusociality has been identified as the pinnacle of social evolution (Wilson, 1978; Wilson & Sober, 1989; Holldobler & Wilson, 2009) and refers to the development of a social structure that allows organisms to cooperate in a number of ways, including such adaptations as the divisions of labor, specialized castes, intentional communication, and complex biological trade-offs to achieve far more collectively than any one organism from the collective could in isolation. In short, these structures serve as force multipliers.[1]

The mechanism by which this cooperative behavior occurs can be explained by Hamilton's Rule, which examines the reproductive efficiency of purely altruistic eusociality.[2] This rule explains the seemingly inherent contradiction in eusocial behavior, what appears to be the willing sacrifice of the individual's self-interest for the collective good. Hamilton demonstrates that collective behavior is not in contradiction to achieving individual interests, as the primary goal of organisms (the expression of genetic material) is furthered by this adaptive behavior.

$$RB > C \qquad\qquad\qquad (1)$$

According to Hamilton's Rule (1), the cooperation that undergirds altruism, the most extreme example of eusociality, can be explained by examining three factors: relatedness (R—degree of shared characteristics at the level of the gene or phenotype), benefit to recipient (B—units of offspring), and cost to altruist (C—sacrifice units of offspring in altruistic individual). When $RB > C$, altruism will spread, as the collective genetic benefit will surpass individual cost.

Why Apply Biological Theory to Nonprofit Organizations?

The fundamental rationale for our choice to rely on biological theory comes from research analyzing the application of game theory in social situations and the nature of nonprofit organizations. While game theory has served as an appropriate way to model decision-making in a number of situations, it often fails to approximate decision-making when actors have the ability to engage in communication before and during the decision-making process, such as social situations; in these cases, cooperation is more common than game theory would predict (Colman, 2003). One explanation for this phenomenon comes from the field of biology, which posits that a predisposition toward cooperation, although seemingly irrational for the individual, could arise through behavior that is both adaptive and rational when viewed from the perspective of collective interests (Gintis, 2003).

We posit that nonprofit organizations have the capacity to overcome pressures toward competition with other organizations in order to derive an advantage through collective action. These organizations will abstain from competition within group in order to achieve greater benefits (individually and in aggregate) by maximizing competitiveness with extra-group organizations (or as judged relative to an external standard of success). In short, cooperating nonprofits will achieve their missions more effectively and efficiently than would have been possible as unitary actors.

We expect cooperative behaviors to differ fundamentally in nonprofit organizations due to critical differences that distinguish these organizations from for-profit firms. Obviously, for-profits operate with the fundamental purpose of profit, or some other measure of benefit to firm owners. This purpose means that the primary mission of these organizations cannot overlap, although organizations certainly might take joint action that serves their mutual benefit. Nonprofits' purposes of achieving some public good are quite different, in that these purposes have the capacity to overlap, as two nonprofits may share missions that are identical. Whether community theaters, social welfare organizations, or art museums, the expressed purpose of these organizations can be identical. We propose that this fundamental difference from for-profit firms will predispose nonprofits toward collaboration when compared to other organizations, with the similarity of organizations' missions increasing their capacity to cooperate (holding other factors constant). For example, for-profit organizations need to act expressly in order to create truly shared interests (such as joint equity) whereas other cooperation relies on arrangements that deliver benefits that accrue to each party (Uzzi, 1997). Nonprofits have the option to enter into these arrangements, but we hold that shared missions serve as a factor preconditioning decisions to cooperate, independent of other factors.

Although we expect our conceptual framework does oversimplify decision-making, we hope the importance of communication and relatedness in our explanation of cooperation makes our adaptation of biological theory a better approximation for this process.

Nonprofit Organizations' Decisions to Cooperate

Collaboration, as conceived in this chapter, is the result of a decision process. Occurring within the organization, this decision relies on a cognitive mechanism. We expect this process will approximate a cost-benefit analysis, with organizations attempting to make rational decisions to pursue their interests, although constrained by imperfect information and decision-making processes (Simon, 1965).

We rely on a version of Hamilton's formula to represent the primary considerations weighed in this cognitive process. How could this biological theory apply to the cooperation of nonprofit organizations? We argue that mechanisms of social technology (cooperation) allow organizations to achieve greater success, making cooperation adaptive under certain environmental conditions. The rationale for this behavior can be understood using a formula similar to that used to understand biological cooperation. This formula utilizes the same terms: relatedness, benefits, and costs. The meaning of these terms in the context of organizations differs from the discussion of genetic heritability and offspring above, and is expressed instead using broad ideas such as organizational similarity, resource costs, and benefits provided. We also use these terms with the understanding that, in practice, these concepts may often be the result of the shared perceptions of individuals within the organization rather than quantifiable and absolute measures.

In biological explanations for cooperation, a focus on altruism is utilized for the purpose of simplification. We expand this theory for the purpose of explication, hoping to explain a broader range of cooperation by expressing all of the key concepts in our model of the decision-making process. Our formula is therefore lengthier, containing additional costs and benefits; as we expect these factors to influence the decision to work with others, as well as the concepts of reliability and the probability of success; so this formula relies on additional terms in order to facilitate a discussion of the factors influencing decisions to cooperate. We also have not reduced the formula in any way, again hoping to emphasize the components of the decision process rather than identify a reduced form.

Formula (2) provides our conceptualization of the decision processes driving cooperation and differs from Hamilton's theory in a few ways. These differences are necessary in order to adapt it to conscious decisions and the flexibility organizations can exercise in their applications of social technology. Specifically, it includes perceptions of success, allowing actors to consciously weight the expected outcomes of the action. Also, we include conceptions of self-benefit and the cost to a potential collaborator/cooperator, so that it might explain joint behaviors ranging from very low cost information-sharing to full blown altruism:

$$((R * B_O) + B_S) * PS_{SO} > (R * (C_O + CC_O)) + (C_S + CC_S) \tag{2}$$

In this formula, R represents *relatedness*, representing organizational similarity or symmetry. We expect factors such as: governance; ends; means; and human, technical, shared experiences, and financial resources will help to foster a sense of relatedness, but the primary component of relatedness will be the result of mission similarity. We expect that relatedness conditions organizations' evaluations of both the cost and benefits of collaboration with potential partners, as the degree of similarity between the organizations will predispose organizations toward cooperation. We differentiate relatedness from trust, as we would expect that trust is an outcome of some combination of relatedness and positive experiences.

Benefits are represented by both B_S (expected benefits to own organization) and B_O (expected benefits to other organization): these benefits are the perceived gains that the respective parties are expected to realize via their collaboration/cooperation. These are measured as the degree to which the cooperative act will allow these organizations to support their interests. This could be via direct gains in program delivery or indirect gains, providing the human, technical, physical, or financial resources that facilitate more effective mission attainment.

The *probability of success*, PS_{SO}, represents the overall likelihood of success expected from the joint endeavor; this would represent whether the venture was considered likely to succeed or inherently more risky than existing operations. This could be due to the presence of a competitive market, the inherent complexity of the endeavor, or other complicating factors. For example, entrepreneurial ventures, novel approaches to fundraising, completely new programs, innovative changes to delivery might reduce expectations for success.

Costs reflect the resources sacrificed in the collaborative effort. These are represented by C_S and C_O, representing the costs realized by the organization and to the potential collaborator/cooperator. These costs could be realized on a number of dimensions, including the direct or indirect benefits to mission fulfillment mentioned above.

Communication costs (CC) are only distinguished from the above to provide clarity in the models of hierarchy below, as these costs will help shape our expectations related to chosen forms of cooperation. These costs include the time and energy that staff dedicate toward the creation and maintenance of the cooperative effort, including communication costs, monitoring, and expertise.

While we concede that this formula is an oversimplification, it provides some conceptual clarity. Our description of the choice to cooperate in nonprofit organizations posits that consciously or unconsciously, decision-makers within organizations utilize these values when choosing to cooperate. Weighing the degree to which any potential cooperative activity serves the organization, the costs of the endeavor, and the nature of potential partners in order to decide when to participate in collective endeavors. This model relies on actors pursuing their own interest, but allowing that they might value the efforts of other organizations hoping to achieve the same goals. We expect the major component of the organizations' interest to be the attainment of their public-serving mission, but allow that other similarities or differences could condition the capacity for one organization to identify with another. For example, similar information systems, management styles, or programming preferences could lead organizations to feel more aligned with potential partners. On its own, this component of our theory does not tell us much about choices to cooperate, except that they will be pursued when the benefits to mission achievement outweigh costs and that these costs and benefits are conditioned by the similarity of organizations' mission, but we expect that the implications of organizational learning related to each of these terms could enlighten our expectations about organizational cooperation.

The Influence of Information

Although the formula above would represent only a singular decision, clearly the factors driving decisions on cooperation would be influenced by communication with potential partners regarding the potential benefit of their efforts, as well as the benefits, costs, and characteristics of their organization. We would also expect that experiences and learning would condition these decisions. Information constitutes a critical component of cooperation decisions, as organizations will continually encounter information that conditions their perceptions of whether potential collective activities are adaptive/maladaptive. This information could come from many sources, but we expect much of this information to be generated by the organization's deliberate communication and experiential learning related to collective organizational behaviors. In this way, initial exploratory

communications with other organizations, while not intentionall'
to cooperative endeavors, could have major implications for futur
directly related to cooperation.

Propositions

Building on these notions, we have some preliminary propositions related
to the influence of information on collaboration:

1   Positive communication experiences reduce perceptions of costs.
2   Positive cooperative experiences reduce perceptions of costs.
3   Positive communication experiences increase perceptions of relatedness.
4   Past positive cooperative experiences increase perceptions of
    relatedness.
5   Past positive cooperative experiences increase perceptions of the prob-
    ability of success.
6   The integration necessary for any cooperative endeavor increases com-
    munication costs linear to the magnitude of the cooperative effort.
7   Past positive collaboration/cooperation experiences create integration,
    reducing communication cost.
8   Formal integration reduces perceptions of costs.
9   Formal integration increases perceptions of relatedness.

We expect that information and the adaptations made as the result of communication and cooperation could contribute to greater cooperation within
the sector due to structural isomorphism, shared information, shared
experiences, and organizations' shared reliance on common-pool resources.
An understanding of this possibility must be nested in an understanding of
the forms of group or cooperative behavior within the sector, which can be
understood as a hierarchy, ranging from solitary behavior to cooperative
behavior that is deliberate and highly structured.

Introduction to a Model of Hierarchy of Mutual Reliance in Nonprofit Organizations

Our description of hierarchy relies on definitions that attempt to distinguish between different forms of solitary, group, or cooperative organizational activities.[3] While we realize this could create confusion due to the
presence of terminology that appears in more than one literature on col-
laboration/cooperation, we hope our attempt to clearly define each stage
and specify our interpretations of existing jargon will be useful. Ultimately,
developing clear definitions of concepts could serve to reduce confusion
when comparing research examining nonprofit collaboration/cooperation
from the perspectives of mergers, partnerships, or networks.

We define mutual reliance as any activity that involves organizational
cooperation or collaboration to achieve an end. This could be structured

or unstructured, but involves two or more organizations using purposeful (or deliberate) communication regarding the nature of cooperation and to choosing a course of action perceived to be beneficial.

Purposeful communication is defined as communication involving deliberate signaling and response toward a cooperative end. The sender initiates and communicates with the expectation that the signal will produce the desired response in the recipient, allowing activity to be coordinated toward goal achievement. In this context, this signaling and response is specifically focused on cooperative activity. This is quite different from our definition of nonpurposeful communication, defined as cuing behavior, actions, or communication that may or may not be intentional, and are not intended to create a specific response.

We use these terms to categorize organizational behaviors based on a number of dimensions, with each category representing a more advanced state of cooperative behavior as seen in Table 5.1. We use the term 'advanced' to describe the complexity of the cooperative institution, without any normative intent.

The first level of hierarchy is solitary action. Solitary organizations do not intentionally aggregate with other organizations to collect information or coordinate activities, although they may communicate with others if necessitated by mission or organizational processes. They also may learn from other organizations by utilizing cues, but do not engage in deliberative communication related to cooperative mission attainment, or deliberately engage with other organizations purely for the purpose of generating information.

Grouping organizations deliberately engage with others, due to the information generated by this activity, distinguishing these organizations from solitary actors. They learn from other organizations, often by receiving cues regarding the other organizations' solutions to problems, which can then be assessed as potential innovations. This communication is not purposeful coordination, as there is no expectation of a specific collaborative/cooperative response by the recipient. Still, the group benefits collectively, as each organization has a potential resource for information when confronted by environmental or organizational change. These connections do not create true cooperation, as activities are not coordinated, information-sharing is largely ad hoc, and there are no limitations placed on the structure, operations, or decision-making of any actors.

Organizations working within these groups are primarily benefitting from information exchanges that would constitute the 'weak ties' in the literature on organizational networks. Beyond generating a list of potential innovations, additional learning does take place when grouping occurs.

We posit that this learning stems from organizations' inability to assess the applicability of others' solutions to their own problems. Evaluating potential innovations requires context, as the likely applicability of a borrowed solution to a problem relies on the similarity of both organizations and problems. When solutions are evaluated, organizations have an incentive to learn about

Table 5.1 Hierarchy of Mutual Reliance in Organizations

Behavior	Mechanism Differentiating from Low State	Maximum Efficiency	Behavioral					Structural				
			Breadth of Task Coordination	Resource Exchanged	Temporal Span	Perspective on Competition	Level of Cooperative Communication	Specialization	Hierarchy	Homogeneity	Organizations' Retained Capacity	Opt-Out Cost
Advanced Coordination	Structural and functional integration	Nonlinear production function	All tasks	Information, tech/human capital, financial	Permanent	Collective	Medium (structure facilitates cooperation)	High	Clearly delineated	High; sometimes approaching unity	Limited	Extremely high/impossible
Coordinated Cooperation	Complex and integrated signalling	Near linear production function	Many tasks	Information, tech/human capital, financial	Extensive	Collective	High	Some/geographic	Team-like (hierarchy by task)	Medium to high	Retained, with focus on utilizing strengths	High
Incipient	Division of labor	Linear	Limited	Information, tech/human capital, financial; all task specific	Length of task	Collective for specific task(s), otherwise individual	Low, due to few cooperative activities, but signalling present related to task	Low/self selection	Little to none	Medium; limited to task	Retained	Limited to task
Grouping	Deliberate association; facilitating international information-gathering	Linear	None	Information	Ad hoc	Individual	Entirely optional/high cues/low and ad hoc intentional signalling	None	None	Low	Retained	None
Solitary		Linear	None		NA	Individual	Only to pursue self-interest or unintentional cue	NA	NA	None	Responsible for all	None

others in their group, resulting in a degree of familiarity with organizations facing loosely similar challenges. This creates an incentive to learn even more about organizations that face very similar challenges. We expect that this incentive will lead to distinct information inequalities pertaining to other organizations in the group, revealing commonalities with some organizations related to organizational goals, processes, needs, or challenges.

In some cases, the information generated by these connections will reveal substantial congruence in goals, processes, needs, and challenges along with potential opportunities to solve problems collectively. While these connections could certainly become apparent among solitary organizations, we expect that the information-sharing that occurs in the group will make these realizations more common among group members, fundamentally acting to facilitate cooperation among some members. This is due to the information provided, which will give organizations more confidence about their evaluations of *relatedness* and *reliability*. As this information accumulates, the risk inherent in deciding to engage in cooperative activity may abate, organizations become more capable of identifying mutually beneficial opportunities, and become more confident of their perceptions of costs and benefits. This reduces the perception of the total level of risk inherent in cooperation, as well as the potential for collectively realized payoffs.

As perceptions of the risk of cooperation subside, organizations will be more willing to engage in cooperation for mutual benefit. This decision is based on the ability of the organization to generate the same amount of mission-related outcomes with fewer resources, with some efficiency resulting from complementary organizational competencies; possibly stimulated by resource deficiencies that threaten organizations' capacities to continue to do so as solitary actors. These decisions will lead to truly cooperative behavior, in which organizations pool their resources in order to carry out at least one task.

The first stage of cooperative behavior is incipient cooperation; in this stage organizations collaborate in order to achieve one or a few tasks collectively. Toward this end, they divide labor in a relatively primitive way, most often utilizing self-selection of tasks and roles based on the self-perceptions of strengths and weaknesses each actor brings to the cooperative endeavor. More than just information is exchanged, with technical, human, financial, and physical resources allocated based on capacity, need, and a process of bargaining. These exchanges reflect the strong ties present in the literature on nonprofit networks. Communication is purposeful, with each party sending signals to the other in order to coordinate these exchanges efficiently. In these arrangements, little hierarchy exists, with both organizations acting like relatively equal partners or leading on various task components according to their strengths. This cooperation is limited to the time needed to complete the task and to the functions required to complete the task, rather than a wide range of organizational activities, meaning that organizations view competition in all other areas as individual. Organizations will need to establish some symmetry of structure and communication related to the task, but will retain the capacity to engage in other aspects of organizational survival independent of this cooperation (such as governance, resource provision, other programming).

**Case—Southeast Asian Human Rights Organizations—
The Development of Cooperation**

An example of the development of incipient cooperation recently occurred among human rights organizations in a country in Southeast Asia that had worked in a loose network to share information about facts on the ground, ensuring organizations were informed about potential conflicts, and facilitating information-sharing among organizations that often lack human and technical capital. When required to make formal reports, many members of this network could not produce the materials required by international organizations. These organizations, having become familiar with the nation's longest serving human rights nongovernmental organization (NGO), realized that this organization could lead efforts to produce required documents in order to improve their odds of getting attention from the international community. Smaller NGOs then willingly allowed this organization to take the lead in reporting, without creating any formal hierarchy to support the arrangement. This cooperation provided benefits to each partner and grew out of a network of weak ties.

Engaging in cooperative behavior, even if limited to a narrow range of activities, will produce side effects that condition organizations' future predispositions toward cooperation. These side effects are the increased information about cooperative organizations and the integration required to carry out the task. We expect this occurs via processes very similar to grouping behavior. Information acts to reduce the uncertainty of perceptions, reducing uncertainty regarding any judgments required to assess future cooperative endeavors with the same organization(s). Integration also has the capacity to directly influence a component of formula (2), as the sunk costs required to functionally integrate organizations in order to achieve successful cooperation will persist over time and can reduce communication costs with the same organization(s) in the future.

Initial cooperation, then, further reduces the perceived costs of cooperation and increases the information organizations possess about their partners. This has the capacity to influence their future judgments about cooperation, with successful efforts predisposing organizations to cooperate further, should opportunities arise. In some cases, organizations will begin to cooperate more broadly with additional partners. As this cooperation builds, organizations' strengths and weaknesses become more apparent to cooperating participants; as cooperation expands, this knowledge naturally predisposes organizations to take the lead according to their capabilities. This division of labor does not create official hierarchy, but a team-like structure, where organizations are allowed to assume positions of leadership in particular areas due to expertise or resource advantages. This allows the cooperators to produce more, but also creates tremendous communication costs, as information-sharing is required to ensure that each party has the capacity to monitor and influence each area of cooperation. It does preserve the formal independence of each actor, although each actor becomes increasingly reliant on their cooperators due to the specialization that develops. The longer this arrangement persists and succeeds, the greater the incentives for organizations to continue to invest in their strengths and weaknesses, the more each actor is likely to learn about their partners, and the more similar cooperators are likely to become due to the increased program integration created by cooperation.

If cooperators possess substantial similarity, these arrangements may lead to the most formal of cooperative arrangements. This structure introduces formal hierarchy, which reduces organizational flexibility and independence, but substantially reduces the communication required for successful cooperation. In these arrangements, true specialization occurs (we speculate geographic specialization would be the most likely structure) with labor divided and rules governing these arrangements. Organizations in these arrangements become extremely integrated in all cooperative functions; in the most advanced hierarchical structures, organizations at the same level might vary in scale and location, but are otherwise similar. These structures are the most efficient cooperative arrangements available, although member organizations sacrifice diversity and independence. We expect these organizations to dominate their environments, outcompeting competitors for resources within their markets.

Implications

Although this model is clearly preliminary, we speculate that the current conditions influencing nonprofit organizations could lead to trends toward increasing cooperation and, ultimately, hierarchy in the nonprofit sector. Nonprofits face many challenges, including an increasingly crowded and competitive sector, for-profit entry into traditionally nonprofit markets, and a stagnant economy that limits the availability of revenues. As these environmental pressures escalate, nonprofits will need to do more with less. With resource scarcity requiring organizations to adapt or risk failure, cooperation is one technology available to do more with less. Given the increasing focus on networking and the benefits of information-sharing via weak ties, organizations have reason to possess more information about their peers than ever before. We can only guess at the impact of these developments on nonprofit organizations, but our attempt to understand decisions to cooperate implies that cooperation and ultimately hierarchy may result.

This would clearly have implications for the diversity of the sector, as we expect the advantages of hierarchical cooperative arrangements would benefit the cooperators, but threaten any other organizations competing in the same resource markets. Ultimately, we may see a sector in which solitary organizations are pushed to the periphery. This would have drastic consequences for range of organizations and services available and, potentially, reduce the capability of the nonprofit sector to serve some of the populations that have historically relied on nonprofits.

Notes

1 One example of how this behavior is manifested among organisms is demonstrated by primitive wasps, which engage in the most simplistic of cooperative behaviors. As these organisms might have difficulty protecting their offspring from predators as solitary actors, they have therefore evolved to achieve greater success through collective defense, with coordinated behavior allowing for some members to forage for their own survival while others protect the young. In this case, each organism produces its own offspring and cooperation allows both the collective and individual output to exceed what would be possible without cooperation. Within their environments, organisms engaging in this or more complex cooperative behaviors dominate, pushing solitary organisms to the periphery (Holldobler & Wilson, 2009). In this way, cooperation serves as a biological solution to environmental pressures, an adaptive mechanism allowing for the collective benefit of the participants. Biologists speculate that the most advanced forms of this adaptive behavior arose from behavioral heterochrony, the genetic variation serving to moderate the timing of maternal instincts (Holldobler & Wilson, 2009).
2 Hamilton's Rule relies on individual-level selection, which is not the only theory to explain this altruism. Other theories hold that group-level, mixed-level, or multilevel selection produce these phenomena, with substantial disagreement over the specific nature of this mechanism. For our purposes, Hamilton's Rule provides the most parsimonious explanation suitable to adopt to conceptualize organizational cooperation (see Wilson & Wilson, 2007).
3 This hierarchy relies on patterns of cooperation and specialization predicted of organisms by biological theory (Hunt, 2011; Johnson & Linksvayer, 2010).

References

Agranoff, R. (2007). *Managing within networks: Adding value to public organizations*. Washington, DC: Georgetown University Press.

Agranoff, R., & McGuire, M. (2001). American federalism and the search for models of management. *Public Administration Review*, 61(6), 671–681.

Agranoff, R., & McGuire, M. (2003). *Collaborative public management: New strategies for local governments*. Washington, DC: Georgetown University Press.

Barnard, C. A. (1968). *The functions of the executive*. Cambridge, MA: Harvard University Press.

Baumgartner, F. R., & Jones, B. D. (1993). *Agendas and instability in American politics*. Chicago, IL: University of Chicago Press.

Brinkerhoff, J. M. (2002). Government–nonprofit partnership: A defining framework. *Public Administration and Development*, 22(1), 19–30.

Burt, R. S. (2004). Structural holes and good ideas. *American Journal of Sociology*, 110(2), 349–399.

Carr, J. B., LeRoux, K., & Shrestha, M. (2009). Institutional ties, transaction costs, and external service production. *Urban Affairs Review*, 44(3), 403–427.

Chen, M. J., & Miller, D. (2012). Competitive dynamics: Themes, trends, and a prospective research platform. *The Academy of Management Annals*, 6(1), 135–210.

Child, C. D., & Grønbjerg, K. A. (2007). Nonprofit advocacy organizations: Their characteristics and activities. *Social Science Quarterly*, 88(1), 259–281.

Christakis, N. A., & Fowler, J. H. (2013). Social contagion theory: Examining dynamic social networks and human behavior. *Statistics in Medicine*, 32(4), 556–577.

Churchman, C. W. (1968). *The systems approach*. New York, NY: Delta.

Colman, A. M. (2003). Cooperation, psychological game theory, and limitations of rationality in social interactions. *Behavioral and Brain Sciences*, 26, 139–198.

Cropanzano, R., & Mitchell, M. S. (2005). Social exchange theory: An interdisciplinary review. *Journal of Management*, 31(6), 874–900.

Das, T. K., & Teng, B. S. (1998). Between trust and control: Developing confidence in partner cooperation in alliances. *Academy of Management Review*, 23(3), 491–512.

DeLeon, P., & Varda, D. M. (2009). Toward a theory of collaborative policy networks: Identifying structural tendencies. *Policy Studies Journal*, 37(1), 59–74.

Drucker, P. F., & Wilson, G. (2001). *The essential Drucker: Selections from the management works of Peter F. Drucker*. New York, NY: Harper Collins.

Dyer, J. H., & Singh, H. (1998). The relational view: Cooperative strategy and sources of interorganizational competitive advantage. *Academy of Management Review*, 23(4), 660–679.

Galaskiewicz, J. (1985). Interorganizational relations. *Annual Review of Sociology*, 11, 281–304.

Gaus, J. M. (1947). *Reflections on public administration*. Tuscaloosa, AL: The University of Alabama Press.

Gazley, B. (2008a). Inter-sectoral collaboration and the motivation to collaborate: Toward an integrated theory. In L. B. Bingham & R. O'Leary (Eds.), *Big ideas in collaborative public management* (pp. 36–54). Armonk, NY: M.E. Sharpe.

Gazley, B. (2008b). Beyond the contract: The scope and nature of informal government-nonprofit partnerships. *Public Administration Review*, 68(1), 141–154.

Gazley, B., & Brudney, J. L. (2007). The purpose (and perils) of government-nonprofit partnership. *Nonprofit and Voluntary Sector Quarterly*, 36(3), 389–415.

Gintis, H. (2003). A critique of team and Stackelberg reasoning. *Behavioral and Brain Sciences*, 26(2), 160–161.

Goldenkoff, R. N. (2001). Opportunities and challenges of public/private partnerships. *The Public Manager*, 30(3), 31–40.

Gulati, R., & Westphal, J. D. (1999). Cooperative or controlling? The effects of CEO-board relations and the content of interlocks on the formation of joint ventures. *Administrative Science Quarterly*, 44(3), 473–506.

Hannan, M. T., & Freeman, J. (1977). The population ecology of organizations. *American Journal of Sociology*, 82(5), 929–964.

Holldobler, B., & Wilson, E. O. (2009). *The Superorganism*. New York, NY: W.W. Norton & Company.

Hunt, J. (2011). A conceptual model for the origin of worker behavior and adaptation of eusociality. *Journal of Evolutionary Biology*, 25, 1–19.

Isett, K. R., LeRoux, K., Mergel, I. A., Mischen, P. A., & Rethemeyer, R. K. (2011). Networks in public administration scholarship: Understanding where we are and where we need to go. *Journal of Public Administration Research and Theory, 21*(S1), 157–173.

Johnson, B., & Linksvayer, T. (2010). Deconstructing the superorganism: Social physiology, groundplans, and sociogenomics. *The Quarterly Review of Biology, 81*(1), 57–79.

Kadushin, C. (2012). *Understanding social networks: Theories, concepts, and findings.* New York, NY: Oxford University Press.

Kamensky, J. M., & Burlin, T. J. (2004). *Collaboration: using networks and partnerships.* Lanham, MD: Rowan & Littlefield.

Kast, F. E., & Rosenzweig, J. E. (1972). General systems theory: Applications for organization and management. *Academy of Management Journal, 15*(4), 447–465.

Kickert, W., & Koppenjan, J. (1997). Public management and network management: An overview. In W. Kickert, E. H. Klijn, & J. Koopenjan (Eds.), *Managing complex networks* (pp. 35–61). London: Sage.

Klijn, E. H., & Koppenjan, J. F. M. (2000). Public management and policy networks: Foundations of a network approach to governance. *Public Management: An International Journal of Research and Theory, 2*(2), 135–158.

Lane, C., & Bachmann, R. (Eds.). (1998). *Trust within and between organizations: Conceptual issues and empirical applications.* Oxford, England: Oxford University Press.

McLaughlin, T. A. (2010). *Nonprofit mergers and alliances.* Hoboken, NJ: John Wiley & Sons.

McPherson, M., Smith-Lovin, L., & Cook, J. M. (2001). Birds of a feather: Homophily in social networks. *Annual Review of Sociology, 27,* 415–444.

Mandell, M. P., & Steelman, T. A. (2003). Understanding what can be accomplished through interorganizational innovations: The importance of typologies, context, and management strategies. *Public Management Review, 5*(2), 197–224.

Miller-Stevens, K., & Gable, M. (2012). Antecedents to nonprofit advocacy: Which is more important—governance or organizational structure? *Journal for Nonprofit Management, 15*(1), 21–39.

Mintzberg, H. (1979). *The structuring of organization: A synthesis of the research.* London, England: Prentice-Hall.

O'Toole, L. J., Jr. (1997). Treating networks seriously: Practical and research-based agendas in public administration. *Public Administration Review, 57*(1), 45–52.

Pfeffer, J., & Salancik, G. R. (1978). *The external control of organizations: A resource dependence perspective.* New York, NY: Harper and Row.

Pisano G. P., & Verganti, R. (2008). Which kind of collaboration is right for you? *Harvard Business Review, 86*(12), 78–86.

Provan, K. G. (1984). Interorganizational cooperation and decision-making autonomy in a consortium multihospital system. *Academy of Management Review, 9*(3), 494–504.

Provan, K. G., Fish, A., & Sydow, J. (2007). Interorganizational networks at the network level: A review of the empirical literature on whole networks. *Journal of Management, 33*(3), 479–516.

Provan, K. G., & Kenis, P. (2008). Modes of network governance: Structure, management, and effectiveness. *Journal of Public Administration Research and Theory, 18*(2), 229–252.

Provan, K. G., & Milward, H. B. (1995). A preliminary theory of interorganizational network effectiveness: A comparative study of four community mental health systems. *Administrative Science Quarterly, 40*(1), 1–33.

Putnam, R. D. (1993). The prosperous community. *The American Prospect, 4*(13), 35–42.

Rethemeyer, R. K. (2009). Making sense of collaboration and governance: Issues and challenges. *Public Performance and Management Review, 32*(4), 565–573.

Rhodes, R. A. W. (1997). *Understanding governance: Policy networks, governance, reflexivity, and accountability.* Buckingham, England: The Open University Press.

Sabatier, P. A., & Jenkins-Smith, H. C. (Eds.). (1993). *Policy change and learning: An advocacy coalition approach.* Boulder, CO: Westview Press.

Sabatier, P. A., & Weible, C. M. (2007). The advocacy coalition framework: Innovations and clarifications. In P. A. Sabatier (Ed.), *Theories of the policy process* (2nd ed., pp. 189–220). Boulder, CO: Westview Press.

Schein, E. A. (1970). *Organizational psychology.* Englewood Cliffs, NJ: Prentice-Hall.

Scott, W. R., Deschenes, S., Hopkins, K., Newman, A., & McLaughlin, M. (2006). Advocacy organizations and the field of youth services: Ongoing efforts to restructure a field. *Nonprofit and Voluntary Sector Quarterly, 35*(4), 691–714.

Senge, P. (2000). *The art and practice of the learning organization.* New York, NY: Doubleday.

Simon, H. A. (1965). Administrative decision making. *Public Administration Review, 25*(1), 31–37.

Singer, M. I., & Yankey, J. A. (1991). Organizational metamorphosis: A study of eighteen nonprofit mergers, acquisitions, and consolidations. *Nonprofit Management and Leadership, 1*(4), 357–369.

Sink, D. W. (1998). Interorganizational collaboration. In J. M. Shafritz (Ed.), *The International encyclopedia of public policy and administration* (pp. 1188–1191). Boulder, CO: Westview Press.

Stone, M. M., & Sandfort, J. R. (2009). Building a policy fields framework to inform research on nonprofit organizations. *Nonprofit and Voluntary Sector Quarterly, 38*(6), 1054–1075.

Thomson, A. M., & Perry, J. L. (2006). Collaboration processes: Inside the black box. *Public Administration Review, 66*(1), 19–32.

Varda, D. M. (2011). Data-driven management strategies in public health collaboratives. *Journal of Public Health Management and Practice, 17*(2), 122–132.

Varda, D., Shoup, J. A., & Miller, S. (2012). A systematic review of collaboration and network research in the public affairs literature: Implications for public health practice and research. *American Journal of Public Health, 102*(3), 564–571.

Varda, D. M., & Talmi, A. (2013). A patient-centered approach for evaluating public health roles within systems of care for children with special healthcare needs. *Frontiers in Public Health Services and Systems Research, 2*(1), 7.

von Bertalanffy, L. (1956). A biologist looks at human nature. *Scientific Monthly, 82*, 33–41.

von Bertalanffy, L. (1959). Human values in a changing world. In A. H. Maslow (Ed.), *New knowledge in human values* (pp. 65–74). New York, NY: Harper.

Uzzi, B. (1997). Social structure and competition in interfirm networks: The paradox of embeddedness. *Administrative Science Quarterly, 42*(1), 35–67.

Valentinov, V. (2007). Some reflections on the transaction cost theory of nonprofit organisation. *Journal for Public and Nonprofit Services, 30*(1), 52–67.

Weiner, M. E. (1990). *Human services management: Analysis and applications,* (2nd ed.). Belmont, CA: Wadsworth.

Weiner B. J., Alexander, J. A., & Zuckerman, H. S. (2000). Strategies for effective management participation in community health partnerships. *Health Care Management Review, 25*(3), 48–66.

Williamson, O. E. (1981). The economics of organization: The transaction cost approach. *American Journal of Sociology, 87*(3), 548–577.

Wilson, D., & Wilson, E. O. (2007). Rethinking the theoretical foundation of sociobiology. *The Quarterly Review of Biology, 82*(4), 327–348.

Wilson, D. S., & Sober, E. (1989). Reviving the superorganism. *Journal of Theoretical Biology, 136*(3), 337–356.

Wilson, E. O. (1975). *Sociobiology: A new synthesis.* Cambridge, MA: Harvard University Press.

Wilson, E. O. (1978). *On Human Nature.* Cambridge, MA: Harvard University Press.

6 Collaborative Management and Leadership

A Skill Set for the Entrepreneur

Madeleine W. McNamara

Introduction

As scarce resources and limited funding continue in today's complex policy landscape, it seems likely that organizations representing the public, private, and nonprofit sectors will continue to work within collaborative arrangements to resolve interconnected problems. Multiorganizational collaboration occurs when two or more organizations leverage information, resources, and expertise to achieve collective goals that a single organization is unable to achieve (Bryson, Crosby, & Stone, 2006). While the utilization of multiorganizational collaboration in the provision of public goods and services is a prominent theme among public administrators and scholars, a managerial roadmap for successful collaboration has yet to be developed.

Collaborative public management is a "process of facilitating and operating in multiorganizational arrangements in order to remedy problems that cannot be solved—or solved easily—by single organizations" (McGuire, 2006, p. 33). A participative management approach is used as the group works together to establish goals. Participants are viewed as equals within the arrangements as no one person has authority or formal power over another (McNamara, 2011). However, there is typically one person who invites relevant stakeholders to the table while creating an atmosphere of open discussion. The title most commonly given to this individual is 'manager' or 'convener' (McNamara & Morris, 2012). While 'collaborative manager' is a term often used to describe a person who facilitates the multiorganizational arrangement (see, for example, Agranoff & McGuire, 2001; Agranoff, 2006; Bryson et al., 2006; Mandell, 1999; Mandell & Steelman, 2003), the term 'manager' can create confusion as it typically involves a directive role (McNamara & Morris, 2012). Another term used to describe this role is 'collaborative convener', which emphasizes facilitation amongst equal partners absent formal authority (McNamara & Morris, 2012). "A convener is someone who works among equal partners to create conditions conducive to successful collaboration" (McNamara & Morris, 2012, p. 87). However, 'convener' does not necessarily take into account the strategic component of bringing together the right participants while acknowledging elements that impact relationships and preparing an environment conducive for collaboration. In other words, collaborative success takes more than facilitating interpersonal relationships. It also requires the deliberative creation of external factors that help create opportunities for success.

Takahashi and Smutny (2002) propose the use of the term 'collaborative entrepreneur' to describe a person that helps participants engage in interactions that address complex problems while creating an environment that further facilitates these interactions (p. 165). In this sense, the entrepreneur serves as a coupling mechanism between a complex problem, relevant stakeholders, and the external environment. It is this role that provides the focus for this chapter as a combination of facilitative and strategic skills better capture the complex atmosphere of bringing together and sustaining collaborative relationships. In their research, Takahashi and Smutny (2002) focus on the role of a collaborative entrepreneur as part of a larger focus on governance structures in three case studies involving small, community-based organizations. This chapter moves beyond their work in two significant ways. First, this chapter incorporates the public policy and collaborative management literatures to create a well-rounded skill set for the collaborative entrepreneur. While Takahashi and Smutny (2002) focus on the public policy literature, they do not tie the idea of a collaborative entrepreneur back into the collaboration literature. This is problematic because the collaboration literature offers important theoretical discussions regarding the management of multiorganizational arrangements that should be part of the broader conversation. Second, this chapter clearly identifies a skill set for the collaborative entrepreneur which was not the focus for Takahashi and Smutny (2002). It is through this skill set that the idea of a collaborative entrepreneur is operationalized and becomes more applicable to practitioners engaging in these types of activities.

Because collaborative arrangements operate outside legal-rational authorities, the ways in which collaborative entrepreneurs cultivate and sustain relationships between participants is worthy of exploration. The skill set for a collaborative entrepreneur can be based on an expansion of the literature's foundation for that of a collaborative manager. The focus of Agranoff and McGuire (2001) on activating, framing, mobilizing, and synthesizing provides a useful starting point for this discussion. The purpose of this chapter is to expand on this framework in a way that incorporates a strategic component acknowledging a need to create favorable environmental conditions for collaborative action.

This gap in the literature is an important area to address for two reasons. The first reason highlights the importance of definitional clarity as a theme within this volume. The development of an entrepreneurial skill set may help us to better understand the interpersonal and contextual conditions that support the formulation and sustainment of successful collaborative relationships. In better understanding these conditions, we may also gain a clearer understanding of collaboration itself and the predetermined nature of collaborative success. As with McGuire's (2006) work on a skill set for a collaborative manager and the work of McNamara and Morris (2012) on the skill set for a collaborative convener, there is a desired skill set for a collaborative entrepreneur. Therefore, it is plausible to suggest that multiorganizational arrangements with access to a person with the desired skill set may be more likely to find success. If a collaborative entrepreneur plays an important role in creating a foundation for the arrangement's success, filling this role with a person holding particular skills becomes an important aspect of an organization's strategic plan and a component of employment decisions.

The second reason highlights the importance of an interdisciplinary approach to collaboration as a theme within this book. Cross-pollination with the public policy literature can help us gain a deeper insight into the role of the collaborative entrepreneur while expanding on the research presented by Agranoff and McGuire (2001). More specifically, including components of a policy entrepreneur, policy window, and the policy subsystem into the skill set of the collaborative entrepreneur better accounts for the strategic context that practitioners often face in multiorganizational domains. Although the literature acknowledges the potential usefulness of collaborative arrangements in resolving complex problems (Harmon & Mayer, 1986; Keast, Mandell, Brown, & Woolcock, 2004; Rittel & Webber, 1973), there is much involved in creating the environmental context that will support the arrangement's agenda.

This chapter is divided into four sections. First, an overview of the collaborative management literature and the activities developed by Agranoff and McGuire (2001) are introduced. Next, themes pertaining to the skill set of the collaborative entrepreneur are explored. Third, the importance in developing this skill set is discussed. The chapter concludes with implications for the theory and practice of public administration.

An Overview of Collaborative Management

In collaborative interactions, organizations establish highly interdependent relationships that evolve as organizations interact with one another to attain long-term goals (Huxham, 2003; Keast et al., 2004; O'Leary & Bingham, 2007; Thomson & Perry, 2006). Interdependence develops as organizations share responsibility for highly complex problems or crises that prevent them from acting alone (Bryson et al., 2006; Gray, 1985; Imperial, 2005; Keast, Brown, & Mandell, 2007). Each organization is considered an essential element of the larger interdependent system (Mandell, 1994).

Collaborative management means managers work with all participants in a multiorganizational arrangement to solve problems that cannot be solved by an individual organization (Agranoff, 2006; McGuire, 2006). It emphasizes equal powers amongst participants and utilizes a participative approach to establish collective goals (McNamara, 2012). Because participant membership is fluid and the environment is often more complex, collaborative arrangements are subject to more variation and uncertainty than hierarchical organizations (O'Toole & Meier, 1999). Rather than formal authority based on position, all participants may lead and mobilize resources in order to attain the objectives of the collective group (McNamara & Morris, 2012). In fact, interpersonal relations between group members can generate informal power that is of greater importance than formal sources of power (Keast et al., 2004). Shared power, flexibility, and diverse perspectives are utilized to attain collective goals.

The literature identifies a key player of the collaborative as the person who establishes and sustains the group (Bryson et al., 2006; McNamara, Leavitt, & Morris, 2010; Wood & Gray, 1991). This person creates legitimacy for the arrangement by identifying an important problem and bringing relevant stakeholders together to address a particular purpose (Bryson et al., 2006; Wood & Gray, 1991). It is through expertise and relationship building that informal powers develop to persuade stakeholder participation, enhance credibility among stakeholders, establish collaborative processes, and identify relevant stakeholders (Gray, 1989; Keast et al., 2004; Wood & Gray, 1991).

While there is much discussion in the literature that compares the skill set between a traditional and collaborative manager, research suggests that today's public administrators must have the skills to work seamlessly in hierarchical or network arrangements (Agranoff, 2006; Hill & Lynn, 2005; Kettl, 2006; McGuire, 2006; McNamara & Morris, 2012). Agranoff (2006) conducted discussions with 150 public officials almost 10 years ago and concluded that managers allocated 20% of their workday to collaborative activities. If replicated today, it seems highly probable that this percentage would be higher based on our increased understanding of collaboration and the highly complicated nature of problems that administrators continue to face. Based on this premise, the role of the individual that forms and sustains this type of relationship is even more important today and is worthy of additional attention.

McGuire (2006) offers a skill set for the collaborative manager based on the processes of activating, framing, mobilizing, and synthesizing that he developed with Agranoff in 2001. Activating focuses on the identification of participants and stakeholders that have access to specific resources or skills needed for the collective arrangement. Framing focuses on developing collaborative support through operational rules, organizational values, and participants' perceptions. Mobilizing focuses on the process of participant engagement to create shared goals and further support for the group. Synthesizing focuses on creating an environment that promotes unifying participants in a collective goal (Agranoff & McGuire, 2001). These activities also provide McNamara and Morris (2012) with a framework for exploring the role of the collaborative entrepreneur.

A Skill Set for the Collaborative Entrepreneur

This section expands on the framework of Agranoff and McGuire (2001) in order to account for the expanded responsibilities of a collaborative entrepreneur. The remainder of this chapter will look to the public policy literature to further describe the existing framework while incorporating the activities of advocating and legitimizing into the process. A process of advocating, activating, legitimizing, framing, mobilizing, and synthesizing is proposed to discuss the role of the collaborative entrepreneur.

Advocating

The advocating activity of a collaborative entrepreneur is included in the framework to provide a focus on generating collaborative opportunities through the development of conditions that are conducive for interaction and change. Takahashi and Smutny (2002) develop this idea by suggesting that a collaborative window opens with convergence of a problematic situation, a resolution to the situation, decision-making with consideration for environmental impacts, and public recognition of the problem. This proposed activity moves beyond the framework of Agranoff and McGuire (2001) to suggest that an intersection of conditions is important to collaborative viability. A strong presence in this activity will require the collaborative entrepreneur to utilize skills of strategic problem-solving, persistence, and marketing. It is through this process that participants are able to see that context for viable interaction is in place before being exposed to the benefits in working together in the activating activity.

The policy literature also uses the idea of opening a window to create opportunities for issues to be placed on the policy agenda. A policy window is created when three streams—problem, policy, and politics—come together to create an opportunity for agenda-setting action (Kingdon, 2002). The convergence of these three streams is based on the identification of a public problem in need of a solution, the availability of a solution through the policy development process, and openness within the political environment for change (Kingdon, 2002). With the problem stream, issues are prioritized for actor attention. Alternatives are developed in the policy stream whereas negotiation and influence impact agenda-setting within the political stream. The opening of a policy window can be difficult to accomplish because the three streams operate on independent paths. Policy goals may be reached when there is an intersection of the streams and a subsequent window opening. This convergence is based on the communication of a compelling problem, occurrence of a focusing event, proactive efforts of a policy entrepreneur, or funding opportunities within the appropriations cycle (Kingdon, 2002).

By incorporating the idea of opening a window for opportunity into the collaboration literature, this section suggests that opportunities for collaboration are created when there is an intersection of conditions in addition to an intersection of interests. Partners share agreement on a problem, establish shared rules, develop a collective purpose, and decide on a course of action (Bryson et al., 2006; Imperial, 2005; Mattessich, Murray-Close, & Monsey, 2001). In addition, beneficial impacts of generating social and political agreement on the problem should not be underestimated. While significant events, such as the Space Shuttle Columbia disaster, hurricanes Rita and Katrina, and the attacks of 9/11, are often used as the backdrop for case studies in the collaboration literature (see Donahue, 2006; Kapucu, 2006; Kiefer & Montjoy, 2006), the impacts these types of events have to focus collaborative efforts are less often discussed. By their very definition, collaborative relationships are used to address complex issues with temporary resolutions vice solutions (Harmon & Mayer, 1986). However, a focusing event can help make a problem tangible for policy-makers, scientists, citizens, and advocates while also creating opportunities for collaborative entrepreneurs to highlight possible resolutions for the problem. A combination of the presence of a focusing event and the efforts of a collaborative entrepreneur to further communicate the problem may result in the availability of funding. The collaboration literature acknowledges the role of a champion and a sponsor (see, for example, Bryson et al., 2006), but it does not link the strategic component of creating a window for change or identifying funding opportunities to the person facilitating and sustaining relationships within the arrangement.

Therefore, a collaborative entrepreneur must recognize and act on opportunities to push forward the agenda of the collective arrangement. Particular skills are needed to accomplish this goal. First, the collaborative entrepreneur must have strong strategic problem-solving skills to assess political and financial feasibility for problem resolution. This includes identifying potential funding streams that align with the problems the arrangement is looking to address and the solutions that the arrangement is able to propose for addressing those problems. Second, the collaborative entrepreneur must have persistence to push the group's agenda while softening the environment until a window for opportunity occurs. Third, marketing skills may help the collaborative entrepreneur garner attention from relevant stakeholders and funders to allow the coupling of problems with solutions and political forces. A focusing event creates opportunities for a window to open but it is up to the collaborative entrepreneur to push the group's ideas forward in order to politically advance the group's agenda and create an environment conducive to change.

Activating

Much like a collaborative convener, the activating role of a collaborative entrepreneur brings relevant stakeholders to the arrangements. Relevancy is based on the desired skills and resources needed within the collective group to achieve goals (McNamara & Morris, 2012). The collaboration literature suggests that it is important to persuade stakeholders to participate in the group in the absence of formal authority (Gray, 1989; Keast et al., 2004; McNamara, 2011; Wood & Gray, 1991). Opportunities for collaboration typically occur when there is an intersection of interests between participants that creates a win-win situation for the partnership. Therefore, participants must perceive a mutually beneficial relationship. For the collaborative entrepreneur, this activity requires skills in strategic messaging, multitasking, and group facilitation.

The policy literature also acknowledges the power of common interests but emphasizes the use of persuasion in bringing people together toward common goals based on overlapping interests. In a policy subsystem, various government and nongovernmental actors participate in the agenda-setting process and interact where common interests are identified (Howlett, 2003). Influential relationships play an important role on those involved as these relationships encourage individuals to support certain interests. Actors outside government, such as interest groups and the public, usually influence the agenda-setting process by bringing problems to the attention of actors inside government (Howlett, 2003). Stone (2001) also explores how people form groups using a polis model. She emphasizes the use of symbols and metaphors to create interpretations for issues in particular ways (Stone, 2001). As a result, these symbols and metaphors can be powerful tools in decision-making as individuals seek outcomes that maximize individual and community benefits.

By incorporating the use of symbols and metaphors into the collaboration literature, this section suggests that these tools can be used to strategically conjure a shared agreement for a particular problem while emphasizing benefits to the community. Policy actors can act like craftsmen in shaping arguments through the presentation of facts and figures to persuade a particular audience (Majone, 1989). The result of this approach can lead to collaborative participation in two ways. First, the collaborative entrepreneur identifies participants with expertise needed to contribute to and benefit from the collective agenda. Second, the same vision can be used to generate political feasibility for particular resolutions in the policy arena.

Therefore, a collaborative entrepreneur must communicate a strategic message to participants within the collaborative arrangement and to potential supporters outside the arrangement. This activity requires multitasking skills for the collaborative entrepreneur as it will require activities with two different groups of people who are engaged in activity simultaneously. In selecting the proper communication techniques for the different groups, partners with diverse resources and expertise will come together to address complex problems while support outside the arrangement continues to grow. Strong communication skills will allow the collaborative entrepreneur to broker the relationships necessary to match problems with people who are able to support resolutions. In addition, the collaborative entrepreneur must have strong skills in group facilitation to help individuals see the benefits in working together and the ways in which diverse contributions are one part of a larger whole.

Legitimizing

The legitimizing activity of a collaborative entrepreneur is added to the framework to provide a focus on building resources, recognition, and trust inside *and* outside the arrangement. This activity requires the collaborative entrepreneur to have strong specialized knowledge in the problem area, negotiation skills to generate political forces, and personal connections to support citizen engagement. The current collaboration literature typically combines an element of legitimacy within the mobilization activity, and the focus for legitimacy is viewed from the perspective of collaborative participants. In other words, legitimacy is about collaborative participants viewing the arrangement as a legitimate vehicle for addressing problems (McNamara, 2008) and the person who brings participants to the table as having a legitimate role in the arrangement (Gray, 1985). Legitimacy for the arrangement is needed to attract participants and resources while legitimacy for the facilitator is needed to develop trusting relationships within and between participants (Gray, 1985). Legitimacy is described as a mindset toward the collective arrangement (Mandell, 1994) and as an "ethic of collaboration" (Thomson & Perry, 2006, p. 25). However, the collaboration literature can incorporate an expanded view of legitimacy to better capture the role of a collaborative entrepreneur.

The policy literature also addresses legitimacy but includes an external orientation to the discussion of legitimacy. For example, Kingdon (2002) acknowledges the influence that actors outside government can have on the agenda-setting process through the policy stream. Interest groups, academic and research communities, and public opinion have abilities to influence agenda items. Certain policy proposals rise to the top of the agenda due to alignment with public opinion and values of members in the policy community (Kingdon, 2002). The job of the policy entrepreneur includes identifying opportunities for agenda-setting.

By incorporating an external source of legitimacy for the collective arrangement into the collaboration literature, this section emphasizes the value of political and citizen participation in collaborative success. Political support can be built through communications with elected officials and their constituents. It is important that well-connected people believe the group's visions and goals provide a legitimate way to resolve the problem at hand. Strong negotiation skills are needed to translate perceived legitimacy into the political force needed to open a collaborative window while generating public involvement. The collaborative entrepreneur must be perceived as a viable source of information and expertise by the citizenry to cultivate trust.

Negotiation within collaborative arrangements is an important skill for the collaborative entrepreneur and underexplored in the literature. Based on the work presented in Chapter 7, a need for negotiation arises when collaborative participants agree on a collective goal but have different ideas on how to achieve that goal. Joannou Menefee explores a framework for resistance in collaborative arrangements and suggests that cultural and communicative differences need to be considered. When applying the premise for her model to this activity, the entrepreneur must also consider the need to resolve conflict through negotiation by acknowledging and respecting cultural and communicative differences. An ability to do so further speaks to the legitimacy for the role.

Citizen engagement can also play a major role in helping the collective group achieve its goals. While Simo and Bies (2007) identify volunteer involvement as an important initial condition in their case study of Hurricane Katrina, the impact on goal attainment is not stressed. The collaborative entrepreneur will rely on professional knowledge to generate public support. Increased knowledge can help citizens advocate for their own interests. Educational campaigns are often used to inform the public of a particular initiative and enhance citizen engagement. Therefore, the collaborative entrepreneur must select participants to interact with the public based on a balanced skill set with specialized knowledge and communication skills that will help the public understand the material presented. The information the public receives and the interactions they experience will impact their level of involvement. Strong personal connections may help an entrepreneur determine strengths of participants while placing them in situations appropriate to these strengths. Perceived legitimacy inside and outside the collaborative arrangement is important for developing a context for successful collaboration. In order for this to happen, people inside and outside the arrangement must believe the entrepreneur is a legitimate source for advocating for the problem.

Framing

Much like a collaborative convener, the framing activity of a collaborative entrepreneur focuses on developing rules for operations, promoting collaborative values, and understanding the contextual environment to know when the collaborative is a viable partnership (McNamara & Morris, 2012). Because participants are part of different organizations with independent missions, the collaborative entrepreneur builds a common vision among participants by creating opportunities for them to learn more about one another (McNamara, 2008). Emphasis is placed on communicating interests through a lens most participants find beneficial to collective and individual goals. The current collaboration literature acknowledges the importance of establishing rules while developing a collaborative spirit among participants (McNamara, 2008). Key stakeholders must establish shared rules, develop a collective purpose, and decide jointly on a course of action (Bryson et al., 2006; Imperial, 2005; McNamara, 2012; Mattessich et al., 2001). For collaborative entrepreneurs, this activity requires skills in facilitating relationships, developing social capital, assessing feasibility, as well as communicating, consensus-building, and problem resolution.

The policy literature also recognizes the importance of promoting values and understanding the contextual environment through the development of a policy subsystem. Various government and nongovernmental actors participate in the agenda-setting process and interact where common interests are identified (Howlett, 2003). The policy literature acknowledges that the way in which the problem is framed depends upon the influence of actors within the subsystem. Participants can influence the agenda-setting process by bringing attention to a particular problem through the use of focusing events. Some power among participants is not equal. Certain problems receive prominence based on the reaction of participants in the subsystem. Therefore, it is possible for a particular subsystem of actors to monopolize interpretation of the problem to ensure it is conceived and discussed in ways that further the subsystem's interests (Kingdon, 2002). In order for the problem, policy, and political streams to converge, major actors must agree on the problem and the viability of potential solutions. Stone (2001) also suggests that the policymaking process is value laden and explores the influence of linkages between members of the community. Because people are influenced by those closest to them, interpretation of values and interests influence policy issues.

By incorporating contextual viability into the collaboration literature, this section suggests that collaborative entrepreneurs consider the dynamic environment that participants are working within and find ways to highlight the importance of connections between individuals based on trust and reciprocity. In addition, the collaborative entrepreneur must scan the multiorganizational environment to ensure the development of social capital is possible. Some amount of social capital is needed to initiate a collaborative effort and the following elements are identified in community-based arrangements: respect and understanding, empathy, commitment and continuity, predictability and dependability, and transparency (see Morris, Gibson, Leavitt, & Jones, 2013). The current collaboration literature can be expanded to link these elements of social capital to a need for the collaborative entrepreneur to operate in an environment that captures at least some of these characteristics. Majone (1989) refers to this skill as assessing feasibility in a political or administrative context. Communication skills are needed to help participants understand one another, which will foster respect and empathy (McNamara & Morris, 2012). In addition, deliberative discussion allows for open communications that will help create transparency among participants. Skills in consensus-building help participants develop a shared vision to enhance commitment to the collective arrangement. Skills in problem resolution allow an entrepreneur to address initial issues while continuing to allow for participants to see that others are there for them in difficult times.

Mobilizing

As with a collaborative convener, the mobilizing activities of a collaborative entrepreneur include motivating participants to develop shared goals and common objectives to secure continued support for the arrangement. Decisions are based on consensus and compromise with the development of a shared agreement in which all participants are involved. With many different viewpoints, it is important for participants to be aligned in problem identification and role assignment. Through the development of long-standing relationships, diverse perspectives are shared and potentially creative solutions developed to obtain collective goals (McNamara, 2008). While DeLeon and Varda (2009) recognize the probability of heterogeneity among network participants, no mention is made regarding a coupling mechanism to bring participants together in a way that most benefits collective and individual interests. The role of a collaborative entrepreneur can address this gap.

When applying the policy literature to the mobilizing activity, the complexity of this activity and potential struggles among participants are better understood. Stone (2001) acknowledges that problem definition can be ambiguous as contradictory interpretations of policy goals develop. Because participants mobilize their interests to influence problem definition and increase support for certain interests, outcomes of the process depend on abilities of the actors to mobilize interests and garner support from a variety of groups. Therefore, it is possible for a particular subsystem of actors to monopolize interpretation of the problem to ensure it is conceived and discussed in ways that further the subsystem's interests. Goal congruence among major actors plays a key factor in the convergence of the problem, policy, and political streams (Kingdon, 2002).

A policy goal can represent different interests to different people (Stone, 2001). Therefore, the process of uniting around common goals should be a deliberative one. Majone (1989) views the process of argumentation as an opportunity to develop consensus regarding policy goals and moral judgments among citizens and policymakers. The collaborative entrepreneur must support relationships between participants by establishing channels that support ongoing discussion and mutual understanding.

Synthesizing

Similar to a collaborative convener, synthesizing activities of a collaborative entrepreneur involve creating an environment that will support positive interactions while removing potential barriers (Agranoff & McGuire, 2001). A common purpose is supported through the reduction of uncertainties and development of incentives (McNamara & Morris, 2012). This particular activity often takes time and a foundation built on long-standing relationships. Prior relationships and open dialogue help participants cultivate trust by enhancing their understanding of organizational missions and looking for opportunities to help one another (Bryson et al., 2006; Huxham, 2003; Mandell, 1999).

From the policy literature, Stone (2001) puts the interests of the collective good above those of individuals. Enjoyment of group membership generates support for interests beyond goal achievement as actors create opportunities to increase support for particular interests through the offering of group membership. People may support particular initiatives because their family or friends support those interests (Stone, 2001). Therefore, it is important to consider the impact of social relationships on political reasoning.

By incorporating the strength of social relationships into the collaboration literature, this section expands on the sense of community that a collaborative entrepreneur must establish within the collaborative as well as with the broader community that the collaborative is looking to help. It is through the sense of community that strong social networks can develop and effect change (Putnam, 2001). While Simo and Bies (2007) identify volunteer involvement as an important initial condition in their case study of Hurricane Katrina, this linkage is worthy of further consideration. Advocacy for community concerns, abilities to effect change, and proposals of new ideas are strengths that a collaborative entrepreneur must find ways to harness in other collaborative arrangements.

Discussion

The use of the term 'collaborative entrepreneur' acknowledges a need to strategize social and contextual impacts on collaborative relationships. This term differs from other terms that have been used to describe this role because it acknowledges the need for a coupling mechanism between a complex problem, relevant stakeholders, and the external environment. It is important for collaborative participants to work with others inside and outside the arrangement to create an environment for success. While the development of internal relationships helps to facilitate trust, open communications, and deliberative discussions to strengthen bonds among participants, the development of external relationships helps to convey the importance of the group while engaging citizens in various ways to better the group as a whole. In both arenas, relationships between individuals and subsequent development of a sense of community further facilitate interactions. The development of personal relationships can enhance collaborative viability and stability as participants feel connected to the work they are doing and learn about one another to develop trust (McNamara, 2008). While the collaboration literature acknowledges the important impact relationships can have on increasing organizational capacities through the diversification of resources and expertise, these connections are far more important in creating a sense of community that strengthens the entire arrangement.

With that being said, it is important to consider that participants have commitments to their respective organizations in addition to the collective arrangement. Memberships to collaborative arrangements do not reduce individuals' loyalties to respective organizations (Keast et al., 2004). Therefore, a collaborative entrepreneur must have a good sense for this delicate

balance while helping participants identify areas where organizational interests intersect with collaborative interests. It is at this intersection that participants will be most engaged and able to assist the collective arrangement. This
is an area that the collaborative entrepreneur may need to revisit frequently
with participants as organizational environments evolve; changes are made as
the arrangement grows, partners change, or the problem domain shifts
(Bryson et al., 2006). This dynamic environment requires frequent monitoring and forecasting by the collaborative entrepreneur.

   While social capital is an important element of collaborative viability,
collaborative entrepreneurs must consider its presence among participants.
Morris et al. (2013) suggest that social capital increases through the act of
collaboration. Therefore, some level of social capital is needed as a precondition for collaboration, but an entrepreneur should also consider how collaborating helps to strengthen social capital. Some of the qualities that help
to facilitate trust within a collaborative arrangement can also be used to
facilitate trust outside the arrangement. For example, developing mechanisms for citizen participation can allow for open communications between
the collaborative arrangement and the citizens it's looking to serve. Active
listening and deliberative discussion may help the collaborative entrepreneur better understand citizens' needs and the availability of community
resources. Over time, transparency and a willingness to share information
will help foster the development of a community.

   This chapter also suggests that the skill set that a collaborative entrepreneur brings to the table can be a powerful precondition for collaborative
viability. According to interviews with federal executives, O'Leary, Choi,
and Gerard (2012) found that effective collaboration is dependent on the
skill set of the administrator even though organizational-level antecedents
are the primary focus of collaboration models within the public administration literature. Despite their important role, specific guidance for collaborative conveners is lacking (McNamara, 2011). Therefore, the following
guidelines are offered to help conveners assess the alignment of initial conditions with collaborative viability:

- Be an entrepreneur to create an environment for change. Seize focusing
  events to create windows for collective action through a softening in
  the environment that may create opportunities to advance politically
  the arrangement's agenda.
- Canvas existing relationships to ensure necessary resources and expertise are represented in the collaborative subsystem.
- Locate a stable funding stream that can be used to support the arrangement and leverage resources amongst participants.
- Ensure all members of the arrangement agree on the problem at hand
  and a plan to address it.
- Cultivate relationships between personnel to establish a sense of
  community.
- Identify creative ways to educate and involve citizens.

The development of a skill set for collaborative entrepreneurs may benefit the practice of public management. This research extends the idea of collaboration being a deliberate process based on the inclusion of people with high levels of competence, interpersonal skills, trustworthiness, and commitment/personal interest. Other research acknowledges that structural or procedural elements may facilitate the development and sustainment of collaboration (see McNamara, 2011; Thomson & Perry, 2006) while administrators invite stakeholders to the table based on a need for particular resources or technical expertise (see McNamara, 2012; McNamara et al., 2010). However, the development and sustainment of collaborative interactions may also be influenced by the skills collaborative entrepreneurs possess and their abilities to facilitate the strategic components of the process.

There is much discussion in the literature concerning success in collaborative arrangements (see, for example, Bardach & Lesser, 1996; Mandell, 1994; O'Toole, 1997; Page, 2004). Thoughts concerning the definition of collaborative success range from the mere existence of a collaborative process (see Feldman & Khademian, 2001) to proven improvements in outcomes (see, for example, Koontz, 2005; Mandell, 1994; O'Leary et al., 2012). This chapter captures the complexity of collaborative success as multiorganizational arrangements often face circumstances beyond any individual's control. Even with the presence of identified preconditions, collaborative success can be limited by outside dynamics or the people involved. These challenges, coupled with seemingly limited accomplishments, may prevent us from hearing about collective endeavors that could further expand our knowledge of multiorganizational relationships. While the very definition of collaboration implies an application to resolving unsolvable problems, this sets a high bar for collaborative success. Perhaps the definition for this term needs to account for the evolving nature of multiorganizational relationships. Practical realities may require a consideration of short- and long-term goals as measurements of success (Cheever, 2006).

Conclusion

This chapter develops the role of a collaborative entrepreneur and acknowledges a strategic component of bringing together the right participants, while acknowledging elements that impact relationships, and preparing an environment conducive for collaboration. In other words, collaborative success takes more than facilitating interpersonal relationships. It also requires the deliberative creation of external factors that help create opportunities for success.

Through a combination of facilitative and strategic skills, the development of a collaborative entrepreneur better captures the complex atmosphere of bringing together and sustaining collaborative relationships. Because the literature emphasizes the enormous effort needed to develop and sustain collaborative arrangements from a theoretical standpoint, it is important to discuss the conditions that contribute to collaborative success as well as practical limitations. It is through these discussions that administrators will be truly prepared to make a determination of collaborative viability in a specific context.

The usefulness of the framework for explaining the skill set of the collaborative entrepreneur may be determined in future empirical research. Application could improve the framework in two ways. First, skills not identified in this chapter may be uncovered and important in facilitating interpersonal relationships while creating external factors that foster opportunities for success. This framework is intended as a starting point for that discussion. Second, ranking the importance of skills for a collaborative entrepreneur is beyond the scope of this paper but could provide valuable information to inform practice and theory. It is through application of this framework that researchers could get a sense for presence and relative importance of each skill. It is possible for a collaborative arrangement to find success in an environment that does not call on the utilization of a specific skill. Documentation of these situations would help theorists and practitioners get a sense for the skills most important to success which could be used to inform training and hiring decisions. Today's collaborative entrepreneurs have a complex role requiring a variety of skills. It is through this framework that discussion regarding a baseline skill set can emerge in future research.

References

Agranoff, R. (2006). Inside collaborative networks: Ten lessons for public managers. *Public Administration Review*, 66(supplement), 56–65.

Agranoff, R., & McGuire, M. (2001). Big questions in public network management research. *Journal of Public Administration Research and Theory*, 11(3), 295–306.

Bardach, E., & Lesser, C. (1996). Accountability in human services collaboration: For what? And to whom? *Journal of Public Administration Research and Theory*, 6(2), 197–224.

Bryson, J., Crosby, B., & Stone, M. (2006). The design and implementation of cross-sector collaborations: Propositions from the literature. *Public Administration Review*, 66(supplement), 44–55.

Cheever, K. (2006). Collaborations in public service: Memphis experience. *International Journal of Public Administration*, 29(7), 533–555.

DeLeon, P., & Varda, D. (2009). Toward a theory of collaborative policy networks: Identifying structural tendencies. *Policy Studies Journal*, 37(1), 59–74.

Donahue, A. (2006). The space shuttle *Columbia* recovery operation: How collaboration enabled disaster response. *Public Administration Review*, 66(Special Issue), 141–142.

Feldman, M., & Khademian, A. (2001). Principles for public management practice: From dichotomies to interdependence. *Governance: An International Journal of Policy and Administration*, 14(3), 339–361.

Gray, B. (1985). Conditions facilitating interorganizational collaboration. *Human Relations*, 38(10), 911–936.

Gray, B. (1989). *Collaborating: Finding common ground for multiparty problems.* San Francisco, CA: Jossey-Bass.

Harmon, M., & Mayer, R. (1986). *Organization theory for public administration.* Boston, MA: Little, Brown and Company.

Hill, C., & Lynn, L. (2005). Is hierarchical governance in decline? Evidence from empirical research. *Journal of Public Administration Research and Theory,* 15(2), 173–195.

Howlett, M. (2003). *Studying public policy: Policy cycles and subsystems.* New York, NY: Prentice Hall.

Huxham, C. (2003). Theorizing collaboration practice. *Public Management Review,* 5(3), 401–423.

Imperial, M. (2005). Using collaboration as a governance strategy: Lessons from six watershed management programs. *Administration & Society,* 37(3), 281–320.

Kapucu, N. (2006). Interagency communication networks during emergencies: Boundary spanners in multiagency coordination. *American Review of Public Administration,* 36(2), 207–225.

Keast, R., Brown, K., & Mandell, M. (2007). Getting the right mix: Unpacking integration meanings and strategies. *International Public Management Journal,* 10(1), 9–33.

Keast, R., Mandell, M., Brown, K., & Woolcock, G. (2004). Network structures: Working differently and changing expectations. *Public Administration Review,* 64(3), 363–371.

Keifer, J., & Montjoy, R. (2006). Incrementalism before the storm: Network performance for the evacuation of New Orleans. *Public Administration Review,* 66(Special Issue), 122–130.

Kettl, D. (2006). Managing boundaries in American administration: The collaboration imperative. *Public Administration Review,* 66, 10–19.

Kingdon, J. (2002). *Agendas, alternatives, and public policies* (2nd ed.). New York, NY: Harper Collins.

Koontz, T. (2005). We finished the plan, so now what? Impacts of collaborative stakeholder participation on land use policy. *Policy Studies Journal,* 33(3), 459–481.

McGuire, M. (2006). Collaborative public management: Assessing what we know and how we know it. *Public Administration Review,* 66(supplement), 33–43.

McNamara, M. (2008). Exploring interactions during multiorganizational policy implementation: A case study of the Virginia Coastal Zone Management Program. *Dissertations and Thesis Full Text,* 69(11), (UMI No. 3338107).

McNamara, M. (2011). Processes of cross-sector collaboration: A case study of the Virginia Coastal Zone Management Program. *Nonprofit Policy Forum,* 1–20.

McNamara, M. (2012). Struggling to untangle the web of cooperation, coordination, and collaboration: A framework for public managers. *International Journal of Public Administration,* 35(6), 389–401.

McNamara, M., Leavitt, W., & Morris, J. (2010). Multiple-sector partnerships and the engagement of citizens in social marketing campaigns: The case of Lynnhaven River "NOW". *Virginia Social Science Journal,* 45, 1–20.

McNamara, M., & Morris, J. (2012). More than a "one-trick pony": Exploring the contours of a multi-sector convener. *Journal for Nonprofit Management,* 15(1), 84–103.

Majone, G. (1989). *Evidence, argument, and persuasion in the policy process.* New Haven, CT: Yale University Press.

Mandell, M. (1994). Managing interdependencies through program structures: A revised paradigm. *American Review of Public Administration, 24*(1), 99–121.

Mandell, M. (1999). The impact of collaborative efforts: Changing the face of public policy through networks and network structures. *Policy Studies Review, 16*(1), 4–17.

Mandell, M., & Steelman, T. (2003). Understanding what can be accomplished through interorganizational innovations: The importance of typologies, context, and management strategies. *Public Management Review, 5*(2), 197–224.

Mattessich, P., Murray-Close, M., & Monsey, B. (2001). *Collaboration: What makes it work.* Saint Paul, MN: Amherst H. Wilder Foundation.

Morris, J. C., Gibson, W. A., Leavitt, W. M., & Jones, S. C. (2013). *The case for grassroots collaboration: Social capital and ecosystem restoration at the local level.* Lanham, MD: Lexington Books.

O'Leary, R., & Bingham, L. (2007). Introduction. *International Public Management Journal, 10*(1), 3–7.

O'Leary, R., Choi, Y., & Gerard, C. (2012). The skill set of the successful collaborator. *Public Administration Review, 72*(SI), 570–583.

O'Toole, L. (1997). Treating networks seriously: Practical and research-based agendas in public administration. *Public Administration Review, 57*(1), 45–52.

O'Toole, L., & Meier, K. (1999). Modeling the impact of public management: The implications of structural context. *Journal of Public Administration Research and Theory, 9*, 505–526.

Page, S. (2004). Measuring accountability for results in interagency collaborative. *Public Administration Review, 64*(5), 591–606.

Putnam, R. (2001). *Bowling Alone.* New York, NY: Simon & Schuster.

Rittel, H. W. J., & Webber, M. M. (1973). Dilemmas in a general theory of planning. *Policy Sciences, 4*(1), 155–169.

Simo, G., & Bies, A. (2007). The role of nonprofits in disaster response: An expanded model of cross-sector collaboration. *Public Administration Review, 67*(Special Issue), 125–142.

Stone, D. (2001). *Policy paradox: The art of political decision making.* New York, NY: W.W. Norton.

Takahashi, L., & Smutny, G. (2002). Collaborative windows and organizational governance: Exploring the formation and demise of social service partnerships. *Nonprofit and Voluntary Sector Quarterly, 31*(2), 165–185.

Thomson, A., & Perry, J. (2006). Collaboration processes: Inside the black box. *Public Administration Review, 66*(supplement), 20–32.

Wood, D., & Gray, B. (1991). Toward a comprehensive theory of collaboration. *Journal of Applied Behavioral Science, 27*(2), 139–162.

7 Conflict in Collaborations

To Resolve or Transform?

Stephanie Joannou Menefee

> Differences are often the source of immense creative potential. Learning to harness that potential is what collaboration is all about.
>
> (Gray, 1989, p. 11)

Introduction

Collaboration is a way for people and organizations to come together to solve bigger problems and create real value. Part of the attraction to collaborations is that all parties to the collaboration tend to be passionate about the end goal. But, part of passion is the inevitability of conflict to arise. The important point to remember in the face of conflict is that conflict can also be a chance for positive growth. If parties to the collaboration understand that idea, then they can use the conflict to drive constructive discourse, and the product of the collaboration could be even greater than any of the parties anticipated. In this chapter, we will discuss collaborations, conflicts, and how the two can come together harmoniously to reach creative and lasting end goals.

A common reason collaborations form is because there is a scarcity of resources (Levine & White, 1961) surrounding a complex issue (O'Toole, 1997). To solve this complex issue, each collaborator comes to the table with resources that other collaborators need to achieve a common end goal (Thomson & Perry, 2006; Chen & Graddy, 2005; Gray, 1989; Gray & Wood, 1991; Pfeffer & Salancik, 1978; Thomson, 2001). However, common goals do not ensure constant agreement along the path to goal achievement.

Barbara Gray (1989), a leading contributor to the field of collaboration, states: "Collaboration operates on the premise that the assumptions disputants have about the other side and about the nature of the issues themselves are worth testing" (p. 13). This statement is what leads to the current question of how conflict presents itself in a collaborative and what measures can be taken to resolve—or even transform—that conflict into a lasting partnership. The goals of this chapter are threefold: the first is to briefly highlight the process of collaboration, noting in particular the non-material issues in collaboration; the second is to define conflict, specifically how conflict manifests itself in collaborations; and the third is to highlight how, through constructive use of communication (driven by culture and emotions), conflict can be transformed into a creative product leading to a lasting collaborative partnership.

Definitions and Context

Collaboration

In her 1989 work, Gray notes several things about collaboration that are central to this exploration. First, there two paths to collaboration: one that comes together in the interest of resolving conflict and one that comes about to achieve a shared vision. The path we are interested in here is the one where the collaborative comes together on its own accord to achieve a shared vision.

Second, there are two types of expected outcomes from a collaborative: exchange of information and joint agreements. In this exploration, the joint agreement is of interest because it is the outcome wherein when combined with the desire to achieve a shared vision, collective strategies are put into place forming groups like public–private partnerships, joint ventures, and labor-management cooperatives, and, when successful, these collaborations form ongoing bodies.

Third, there are five features critical to collaboration: stakeholders are interdependent; solutions emerge by dealing constructively with differences; joint ownership of decisions is involved; stakeholders assume collective responsibility for the future direction of domain; and collaboration is an emergent process. The feature central to this exploration is the second, dealing constructively with differences.

Additionally, Thomson and Perry (2006) identify two competing political traditions surrounding collaboration in the context of an American public ethos, classic liberalism and civic republicanism. This chapter focuses on collaboration in a civic republicanism context, which views collaboration as "an integrative process that treats differences as the basis for deliberation in order to arrive at 'mutual understanding, a collective will, trust and sympathy, [and the] implementation of shared preferences'" (p. 20).

In sum, the goal of this paper is reconciling what happens when difference presents itself in shared visions whose expected outcome is a joint agreement. There is a deep body of literature addressing the motivations, conditions, and hardships of forming and maintaining a collaborative, but the body of literature on how to navigate those hardships toward a successful and lasting collaborative is extremely small (Takahashi & Smutny, 2002).

There is no doubt that successfully advancing the shared vision of a collaborative requires multiple stakeholders, each of whom holds a piece of the resources necessary to achieving goal completion (Gray, 1989). But it is important to note that these stakeholders can come from different locations, cultures, and perspectives. These locations, cultures, and perspectives combined have the ability to produce the ideal environment for harnessing creative potential if cultivated properly; but they also have the ability to produce a conflict-ridden environment where the only solution is to dissolve what could have been an extremely successful, ongoing venture. Therefore, this exploration has been constructed based on the following stream of logic: the success of Gray's collaboration definition seen throughout the other chapters in this book depends largely on communication (non-verbal and verbal), which can determine—through culture (a significant driver of emotion)—how people in a collaborative environment respond to conflict. Because of the nature of the above statement, the following assumptions are held throughout the exploration: collaboration is voluntary, parties are interdependent, stakeholders are equal, accountability is shared, and once a collaborative is formed successfully there is a high level of trust between stakeholders (Bardach, 1998; Logsdon, 1991; Ostrom, 1990; Gray, 1989)

Many writers in the collaboration literature agree "the sincere practice of collaboration dictates that all parties involved will take part in the decision making" (Davoli & Fine, 2004, p. 268); which means that in order for a collaboration to be successful, obstacles must be faced as they arise. The best way to begin to address these obstacles is through a comprehensive understanding of the conflict literature.

Conflict

The potential for conflict is everywhere, and whereas some believe that conflict is a bad thing, others believe it to be something that can promote positive change. Conflict arises in two ways in a collaborative. One way is in deciding how the vision should be carried out, and the second is in the implementation of agreements (Gray, 1989). When stakeholders from different backgrounds and beliefs are present in a collaborative, it is very easy to meet resistance with decisions.

According to Pruitt and Kim (2004), conflict is "a perceived divergence of interest" (p. 15) between individuals (known as party and other)— 'interest' meaning feelings about what is desirable. Interests are central to thinking and action, driving attitudes, goals, and intentions. Interests are translated to aspirations (things party must achieve); and conflict exists when party sees others' aspirations as incompatible to their own.

Because we know that "conflict arises from resource limitations, high-stakes consequences, uncertainty, [and] goal conflict among stakeholders..." (Xiao et al., 2007, p. 171), the best answer to the question of why divergence of interests would present themselves in a collaborative lies in Pruitt and Kim's (2004) "Lack of Normative Consensus" (p. 26), which falls under features of the community, the fourth category of proposed conditions that encourage conflict.

> When communities lack normative consensus, some community members will have aspirations that are incompatible with those of others, and conflict will be common.... Low conflict communities have particularly clear norms governing those interpersonal relationships that are most prone to conflict, such as authority and status relationships.
>
> (Pruitt & Kim, 2004, pp. 26–27)

Speaking to authority and status relationships, it is understood that true collaborations do not have vertical hierarchies. However, there is still a structure, and how the stakeholders come together to form that structure is crucial. Takahashi and Smutny (2002) conducted a case study of the people in three small, community-based organizations who formed a collaborative to address HIV and AIDS issues in Orange County, California. The study found that a gradual demise of relationships was attributed to the initial governance structure's inability to adapt to the changing conditions of the collaborative, eventually leading stakeholders to look elsewhere for partnership. This study shows that there was a problem with relationships—potentially related to authority and status because the stakeholders were inflexible to the changing needs of the collaborative.

Let us go to John Paul Lederach's (2003) explanation of how conflict is experienced for a deeper understanding. First, it is noticed that something is not "right"—a feeling of dis-ease is experienced. Second, things previously taken for granted are noticed—the relationship all of a sudden becomes difficult. Then, communication becomes difficult—those individuals not in agreement go unheard and the feeling is that everyone who is not in alignment with the majority is "up to no good." Finally, there is a change in physiology—a shift from experiencing anxiety to experiencing pain, anger, and frustration (p. 7). It is at this point that stakeholders in a collaborative will focus efforts elsewhere, leaving the venture to crumble.

Pruitt and Kim (2004) mention community as the body who has this lack of normative consensus. It is proposed here that stakeholders in a collaborative treat themselves as a community to foster an increased sense of belonging. Community can be defined as "A group of people with diverse characteristics who are linked by social ties, share common perspectives, and engage in joint action in geographical locations or settings.... Community [is] defined similarly but experienced differently by people with diverse backgrounds" (MacQueen et al., 2001). If stakeholders are viewed as the initial community members, then as the collaborative expands, the community expands to those others who join the collaborative, regardless of role responsibility.

After a collaborative built to serve the needs of at-risk youth failed, it was noted that one of the reasons was too much focus on getting the groups to work together, and not enough focus on repairing the actual problems the collaborative was formed to address. "Collaboration should not be seen primarily as a problem of getting professionals and human service agencies to work together more efficiently and effectively" (White & Wehlage, 1995, p. 36).

Along the lines of Pruitt and Kim, collaboration literature supports the normative community approach, which it proposes helps create and sustain a sense of being (Sanchez, 2012). Although in the traditional sense the community approach focuses on more than just the stakeholders, as mentioned above, it is proposed that in the start-up process, stakeholders treat themselves as the beginning of a larger community unit, believing in the claim that "within-group conflict often fosters long-run group solidarity, that is, unity between the group members who have come into conflict" (Pruitt & Kim, 2004, p. 11).

Further investigation by Gray (2004) found that stakeholders set up collaboration success or failure based on the way they frame issues and interactions with, and views of, each other. Framing revolves around the "lenses stakeholders use to make sense of the conflict" (Gray, 2004, p. 167). The more diverse the framing, the harder it becomes to find agreeable solutions among the stakeholders, causing the collaborative to split and crumble.

Along with mediation (third-party aided negotiation), framing, and reframing are proposed solutions to conflict in collaborations, but often come at a time when it is too late to make the intended impact. In a study of what made an 18-month mediation fail, Gray notes that the job of a mediator is to reframe the issues of the conflict so all parties can find an agreeable solution. However, she also notes that collaborative partnerships will eventually succeed or fail based on stakeholder ability to frame and reframe. Knowing that conflict in the collaborative process is so inherent solidifies a bigger need for putting a mechanism into place that will address issues early enough to save the collaborative.

Communication and Culture

Dialogue is a "direct interaction between people or groups" (Lederach, 2003, p. 21) that promotes constructive change (Leavitt, 2010; Lederach, 2003; Eadie & Nelson, 2001). Simply put, the differences individuals have in relation to culture can be overcome through communication. While it has been noted, "communication and language are intertwined with and are inseparable from culture" (Leavitt, 2010, p. 61), it has also been noted, "emotion drives conflict and communication is the means by which individuals understand emotion" (Eadie & Nelson, 2001, p. 6).

The collaboration literature mentions that collaborations thrive in a setting where it feels natural—a social, educational, and business environment that fosters, values, and prizes cooperative behavior over competition; and that fundamental value differences increase conflict in the collaborative process (Marlowe, Jastroch, Nousala, & Kirova, 2011).

So, how do we cultivate our values? Through behaviors and interactions we have with others that we accept as our own—also known as culture.

Culture is "a set of shared and enduring meanings, values, and beliefs that characterize national, ethnic, or other groups" (Pruitt & Kim, 2004, p. 56). The two main types of culture are individual and collective (Triandis, 1995). The primarily North American Individual culture values independence, freedom, rights, and equity; and members of this culture view themselves as independent of each other, personal goals taking precedence over group interests (Triandis, 1995). The primarily East Asian Collective culture is characterized by interdependence with others, where group goals precede individual goals and group harmony and group equality are most valued (Triandis, 1995).

We know that individualist culture prefers to confront conflict rather than avoid it, and sees most human relationships as horizontal, accepting equality as a given. Because of these views, individualists see conflict as necessary and therefore not inherently negative. Collectivists, on the other hand, are vertically ordered and very aware of rank, desiring group harmony and viewing conflict as dangerous (Pruitt & Kim, 2004). Because of these views, one trait of a collective culture is the tendency to have third parties involved in conflict settlement, and negotiation (more of an indirect approach to conflict resolution). Collectivists also engage in high context communication, and rely less on spoken messages and more on unspoken signs. For example, if a collectivist says "yes," it could mean many things, including "go on, I'm listening"—if an individualist says "yes," it means, "yes, I agree." Where individualists do not fear saying no, collectivists worry that saying no will cause severe disruption in the group harmony (Pruitt & Kim, 2004). The individualist/collectivist culture idea is a broad one, roped in only slightly with the addition of Elazar's Political Cultures (Elazar, 1972; Johnson, 1976; Wirt, 1991). However, inclusion of Elazar aids in narrowing this large-scale view to the field of collaborative public administration.

"Collaboration typically requires great levels of commitment and time as stakeholders within a particular arrangement interact frequently to develop shared norms, rules, and processes used to make collective decisions impacting mutual interests" (McNamara, 2010, p. 129). A case study surrounding organizations involved in the Virginia Coastal Zone Management Program showed: (1) horizontal linkages created sustained feelings of collaboration across government organizations; (2) the presence of a convener was positive—as was developing a new program structure (a horizontal rather than a vertical one); and (3) "Southern states embrace policy innovation [and] collaborative approach is possible in southern states when balanced with the traditionalistic political culture" (McNamara, 2010, p. 144). The program was established via executive order by the Governor of Virginia, identifying two groups—one responsible for assisting with the program, and another responsible for implementing the program policies. Even though the collaboration was mandated, there was no command and control structure put in place by the order, thereby allowing the groups to decide how and to what extent each would work together during implementation of the program. The promising part of this finding to transforming conflict in a collaborative is that while command and control is expected in southern states, people were able to move beyond that using personal relationships to create "vibrant collaborative interactions" (McNamara, 2010, p. 145).

While understanding the difference between the types of large-scale culture is only chipping the iceberg to deeper issues involving how each individual stakeholder in a collaboration views the issues crucial to the set-up and maintenance of the collaborative, it leads us to an important point worth noting in this exploration—the importance of how each stakeholder views cultural difference is to the overall collaborative process. Shown in Figure 7.1 below, Milton Bennett's (1986) Continuum of Cultural Competence, updated by Leavitt (2010) is of great aid here because it shows us where stakeholders lie in their beliefs that culture has a role, if any, in the collaborative process, and gives us something to work with in terms of the strategy used to get all stakeholders on the same page where the cause of conflicts are concerned. For example, someone who is in the avoidance stage will not believe that there is a breakdown in communication because his or her body language is different than another persons'; but someone in the integration stage will be well aware of body language and perhaps feel frustration that his or her efforts to include others' norms in the collaborative set-up process is not proving effective.

Tying this idea that culture inevitably dictates our actions back into the collaborative process using Putnam's (2001) idea of conflict orchestration and keeping in mind that stakeholders in a collaborative have a degree of interdependence, we "[allow] the participants in the conflict to gain new insights about the causes and manifestations of the conflict and [to] produce the types of creative solutions that keep the organization and its members operating in a productive manner" (Eadie & Nelson, 2001, p. 3). Some may call this orchestration an act of incivility, however, what we are calling 'uncivil' is actually our interpretation of the linguistic behavior we

Ethnocentric	1. Denial/avoidance: denies that cultural differences exist, things everyone shares same worldview 2. Defense/protection: acknowledges differences, but considers them threatening to sense of self; leading to thoughts of superiority 3. Minimization: trivializes cultural differences and focuses on assumed similarities
Ethno-relative	4. Acceptance: cultural worldviews are accepted but focus is on behaviors rather than values 5. Adaptation: interaction and communication skills are improved in the interest of cross-cultural relations 6. Integration: a range of cultures are valued and individuals try to integrate aspects of all cultures into practice

Figure 7.1 Milton Bennett's Continuum of Cultural Competence (source: Bennett, 1986).

call anger; so rather than try to eradicate it, why not try to understand it through transformative methods?

Application and Practice

The Framework: Use of Culture and Communication as Tools to Reframe and Transform Conflict in Collaborations

Overall, there is merit in the idea that conflict contributes to the value and creative potential of the collaboration. Because creativity arises out of conflict, instead of bringing in a facilitator to manage disagreements, why not deliver a method that would allow collaborators to work through conflict on their own? The proposed framework below suggests a way to equip the stakeholders in a collaboration with the tools to solve conflict independently.

After having an experience in South America where people there said resolution carried "a danger of co-optation," attempting to get rid of conflict rather than confront it, John Paul Lederach (2003) thought more about going beyond the typical resolution, putting transformation principles into place. "Rather than seeing peace as a static 'end-state,' conflict transformation views peace as a continuously evolving and developing quality of relationship" (Lederach, 2003, p. 20), taking conflict past the point of traditional reconciliation, where the goal is to de-escalate and solve the current problem only, and into the realm of engaging conflict in a quest for constructive, core-centered change.

This engagement means identifying not only the current issue, but also the roles, structures, systems, cultures, and strategies that underlie what cultivated the conflict (Lederach, 2003; Cloke & Goldsmith, 2000). According to Takahashi and Smutny (2002), "Conditions leading to the formation of collaborations may sow the seeds of their demise in the relative short term" (p. 166). Rather than ignoring these conditions, they should be embraced and integrated into the start-up process.

Conflict transformation is based on two principles: the ability to see conflict as a positive, expected occurrence, and a willingness to respond to this occurrence in ways that promote positive change (Lederach, 2003; Galtung, 1996). In order to achieve useful, creative, and positive solutions when conflict arises in a collaborative setting, the following framework is proposed (see Figure 7.2).

The word 'framework' is used here because each step together comprises a basic structure that, when used together, has the ability to underlie various contexts. In this framework, when a conflict arises, all parties in the collaboration should first work to frame and reframe the conflict. According to Mayer (2000), framing is how the conflict is presented in its original state, while reframing is "changing the way a thought is presented so that it maintains its fundamental meaning but is more likely to support resolution efforts" (p. 132).

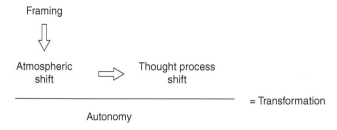

Figure 7.2 Framework for Conflict Transformation Within a Collaborative Network.

Once the conflict is reframed, an atmospheric shift may then take place that allows successful communication of emotions. In professional settings, emotional expression is often stifled (Jameson, Bodtker, Porch, & Jordan, 2009; Cloke & Goldsmith, 2000; Jones, 2000). Because emotion can be a facilitator of successful conflict transformation, it is important for all parties to experience this shift in environmental context (Jameson et al., 2009). The atmospheric shift is also the point where culture comes into play. If each stakeholder to the collaboration is able to place his or her individual cultures aside in favor of a new group culture, then the atmospheric shift will be robust.

As a result of atmospheric shift, the thought processes (Kalishman, Stoddard, O'Sullivan, 2012) of each party can then move from 'parallel play' (resolving the conflict from personal perspective) to 'interdisciplinary work' (how can we solve the problem together). Because the power distribution in a collaborative setting is equal, this step should be easily achieved for all parties.[1]

Underlying the components of framing, atmospheric shift, and thought processes, is autonomy (Jameson et al., 2009). Decision-making ability absent duress leads to more confident participation in resolving conflict. To provide a better perspective on this proposed framework, it helps to view it in the context of combining Gray's (1989) three-phase process with Tuckman's (1965) model of group cohesion.

Breathing Life into the Framework

In 1965, Bruce Tuckman proposed that groups are predictable; and if certain procedures are practiced during formation, then group cohesion can be achieved. The overall idea is that a group not only needs to set norms, but also (as a whole) be self-aware enough to practice those norms. In the end, if all stages are completed as designed, then there is success; and that success continues to thrive within stages two, three, and four as long as the group stays in place. More recently, a fifth step, adjourning, has been added to Tuckman's work. However, this exploration is not concerned with that step because it does not apply to the interests of a sustainable collaborative (Ring & Van de Ven, 1994).

Barbara Gray (1989) provides the collaboration literature with a three-phase process by which a collaborative is formed, noting, "the importance of process can not be overemphasized in planning and conducting successful collaborations" (p. 93). Gray goes on to note that good intention alone is not sufficient to establish a successful collaborative, rather ample attention should be given to the design and management of the process. Figure 7.3 illustrates the ideal process put forth by Tuckman combined with Gray's Collaborative Process.

This combination can be considered a model, because it is simple to follow, prescriptive, and has a narrow, specific scope. The purpose of combining the two separate models is to add the element of the unseen (culture and the resultant emotions) to the collaboration process. While it is possible that there may be some universals of development within these models, it is necessary to take into account things that prevent this from being a universal model. These things are namely the cultural and communicative differences that may be present in each of the stakeholders that, if unaddressed in the early stages, could cause conflict and eventual dissolution of the collaborative.

A very positive aspect of conflict transformation is that a transformational approach can be used to realize that a quick resolution of the

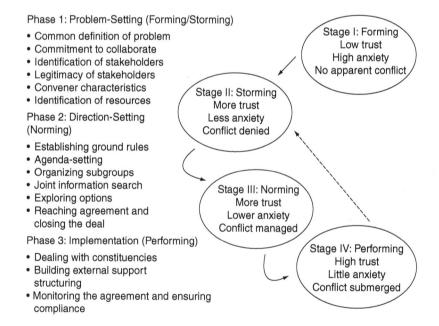

Phase 1: Problem-Setting (Forming/Storming)
- Common definition of problem
- Commitment to collaborate
- Identification of stakeholders
- Legitimacy of stakeholders
- Convener characteristics
- Identification of resources

Phase 2: Direction-Setting (Norming)
- Establishing ground rules
- Agenda-setting
- Organizing subgroups
- Joint information search
- Exploring options
- Reaching agreement and closing the deal

Phase 3: Implementation (Performing)
- Dealing with constituencies
- Building external support structuring
- Monitoring the agreement and ensuring compliance

Stage I: Forming
Low trust
High anxiety
No apparent conflict

Stage II: Storming
More trust
Less anxiety
Conflict denied

Stage III: Norming
More trust
Lower anxiety
Conflict managed

Stage IV: Performing
High trust
Little anxiety
Conflict submerged

Figure 7.3 Combining Tuckman's Stages of Group Formation with Gray's Phases of the Collaborative Process to Address the Non-Material Issues in Collaborations (sources: Gray, 2004; Tuckman, 1965).

problem is all that is needed, but the same cannot be done with conflict resolution because transformation is then not an option. Knowing these things, it is also important to know that not every conflict must result in transformational discussion. However, if and when collaborations want to pursue transformational discussion, the potential to affect positive change as a result can only be harnessed if a framework for that change is already present. Let's review an example to gain more perspective. This example is based in my experience working in the public sector, but the names of individuals and organizations have been suppressed and/or changed to protect the integrity of the program.

Consider the hypothetical organization, Pax. Pax is a conglomeration of seven different stand-alone organizations whose leadership has come together with the intent to solve the recidivism problem in their area. All of the organizations have come together of their own volition, but each of the seven stakeholders has a different interpretation of the problem and its causes, and several value different things as far as solutions and goals. The idea to collaborate came out of a conversation where the leadership of all seven organizations was discussing how they could do more for their client base if they teamed up with one another. They collectively applied for a grant, and were awarded full funding to establish their organization and hire a team of people from each of their agencies who would bring their ideas to life.

In Phase I of the Gray/Tuckman model, the collaborators are able to come to a common definition of the problem: that there is a lack of resources for those either coming back to the city after a stint with the Department of Corrections or for those leaving City jail; they have all committed to the collaboration; the stakeholders have been identified as the organizations and individuals who will be working together to combat the recidivism problem—each being a legitimate addition to the collaboration; resources have been identified; and because the leadership of each party is a convener of this new organization, each has been doing his or her best to be respectful to the other parties in the interest of the greater goal. In this phase, there is relatively low trust and high anxiety between and among the stakeholders, but no apparent conflict, because stakeholders are still settling into the group and have yet to fully assert opinions. Think of this stage in terms of getting a new roommate. In the beginning, you are excited, everything is fun, and everyone is polite to each other. It is not until you get settled a bit more into your living situation that problems begin to present themselves.

In Phase II of the Gray/Tuckman model, trust levels are rising and anxiety levels are falling—but conflict is beginning to present itself. While the group brought together by the conveners to carry out stated goals surrounding recidivism is establishing ground rules and exploring their options, values begin to emerge. Some of the group members believe that Pax should be implementing more programming within the jail system; others believe that the point of exit from the jail is the most important; and the remainder of the members believe that regardless of where programming is targeted, following the research showing best practices is the only way to make Pax a success. To add to this inter-group conflict, there is a consultant who has been hired to lead the group via best practices to an effective outcome—the only problem is that he seems very disconnected from practice.

Typically in this phase, conflict is managed. Management can range from avoidance of the conflict to proactive discourse; but in this situation, all stakeholders in the collaboration resorted to conflict avoidance. The individuals brought together by the conveners to implement the program had a lot of problems working together, and while the conveners did their best to mediate those problems, it began to show that they also had slightly differing ideas of how implementation should be handled.

Thus, Phase III of the Gray/Tuckman model was challenging, to say the least. While the program the conveners of Pax created was being implemented, the trust between stakeholders began to wane as various conflicts continued to fester under the surface of everyday operations. Interactions with program recipients became strained, as did building external support for the program recipients. Both the grant and the outside consultant monitored the program, and while the program was off to a slow start, on paper it showed a lot of promise. Unfortunately in the long run, a program formed to make a real difference in the community turned into a lesson in the importance of addressing and transforming conflict within collaborations.

While Pax and its program are both still in effect today, the original grant funding has run out and the program is standing on unstable footing at best. The framework introduced in this chapter fits squarely within Phase II of the Gray/Tuckman model. Its use in the very critical time where conflict can be transformed into a creative and effective product may have helped propel Pax into the realm of goal achievement it set out to reach, and the 'why' can be found in the following set of propositions:

1   Framing helps change the presentation of thoughts. The more times we frame our interests using different words, the more likely we are to find a common interest with seemingly opposing parties that we can further explore in hopes of reaching creative resolution.
2   Atmospheric shift is necessary in terms of team cohesion. When a group of people from different organizations comes together, they bring with them the values and ideas of their respective organizations. Part of a successful conflict transformation within a collaboration is forming a subculture with stakeholders where emotions can be communicated successfully. Thus, the more a collaboration sees itself as a unit, the easier it is for the stakeholders in the collaboration to communicate effectively.
3   The more stakeholders in a collaboration believe themselves to be a team, the easier it is for them to practice 'interdisciplinary work' (solving a problem together).

4 Underlying each of the above three propositions is one important concept: autonomy. The less duress present in the decision-making process for each stakeholder, the more confident each will be in participating in resolving a conflict.

The aim of this chapter has been to examine how conflict presents itself in a collaboration and to deconstruct the underlying causes so that both future research and practice may grow and benefit from the ideas presented here. The overall belief is that the success of Gray's collaboration definition depends largely on a combination of culture (both general and political) and communication (non-verbal and verbal), which together can determine, through emotions, how we handle conflict. While it is not proposed that other forms of conflict resolution should be set aside in favor of conflict transformation, it should be noted that the collaboration literature shows that the appearance of these other means (mediation and framing) have come into the fold at times when the damage has proven to be irreparable. Overall, there is a noticeable gap in the collaboration literature where conflict is concerned; and adding conflict analysis and transformation to the field of collaboration can only increase its value and contribution to both public administration and society in general.

Conclusion

This chapter has been an overview of how, when treated carefully and appropriately, conflict can be tapped into to create a sustainable and cohesive collaborative environment. Individuals or whole organizations of individuals coming together to solve larger problems can easily find differences among themselves that could stifle the collaborative effort. However, if each person is to take into account their individual culture and their resultant communication style, and direct their passion for the larger goal into creating a cohesive environment where conflict is not the enemy, but rather a means to creative goal achievement, then there is a very real possibility the overarching goal can be achieved successfully.

As stated in the beginning of the chapter, collaboration is a way for people and organizations to come together to solve bigger problems and create real value. And while many collaborative efforts do just that without crumbling from inner conflicts, many do not. Thus, there is a real and immediate need to build a conflict resolution framework into the extant collaboration literature that will help both theorists and practitioners alike navigate conflicts as they arise within collaborative efforts. As this chapter is highly theoretical, with it comes the hope that it will be a catalyst for empirical research. The field of collaboration is a highly practical one, and the better scholars are at connecting theory with practice, the better the chance there is of implementation of successful collaborative efforts.

Note

1 Human social interactions are generally thought of as unbalanced in regard to power distribution (Curle, 1971).

References

Bardach, E. (1998). *Getting agencies to work together: The practice and theory of managerial craftsmanship*. Washington, DC: Brookings Institution Press.
Bennett, M. J. (1986). A developmental approach to training for intercultural sensitivity. *International Journal of Intercultural Relations, 10*(2), 179–196.
Chen, B., & Graddy, E. A. (2005). *Interorganizational collaborations for public service delivery: A framework of preconditions, processes, and perceived outcomes*. Paper presented at the Association for Research on Nonprofit Organizations and Voluntary Action, Washington, DC.
Cloke, K., & Goldsmith, J. (2000). *Resolving personal and organizational conflict*. San Francisco, CA: Jossey-Bass.
Curle, A. (1971). *Making peace*. London, England: Tavistock.
Davoli, G. W., & Fine, L. J. (2004). Stacking the deck for success in interprofessional collaboration. *Health Promotion Practice, 5*(3), 266–270.
Eadie, W. F., & Nelson, P. E. (2001). *The language of conflict and resolution*. Thousand Oaks, CA: Sage Publications, Inc.
Elazar, D. (1972). *American federalism: A view from the states*. New York, NY: Thomas Y. Crowell.
Galtung, J. (1996). *Peace by peaceful means: Peace and conflict development and civilization*. Thousand Oaks, CA: Sage.
Gray, B. (1989). *Collaborating: finding common ground for multiparty problems*. San Francisco, CA: Jossey-Bass.
Gray, B. (2004). Strong opposition: Frame-based resistance to collaboration. *Journal of Community & Applied Social Psychology, 14*(3), 166–176.
Gray, B., & Wood, D. (1991). Collaborative alliances: Moving from practice to theory. *Journal of Applied Behavioral Science, 27*(1), 3–22.
Jameson, J. K., Bodtker, A. M., Porch, D. M., & Jordan, W. J. (2009). Exploring the role of emotion in conflict transformation. *Conflict Resolution Quarterly, 27*(2), 167–192.
Johnson, C. A. (1976). Political culture in American states: Elazar's formulation examined. *American Journal of Political Science, 20*(3), 491–509.
Jones, T. S. (2000). Emotional communication in conflict: Essence and impact. In W. Eadie & P. Nelson (Eds.), *The language of conflict and resolution* (pp. 81–104). Thousand Oaks, CA: Sage.
Kalishman, S., Stoddard, H., & O'Sullivan, P. (2012). Don't manage the conflict: Transform it through collaboration. *Medical Education, 46*(10), 926–934.
Leavitt, R. (2010). Exploring cultural diversity: Eliciting a client's ethnography. In R. Leavitt (Ed.), *Cultural Competence: A lifelong journey to cultural proficiency* (pp. 51–76). Thorofare, NJ: Slack, Inc.
Lederach, J. P. (2003). *The little book of conflict transformation*. Intercourse, PA: Good Books.
Levine, S., & White, P. E. (1961). Exchange as a conceptual framework for the study of interorganizational relationships. *Administrative Science Quarterly, 5*(4), 581–601.

Logsdon, J. M. (1991). Interests and interdependence in the formation of social problem-solving collaborations. *Journal of Applied Behavioral Science, 27*(1), 23–37.

McNamara, M. W. (2010). Collaborative environmental management within a traditionalistic political culture: An unconventional approach to solving "wicked" problems. In G. A. Emison & J. C. Morris (Eds.), *Speaking green with a southern accent: Environmental management and innovation in the "South"* (pp. 129–148). Plymouth, England: Lexington Books.

MacQueen, K. M., McLellan, E., Metzger, D. S., Kegeles, S., Strauss, R. P., Scotti, R., et al. (2001). What is community? An evidence-based definition for participatory public health. *American Journal of Public Health, 91*(12), 1929–1938.

Marlowe, T., Jastroch, N., Nousala, S., & Kirova, V. (2011). The collaborative future. *Systemics, Cybernetics, and Informatics, 9*(5), 1–5.

Mayer, B. S. (2004). *Beyond neutrality: Confronting the crisis in conflict resolution.* San Francisco, CA: Jossey-Bass.

Ostrom, E. (1990). *Governing the commons: The evolution of institutions for collective action.* Cambridge, MA: Cambridge University Press.

O'Toole, L. J., Jr., (1997). Treating networks seriously: Practical and research-based agendas in public administration. *Public Administration Review, 57*(1), 45–52.

Pfeffer, J., & Salancik, G. R. (1978). *The external control of organizations: A resource dependence perspective.* New York, NY: Harper & Row.

Pruitt, D. G., & Kim, S. H. (2004). *Social conflict: Escalation, stalemate, and settlement* (3rd ed.). New York, NY: McGraw-Hill Companies.

Putnam, L. (2000). The language of opposition: Challenges in organizational dispute resolution. In W. F. Eadie & P. E. Nelson (Eds.), *The language of conflict and resolution* (pp. 10–20). Thousand Oaks, CA: SAGE Publications.

Ring, P. S., & Van de Ven, A. H. (1994). Development and processes of cooperative organizational relationships. *Academy of Management Review, 19*(1), 90–118.

Sanchez, M. (2012). A collaborative culture: Collaboration is not something organizations do, but a way of being. *Organization Development Practitioner, 44*(2), 7–12.

Takahashi, L. M., & Smutny, G. (2002). Collaborative windows and organizational governance: Exploring the formation and demise of social service partnerships. *Nonprofit and Voluntary Sector Quarterly, 31*(2), 165–185.

Thomson, A. (2001). *Collaboration: Meaning and measurement.* Bloomington, IN: Indiana University.

Thomson, A., & Perry, J. L. (2006). Collaboration processes: Inside the black box. *Public Administration Review, 66*(s1), 20–32.

Triandis, H. (1995). *Individualism and Collectivism.* Boulder, CO: Westview.

Tuckman, B. W. (1965). Developmental sequence in small groups. *American Psychological Association, 63*(6), 384–399.

White, J. A., & Wehlage, G. (1995). Community collaboration: If it is such a good idea, why is it so hard to do? *Educational Evaluation and Policy Analysis, 17*(1), 23–38.

Wirt, F. M. (1991). Soft concepts and hard data: A research review of Elazar's political culture. *Publius: The Journal of Federalism, 21*(2), 1–13.

Xiao, Y., Kiesler, S., Mackenzie, C. F., Kobayshi, M., Plasters, C., Seagull, F. J., et al. (2007). Negotiation and conflict in large scale collaboration: A preliminary field study. *Cognition, Technology and Work, 9*(3), 171–176.

8 A New Model of Collaborative Federalism From a Governance Perspective

Katrina Miller-Stevens, Tiffany Henley, and Luisa Diaz-Kope

Introduction

In a networked world, collaboration is rapidly becoming a mode of choice to solve 'wicked problems' (Meek & Thurmaier, 2011; Rittel & Webber, 1973). Governments are seeking outside counsel and policy actors to assist in providing public goods and services (Berardo, 2014). As modern society and technology have advanced, complex dilemmas have infiltrated the public sphere. With widespread complex dilemmas, most federal governmental systems lack the capacity to resolve pressing issues independently due to overlapping jurisdictional authority at the state and local level and problems that transcend multiple boundaries (Feiock, Steinacker, & Park, 2009; Mandarano, Featherstone, & Paulsen, 2008).

Collaboration is best suited for a variety of dilemmas involving multiple stakeholders with shared interests, lack of resources, disagreements over the means of alleviating a problem, individuals with variable degrees of expertise, and previous attempts or inadequate governance processes in place to handle a problem (Gray, 1989). American federalism, in its current state, is fragmented and polarized, which renders traditional processes of governance insufficient to handle complex problems (Pickerill & Bowling, 2014). The coupling of wicked problems, a fragmented and polarized federal system, and ideal circumstances supporting the use of collaboration has opened a window to develop a model to explore the utility of collaborative federalism in the United States (U.S.). Models of collaborative federalism have primarily been applied to a Canadian, Australian, and European context. In Canada, collaborative federalism is conceptualized as a governance structure involving two levels of government that are working together to create national policy (Cameron & Simeon, 2002). Collaborative federalism in Australia is perceived as a formal agreement demarcating an issue, purpose, procedures for resolving a problem, and time limitations. The agreements are made by different levels of government including the Commonwealth (the federal government), states, and two self-governing territories (Saunders, 2002). Additionally, the different levels of government collectively share in accountability, administrative responsibility, and implementation protocols (Baracskay, 2012).

In Europe, collaborative federalism is practiced with much trepidation through negotiations with member states comprising the European Union with consideration of multiple layers of government (Stame, 2008). Collaborative federalism is typically seen in programs seeking to enhance economic and social growth by decreasing disparities across Europe through collaborative partnerships financed entirely or co-financed by the European Union (Bachtler & Mendez, 2007; Stame, 2008). While other countries have engaged and established protocols for instituting collaboration at the national level, the literature on collaborative federalism in the United States is limited in scope and has yet to be fully explored. This chapter presents a model of collaborative federalism within a United States context. The model explores collaborative federalism in the U.S. through the lens of three types of governance structures including interagency, cross-sector, and grassroots governance (see Bonner, 2013; Bryson, Crosby, & Stone, 2006; Diaz-Kope & Miller-Stevens, 2014; Dienhart, 2010; Mullin & Daley, 2010; Paul, 1989).

This chapter augments existing collaboration frameworks on several fronts. First, it sheds light on the operation of collaborative federalism in the U.S., a topic that is significantly underdeveloped. Second, this chapter supports the emphasis of Part II of this volume to advance collaboration theory by building upon existing studies to develop a model of collaborative federalism that helps explain the processes of formulation and implementation in a collaborative partnership. Third, creating a new model of collaborative federalism through a governance perspective allows scholars to engage in theoretical testing with an emphasis on the role of governance structures in collaborative arrangements. Fourth, the model is generalizable to a variety of policy domains and settings utilizing collaboration as a mode of governance.

We begin this chapter with a literature review focusing on a primer of federalism. Next, we discuss governance within the context of collaborative arrangements, and introduce the concepts of interagency, cross-sector, and grassroots governance. This is followed by an overview of the characteristics and elements that influence governance and collaborative arrangements. We then introduce our new model of collaborative federalism through a governance perspective and provide exemplars in two policy arenas to further support the utilization of our model. We conclude with final thoughts and suggestions for future research and application of the model.

A Federalism Primer

The meaning of federalism is a discussion that has endured from the founding of the U.S. to present day. The meanings and terms are diverse and include dual federalism, centralized federalism, cooperative federalism, new federalism, horizontal federalism, bimodal federalism, national federalism, mature federalism, and collaborative federalism, among others.

This chapter focuses on a new approach to collaborative federalism through a governance perspective. Before this approach can be discussed, it is important to understand the meanings of two foundational approaches to federalism including dual and cooperative federalism. Dual federalism (or layer-cake) is a common interpretation of federalism and can be traced to the Framers of the American Constitution. Landau (1973) states:

> Dual federalism specifies a fixed relationship between two domains of independent authority in the same territorial unit, each of which possesses an exclusive jurisdiction, neither of which is subordinate to the other and neither of which can be stripped of its authority by the other.
>
> (p. 174)

Dual federalism emphasizes the division of power between the national- and state-level governments where the two rarely interfere or overlap with one another's regulatory powers (Zimmerman, 2001).

In contrast, cooperative federalism (or marble-cake) is conceptualized as national-, state-, and local-level governments working together to regulate and address policy issues. This approach to federalism can be traced to Roosevelt's New Deal when the federal government increased its presence in administering and funding state-level programs, resulting in more coordination between national- and state-level governments (Elazar, 1962; Staten, 1993). "From a federalist perspective, the most important reason for the development of the theory of cooperative federalism was that it enabled federalism to survive in a period of growing federal-state interdependence" (Elazar, 1991, p. 65). Cooperative federalism rests on two primary notions: that American society is dynamic, and there is sharing and bargaining between levels of government (Elazar, 1991). These elements are important in that they lead us away from the bifurcated system of dual federalism to a more coordinated system of cooperative federalism. This in turn leads us to the concept of collaborative federalism.

Collaborative federalism focuses on the networks and common interests between all levels of government and sectors of society to address complex policy issues (Cameron & Simeon, 2002). "Collaborative federalism facilitates understanding of how administrative responsibilities, accountability for a policy sphere and the process of implementation are collectively shared" (Baracskay, 2012, p. 318). The collaborative approach emphasizes shared decision-making between the national, state, and local governments and the public, nonprofit, and private sectors where no level of government or sector is mutually exclusive, but, rather, all levels of government and sectors work together to solve policy problems (Graefe & Bourns, 2008).

To date, collaborative federalism has been used to examine a myriad of contexts across the globe. For example, Lenihan (2002) explores the Canadian government (provinces and territories) and working sectors' efforts to address implementation of public policies regulating immigrants entering the labor market. In another study, Baracskay (2012) compares collaborations between government and nongovernmental organizations in the implementation of health policies related to the H1N1 influenza pandemic in Australia, Malaysia, and the United States. In another recent study, Morris, Gibson, Leavitt, and Jones (2014) apply collaborative federalism to explore the partnerships of nongovernmental organizations and local governments in the implementation of policies protecting the Chesapeake Bay from water pollutants.

With this shared environment, government agencies and private and nonprofit organizations develop collaborative arrangements to address both short- and long-term policy issues, and within these collaborations governance becomes an important concern. With the varying degrees of participation and resources allocated to collaborative arrangements, the management and governance processes of collaborations have remained largely unknown or misunderstood (Agranoff & McGuire, 2001; Imperial, 2005). It is with this context in mind that we turn to a discussion of the relationship between governance and collaboration arrangements.

Governance and Collaboration Arrangements

The complexities of governing in the 21st century require government to use innovative policy strategies to address 'messy' problems (Kettl, 2002). Environmental uncertainties and instability create interdependency between governmental units and non-state actors (Emery & Trist, 1965; Gray, 1985). Fiscal pressures at the federal, state, and local levels continue to constrain governmental resources and impact the efficacy of national policy goals (Gamkhar & Pickerill, 2012). Recently, congressional debates over federal spending resulted in across-the-board cutbacks in federal funding for domestic programs implemented at the state and local levels (see Prah, 2012). The culmination of political, economic, and societal pressures have changed the landscape of democratic governance (Kettl, 2002, 2006).

Federalism scholars argue that the state of American federalism is evolving into a complex web of intergovernmental relations (Bowling & Pickerill, 2013; Gamkhar & Pickerill, 2012; Weissert & Schram, 1998). The infrastructure of today's federal systems are more complex and dynamic, thus neccessitating new governance systems. Nestled within the concept of collaborative federalism is the notion of collaborative governance. Emerson, Nabatchi, and Balogh (2011) broadly define collaborative governance as the:

[p]rocesses and structures of public decision making and management that engage people constructively across the boundaries of public agencies, levels of government, and/or the public, private and civic spheres in order to carry out a public purpose that could not otherwise be accomplished.

(p. 2)

The term 'collaborative governance' captures a wide array of integrative governing systems where state and non-state actors with common interests work across institutional boundaries within a policy area or problem domain.

Collaborative governance is increasingly becoming the new mode of governing in the 21st century (Kettl, 2006; Purdy, 2012), yet it is only one perspective of many definitions of governance (Lynn, 2010). As Lynn (2010) notes, academics have most often defined governance as a broad and overarching term to explain "how actors are organized and managed in order to accomplish purposes on which they agree or which they have in common" (p. 6). This definition has been applied to a variety of contexts from expansive discussions of the role of government versus governance in public administration (Kettl, 2002), to implementation and regulation issues of public policies on the private and nonprofit sectors (Hajer & Wagenaar, 2003; Sørenson, 2006), to more specific discussions of corporate or nonprofit board governance (Brown, 2002). Imperial (2005) argues that governance is important in that it guides institutional decisions regarding the allocation of resources, the role and responsibilities of actors, operational activities, and the objectives of institutions. Governance is the mechanism that binds social institutions. With such varying interpretations of governance, it is important to note that collaborative governance is one take on a well studied, yet somewhat elusive, concept.

The concept of collaborative governance is integral to understanding collaborative federalism. In the realm of collaborative federalism, evidence of 'multipartner governance' is found in numerous policy arenas including environment, health, education, and economic development policy (see Bowling & Pickerill, 2013; Emerson et al., 2011; Gamkhar & Pickerill, 2012; Morris et al., 2014). The collaboration literature reveals that within the rubric of collaborative federalism there are different types of governance structures (see Diaz-Kope & Miller-Stevens, 2014; Margerum, 2011; Morris et al., 2014; Provan & Kenis, 2007; Purdy, 2012). For example, in the realm of watershed collaboration groups, Diaz-Kope and Miller-Stevens (2014) identify three different types of collaborative governance structures including interagency governance, cross-sector governance, and grassroots governance. The following provides a brief discussion of the three types of governance structures operating in collaborative arrangements, and they are also illustrated in Table 8.1.

Diaz-Kope and Miller-Stevens (2014) define interagency goverance as collaboratives that have "…institutional policies and procedures shared among a network of multilevel stakeholders that coordinate their activities and share their resources to address complex policy problems within a problem domain" (p. 2). Collaboratives with interagency governance typically operate in policy networks and coordinate their activities to address complex policy issues at the regional and national levels (Margerum, 2011). Collaboration arrangements operating under interagency governance are typically comprised of high-level governmental actors operating

Table 8.1 Typology of Collaborative Federalism Activities

Governance Structures Operating Simultaneously Within Problem Domain	Makeup of Collaborative Arrangement	Policy Objectives
A. Interagency Governance	Public-sector agencies and institutions (federal, state, and local levels)	Formulate, implement, and regulate federal policies at the national, state, and local levels
B. Cross-Sector Governance	Public-sector agencies and institutions, private sector companies, and nonprofit sector organizations	Implement and regulate federal policies at the state and local levels
C. Grassroots Governance	Citizens' groups, civic leagues, grassroots associations, and local nonprofit agencies	Influence and implement federal policies at the local level

across mulitlevel networks (Diaz-Kope & Miller-Stevens, 2014). In addition, government plays a central role in the policymaking process, and decision-making activities occur at different institutional levels (Heikkila & Gerlak, 2005; Margerum, 2011).

Institutional actors operating under cross-sector governance are comprised of a diverse set of stakeholders including governmental agencies, nonprofit, and nongovernmental organizations (NGO), as well as businesses operating in the private sector (Hardy & Koontz, 2009; Margerum, 2011). Collaborative arrangements using cross-sector governance are critical to the implementation of federal policies at the state and local levels (Bryson et al., 2006; Imperial, 2005; Margerum, 2011). In this setting, government plays a central role in the coordination of resources and the implementation of activities across sector boundaries. In addition, citizens' inputs are integral in the policy decision-making process. Due to the breadth of stakeholders, these collaboratives are able to pool a wide variety of resources including funding as well as knowledge, technological and social capital in order to achieve the collaborative's organizational goals. Further, the diverse composition of the stakeholders in these arrangements allow these governance bodies to circumvent political red tape (Margerum, 2011).

Collaborative arrangements operating under grassroots governance structures are comprised of organized groups of citizens working collectively to address policy issues at the local level (Kenney, 1997). The role of government is that of supporting actor rather than partner. Governance activities center on improving the quality of life in local communities through public outreach programs and social marketing campaigns (McNamara, Leavitt, & Morris, 2010; Morris et al., 2014). In contrast to interagency and cross-sector governance, decision-making is conducted by citizen boards, steering committees, and civic leagues. Moreover, resources are limited and the sustainability of these collaboratives are highly reliant on community support and leveraging social capital in order to achieve the collaborative's organizational goals (Morris, Gibson, Leavitt, & Jones, 2013).

Building on Diaz-Kope and Miller-Stevens's (2014) watershed governance typology identifying three types of governance structures within watershed collaborations, we propose a new model of collaborative federalism through a governance perspective. The model depicts how interagency governance, cross-sector governance, and grassroots governance help explain the broader spectrum of collaborative federalism. In our view, collaborative federalism can be best understood as a nested system of three governance approaches that operate simultaneously within a problem domain.

In line with the basic systems approach discussed in Chapter 2, scholars of collaboration have created frameworks to identify nested dimensions of collaboration within larger systems contexts. For example, Emerson et al. (2011) develop a framework of collaborative governance that explores the linkages between operational contexts of collaborations made up of private, public, and nonprofit sector organizations and the broader context of "a host of political, legal, socioeconomic, environmental, and other influences" (p. 20). Their framework identifies three nested dimensions of collaborative governance as the collaborative governance regime (actions and impacts of cross-boundary collaboration), surrounded by systems contexts (external influences) that create opportunities and constraints on the collaboration, and the drivers that impact the nature of the collaborations (leadership, consequential incentives, interdependence, and uncertainty) (pp. 5–6).

The model proposed in this chapter adopts the systems approach to explain nested dimensions of collaborative federalism through a governance perspective. Before delving into the proposed model, elements of collaborative arrangements with interagency governance, cross-sector governance, and grassroots governance must first be addressed. While it is important to address each of these elements for a broader understanding of collaborative arrangements and governance, it must be noted that due to the complexity of collaboration, not all elements are depicted in the proposed model. Regardless, these underlying elements are consistently impacting the nature of collaborative federalism and the collaboratives' governance structures.

Elements of Collaborative Governance

Stakeholders working in a collaboration are first tasked with identifying the problem domain and the objective of the collaboration. The problem domain refers to the way the problem is conceptualized (Gray, 1989; Trist, 1983), and this conceptualization can be influenced by multiple elements.

While many of these elements have been explored by scholars of collaboration (see Ansell & Gash, 2007; Moore & Koontz, 2003; Moss & Newig, 2010), Diaz-Kope and Miller-Stevens (2014) narrow the list to five prominent elements in the literature, including resource capacity, decision-making, institutional activities, the role of government, and the complexity of the nature and scope of the issue. This list is drawn from cases of collaboration discussed in the watershed literature that provided elements that are broad and overarching, and are thus presumed to be present in other collaborative environments. It is important to identify the relationship between these underlying elements within the context of collaborative federalism in order to fully understand the proposed model in Figure 8.1. Before delving into these five elements, the following discussion provides a description of the model.

Figure 8.1 outlines the Collaborative Federalism Governance Model. The model conceptualizes the formulation and implementation of federal policies through three governance structures that operate within a problem domain. In the abstract, the model depicts collaborative federalism as a three-tiered nested system comprised of three distinctive

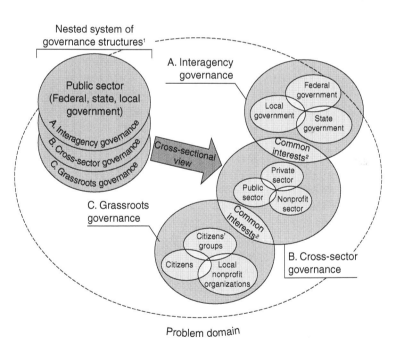

Figure 8.1 Collaborative Federalism Governance Model.

Notes
1 Actors within each governance structure collaborate to define, formulate, and implement policy objectives at the national, state, and local levels.
2 Each governance structure is connected by mutual common interests that serve as an impetus to jointly address a problem.

governance structures: (A) interagency collaborative governance; (B) cross-sector collaborative governance; and (C) grassroots collaborative governance. The governance structures are linked by mutual common interests resulting from a need to address a complex issue emanating from the problem domain. The complexities of the issue render traditional centralized modes of governance ineffective at addressing the problem. Consequently, federal initiatives are designed to encourage collaborative arrangements between state and non-state actors.

Viewing the model from the top down, interagency collaborative governance (A) is comprised of federal, state, and local governmental agencies working together to formulate state and local implementation strategies in order to achieve federal policy objectives. The linkage between interagency and cross-sector collaborative governance (B) occurs at the policy implementation process. Governmental units operating in interagency collaborative governance structures build institutional capacity through cross-sector collaborative governance structures (B). The linkage between cross-sector collaborative governance (B) and grassroots collaborative governance (C) occurs at the local community level.

To illustrate the linkages between the three governance structures, the model displays a cross-sectional view of interagency collaborative governance (A), cross-sector collaborative governance (B) and grassroots collaborative governance (C). As shown in the model, cross-sector collaborative governance (B) is nestled between interagency collaborative governance (A) and (C) grassroots collaborative governance. The model shows cross-sector collaborative governance (B) as comprised of organizations operating in the private, public, and nonprofits sectors. Actors operating in this governance structure focus on implementing federal policies at the state and local levels.

Working at the community level is grassroots collaborative governance (C) which is comprised of various community organizations including citizens' groups, civic leagues, and local nonprofit 501(c) organizations working collectively to address problems at the local level. The cross-sectional illustration shows the relational overlap between interagency collaborative governance (A), cross-sector collaborative governance (B), and grassroots collaborative governance (C), noted in the figure as the common interests shared between the governance structures to address the problem. The three governance structures operate simultaneously within the problem domain as shown by the dotted line in the model.

Five Prominent Elements of Collaborative Governance

As noted previously, the model applies five prominent elements of collaborative governance. In the collaboration literature, resource capacity refers to the capabilities of existing institutions and individuals to address problems (Wood & Gray, 1991). Examples of individual resource capacity include knowledge and expertise, whereas examples of institutional capacity include funding and technology. The resources each individual and institution has to offer are assessed within the collaboration, and the allocation of resources impacts the governance structure of the collaboration (Diaz-Kope & Miller-Stevens, 2014).

A second element of collaborative governance is decision-making. The process of decision-making within a collaboration depends in large part on the stakeholder composition of the collaboration (Margerum, 2011). Collaborations composed of stakeholders from the government will be more likely to follow a formal decision-making process (Margerum, 2011). Collaborations with grassroots and citizen stakeholders will be more likely to follow decision-making processes that are informal with less structure (Morris et al., 2013).

The third element impacting collaborative governance is institutional activities. Institutional activities relate directly to the actions of stakeholders within a collaboration. As noted by Diaz-Kope and Miller-Stevens (2014), the actions of government agencies will be formally coordinated following the standards and expected processes of government rules and norms. Conversely, actions of grassroots stakeholders will include less formalized activities such as raising awareness through social media or organizing community events.

The fourth and fifth elements are the role of government and complexity of the nature and scope of the issue. The role of government in a collaboration varies depending on whether a problem impacts a large or small regional area (Kenney, 1997; Margerum, 2011). Government agencies are more likely to be involved in a collaboration if the problem is large and complex, or if the problem directly impacts government property. Government agencies are less likely to be involved in localized problems that impact small groups of citizens. Similarly, problems that are less complex and narrow in scope will be more likely to initiate collaborations at the local or grassroots levels.

It must also be noted that political, economic, and social forces from different levels of government (federal, state, local) and all sectors of society (private, public, nonprofit, and citizens) consistently impact the problem domain, and each of these factors influences the interpretation of the problem the collaboration seeks to address. Given this complexity, it is necessary to develop a model to interpret these interactions and relationships between collaborative federalism and collaborative governance.

The Collaborative Federalism Governance Model

Figure 8.1 provides a graphical representation of our Collaborative Federalism Governance Model. The model builds upon Diaz-Kope and Miller-Stevens's (2014) typology on watershed governance. Collaborative federalism is conceptualized as a nested system of governance structures (interagency, cross-sector, and grassroots) operating in a policy domain. Each structure plays a role in policy formulation and implementation. At the formulation stage, planning occurs through consensus-building and participatory discourse (Margerum, 2011). The three governance structures are not autonomous, but rather they operate simultaneously according to the problem domain. They are connected by the presence of a common interest and implementation practices are contingent upon the nature, scope, scale, and availability of resources affecting the problem through participatory decision-making (Heikkila & Gerlak, 2005).

The role of the federal government varies based on external pressures and the degree of support from the government, and is decided during the formulation stage of the policy process. Stakeholders within the collaborative are involved at every decision point and responsibility is shared amongst the whole collaborative arrangement and within each governance system (Ansell & Gash, 2007). Additionally, a convener or convening organization directs the collaborative arrangement by mobilizing stakeholders to participate while facilitating efforts to implement agreed upon goals of the collaborative (Gray, 1989).

Our conception of collaborative federalism is a synthesis of existing literature based on the collaborative governance structures depicted in both Table 8.1 and Figure 8.1. Our model recognizes the interaction between interagency, cross-sector, and grassroots governance as they work together to solve social and environmental problems. Within each governance structure, our model considers the role of the federal, state, and local governments in addition to nongovernmental agencies and citizens in the collaborative arrangements. The model is not impacted by conflicting views of policy formulation and implementation because the collaborative operates under the following assumptions: a common interest is present, information is freely available and shared, power is decentralized, trust is established, and stakeholders are committed (Bryson et al., 2006; Shaw, 2003). The assumptions of this model are consistent with the literature on collaboration and present us with the opportunity to synthesize the literature on governance structures and collaborative federalism. The next section provides a detailed description of the major facets of the model.

Interagency Governance

As shown in Figure 8.1 under interagency governance (A), the federal government and state and local agencies work together to address a specific problem at the national level. Governmental interagency collaboration is increasingly occurring due to budget constraints, an increase in societal needs, sequestration, and limited resources as federal, state, and local governments work collectively to enforce regulations and implement policies (Bonner, 2013; Mullin & Daley, 2010). While governmental agencies are striving to maintain their core missions, the forces driving interagency collaboration include reducing costs through pooling agencies' resources, building institutional capacities across jurisdictional boundaries, and federal mandates (Bonner, 2013). Shared responsibility for complex problems may be addressed across agencies within one governmental institution in a horizontal manner or across different levels of governments with overlapping missions and functions between governmental agencies (Mullin & Daley, 2010). The conditions in which an interagency unit takes a lead role in a collaborative federal arrangement typically occur when the federal government is receiving pressure from external factors such as the public, media, or policymakers, and action is required through legislation (Kenney, 1997).

Under such conditions, an interagency unit is the convener. Federal agencies oversee the coordination of state and local government entities with the granting of external authority (Diaz-Kope & Miller-Stevens, 2014; Page, 2004). A variety of agencies, community leaders, and local grassroots organizations may be called upon within a problem domain to assist government agencies with implementation of policy initiatives (Page, 2004). Decision-making is centered upon rules, regulations, and procedures for broad implementation strategies within a hierarchical structure with an overlay of lateral associations from nongovernmental agencies and citizens at the formulation stage (Agranoff, 2006; Hardy, 2010). During formulation, this collaborative arrangement can be tightly controlled; however, boundaries are established to allow participants of the arrangement to operate with the ability to execute tasks that are required to serve the purpose of the collaborative while common interests are met (Keast, Mandell, Brown, & Woolcock, 2004). The efforts to maintain this collaborative at the implementation level are typically permanent, coordination is stable, and the exchange of resources is widespread (Mandell, 1999; McGuire, 2006).

Cross-Sector Governance

Cross-sector governance plays a leading role in collaborative network systems when various institutional structures or sectors such as governments, businesses, and nonprofits do not have the capacity, legitimacy, or support to achieve certain functions alone (Bryson et al., 2006; Dienhart, 2010). As depicted in Figure 8.1 (B), this governance structure may have a multitude of actors collaboratively engaged in addressing transboundary problems. Collaboration can occur in an episodic and informal manner or through formalized agreements between multiple sectors (Simo & Bies, 2007). Under a collaborative federalist system, a cross-sector collaborative may take the role of a convening organization.

An acting role as a convener and the structure of the cross-sector governance system allows for a higher degree of influence over policy implementation amongst the interagency and grassroots governance systems (Leach & Pelkey, 2001). The federal government is actively engaged and activities are coordinated through comprehensive strategic approaches to manage the purposes of the collaborative between the participants of the collaborative to guide implementation (Bryson et al., 2006; Margerum, 2011; Morris et al., 2013).

Implementation of collaborative objectives occurs in an expeditious manner when the cross-sector governance system is playing a leading role because the structure is flexible and more responsive to public problems than the interagency governance system (Shaw, 2003). Stakeholders have access to a variety of resources and the ability to mobilize volunteers as a result of their connections with the community and political leaders, thus generating the participation of a wide array of stakeholders to resolve the problem (Hardy, 2010; Kiefer & Montjoy, 2006; O'Toole & Meier, 2004). The development of interpersonal relationships with grassroots associations and interagency organizations further supports the mission of the collaborative (Hardy, 2010; Leavitt & Morris, 2007). This collaborative arrangement is marked by bargaining between actors, enduring partnerships, emphasis on interpersonal relationships, and accountability for outcomes that are typically shared when the cross-sector governance system is participating in a principal role (Gazley & Brudney, 2007; Leavitt & Morris, 2007).

Grassroots

Grassroots organizations are both formally and informally organized at the local level and members are typically dedicated to a single cause as shown in Figure 8.1 under grassroots governance (C). Participants of the grassroots governance system include citizens' groups, civic leagues, and various 501(c) nonprofit organizations. These organizations are responsive to the needs of the community and are able to adapt easily to a changing environment. Additionally, grassroots organizations are able to achieve accountability for results due to their proximity, knowledge, and expertise to local problems (Paul, 1989). Grassroots associations or local nonprofit organizations may play a convening role, when a local approach is needed to tackle a policy issue at the formulation stage in the collaborative federalism model.

The role of government is supportive through funding and the provision of specialized resources and citizens are actively engaged through civic activism to influence governmental responses to local problems (Cooper, Bryer, & Meek, 2006; Margerum, 2011). Grassroots associations or local nonprofit organizations may be regarded as a referent body with a specialized knowledge base acting as a center for information exchanges. As a convener, this group operates within the grassroots governance system and supports member relations within the entire collaborative by making connections based on common interests in accordance with a local problem domain (McNamara et al., 2010; Parisi, Taquino, Grice, & Gill, 2004). Decision-making is consensus oriented and deliberative and includes all stakeholders, but the development of strategies for resolution of a problem can be prolonged due to a low degree of influence at the formulation stage of federal policy (Cooper et al., 2006; Diaz-Kope & Miller-Stevens, 2014). However, the grassroots governance system wields great influence at the implementation level in that it bypasses the hierarchical relationships that may be found in the interagency and cross-sector collaborative governance systems by mobilizing citizens to support the execution of policies in a problem domain and garnering compliance (Morris et al., 2014). When a convener within the grassroots governance structure plays a leading role, the collaborative arrangement can be temporary, relationships between members of the entire collaborative can be weak, and implementation may focus on building social networks and sharing information (Mandell, 1999; Morton, 2008; Parisi et al., 2004).

As demonstrated in both Table 8.1 and Figure 8.1, the three governance structures simultaneously work within a federalist system to address widespread social and environmental issues. The nested governance systems are connected through common interests, but essential elements such as resource capacity, decision-making processes, institutional activities, and the nature and scope of the problem encourage and support the use of collaboration to address the issue involving action at multiple levels of government and the use of nongovernmental organizations and citizens. The following section illustrates the utility of The Collaborative Federalism Governance Model and its ability to bridge the gap between theory and practice by explaining the interactions between nested systems of governance while highlighting processes of formulation and implementation in a federal collaborative. This model can be applied to a variety of policy domains as illustrated in the following section.

Applications of the Collaborative Federalism Governance Model

We argue that our Collaborative Federalism Governance Model is generalizable to a multitude of policy settings and can assist scholars in offering an explanatory analysis of collaborative federalism. The uniqueness of our model stems from the identification of three nested governance structures collaboratively addressing a national problem. The subsequent section will demonstrate the utility of our model by examining two national initiatives utilizing collaborative measures to address a problem from the arena of health policy and domain of watershed policy.

The Community-Based Child Abuse Prevention Program

Collaborative federalism is a common mode of governance in the health policy arena. There are a variety of federal government initiatives that have called upon states and local communities to participate in national programs. This exemplar will examine the Community-Based Child Abuse Prevention Program (CBCAP) and apply our Collaborative Federalism Governance Model while concentrating on the interactions between interagency, cross-sector, and grassroots governance systems. The CBCAP under the authority of the U.S. Department of Health and Human Services and supervised by The Children's Bureau was created in response to the Child Abuse Prevention and Treatment Act (CAPT) of 1974 (Lim Brodowski et al., 2014; Stein, 1984). The objective of CAPT is "to provide financial assistance for demonstration programs for the prevention, identification and treatment of child abuse and neglect to establish a National Center on Child Abuse" (Light, 1974, p. 46). The Act requires States to participate in mandated reporting, monitoring, and investigations of child abuse and neglect (Stein, 1984).

Following the enactment of CAPT, implementation of the Act throughout the 1980s focused on reporting measures, education, and creating public awareness (Child Welfare Information Gateway, 2011). However, despite an overall decline in physical and sexual abuse, three million children were estimated to have been mistreated in any given year (Finkelhor, Jones, & Shattuck, 2011; U.S. Department of Health and Human Services, Administration on Children, Youth and Families, & Children's Bureau, 2010). Interventions created to address the problem of child abuse and neglect focused on individual-level programs; however, prevention strategies placing emphasis on changing behavior at the community level arose due to an inability to address the needs of vulnerable populations with an increased risk of child maltreatment (Daro, 2000; Daro & Dodge, 2009).

In recognition of identifying strategies targeted at the community level, the federal government called for new ways of preventing child abuse through collaboration (Lim Brodowski et al., 2014). Our Collaborative Federalism Governance Model explains the structure of the CBCAP and the essential elements that have contributed to the interaction of the nested governance systems illustrated in the model operating under the entire collaborative. Part (A) of our model is comprised of the federal government, state government, and local governments working collaboratively through the interagency governance system.

In the case of CBCAP, the Children's Bureau is the federal agency that is tasked with overseeing the entire program. The Children's Bureau is responsible for improving the welfare of children and families through prevention, assessment, treatment, and investigational pursuits. In order to achieve their organizational objectives, the Children's Bureau establishes partnerships with state, local, and tribal agencies. Additionally, the Children's Bureau is responsible for administering formula-based grants to all states in the implementation of child abuse and neglect programs (Children's Bureau, 2012; National Alliance of Children's Trust & Prevention Funds, 2009). The governor of each state must assign a lead agency to formulate and implement prevention activities while disseminating funds to partners such as community agencies, private businesses, or nonprofit organizations working together to prevent child abuse (Children's Bureau, 2012; Missouri Children's Trust Fund, 2014). At the interagency level, the Children's Bureau, state, local, and tribal agencies work together to formulate, implement, and finance prevention strategies that are tailored to the needs of states and targeted local communities where there are high incidences of child abuse and neglect.

The common interest linking the interagency governance system to the cross governance system is the recognition that support for the prevention of child abuse requires many actors and expertise from a diverse set of organizations with valuable resources. Part (B) of our model includes the cross-sector governance system consisting of the public sector, the federal government, nongovernmental organizations, and private businesses. The organizations that are represented in the cross-sector governance system collaborate based on federal mandates, memorandums of understanding, contracts, or informal agreements (National Alliance of Children's Trust & Prevention Funds, 2009). With the enactment of CAPT, the federal government mandates the establishment of a national resource center and the nonprofit organization Family Resource Information, Education and Network Development Services (FRIENDS) has been fulfilling that role for the past 15 years, renewing the agreement on a yearly basis (Family Resource Information, Education and Network Development Services, 2014; Light, 1974; Lim Brodowski et al., 2014). Leading state agencies will contact FRIENDS to provide material on evidence-based practices, training, and support for programs for implementation purposes aimed at preventing child abuse and neglect, utilizing identified partners in the collaborative (Family Resource Information, Education and Network Development Services, 2014).

Every state has a network of collaborating partners operating in the cross-sector governance system. For instance, in Missouri partners who have received funding from the leading state agency the Children's Trust Fund included community agencies such as the Missouri Valley Community Agency, the Columbia-Boone County Community Partnership, and the Washington County Community Partnership. Faith-based organizations that have received funding involved organizations such as Lutheran Family & Children's Services of Missouri, St. Joseph Youth Alliance, and Catholic Charities of Kansas City. Other organizations that have received funding have included the University of Missouri and a plethora of nonprofit agencies that have provided services to at-risk children and parents (Missouri Children's Trust Fund, 2014).

In addition to a variety of agencies receiving funding from the Children's Trust Fund, private and public agencies have also been involved in the cross-sector collaborative (Child Abuse Prevention Association, 2011; Missouri Department of Social Services, 2009). The Annie E. Casey Foundation is a private philanthropic organization that provides grants to states, federal agencies, and neighborhoods to support cost-effective and innovative projects affecting disadvantaged children (Annie E. Casey Foundation, 2014). The Missouri Coordinating Board for Early Childhood is a public/private entity that coordinates early intervention and child development programs for children up until the age of five (Missouri Department of Social Services, 2009). The Missouri Department of Social

Services is a public organization that handles complaints, investigations, and reports of child abuse and neglect (Missouri Children's Trust Fund, 2014; Missouri Department of Social Services, 2009). These entities fall under the cross-sector set of actors by contributing services, grants, and information to alleviate child maltreatment.

The organizations operating in a cross-sector collaborative governance system pool their resources and work collaboratively together to prevent child abuse and neglect, utilizing evidence-based practices with the assistance of FRIENDS that target an entire population and at-risk groups (Missouri Children's Trust Fund, 2014). At the cross-sector level, each state has a network of actors that are working with the specially appointed lead agency. Through this arrangement, funding for new and existing initiatives are submitted to the Children's Bureau by the leading state agency to determine the amount of federal funding per state for the CBCAP. This process involves input from actors from the interagency and grassroots governance systems.

Implementation of evidence-based practices affecting an entire population requires the efforts of many stakeholders. Under CBCAP, the common interests (noted in the cross-sectional display in Figure 8.1) linking the cross-sector governance system and the grassroots governance structure is the need to create awareness and mobilize groups to participate in implementing evidence-based programs at the community level. These programs are targeted towards preventing child abuse and neglect. Part (C) of our Collaborative Federalism Governance Model consists of nonprofit organizations, nongovernmental organizations, community leaders, and citizens working together in the grassroots governance system. Leading state agencies are able to increase their capacity by including actors in the grassroots governance system, thus enhancing the formulation and implementation of evidence-based initiatives (National Alliance of Children's Trust & Prevention Funds, 2009).

The maximization of increased capacity by utilizing agents at the grassroots governance level has increased the impact of the collaborative. For example, the leading state agency of New York hosted a series of community cafes with community leaders, members, and organizations to promote constructive discourse on strategies to protect children from abuse and neglect (New York State Office of Children and Family Services, 2012). In Wisconsin, the leading state agency has partnered with the Zilber Family Foundation, which has committed 50 million dollars to improving Milwaukee neighborhoods through organizational development, planning and assessment, technical assistance, operating expenditures, and implementation projects (Wisconsin Children's Trust Fund, 2014; Zilber Family Foundation, 2014). At the grassroots governance level, the actors in this collaborative structure work directly with organizations in the cross-sector governance system in providing services and raising awareness of child abuse and neglect. Additionally, grassroots actors provide valuable information to participants of both the interagency and cross-sector governance structures due to their proximity to the problem and insight into systematic issues that may arise while combating child maltreatment.

The application of our Collaborative Federalism Governance Model to the Community Based Prevention Program captures the process through which individual collaborative governance structures come together under a national initiative to prevent child abuse and neglect. Each governance structure serves an important role in the formulation and implementation of prevention initiatives and the strengths of each system are maximized at certain decision points within the collaborative. This exemplar demonstrates that the leading state agency appointed by the governor of each state at the cross-sector collaborative governance level serves as a convener facilitating the entire collaborative. The interagency collaborative governance system appropriates funds across states and plays a supportive role in the collaboration. The grassroots collaborative governance structure performs an important role by promoting action at the community level. While the roles of each governance system are defined and present within the collaborative, decisions, interests, and information are freely shared.

The Healthy Watersheds Initiative Program

In the realm of U.S. watershed policy, collaborative federalism plays a central role in policy formulation and implementation. Watershed policy encompasses a wide array of policy issues including protection of water quality, recreational usage, agriculture, public land management, nonpoint source pollution control, wetland protection, and habitat conservation (Goldfarb, 1994; Woolley & McGinnis, 1999). The transboundary nature of watersheds poses unique challenges for the federal government as to how to address environmental issues that span jurisdictional boundaries (Goldfarb, 1994; Kenney, 1997).

The nature and scope of watershed policy has resulted in the formulation of numerous watershed initiatives sponsored by the Environmental Protection Agency (EPA) including the Clean Lakes Program, the National Estuary Program, the Chesapeake Bay Initiative, the Targeted Watershed Grants Program, and the Healthy Watersheds Initiative (Goldfarb, 1994; U.S. Environmental Protection Agency, 2011; 2012b; 2014). These policy initiatives are designed to achieve a broad spectrum of federal environmental watershed policy objectives through establishing collaboration arrangements with national, state, and local actors (Kenney, 1997; Margerum, 2008; Sabatier, Weible, & Ficker, 2005). The following applies the Collaborative Federalism Governance Model to the EPA's Healthy Watersheds Initiative and discusses the three nested collaborative governance approaches operating in this problem domain.

The EPA's Healthy Watersheds Initiative uses the multilayered collaborative governance approach illustrated in Figure 8.1 to address different types of watershed issues impacting the quality of U.S. waterways. The EPA's Healthy Watershed Initiative is designed to tackle the problem of the rapid rate of increase in the degradation of the environmental quality of America's watersheds and the impairment of the aquatic ecosystem (U.S. Environmental Protection Agency, 2012a). The causes for watershed degradation emanate from multiple fronts derived from point (i.e., industrial activities) and nonpoint source pollution (i.e., runoff from residential and agricultural use of pesticides) (U.S. Environmental Protection Agency, 2012c). In response to the pervasiveness and complexity of watershed pollution the EPA has recently created new policy strategies aimed at building strategic collaborative alliances with a wide array of stakeholders.

The Healthy Watersheds Initiative (HWI) was established in 2011, and falls under the purview of the EPA and their federal partners (U.S. Environmental Protection Agency, 2014). The HWI program seeks to promote and support the formation of collaborative arrangements between federal, state, and local agencies and nongovernmental actors in its implementation of identifying and assessing healthy watersheds and developing state-wide strategic plans to protect and restore the quality of the nation's watersheds (see U.S. Environmental Protection Agency, 2012a). The implementation of this program involves the participation of interagency, cross-sector, and grassroots watershed collaborative governance structures.

The policy goal of the initiative is to "…protect and maintain a network of healthy watersheds and supportive green infrastructure habitat networks across the United States" (U.S. Environmental Protection Agency, 2011, p. 8). The policy program's objective is to use a systematic integrative approach, through collaborative partnerships, to implement state-wide strategic watershed plans and "…local protection programs based on priorities from state and local assessements…" (U.S. Environmental Protection Agency, 2011, p. 8). This initiative supports a holistic approach to evaluate the different characteristics, functions, and processes of watersheds in order to formulate and implement watershed policies that target specific regional and local watershed issues (U.S. Environmental Protection Agency, 2013).

Healthy Watersheds Initiative interagency collaborative governance structures consist of EPA administrators, state governors, and input from local governments, as depicted in interagency collaborative governance (A) of the model. The EPA's central headquarters takes the lead role on policy issues and regulatory guidance in each of the states' HWI interagency collaborative arrangements (U.S. Environmental Protection Agency, 2011). Participation in HWI is voluntary, and interagency collaborative partnerships are established through Memorandums of Understanding (MOUs).

At the interagency collaborative governance level, EPA regional administrators and their partners work with state governments along with the input of local governments to develop comprehensive strategic watershed plans that are tailored to the environmental and economic interests of a particular region (U.S. Environmental Protection Agency, 2011). States participating in HWI receive funding and technical assistance for their particular watershed projects from the EPA. Since 2011, five states have established HWI interagency collaborative agreements with the EPA including Alabama, California, Wisconsin, Tennessee, and Virginia (U.S. Environmental Protection Agency, 2013).

The common interests (noted in Figure 8.1) that link HWI interagency and cross-sector collaborative governance structures is the recognition that preserving and restoring America's watersheds is critical to protecting the environment for future generations, and is neccessary for the health of both national and state economic growth (U.S. Environmental Protection Agency, 2012a, 2012d). As shown in the cross-sectional view of the model, the role of cross-sector collaborative governance (B) in the initiative is the implementation of each states' HWI watershed plans through cross-sector partnerships that are comprised of federal, state, and local agencies, non-governmental organizations (NGOs), private business firms, nonprofit organizations, and local watershed groups (U.S. Environmental Protection Agency, 2009). For example, Tennessee's Healthy Watershed Initative (THWI) is a cross-sector collaborative goverance structure whose partners include the Association of Clean Water Administrators (ACWA), Tennessee Water Authority (TVA), The Tennessee Department of Environment and Conservation (TDEC), the Tennessee Chapter of the Nature Conservancy (TNC), and the West Tennessee River Basin Authority (WTRBA). The THWI collaborative operates under formalized MOUs (Association of Clean Water Administrators, 2013).

State HWI cross-sector governance collaboratives and grassroots governance collaborative structures share mutual interests in that local communities' quality of life are directly impacted by the quality of sub-basin waterways. Furthermore, the efficacy of the EPA's HWI state-wide watershed goals are linked to changing the behavior of citizens and their compliance to local watershed plans. As illustrated by the model, grassroots collaborative governance (C) operates at the local community level where regional EPA representatives take on a supportive role through providing community-based groups technical support and updated assessment tools to identify and assess healthy watersheds at the community level. HWI technical support provides a range of activities at the community level including assistance with local watershed protection plans, staff training and public educational programs that promote healthy watershed protection, and developing outreach programs (U.S. Enivronmental Protection Agency, 2011).

Applying the Collaborative Federalism Governance Model to the EPA's Healthy Watershed Initiative demonstrates the linkages between the three collaborative governance structures and the formulation and implementation of federal watershed programs. The analysis reveals the critical role that interagency, cross-sector, and grassroots collaborative goverance structures play in achieving the EPA's goal of identifying and assessing healthy watersheds. This exemplar captures the different levels of coordination and integration that occur within a collaborative federalism context and the three levels of collaborative governance structures that are operating in the problem domain of watershed policy.

Conclusion

This chapter offers the Collaborative Federalism Governance Model as one conceptualization of the multidimensional nature of collaborative federalism. We argue that collaborative federalism is best understood as a nested governance system comprised of three types of governance structures operating within a problem domain, identified by Diaz-Kope and Miller-Stevens (2014) as interagency governance, cross-sector governance, and grassroots governance. These structures simultaneously operate and intersect at different points of policy formulation and implementation processes (Margerum, 2011; Sabatier et al., 2005).

This model offers researchers, policy analysts, public managers, and policymakers a nuanced approach to explain and study collaborative federalism through a governance perspective. This perspective provides a new lens to help understand complex social and policy issues and the collaborations that form to solve these issues. The model helps unpack the complicated inner workings of the public, private, and nonprofit sectors and the implications of federalism across the sectors.

As noted by Lynn (2010), governance has been a difficult and somewhat unwieldy concept to solidify in the academic literature. We hope to advance this discussion by providing a model to illustrate the relationship between collaborative governance and a federalist system of government. In addition, the model offers a perspective to view the role of grassroots organizations in a federalist system. Further research could explore the role of grassroots organizations by conducting empirical studies on nonprofit organizations and the nonprofit sector's role in the policy formulation and implementation processes. While many studies examine the role of nonprofit organizations in the policy process, few approach this topic from the perspective of collaborative federalism or collaborative governance. With the nonprofit sector's active involvement in recent major disasters (e.g., the BP oil spill in Louisiana, wildfire disasters in California and Colorado), there are numerous opportunities to study the nonprofit sector's role in collaborative activities that are driven by government.

Additional research could also look more closely at the governance activities organizations undertake in collaborations that are driven primarily by government entities. The specific roles and actions of organizations in these types of collaborations have yet to be explored in detail. Topics for that discussion might include the decision-making processes of organizations involved in collaborative federalism, whether the collaboration is governed more like a network or hierarchy, how the collaborations function when they are driven by the federal government versus local government, and what role the convener plays in collaborative activities within a federalist system. Further research could also apply the model to explore the policy areas of national and state security issues, management of widespread health epidemics, or environmental disaster management, among many others.

This chapter aims to provide a clearer understanding of the intersection of collaboration, federalism, and governance. However, we recognize the complexities of each of these concepts when they are individually discussed. This complexity provides limitations, but also gives researchers the flexibility of interpretation. It is our hope that the Collaborative Federalism Governance Model will refine the discussion of collaborative federalism and governance, and that both practitioners and researchers will have a meaningful model that can help explain the relationships between the public, private, and nonprofit sectors.

References

Agranoff, R. (2006). Inside collaborative networks: Ten lessons for public managers. *Public Administration Review*, 66(s1), 56–65.

Agranoff, R., & McGuire, M. (2001). Big questions in public network management research. *Journal of Public Administration Research and Theory*, 11(3), 295–326.

Annie E. Casey Foundation. (2014). *About us*. Retrieved from www.aecf.org/about/.

Ansell, C., & Gash, A. (2007). Collaborative governance in theory and practice. *Journal of Public Administration Research and Theory*, 18(4), 543–571.

Association of Clean Water Administrators. (2013, March 5). *State water agencies, the Nature Conservancy and EPA join to protect healthy watersheds*. Retrieved from www.tn.gov/environment/water/docs/mar2013_hwi_mou_press_release.pdf.

Bachtler, J., & Mendez, C. (2007). Who governs EU cohesion policy? Deconstructing the reforms of the structural funds. *JCMS: Journal of Common Market Studies*, 45(3), 535–564.

Baracskay, D. (2012). How federal health-care policies interface with urban and rural areas: A comparison of three systems. *Global Public Health*, 7(4), 317–336.

Berardo, R. (2014). Bridging and bonding capital in two-mode collaboration networks. *Policy Studies Journal*, 42(2), 197–225.

Bonner, P. (2013). Balancing task with relationship to create interagency collaboration. *Public Manager*, 42, 30–32.

Bowling, C., & Pickerill, M. (2013). Fragmented federalism: The state of American federalism. *Publius: The Journal of Federalism*, 43(3), 315–346.

Brown, W. A. (2002). Inclusive governance practices in nonprofit organizations and implications for practice. *Nonprofit Leadership and Management*, 12(4), 369–385.

Bryson, J., Crosby, B., & Stone, M. (2006). The design and implementation of cross-sector collaborations: Propositions from the literature. *Public Administration Review*, 66(Special Issue), 44–53.

Cameron, D., & Simeon, R. (2002). Intergovernmental relations in Canada: The emergence of collaborative federalism. *Publius: The Journal of Federalism*, 32(2), 49–71.

Child Abuse Prevention Association. (2011). *Capa's sponsors*. Retrieved from www.childabuseprevention.org/content/how-you-can-help/our-sponsors.

Children's Bureau. (2012, May 17). *Community-based grants for the prevention of child abuse and neglect (CBCAP)*. Retrieved from www.acf.hhs.gov/programs/cb/resource/cbcap-state-grants.

Child Welfare Information Gateway. (2011). *Child maltreatment prevention: Past, present, and future.* Washington, DC: U.S. Department of Health and Human Services, Children's Bureau, 1–14.

Cooper, T. L., Bryer, T. A., & Meek, J. W. (2006). Citizen-centered collaborative public management. *Public Administration Review, 66*(s1), 76–88.

Daro, D. A. (2000). Child abuse prevention: New directions and challenges. *Nebraska Symposium on Motivation. Journal on Motivation, 46,* 161–219.

Daro, D., & Dodge, K. A. (2009). Creating community responsibility for child protection: Possibilities and challenges. *Future of Children, 19*(2), 67–93.

Diaz-Kope, L., & Miller-Stevens, K. (2014). Rethinking a typology of watershed partnerships: A governance perspective. *Public Works Management & Policy,* published online, 1–20. doi: 10.1177/1087724X14524733

Dienhart, J. W. (2010). Sustainability, cross-sector collaboration, institutions, and governance. *Business Ethics Quarterly, 20*(4), 725–728.

Elazar, D. J. (1962). *The American partnership: Intergovernmental cooperation in the nineteenth-century United States.* Chicago, IL: The University of Chicago Press.

Elazar, D. J. (1991). Cooperative federalism. In D. A. Kenyon & J. Kincaid (Eds.), *Competition among states and local governments: Efficiency and equity in American federalism* (pp. 65–86). Washington, DC: The Urban Institute Press.

Emerson, K., Nabatchi, T., & Balogh, S. (2011). An integration framework for collaboration governance. *Journal of Public Administration Research and Theory, 22*(1), 1–19.

Emery, F., & Trist, E. (1965). The casual texture of organizational environments. *Human Relations, 18*(1), 21–32.

Family Resource Information, Education and Network Development Services. (2014). *National resource center for community-based child abuse prevention.* Retrieved from http://friendsnrc.org/.

Feiock, R. C., Steinacker, A., & Park, H. J. (2009). Institutional collective action and economic development joint ventures. *Public Administration Review, 69*(2), 256–270.

Finkelhor, D., Jones, L., & Shattuck, A. (2011). Updated trends in child maltreatment, 2009. *Crimes Against Children Research Center.* Retrieved from www.unh.edu/ccrc/pdf/Updated_Trends_in_Child_Maltreatment_2009.pdf.

Gamkhar, S., & Pickerill, M. (2012). The state of American federalism 2011–2012: A fend for yourself and activist form of bottom-up federalism. *Publius: The Journal of Federalism, 42*(3), 357–386.

Gazley, B., & Brudney, J. L. (2007). The purpose (and perils) of government-nonprofit partnership. *Nonprofit and Voluntary Sector Quarterly, 36*(3), 389–415.

Goldfarb, W. (1994). Watershed management: Slogan or solution? *Boston College Environmental Affairs Law Review, 21*(3), 483–510.

Graefe, P., & Bourns, A. (2008). The gradual defederalization of Canadian health policy. *Publius: The Journal of Federalism, 39*(1), 187–209.

Gray, B. (1985). Conditions facilitating interorganizational collaboration. *Human Relations, 38*(10), 911–936.

Gray, B. (1989). *Collaborating: Finding common ground for multiparty problems.* San Francisco, CA: Jossey-Bass.

Hajer, M., & Wagenaar, H. (2003). Introduction. In M. A. Hajer and H. Wagenaar (Eds.), *Deliberative policy analysis: Understanding governance in the network society* (pp. 1–32). Cambridge, England: Cambridge University Press.

Hardy, S. D. (2010). Governments, group membership, and watershed partnerships. *Society and Natural Resources, 23*(7), 587–603.

Hardy, S., & Koontz, T. (2009). Rules for collaboration: Institutional analysis of group membership and level of action in watershed partnerships. *The Policy Studies Journal, 37*(3), 393–414.

Heikkila, T., & Gerlak, A. (2005). The formation of large-scale collaborative resource management institutions: Clarifying the roles of stakeholders, science and institutions. *The Policy Studies Journal, 33*(4), 583–612.

Imperial, M. T. (2005). Using collaboration as a governance strategy: Lessons from six watershed management programs. *Administration & Society, 37*(3), 281–320.

Keast, R., Mandell, M. P., Brown, K., & Woolcock, G. (2004). Network structures: Working differently and changing expectations. *Public Administration Review, 64*(3), 363–371.

Kenney, D. (1997). *Resource management at the watershed level: An assessment of the changing federal role in the emerging era of community-based watershed management.* Boulder, CO: Natural Resource Law Center, University of Colorado School of Law.

Kettl, D. (2002). *The transformation of governance: Public administration for twenty-first century America.* Baltimore, MD: The John Hopkins University Press.

Kettl, D. (2006). Managing boundaries in American administration: The collaboration imperative. *Public Administration Review, 66*(Special Issue), 10–19.

Kiefer, J. J., & Montjoy, R. S. (2006). Incrementalism before the storm: Network performance for the evacuation of New Orleans. *Public Administration Review, 66*(s1), 122–130.

Landau, M. (1973). Federalism, redundancy and system. *Publius: The Journal of Federalism, 3*(2), 173–196.

Leach, W. D., & Pelkey, N. W. (2001). Making watershed partnerships work: A review of the empirical literature. *Journal of Water Resources Planning and Management, 127*(6), 378–385.

Leavitt, W. M., & Morris, J. C. (2007). Public works service arrangements in the 21st Century: The multiple-sector partnership as an alternative to privatization. *Public Works Management & Policy, 12*(1), 325–330.

Lenihan, D. (2002). *Collaborative federalism: How labour mobility and foreign qualification recognition are changing Canada's intergovernmental landscape.* Ottawa, ON: Public Governance International.

Light, R. J. (1974). Abused and neglected children in America: A study of alternative policies. *Harvard Educational Review,* (9), 556–598.

Lim Brodowski, M., Counts, J. M., Gillam, R. J., Baker, L., Spiva Collins, V., Winkle, E., et al. (2013). Translating evidence-based policy to practice: A multilevel partnership using the interactive systems framework. *Families in Society: The Journal of Contemporary Social Services, 94*(3), 141–149.

Lynn, L. (2010). Foundations of public administration: Governance. *Public Administration Review,* 1–40.

McGuire, M. (2006). Collaborative public management: Assessing what we know and how we know it. *Public Administration Review, 66*(s1), 33–43.

McNamara, M., Leavitt, W., & Morris, J. (2010). Multiple-sector partnerships and the engagement of citizens in social marketing campaigns: The case of Lynnhaven River "NOW". *Virginia Social Science Journal, 45*, 1–20.

Mandarano, L. A., Featherstone, J. P., & Paulsen, K. (2008). Institutions for inter-state water resources management. *Journal of the American Water Resources Association, 44*(1), 136–147. doi:10.1111/j.1752-1688.2007.00143.x.

Mandell, M. P. (1999). Community collaborations: Working through network structures. *Policy Studies Review, 16*(1), 42–64.

Margerum, R. (2008). A typology of collaboration efforts in environmental man-agement. *Environmental Management, 41*(4), 487–500.

Margerum, R. D. (2011). *Beyond consensus: Improving collaborative planning and management.* Cambridge, MA: The MIT Press.

Meek, J. W., & Thurmaier, K. (Eds.). (2011). *Networked governance: The future of intergovernmental management.* Washington, DC: CQ Press.

Missouri Children's Trust Fund. (2014). *CBCAP federal grant.* Retrieved from http://ctf4kids.org/program-partners/cbcap/.

Missouri Department of Social Services. (2009, July 02). *Annual progress of child welfare continuum of services.* Retrieved from http://dss.mo.gov/cd/cfsplan/cont_serv.htm.

Moore, E., & Koontz, T. (2003). A typology of collaborative watershed groups: Citizen-based, agency-based, and mixed partnerships. *Society & Natural Resources, 16*(5), 451–460.

Morris, J. C., Gibson, W. A., Leavitt, W. M., & Jones, S. C. (2013). *The case for grassroots collaboration: Social capital and ecosystem restoration at the local level.* Lanham, MD: Lexington Books.

Morris, J. C., Gibson, W. A., Leavitt, W. M., & Jones, S. C. (2014). Collaborative federalism and the emerging role of local nonprofits in water quality implemen-tation. *Publius: The Journal of Federalism, 44* (3), 499–518.

Morton, L. W. (2008). The role of civic structure in achieving performance-based watershed management. *Society and Natural Resources, 21*(9), 751–766.

Moss, T., & Newig, J. (2010). Multilevel water governance and problems of scale: Setting the stage for a broader debate. *Environmental Management, 46,* 1–6.

Mullin, M., & Daley, D. M. (2010). Working with the state: Exploring interagency collaboration within a federalist system. *Journal of Public Administration Research and Theory, 20*(4), 757–778.

National Alliance of Children's Trust & Prevention Funds. (2009). *Honoring our past, building our future: 1989–2009.* Retrieved from www.ctfalliance.org/images/about/Honoring Our Past.pdf.

New York State Office of Children and Family Services. (2012). *New York State children and family trust fund.* Retrieved from www.ocfs.state.ny.us/main/reports/2012%20Trust%20Fund%20Annual%20Report%204-19-13.pdf.

O'Toole, L. J., & Meier, K. J. (2004). Desperately seeking Selznick: Cooptation and the dark side of public management in networks. *Public Administration Review, 64*(6), 681–693.

Page, S. (2004). Measuring accountability for results in interagency collaboratives. *Public Administration Review, 64*(5), 591–606.

Parisi, D., Taquino, M., Grice, S. M., & Gill, D. A. (2004). Civic responsibility and the environment: Linking local conditions to community environmental active-ness. *Society and Natural Resources, 17*(2), 97–112.

Paul, S. (1989). Poverty alleviation and participation: The case for government-grassroots agency collaboration. *Economic and Political Weekly, 24*(2), 100–106.

Pickerill, J. M., & Bowling, C. J. (2014). Polarized parties, politics, and policies: Frag-mented federalism in 2013–2014. *Publius: The Journal of Federalism, 44*(3), 369–398.

Prah, P. (2012, January 10). *State and consumer initiatives: Washington and the states: A year of uncertainty and foreboding.* Retrieved from www.pewstates. org/projects/stateline/headlines/washington-and-the-states-a-year-of-uncertainty-and-foreboding-85899376387.

Provan, K., & Kenis, P. (2007). Modes of network governance: Structure, management, and effectiveness. *Journal of Public Administration Research, 18*(2), 229–252.

Purdy, J. (2012). A framework for assessing power in collaborative governance processes. *Public Administration Review, 72*(3), 409–417.

Rittel, H. W., & Webber, M. M. (1973). Dilemmas in a general theory of planning. *Policy Sciences, 4*(2), 155–169.

Sabatier, P., Weible, C., & Ficker, J. (2005). Eras of water management in the United States: Implication for collaboration watershed approaches. In P. Sabatier, M. Focht, M. Lubell, Z. Trachtenberg, A. Vadlitz, & M. Matlock (Eds.), *Swimming upstream: Collaborative approaches to watershed management* (pp. 23–51). Cambridge, MA: The MIT Press.

Saunders, C. (2002). Collaborative federalism. *Australian Journal of Public Administration, 61*(2), 69–77.

Shaw, M. M. (2003). Successful collaboration between the nonprofit and public sectors. *Nonprofit Management and Leadership, 14*(1), 107–120.

Simo, G., & Bies, A. L. (2007). The role of nonprofits in disaster response: An expanded model of cross-sector collaboration. *Public Administration Review, 67*(s1), 125–142.

Sørenson, E. (2006). Metagovernance: The changing role of politicians in processes of democratic governance. *American Review of Public Administration, 36,* 98–114.

Stame, N. (2008). The European project, federalism and evaluation. *Evaluation, 14*(2), 117–140.

Staten, C. L. (1993). Theodore Roosevelt: Dual and cooperative federalism. *Presidential Studies Quarterly, 23*(1), 129–143.

Stein, T. J. (1984). The child abuse prevention and treatment act. *The Social Service Review, 58*(2), 302–314.

Trist, E. L. (1983). Referent organizations and the development of interorganizational domains. *Human Behavior, 36*(3), 247–268.

U.S. Department of Health and Human Services, Administration for Children and Families, Administration on Children, Youth and Families, Children's Bureau. (2010). *Child maltreatment 2009.* Retrieved from www.acf.hhs.gov/programs/cb/stats_research/index.htm#can.

U.S. Environmental Protection Agency. (2009, July). *EPA's healthy watersheds initiative.* Retrieved from http://water.epa.gov/polwaste/nps/watershed/upload/2009_08_05_NPS_healthywatersheds_highquality_hwi.pdf.

U.S. Environmental Protection Agency. (2011). *Healthy watersheds initiatives: National framework and action plan.* Retrieved from http://water.epa.gov/polwaste/nps/watershed/upload/hwi_action_plan.pdf.

U.S. Environmental Protection Agency. (2012a, February). *Indentifying and protecting healthy watersheds.* Retrieved from http://water.epa.gov/polwaste/nps/watershed/upload/hwi-watersheds-ch1.pdf.

U.S. Environmental Protection Agency. (2012b, March 21). *Water: Targeted watersheds grant program.* Retrieved from http://water.epa.gov/grants_funding/twg/initiative_index.cfm#va.

U.S. Environmental Protection Agency. (2012c, August 27). *Water: Polluted runoff.* Retrieved from http://water.epa.gov/polwaste/nps/whatis.cfm.

U.S. Environmental Protection Agency. (2012d, April). *The economic benefits of protecting healthy watersheds.* Retrieved from http://water.epa.gov/polwaste/nps/watershed/upload/economic_benefits_factsheet3.pdf.

U.S. Environmental Protection Agency. (2013, winter). *EPA healthy watersheds news.* Retrieved from http://water.epa.gov/grants_funding/twg/initiative_index.cfm#va.

U.S. Environmental Protection Agency. (2014, August 23). *Water: Healthy watersheds.* Retrieved from http://water.epa.gov/polwaste/nps/watershed/hwi_action.cfm.

Weissert, C., & Schram, S. (1998). The state of American federalism, 1997–1998. *Publius: The Journal of Federalism, 28*(1), 1–22.

Wisconsin Children's Trust Fund. (2014). *Supportive communities and schools.* Retrieved from http://wichildrenstrustfund.org/index.php?section=prevention~supports.

Woolley, J., & McGinnis, M. (1999). The politics of watershed policymaking. *Policy Studies Journal, 27*(3), 578–594.

Wood, D. J., & Gray, B. (1991). Toward a comprehensive theory of collaboration. *Journal of Applied Behavioral Science, 27*(2), 139–162.

Zilber Family Foundation. (2014). *Zilber neighborhood initiative.* Retrieved from www.znimilwaukee.org/overview.html.

Zimmerman, J. F. (2001). National-state relations: Cooperative federalism in the twentieth century. *Publius: The Journal of Federalism, 31*(2), 15–30.

9 A Life-Cycle Model of Collaboration

Christopher M. Williams, Connie Merriman, and John C. Morris

Introduction

The past three decades have seen a plethora of scholarly work on the topic of collaboration. From Barbara Gray's (1985) early work to the present, the extant literature is rife with books and articles that examine the preconditions, processes, and outcomes of collaboration in a variety of settings and circumstances. An important assumption in most of this work is that collaborative arrangements require certain inputs, process those inputs in a specific manner, and produce measurable and tangible goods or services as a result of that effort. In short, collaboration is often conceived of as a form of organization.

However, the intellectual roots of collaboration are often attributed to the network theory literature (see Agranoff & McGuire, 2003; Mandell, 2001; Meier & O'Toole, 2004). In this conception, collaboration is the result of a group of loosely connected individuals who share common interests, and work together to achieve common goals. Depending on its specific form, collaboration may consist of like-minded individuals, like-minded agencies (or other more traditional organizations), or a combination of the two (Moore & Koontz, 2003). For collaborations that fall into the latter two categories, there are often clear elements of interorganizational theory present in the setting, as collaboration effectively becomes a form of interaction between organizations in a given environment.

Often overlooked in these efforts, however, is an important observation: collaboration often carries network theory beyond its boundaries into something that takes on the characteristics of a traditional organization. Thomson and Perry (2006), for example, conceive of collaboration as a set of inputs and preconditions, which in turn lead to a series of identifiable work and management processes, which results in the production of outputs. This same conceptual 'picture' has been adopted by many others, including Wood and Gray (1991), Morris, Gibson, Leavitt and Jones (2013) and Sabatier et al. (2005). In a sense, these collaborations exhibit more of the characteristics of more traditional (and formal) organizations, and fewer of the characteristics of networks. While we would certainly not dismiss the importance of networks, particularly in the early formation of the group, the extant literature tends to ignore collaboration as an organizational form.

It is our contention that collaborations may be thought of in terms of organizational theory. To that end, this chapter makes an argument that functioning collaborations are, in principle and fact, organizational forms. If this is the case, then we suggest that there is much to be learned about collaboration through the application of the literature in organization theory as a means to more fully understand collaboration. This chapter provides an extension of the literature by testing the efficacy of collaboration as a form of organization, and thus extending our knowledge and understanding of collaboration. Our case in point for this chapter is the application of Anthony Downs's (1967) concept of the "life cycle" of organizations.[1] Downs's notion that organizations move through discrete and identifiable phases during their existence provides the basis for our exploration into the applicability of the organization theory literature to collaboration. Because Downs's model captures a variety of organizational processes, a comparison of these processes to those found in collaboration will provide an indication of the viability of the exercise. It is important to note that the formal study of collaboration is relatively new, as is the use of collaboration (as we know it) in the U.S. context. Because of this, the ability to identify and study existing collaborations that have been in existence long enough to empirically test Downs's model is exceptionally limited. Although life-cycle models have been applied to many kinds of organizational settings, including hospitals (Burns, 1982; Burns & Mauet, 1984), city councils (Waste, 1983), the National Aeronautic and Space Administration (McCurdy, 1991), and for-profit businesses (Lester, Parnell, Crandall, & Menefee, 2008), it does not appear that the life-cycle model has been applied to collaborative settings. To that end, the purpose of this chapter is to theorize about how a life-cycle model of organization might be applied to collaboration.

This chapter begins with a review of Downs's (1967) model, along with some other empirical studies that have applied the life-cycle model in more traditional organizational settings. We then present a model of the life cycle of collaboration, drawing on Downs's work to examine the degree to which his model can inform our knowledge of collaboration. We conclude with some observations about the viability of this comparison, and some suggestions about how organization theory may provide additional insights into collaborative processes and outcomes.

Linking Collaboration Theory and Organization Theory

At the outset of this chapter, we are compelled to offer some important definitions and assumptions that undergird this work. To begin with, we assume that collaboration represents a form of organization that can be reasonably studied, and to which both descriptive and explanatory theory might be applied. Our argument to this effect is drawn from a combination of existing literature and direct observation.

The Nature of Collaboration

As noted at the outset of this chapter, there is a large (and growing) academic literature that examines collaboration from a variety of perspectives. Collaboration is variously described as a management process (e.g., Agranoff & McGuire, 2001), a performance tool (e.g., Agranoff, 2005), a governance choice (e.g., Ansell & Gash, 2007), a policy choice (e.g., Koontz & Thomas, 2006), and as an extension of network theory (e.g., Mandell, 2001).

A useful distinction about the nature of collaboration is that offered by Moore and Koontz (2003). In their examination of watershed collaboration efforts, Moore and Koontz note that collaborations generally fall into one of three categories: agency-based, citizen-based, or mixed. In agency-based collaboration, the primary participants are representatives of existing organizations, and organizations contribute resources (people, money, etc.) directly to the collaborative effort. Citizen-based groups are primarily composed of individual, interested citizens who come together because of a shared interest. Finally, mixed collaborations fall somewhere in between (Moore & Koontz, 2003). When applied to interorganizational theory, the overlap, particularly with agency-based collaboration, is striking. An agency-based collaboration may begin life as a form of interorganizational interaction. As the collaborative activity becomes more regularized, it may take on organizational characteristics of its own, including structure, goals, rules, and organizational processes. In other words, what begins as an interorganizational interaction between several distinct organizations can become an organizational form unto itself. It may still be dependent on its 'parent' organizations for resources, but the ability to operate in all other respects as a largely autonomous body suggests that the collaboration may be treated as a separate entity. As other separate organizations join the collective effort, the collaboration develops its own interorganizational identity. The same is likely true of both mixed- and citizen-based collaboration. Because all three forms of collaboration engage in the same basic activities, it follows that they can be considered as organizational forms in their own right.

The Link Between Intra- and Interorganizational Theory

According to Harmon and Mayer (1986, p. 30), intraorganizational theory is concerned with "...order and control, efficient attainment of goals, coordination, and the maintenance of effective communication." The internal focus apparent here means that issues of structure and process are particularly important, as is the difference between formal and informal organization. Many theorists in this tradition make assumptions of rationality and instrumentality in decision-making, although a substantial literature exists that critiques these basic assumptions. In either case, however, the focus is clearly on elements of management and structure within a single organizational setting.

Conversely, interorganizational theory focuses on relationships between organizations as they occur in a particular setting. These relationships can be formally defined, or they can adopt a more informal character (Harmon & Mayer, 1986, p. 28). In either case, the interactions are treated as "organization to organization," and the unit of analysis becomes the organization. Interorganizational theory also places a great deal of emphasis on the nature of the environment in which the interactions occur. This environment is often conceived of as uncertain and turbulent (see Emery & Trist, 1965; Morris & Burns, 1997; Terreberry, 1968), and the focus is often on how organizations operate in such a complex and uncertain setting (Aldrich, 1967; Lawrence & Lorsch, 1969; Nutt & Backoff, 1995). Coupled with a focus on resource dependency (Aldrich, 1967; Dunford, 1987; Lawrence & Lorsch 1969), this literature examines the effects of the environment on organizational structure (e.g., Thompson, 1967), decision-making (e.g., Lawrence & Lorsch, 1969), and rules (e.g., Ostrom, 1990; Raelin, 1982; Schopler, 1987).

Collaboration creates an interesting definitional dilemma for organization theorists. Because much of the collaboration literature is grounded in the network theory literature, and networks can be thought of as informal examples of interorganizational theory (see Harmon & Mayer, 1986), then it would appear at first glance that collaboration can be treated in the tradition of interorganizational theory. This is especially true if the nature of the collaboration is agency-based or "mixed" (Moore & Koontz, 2003). The interactions take place between organizations in a defined environment, in a reasonably informal manner. However, the literature treats collaboration as much more than an informal association of like-minded participants. Collaborative efforts are often reported to develop goals (Morris et al., 2013), decision and managerial processes (Agranoff & McGuire, 2001; Thomson & Perry, 2006), leadership roles (Bryson, Crosby, & Stone, 2006; Heikkila & Gerlak, 2005), accountability mechanisms (Bardach & Lesser, 1996; Purdy, 2012), and outcomes (Koontz & Thomas, 2006; Rogers & Weber, 2010). In short, collaborations develop all the characteristics of organizations from an intraorganizational perspective. As is the case with intraorganizational theory, these foci tend to change the unit of analysis from the organizational level to the individual level. If our observation is correct, then there must be a point at which collaborative activity transforms from an interorganizational to an intraorganizational interaction. The exact moment at which this occurs is not irrelevant, but it is also largely unimportant for our current purposes. The salient point is that the collaboration literature ends up looking very similar in many respects to the organization theory literature.

If our argument holds, then it follows that we may reasonably apply organizational models to better understand collaborative activity. To test this proposition, we turn to Downs's (1967) life-cycle model of organization. As noted in the preceding paragraphs, most collaborations are relatively young, and therefore little is known about the long-term viability of collaboration as an organizational form. Downs's model provides us with a means to consider the question of long-term survival and viability of collaborative arrangements.

A Life-Cycle Model of Organization

In his seminal book *Inside Bureaucracy*, Anthony Downs (1967) presents the reader with a model through which to view organizational development and growth. Although his overall purpose is "...to develop a useful theory of decision making" (Downs, 1967, p. 1), his work is perhaps best known for the development of a typology of the bureaucratic behavior of individuals. His model of decision-making is predicated on an assumption of rational self-interest on the part of bureaucratic officials. Downs notes that, at different phases of their development and operation, bureaus tend be dominated by certain types of bureaucratic "personalities." By comparing the role of these different "personalities" in an organizational setting, Downs is able to develop propositional statements about the decision-making behavior of these officials.

The life-cycle model offered by Downs (1967) appears to identify five phases of the organizational life cycle—birth, rapid growth, stasis, decline, and eventual death. Although the parallel to biological organisms is striking (see Kaufman, 1991), Durham and Smith (1982) note that organizational life cycles may not occur in a linear fashion, and that they may actually repeat phases at different points in their existence (Burns & Mauet, 1984). While some scholars note a general lack of conceptual clarity in the specification and application of life-cycle models (see Greiner, 1972; Quinn & Cameron, 1983; Whetten, 1987), it is also the case that the number of phases present in the different models varies widely (Cameron & Whetten, 1981). There appears to be general agreement that at least two phases, growth and decline, are present; much of the rest of the variation tends to focus on ways to subdivide these two phases.

Recent scholarly work (Morris et al., 2013; Sabatier et al., 2005) explains collaboration processes through a systems theory lens.[2] Although these models explain collaboration activities quite well, they are presented as cyclical processes that limit their ability to explain collaboration from a life-cycle perspective. Specifically, both scholarly models do not explain the phases of a collaboration's demise. Therefore, this chapter endeavors to explain the collaboration life cycle through an organizational theory lens while comparing the distinct phases that manifest to the model put forth by Morris et al. (2013).

The model proposed by Morris et al. (2013) is based on a systems model approach to collaboration. Their model consists of a series of contextual variables that serve as inputs into the collaboration process (see Figure 9.1). The collaboration process, consisting of resources, rules, and governance structures, leads to three different kinds of outputs. One output of the collaboration process is social capital, which in turn feeds back to

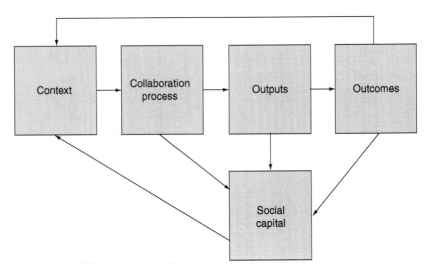

Figure 9.1 A Systems Model Approach to Collaboration (source: adapted from Morris et al., 2013).

the contextual variables. Intermediate outputs include plans, programs, decisions, reports, and partnerships, which in turn lead to long-term outcomes—changes in behaviors and in the physical environment. Both intermediate outputs and long-term outcomes also build social capital, and long-term outcomes also feed directly back to the contextual variables (Morris et al., 2013). It is important to note that this model of collaboration assumes perpetual collaborative activity; the model contains no provision for the cessation of the collaborative effort. Although we believe this is a weakness of the model, it is a weakness shared by other systems-like models.

The Collaboration Life Cycle

Following Downs's (1967) life-cycle model of bureaus, and with influence from other organization life-cycle scholars (Adizes, 1979; Lester, Parnell, & Carraher, 2003), we suggest a model that includes six phases: issue, assembly and structure, productivity, rejuvenation, decline, and dissipation. A commonality found in the organization life-cycle literature is that organizations include a distinct beginning, a period of growth, a phase of relative productivity followed by a decline, and, if no new energy is introduced, an ultimate dissolution.

Collaborations are formed when there is a need to tackle tough issues that cannot be resolved efficiently by one individual or agency acting on its own (Gray, 1989). Therefore, multiple actors will develop the idea of handling a problem through a collaborative effort. Shortly after establishment,

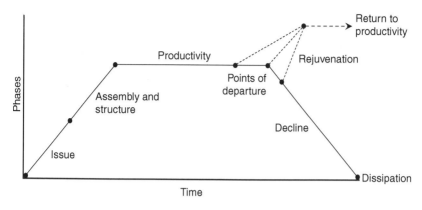

Figure 9.2 The Collaboration Life Cycle.

a collaboration will begin to assemble its actors and structure itself to com-
mence its productivity phase. The productivity phase will last as long as
there are interested stakeholders and at least one issue requiring resolution.
Without a common cause or stakeholder interest, collaborations are faced
with finding new issues to champion or diminish until they no longer exist.
Figure 9.2 illustrates the six distinct phases of a collaboration.

Issue Phase

The issue phase begins with a problem that is so complex no individual or
group believes it can be overcome by the actions of a single actor or organization. This is a brief phase where one or a few founding members, considered collaboration sponsors (Policy Consensus Initiative, 2014), identify
an issue to resolve and recognize the need for stakeholders' support.
Morris et al. (2013) point out that issues that serve as a stimulus for collaboration are contextual in nature and can stem from a multitude of
problem areas such as environmental concerns, public policy matters, and
outcries from citizens and groups who demand public action. These issues
are, in fact, wicked problems (Rittel & Webber, 1973) requiring comprehensive solutions that governments may have not considered. Hence, multiple actors from any combination of nonprofit, public, and private sector
organizations will organize themselves into a collective in order to tackle
the issue at hand. Therefore, the entry criterion for the issue phase is a
salient problem that has a negative impact on multiple actors. The Choose
Clean Water Coalition, for example, came about to take on the seemingly
impossible task of cleaning up rivers and streams that empty into the
Chesapeake Bay.[3]

At this burgeoning juncture in the collaboration life cycle, the group
is small and lacking momentum. The collaboration can either blossom
or fail. Decision-making remains in the hands of a few entrepreneurial

thinkers. The primary concern is planning how to move ahead by acquiring support from multiple actors. The amount of social capital that exists in the issue phase serves as a baseline that directly impacts future development. This baseline is an important precursor to collaboration establishment and growth (Koontz & Thomas, 2006; Morris et al., 2013). The higher the amount of social capital in the issue phase, the more inclined actors are to support the collaborative cause, and the more successful the collaboration will be at transitioning to the next phase in the life cycle. Comparing this phase to the model put forth by Morris et al. (2013), the issue phase encompasses the context variables group with some spillover into the collaboration process group. Additionally, this comparison corroborates the importance of issue context and social capital in the nascent phases of a collaboration as found in the recent literature (Morris et al., 2013; Sabatier et al., 2005).

Towards the end of the issue phase, collaboration members will begin rallying for additional stakeholder support. Prospective stakeholders will start to gain interest and the collaboration will pick up momentum by adding members. The increase in membership and prospective stakeholder interest is the departure point from the issue phase. Gaining collective interest and active involvement from a sufficient number of stakeholders that permits strategic planning marks the exit of the issue phase and entry into the assembly and structure phase.

Assembly and Structure Phase

Lester et al. (2003) describe an organization's survival phase and point out that organizations must amass sufficient resources in order to sustain themselves. In this regard, collaborations are very similar to organizations. Throughout the assembly and structure phase, a collaboration runs the risk of an early termination stemming from a lack of resources. Therefore, upon entering the assembly and structure phase, collaborations are focused primarily on growth, building a network of stakeholders, and amassing resources. In order to rally support, collaborative actors who are passionate about the cause, or zealots (Downs, 1967), play a key role in drumming up resources and membership. Additionally, zealots recruit other actors known as "convenors ... [who] appreciate the potential for mutual exchange and envision a mission which can be fulfilled through joint participation" (Gray, 1985, p. 924). The convenors carry the message to potentially interested parties to drum up further support. Although securing new members and resources is pronounced in the assembly and structure phase, this effort will persist to some degree throughout the life cycle.

In addition to the need for resources, there is also a need for an agreed upon structure within the collaboration. However, in order to institute a structure and a division of labor, the collaboration must define its goals. Hilda Tellioğlu (2008) identifies three tasks that must be accomplished at this phase: "define the common goal of the collaboration, define roles for collaborating members, [and] set up a coordinated work environment" (p. 360). Given that a collaboration is likely to contain multiple sets of actors with different agendas, collaborative goals must be collectively decided upon. Once the goals are set, the collaboration can determine what functions must be carried out for goal attainment, sustainment, and survival.

At this point, the responsibilities for carrying out collaborative functions are assigned to an agreed upon set of actors. This structure may change throughout the life cycle, but the initial structure permits the collaboration to establish a set of business rules defining routine operations focused on achieving its overall goals. Comparison with the Morris et al. (2013) model shows that the assembly and structure phase of the life cycle begins in the collaboration process variable group and transcends into the outputs group. The interactions between stakeholders when assembling and developing structure are expected to yield social capital, but exactly how much remains unclear. However, the social capital produced in this phase appears to be relative to inter- and intraorganizational relationships. Once a coordinated work environment is established, the collaboration has reached this phase's exit criteria and has entered the productivity phase.

Productivity Phase

The productivity phase begins when the collaboration is sufficiently staffed and resourced to begin carrying out its primary focus. This phase, which is in fact the business end of any collaboration, encompasses the remainder of the collaboration model developed by Morris et al. (2013). The efforts of the productivity phase result in outputs which in turn affect social capital and produce environmental outcomes that ultimately feed back to the context of the issue. These feedback loops are called out in the collaboration process models offered by Morris et al. (2013) and others. Productivity is not a simple phase in the life cycle. It is a complex phase where four distinct functions are constantly occurring: communication, learning, decision-making, and managing stability.

Communication

Communication is an important variable for the success of a collaboration. Writing on organizational communication, Gortner, Nichols, and Ball (2007) state that "successful communication processes ensure commonality of purpose" (p. 156) in an organization. This "commonality of purpose" embodies the foundation of a collaboration. During the preceding phases and in the beginning of this phase, communication is used to establish the collaboration's initial focus. The point in which commonality of purpose is attained marks the point where formal communication pathways becomes less interorganizational and more intraorganizational. Hence, the component actors or organizations become one collaboration. It is unclear exactly where this shift occurs in the collaboration life cycle, but we believe it occurs somewhere between the assembly and structure and productivity phases. As the collaboration progresses and its focus adapts to changing environments, healthy communication becomes essential to maintaining a commonality of purpose.

Learning

Learning in a collaboration is a collective process that is closely linked to communication. Members of a collaboration learn through communication at the individual level, information dissemination at the collaboration level, and through trial and error. Gerlak and Heikkila (2011) define this type of learning as collective learning:

> Acquiring information through diverse actions (e.g. trial and error), assessing or translating information, and disseminating knowledge or opportunities across individuals in a collective, and 2) collective products that emerge from the process, such as new shared ideas, strategies, rules, or policies.
>
> (p. 5)

The second part of Gerlak and Heikkila's definition underscores the importance of collective learning. A collaboration must consider the various stakeholders' viewpoints and desires when deciding upon a course of action. Collective learning, therefore, helps to ensure that all members have equal access to the knowledge necessary in developing a collaborative solution or a way ahead. Collective learning is indeed a fundamental necessity to the success of any collaboration.

Decision-Making

Good decision-making is another influential factor of a collaboration's success. The method of decision-making, whether it be through rational choice (Downs, 1957), incrementalism (Lindblom, 1959), satisificing (Simon, 1956), the garbage can model (Cohen, March, & Olsen, 1972) or some other means, is largely based on collaboration objectives and context. Randolph and Bauer (1999) put forth three objectives of collaborative environmental decision-making that are relevant to a collaboration life cycle: to "resolve conflict," to "develop a shared vision," and to "formulate creative solutions" (p. 174). Some collaborations can bring stakeholders together to identify and work through differences rather than jointly dealing with societal issues. Therefore, in the context of resolving conflicts, stakeholders come together to work towards a mutual understanding that supports coexistence in a certain environment.

Randolph and Bauer's (1999) last two objectives are essentially the same context; collectively formulating creative solutions for issues that impact multiple actors. However, in order to formulate creative solutions as a collaboration, the majority of stakeholders must share a common understanding of what is wrong and what needs to occur to make it right. Therefore, these two objectives, developing a shared vision and formulating creative solutions, are achieved through sound communication pathways and robust collective learning environments. It is no coincidence that each of the functions in the productivity phase lay the foundation for subsequent functions, which ultimately impacts a collaboration's health. Consequently, without the first three functions it would be extremely difficult to carry out the last function in the proposed model (managing a collaboration's stability).

Managing Stability

Tellioğlu (2008) believes that managing change "is one of the most important but underestimated issues in collaborative work environments" (p. 7). New policies can be enacted that impact existing collaboration efforts, actors can depart thereby reducing available resources, and changes to the environment can demand a shift in a collaboration's direction. Hence, during the productivity phase, many elements can change that call for creative approaches to problem-solving. It is difficult to imagine every possible stimulus of change. The point is that the productivity phase is not a static setting. Collaborations live and die by being able to respond and adapt to change. Collaborations that cannot manage change are destined to decline, and those that are successful have a real chance at survival.

A collaborative organization that exemplifies a well-orchestrated productivity phase, and an overall collaboration for that matter, is Lynnhaven River NOW (LRN). In 2002, LRN began as a group of citizens concerned with pollution in the Lynnhaven River, a watershed located in southeastern Virginia. In the beginning their goal was simple: obtain and apply public and private resources to clean the river so that oysters could be harvested within five years. Morris et al. (2013) point out that the success of LRN is most likely attributable to the functions of the productivity phase: positive and enthusiastic communications within and external to the collaboration; collective learning made effective by soliciting members with scientific backgrounds; a culture of collective decision-making; and using feedback signals to manage change. In fact, LRN was originally called Lynnhaven River 2007, but after achieving its original goal the collaboration changed its name to Lynnhaven River NOW, which appropriately defines its current mission: maintenance of the water quality in the Lynnhaven River. Perhaps the largest output from LRN's efforts is the social capital that comes with its success. LRN hosts annual oyster roasts, using oysters from the Lynnhaven River, which serves as a venue to raise money and citizens' awareness while soliciting new members.

Exiting the Productivity Phase

The productivity phase is by far the most important phase in the life cycle of a collaboration. This is the point at which collaborative products and processes determine the destiny of the collaboration. One of two paths will be followed at the end of the productivity phase. The collaboration will begin to decline until complete dissipation, or it will rejuvenate itself somewhere between the productivity phase and complete dissipation. If communication and collective learning are weak, the collaboration could be short-lived. Poor decisions will also lead a collaboration to the decline phase. Similarly, attainment of collaborative goals could be the cause for a collaboration to dissipate. In fact, there are many reasons a collaboration can enter the decline phase, but there is only one way to circumvent a complete dissipation: a collaboration can adapt to changing environments in order to receive new energy and continue its existence. Because of the lack of literature on collaboration demises, it is unclear exactly how a collaboration reacts to the prospect of imminent death. We believe a collaboration will be presented with one or more pathways as it reaches the end of the productivity phase. Figure 9.2 illustrates three points of departure that represent the optional pathways for a collaboration to rejuvenate and return to productiveness from either the productivity or the decline phase, or to decline fully into a complete dissipation. We begin by discussing the rejuvenation phase before explaining how collaborations decline into complete dissipation.

Rejuvenation

Despite Weitzel and Jonsson's (1989) contention that action at any of the first four phases of their model can halt or reverse the decline, successful intervention is more likely at the very early phases of decline. Rejuvenation of a collaboration experiencing decline could result from what Downs (1967) described as the "Growth Accelerator Effect," (p. 11), a phenomenon that occurs when the function of an essentially stagnant organization suddenly increases in value or importance. The resulting influx of attention, resources, and energy will reverse the downward direction of the collaboration and generate a new productivity phase. Rejuvenation in collaborations may also be similar to the "recycling phenomenon" that occurs when formal groups in the later phases of development encounter crises (Cameron & Whetten, 1981). Likewise, organizations (and collaborations) may experience crisis-like changes such as decrease in resources or loss of key advocates that cause them to return focus to an earlier point in their productivity phase.

If a collaboration is in decline because the initial objective has been met or the original purpose is no longer relevant, a change in focus will be required to prevent dissipation. A collaboration that is able to innovate and expand its original functions by embracing new ones (Downs, 1967) will attract fresh participants and garner additional resources to fuel a rejuvenation. If, however, potential participants perceive barriers related to the "age lump," whether excessive conservatism or insurmountable resistance to change, rejuvenation will be threatened.

Some inherent effects of decline negatively affect the potential success of rejuvenation. It is widely agreed that decline produces dysfunctional consequences for individuals, as well as the collaborative (Whetten, 1987). These consequences include an increase in conflict, secrecy, scapegoating, and splintering, and a decrease in creativity, morale, participation, and long-term perspectives.

Decline Phase

With few exceptions, decline occurs by degrees. Weitzel and Jonsson (1989) identified five distinct phases of decline ranging from "blinded" to "dissolution and death." At all phases except dissolution, action may be taken to halt or reverse the decline; although the success of interventions becomes increasingly difficult in the latter phases.

According to this model, decline begins at the Blinded phase, when participants and leadership fail to recognize adverse changes—signals or indicators that survival is being threatened. In collaborations, these indicators include an increase in conflict (Jones, 2013) and reduced ability to make decisions, especially decisions requiring consensus. If the Blinded phase continues unchecked, the organization moves to what Weitzel and Jonsson (1989) term the "Inaction phase." At this phase, the decline has reached a level of visibility sufficient for awareness; however, individuals in a position to take corrective action choose not to do so. This inaction may reflect a misinterpretation of the evidence or a belief that the circumstances are the result of a short-term environmental change that will self-correct over time. Inaction may also occur because individuals in leadership roles are pursuing self-interests at the expense of other participants or the collaboration as a whole (Jones, 2013).

As the Inaction phase continues, the collaboration moves farther away from optimum productivity. Unless this trend is recognized and prompt appropriate action is taken, the decline will continue to the Faulty Action phase. Everyone involved agrees there is a problem and that 'something' must be done. Unfortunately, the ensuing panic results in ineffective response, exemplified by poor decisions, made without consideration of consequences (Dark III, 2007; Jones, 2013). By definition, it seems that the Inaction phase must inevitably lead to the Crisis phase. Internal disunity increases as individuals recognize that drastic action is needed, but not occurring. By this point, even the staunchest advocates will have begun to abandon the collaboration and only radical changes can stop the decline from continuing to the Dissolution phase. Reform efforts have failed, stimulating intense internal conflict and the exit of key members. Regardless of effort level, demise can no longer be avoided.

Despite the proliferation of organizational life-cycle models and the differing opinions regarding the number and nature of the inherent phases,
there is some evident consensus about sequential movement through the
early phases (Whetten, 1987). This may be because most organizational
life-cycle models focus almost exclusively on the formative and growth
phases, with a recognizable reluctance to apply fully the biological life-
cycle phases of decline and death to social systems. Greiner (1972), for
example, presents an aging/growth process where organizations evolve in
strict linear fashion through five phases, requiring an identifiable "revolution" or crisis before being able to progress along the continuum. Likewise, the model of collaboration presented by Morris et al. (2013),
although cyclical rather than linear, does not identify a decline phase.
Rather, this model describes a phase of watershed outcomes that trigger a
change of context that in turn renews the collaboration. In life-cycle
models where decline is considered, such as Downs's (1967) life cycle of
bureaus, it is typically discussed concurrently with growth. This tendency
ignores key findings in organizational life-cycle research that indicates
decline and recovery (or death) can result from causes not linked to the
birth and growth phases (Cameron, Whetten, & Kim, 1987; Nystrom &
Starbuck, 1984). Jones (2013) is one of the few to identify distinct decline
and death phases, offering a simple bell-shaped model with four organizational life-cycle phases—birth, growth, decline, and death. He acknowledges that organizations experience these phases at different rates and
many do not experience all of the phases. He further notes that others have
identified sub-phases of decline where organizations have the opportunity
to take corrective action.

It has been stated that collaborations possess many of the characteristics
of other types of organizations. For collaborations established for a concrete,
time-delimited purpose or to resolve a narrow, distinct problem, decline and
dissipation are almost inevitable. This is similar to the type of decline in
public organizations caused by problem depletion (Levine, 1978). Problem
depletion is characterized by a cycle that includes identification of a critical
issue, followed by an influx of commitment and resources. At some point,
the crisis is eliminated, alleviated, redefined, or diminishes significantly in
relation to other issues. In most instances, the resulting decline will likely be
brief, leading directly into dissipation. One possible exception is with redefi-
nition, where a collaboration that is sufficiently flexible would be able to
redirect its focus and enter a period of rejuvenation. Other parallels can be
identified between the decline and dissolution phases of collaborations and
those same phases in other organizations.

One impediment to applying organizational life-cycle discussions of
decline is the lack of an agreed upon definition of 'organizational decline.'
There is a tendency to focus on quantifiable inputs such as financial
resources and numbers of employees which serve as indicators of the perceived worth of the unit. While these measures might signal that a collaboration is entering decline, there could be other less easily measured

indicators such as self-removal, stagnation of ideas or efforts, or minimization by those outside the collaboration. Consequently, decline could be attributed to changes occurring in the environment within which the collaboration functions or linked to changes associated with the participants.

Environmental Changes

Downs (1967) found that the major causes of decline in bureaus are rooted in "exogenous factors in their environment" (p. 10). He acknowledged that rapid growth of an organization, despite the rewards that are produced, ultimately produces obstacles to further growth. This restricted growth may result in stagnation and, in some cases, "death" of the organization (Waste, 1983). The obstacles identified by Downs also have the potential to affect collaborations. As societal values change over time, the significance of the core issues of the collaboration may dissipate. Conversely, if the central focus of the collaboration rises to a greater level of importance with society in general, new collaborations may become a source of competition; not only for external resources but also for the energy and attention of internal collaborators (Jones, 2013). The cumulative impact of these obstacles, according to Downs (1967), is a "decelerator effect" characterized by a period of stagnation and, potentially, decline.

Greiner (1972) presented a model of organizational growth describing an evolutionary process of five phases, each ending in a crisis due to a major problem faced by the organization. According to Greiner's model, in order to advance to the next phase of growth, an organization must successfully change in a way that solves the problem associated with the crisis (as cited in Jones, 2013). Similarly, crises will inevitably affect any of the ongoing functions of the collaboration productivity phase. These crises will lead to decline if they do not stimulate a change in strategy or structure (Jones, 2013). In this context, decline is defined as the life-cycle phase that occurs when there is a failure to "anticipate, recognize, avoid, neutralize, or adapt to external or internal pressures that threaten long-term survival" (Weitzel & Jonsson, 1989, p. 94).

In collaborations, external pressures arise from uncertainty in the environment. Sources of uncertainty include complexity, the number of different 'masters' being served; scope, the degree to which the environment is changing; and wealth, the amount of resources available, including both financial and human resources. Depending upon their purpose, collaborations can be fragile and susceptible to reductions in monetary support as well as participant enthusiasm and commitment. Reduction of financial resources is often the result of environmental atrophy that occurs when the capacity of the external environment to support the collaboration at traditional levels of activity erodes (Levine, 1978). Similarly, the collaborative may experience organizational atrophy, a condition caused by numerous factors, including role confusion, unclear assignment of responsibilities, high member turnover, and strict adherence to established routines despite the occurrence of new or changing problems.

Participant Changes

Contemporary literature on collaboration seems to reflect the competing views about its underlying motivators—classic liberalism, which places emphasis on private interests, and civic republicanism, which emphasizes a shared commitment to something larger than the individual actor (Thomson & Perry, 2006). Huxham (1996) posits that the self-interest motive is a critical requirement for a successful collaboration. He suggests that individuals must first justify their involvement in a collaboration by identifying how such involvement will facilitate achievement of personal or organizational goals. Downs (1967) noted survival ultimately depends on the ability to continually demonstrate that what is being accomplished is worthwhile to those with influence over necessary resources. In collaborations where participation is voluntary, continued vitality may also depend upon the extent to which accomplishments are deemed worthwhile by participants. Even if the core concerns continue to be relevant, other more critical issues or events may distract participants from the mission of the collaboration.

In the best-case scenario, collaboration decline occurs because the 'something larger,' or collective objective has been achieved. However, decline may also occur when individual actors believe their private interests are not being served, their concerns and opinions are not being heard, or because the individual passion for the collective objective diminishes. Stagnation and decline will also occur if the number of new participants is severely limited, creating what Downs (1967) referred to as the "Age Lump Phenomenon" (pp. 20–21). This occurs when a large proportion of the membership is comprised of individuals who joined during formation or high productivity. This "lump" of actors may become more conservative or complacent and be resistant to the changes necessary to continue the viability and productivity of the collaboration. A new group of "zealots" becomes critical to the survival of the organization; however the presence of the "age lump" may deter potential new members.

Conversely, in some instances, zealots who initially advocated for the creation of the collaboration and were fully involved in pursuing the vision choose to abandon the effort (Bauroth, 2008). This may be the result of disenchantment or disenfranchisement that occurs when new actors enter the collaborative and change becomes inevitable. Similarly, individuals attracted into the collaboration because of leadership charisma may withdraw if there is a change of leadership. This outflow of organizational memory may result in decline until the new and remaining participants are able to achieve the cohesion necessary to restart productivity.

Organizations may have difficulty responding to environmental changes due to "organizational inertia" or forces inside the organization that make it resistant to change (Jones, 2013, p. 355). One of the primary 'human' factors contributing to inertia is risk aversion—individuals or groups of individuals are unwilling to assume the uncertainty that accompanies change. This tendency to protect the status quo can multiply over time, bringing the productivity phase to a halt and ultimately leading to decline. At times, risk aversion is a manifestation of the desire to protect power and status (Jones, 2013) or maximize the potential for success by using only strategies with a history of success. These entities experiencing inertia may simply not have the ability to change strategy or structure quickly or easily enough to avoid (or reverse) decline.

Dissipation

It seems unlikely that collaborations have the ability to outlive all iterations of their usefulness. Some collaborations may fully dissolve simply because they have reached the end of their usefulness. The assigned work has been accomplished and the collective talents and abilities of the participants cannot be fitted to a new cause. Some subsets of the existing group may splinter away intact to join others in a new collaboration; however, the original ceases to exist. Tellioğlu's (2008) Collaboration Life Cycle is a model specific to collaboration among individuals with a common goal, providing a framework with a distinct "decomposition" or end phase. This phase will occur when the goals of the collaboration are achieved or members lose interest in the collaboration. It initially appears that with this model, dissipation is inevitable. However, a more detailed view provides opportunities at the Decomposition phase to "hold contact," sustaining the collaboration by preserving the participant network.

The Organizational Decline Model (Weitzel & Jonsson, 1989) discussed earlier concludes with Phase 5—Dissolution. Simply stated, if collaborations that have not purposefully concluded their work fail to adapt to changing environment, death is inevitable. If all efforts to reverse decline and rejuvenate the collaboration have been unsuccessful, internal stakeholders will begin to view their connection to the organization as temporary (Jones, 2013). Eventually external support and resources will be fully withdrawn and internal and external linkages will be severed.

Whether we apply the term 'dissipation,' 'dissolution,' or 'death,' this final phase of the life cycle is rarely abrupt and may, at times, not be truly 'final.' Downs (1967), for example, suggests that when a bureau's death coincides with some of its functions being absorbed by another agency, the bureau "continues to live after a fashion" (p. 22). Similarly, even though a collaborative fully dissolves because of lack of resources, participation, or attention, one or more of the actors may have residual interest in the issue or problem. Given the right environment, this spark could be rekindled into a new collaboration that is substantially similar to its predecessor, essentially restarting the life cycle.

Conclusion

The purpose of this chapter has been to explore the utility of organization theory in the study of collaboration. While an underlying premise of collaboration is a connection to network theory, there is much to be learned about collaboration through an organizational lens. Our use of Downs's (1967) life-cycle concept underscores this utility: although we do not yet have a great deal of evidence about the long-term viability of collaboration, there is ample evidence to suggest that such a lens can provide insights missing from the current approaches to the subject. As other chapters in this volume conclude, collaboration as a field of study is still somewhat in its infancy. Basic questions of definition are unsettled, and we have yet to discover a framework through which to view collaboration that seems to have utility across multiple settings. These conditions are not in and of themselves problematic in the short term, but they do suggest a distinct lack of theoretical development.

There are several implications that can be drawn from this chapter. First, a return to the 'roots' of organization theory may well be a fruitful exercise. If we are correct in our observation that collaboration eventually adopts characteristics more readily associated with traditional intraorganizational theory, then it makes sense that to apply some of these time-tested frameworks is likely to yield important insights into the nature of collaborative interactions. Second, it appears as though there may be a transition point at which collaboration morphs from an interorganizational interaction to an intraorganizational interaction. While the specific terms of that transition are beyond the scope of this paper, it seems likely that such transition happens in the growth portion of the life cycle, perhaps in the 'assembly and structure' or 'productivity' phases. As the collaborative structure begins to develop more regularized activity patterns and routines, it becomes more identifiable as a separate organization.

Relatedly, we suggest that an organization-based theory of collaboration will likely include elements of both interorganizational and intraorganizational theory. It is difficult to deny the interorganizational nature of collaboration, whether the collaboration is agency based or citizen based, or both (Moore & Koontz, 2003). The very nature of collaboration involves a multi-actor effort to address a wicked problem in which the participants share common goals (Morris et al., 2013). The existence of a wicked problem (Rittel & Webber, 1973) is critical, in that it provides justification for collective action. In the final analysis, the collective nature of the effort is, at its heart, an issue of interorganizational theory. The ways in which participants interact with each other in a complex interorganizational environment (Emery & Trist, 1965; Terreberry, 1968) is fundamentally the same question addressed in the collaboration literature. In the end, the difference is in the nature of interaction: while traditional interorganizational theory tends to treat the environment as highly competitive (see Lawrence & Lorsch, 1969;

Thompson, 1967), collaboration views the interactions as mutually supportive, interdependent, and communitarian in nature (Gray, 1989; Morris et al., 2013). At the same time, the routinization, structure, rules, processes, and outputs of collaboration suggest a natural tie to traditional intraorganizational theory. Although much of the traditional intraorganizational theory focuses on bureaucratic structures (see, for example, Downs, 1967), there is a body of literature that approaches the topics from less traditional premises (see Harmon & Mayer, 1986; Morgan, 2006). In the end, it may be that collaboration is much more akin to organic forms of organization.

Finally, our examination of the life-cycle model in a collaborative context suggests to us that such a model can be useful as a means to achieve a deeper understanding of the development, life, and eventual demise of collaborative efforts. Indeed, a life-cycle model provides a theoretical basis for the dissolution (or failure) of collaborative efforts, an area in which the field suffers from a notable lack of both theoretical and empirical work. While we know that collaboration does occasionally fail, we know little about the causes of failure. As a starting point in an effort to apply organization theory to collaboration, the life-cycle model is general enough to be readily adaptable to collaboration, yet it is detailed enough to provide direct and specific connections to existing models of collaboration. Ultimately, the utility of the life-cycle approach will need to be addressed through empirical study, and such study is the subject of future research.

Notes

1 Anthony Downs (1967) used the term "bureaus" to describe the public organizations that were the focus of his study. Because the term 'bureau' is less commonly used today, we employ the term 'organization' throughout this chapter, except in cases where we refer directly to Downs's original work.
2 David Easton (1965) conceived of the policy process as continual action, in which inputs feed into a process which in turn results in a series of outputs. These outputs serve to modify future demands, which thus feed back into the process as new inputs. This 'feedback' process results in an interaction that is cyclical and continuous.
3 Today, more than 100 organizations make up the coalition and help with restoring the Chesapeake Bay estuary system.

References

Adizes, I. (1979). Organizational passages: Diagnosing and treating lifecycle problems of organizations. *Organizational Dynamics*, 8(1), 3–25.
Agranoff, R. (2005). Managing collaborative performance: Changing the boundaries of the state? *Public Performance & Management Review*, 29(1), 18–45.
Agranoff, R., & McGuire. M. (2001). Big questions in public network management. *Journal of Public Administration Research and Theory*, 11(3), 295–326.
Agranoff, R., & McGuire. M. (2003). *Collaborative public management: New strategies for local governments*. Washington, DC: Georgetown University Press.

Aldrich, H. E. (1967). Resource dependence and interorganizational relations: Local employment service offices and social services sector organizations. *Administration & Society, 7*, 419–454.

Ansell, C., & Gash, A. (2007). Collaborative governance in theory and practice. *Journal of Public Administration Research and Theory, 18*, 543–571.

Bardach, E., & Lesser, C. (1996). Accountability in human services collaborative: For what? And to whom? *Journal of Public Administration Research and Theory, 6*(2), 197–224.

Bauroth, N. (2008). The life-cycle of special districts governments: A Downsian approach. *Paper presented at the annual meeting of the MPSA Annual National Conference, Palmer House Hotel, Hilton, Chicago, IL, published online.* Retrieved from http://citation.allacademic.com/meta/p268788_index.html.

Bryson, J., Crosby, B. C., & Stone, M. M. (2006). The design and implementation of cross-sector collaborations: Propositions from the literature. *Public Administration Review, 66*(Special Issue), 44–53.

Burns, M. (1982). Domain consensus in Alabama health systems: An empirical assessment. *Administration & Society, 14*(3), 319–342.

Burns, M., & Mauet, A. (1984). Administrative freedom for interorganizational action: A life-cycle interpretation. *Administration & Society, 16*, 289–305.

Cameron, K. S., & Whetten, D. A. (1981). Perceptions of organizational effectiveness over organizational life cycles. *Administrative Science Quarterly, 26*(4), 525–544.

Cameron, K. S., Whetten, D. A., & Kim, M. U. (1987). Organization dysfunctions of decline. *The Academy of Management Journal, 30*(1), 126–138.

Cohen, M. D., March, J. G., & Olsen, J. P. (1972). A garbage can model of organizational choice. *Administrative Science Quarterly, 17*(1), 1–25.

Dark, T. E., III. (2007). Organizational theory and phases of decline: The case of the AFL-CIO, 1955–2005. *International Journal of Organization Theory and Behavior, 10*(2), 213–244.

Downs, A. (1957). *An economic theory of democracy.* New York, NY: Harper & Row.

Downs, A. (1967). *Inside bureaucracy.* Boston, MA: Little, Brown.

Dunford, R. (1987). The suppression of technology as a strategy for controlling resource dependence. *Administrative Science Quarterly, 32*, 512–525.

Durham, J. W., & Smith, H. (1982). Toward a general theory of organizational deterioration. *Administration & Society, 14*, 373–400.

Easton, D. (1965). *A framework for political analysis.* Englewood Cliffs, NJ: Prentice Hall.

Emery F., & Trist, E. (1965). The causal texture of organization environments. *Human Relations, 18*, 21–32.

Gerlak, A. K., & Heikkila, T. (2011). Building a theory of learning in collaboratives: Evidence from the Everglades restoration program. *Journal of Public Administration Research and Theory, 21*, 619–644.

Gortner, H. F., Nichols, K. L., & Ball, C. (2007). *Organization theory: A public and nonprofit perspective* (3rd ed.). Belmont, CA: Wadsworth.

Gray, B. (1985). Conditions facilitating interorganizational collaboration. *Human Relations, 38*(10), 911–936.

Gray, B. (1989). *Collaborating: Finding common ground for multiparty problems.* San Francisco, CA: Jossey-Bass.

Greiner, L. E. (1972). Evolution and revolution as organizations grow. *Harvard Business Review, 4*, 37–46.

Harmon, M. M., & Mayer, R. T. (1986). *Organization theory for public administration.* Boston, MA: Little, Brown.

Heikkila, T., & Gerlak, A. (2005). The formation of large-scale collaborative resource management institutions: Clarifying the roles of stakeholders, science, and institutions. *Policy Studies Journal, 33,* 583–612.

Huxham, C. (Ed.). (1996). *Creating collaborative advantage.* Thousand Oaks, CA: Sage.

Jones, G. R. (2013). *Organizational theory, design, and change* (7th ed.). Upper Saddle River, NJ: Pearson.

Kaufman, H. (1991). *Time, chance, and organizations: Natural selection in a perilous environment* (2nd ed.). Chatham, NJ: Chatham House.

Koontz, T. M., & Thomas, C. W. (2006). What do we know and need to know about the environmental outcomes of collaborative management? *Public Administration Review, 66*(Special Issue), 111–121.

Lawrence, P. R., & Lorsch, J. W. (1969). *Organization and environment: Managing differentiation and integration.* Homewood, IL: R.D. Irwin.

Lester, D. L., Parnell, J. A., & Carraher, S. (2003). Organizational life cycle: A five-phase empirical scale. *International Journal of Organizational Analysis, 11*(4), 339–354.

Lester, D. L., Parnell, J. A., Crandall, W., & Menefee, M. L. (2008). Organizational life cycle and performance among SMEs: Generic strategies for high and low performers. *International Journal of Commerce and Management, 18*(4), 313–330.

Levine, C. H. (1978). Organizational decline and cutback management. *Public Administration Review, 38*(4), 316–325.

Lindblom, C. E. (1959). The science of "muddling through." *Public Administration Review, 19*(2), 79–88.

McCurdy, H. (1991). Organizational decline: NASA and the life cycle of bureaus. *Public Administration Review, 51*(4), 308–315.

Mandell, M. (Ed.). (2001). *Getting results through collaboration: Networks and network structures for public policy and management.* Westport, CT: Quorum Books.

Meier, K. J., & O'Toole, L. J. (2004). Desperately seeking Selznick: Cooptation and the dark side of public management in networks. *Public Administration Review, 64*(6), 681–693.

Moore, E., & Koontz, T. (2003). A typology of collaborative watershed groups: Citizen-based, agency-based, and mixed partnerships. *Society and Natural Resources, 16*(5), 451–460.

Morgan, G. (2006). *Images of organization.* Thousand Oaks, CA: Sage.

Morris, J. C., & Burns, M. (1997). Rethinking the interorganizational environments of public organizations. *Southeastern Political Review, 25*(1), 3–25.

Morris, J. C., Gibson, W. A., Leavitt, W. M., & Jones, S. C. (2013). *The case for grassroots collaboration: Social capital and ecosystem restoration at the local level.* Lanham, MD: Lexington Books.

Nutt, P. C., & Backoff, R. W. (1995). Strategy for public and third-sector organizations. *Journal of Public Administration Research & Theory, 5,* 189–211.

Nystrom, P. C., & Starbuck, W. H. (1984). To avoid organizational crises, unlearn. *Organizational Dynamics, 12*(4), 53–65.

Ostrom, E. (1990). *Governing the commons: The evolution of institutions of collective action.* New York, NY: Cambridge University Press.

196   C. M. *Williams et al.*

Policy Consensus Initiative. (2014, July 14). *What is collaboration governance?* Retrieved from http://policyconsensus.org/publicsolutions/ps_1.html.

Purdy, J. (2012). A framework for assessing power in collaborative governance processes. *Public Administration Review, 72*(3), 409–417.

Quinn, R. E., & Cameron, K. (1983). Organizational lifecycles and shifting criteria of effectiveness: Some preliminary evidence. *Management Science, 29*(1), 33–51.

Raelin, J. A. (1982). A policy output model of interorganizational relations. *Organizational Studies, 3*, 243–267.

Randolph, J., & Bauer, M. R. (1999). Improving environmental decision-making through collaborative methods. *Policy Studies Review, 16*(3/4), 168–191.

Rittel, H. W. J., & Webber, M. (1973). Dilemmas in a general theory of planning. *Policy Sciences, 4*, 155–169.

Rogers, E., & Weber, E. P. (2010). Thinking harder about outcomes for collaborative governance arrangements. *American Review of Public Administration, 40*(5), 546–567.

Sabatier, P. A., Focht, W., Lubell, M., Trachtenberg, Z., Vedlitz, A., & Matlock, M. (Eds). (2005). *Swimming upstream: Collaborative approaches to watershed management*. Cambridge, MA: MIT Press.

Schopler, J. (1987). Interorganizational groups: Origins, structure, and outcomes. *Academy of Management Review, 12*, 702–713.

Simon, H. A. (1956). Rational choice and the structure of the environment. *Psychological Review, 63*(2), 129–138.

Tellioğlu, H. (2008, May). Collaboration life cycle. In W. K. McQuay & W. W. Smari (Co-chairs), *2008 International symposium on collaborative technologies and systems*. Symposium conducted at the meeting of Collaborative Technologies and Systems in Irvine, CA.

Terreberry, S. (1968). The evolution of organizational environments. *Administrative Science Quarterly, 12*, 590–613.

Thompson, J. D. (1967). *Organizations in action: Social bases of administrative theory*. New York, NY: McGraw Hill.

Thomson, A., & Perry, J. (2006). Collaboration processes: Inside the black box. *Public Administration Review, 66*(Special Issue), 20–32.

Waste, R. J. (1983). The early years in the life cycle of city councils: A Downsian analysis. *Urban Studies, 20*(1), 73–81.

Weitzel, W., & Jonsson, E. (1989). Decline in organizations: A literature integration and extension. *Administrative Science Quarterly, 34*(1), 91–109.

Whetten, D. A. (1987). Organizational growth and decline processes. *Annual Review of Sociology, 13*, 335–358.

Wood, D. J., & Gray, B. (1991). Toward a comprehensive theory of collaboration. *Journal of Applied Behavioral Science, 27*(2), 139–162.

Part III
Collaboration in Action

10 Nonprofit Collaborative Advocacy

An Exploratory Study of State Nonprofit Associations

Jason S. Machado, Katrina Miller-Stevens, and Stephanie Joannou Menefee

Introduction

The nonprofit sector has witnessed tremendous growth over the last 60 years as nonprofit organizations have responded to a growing movement to reduce citizen dependence on government provision of public goods and services (Berry & Arons, 2003; Salamon, 2002). In this effort, many nonprofit organizations have established an influential position in the formulation of public policies and have taken on the role of advocate for those less fortunate (Child & Grønbjerg, 2007). As a result, nonprofit organizations have a complex relationship with policymakers and deep stakes in the formulation and implementation of public policies (Child & Grønbjerg, 2007).

To become successful in the policy arena, Berry and Arons (2003) argue nonprofit organizations must strengthen their organizational resources while building collaborations with other organizations in the public and nonprofit sectors. While Berry and Arons (2003) emphasize collaboration for the purpose of influencing public policy, most studies on nonprofit collaboration focus on the benefits and motivations of collaborative efforts to improve service delivery and program outcomes (Selden, Sowa, & Sandfort, 2006). Sowa (2009) argues that nonprofit organizations participate in collaborative activities with other organizations to benefit the program "services being delivered and the organizations as a whole" (p. 1006). Collaboration improves service delivery by leveraging resources and knowledge to mitigate resource and institutional pressures; whereas organizational-level benefits include prolonging survival, achieving legitimacy, and improving strategic positions (Sowa, 2009). The benefits of collaboration are derived directly from motivations, with solved problems, shared norms, and a sustained alliance all being desired outcomes of collaboration and indicators of a successful effort (Wood & Gray, 1991).

Additional studies show that an organization's need to acquire resources, leverage new ideas and expertise, and satisfy institutional pressures to maximize dollars are also significant motivations for nonprofit organizations to participate in collaboration (Sowa, 2009). Government mandate of collaboration, either as a way to increase an organization's strengths, as a decreed duplication of services, or as an increased measure in evaluation, has shown to be not only a method of classification of collaboration types, but also a key motivation for why organizations participate in collaboration (Leroux & Goerdel, 2009).

Shifting from the trends of program outcomes and motivations in research on nonprofit collaboration, this study focuses on the organizational resources necessary to participate in collaboration and how these resources impact collaborative advocacy activities. Specifically, we seek to identify whether organizational characteristics impact the likelihood of a nonprofit organization to collaborate with nonprofit or public-sector organizations to lobby or advocate for public policy issues, and whether this method of collaboration is perceived as effective. The chapter is included as an exemplar in the third part of this volume in that it illustrates an advocacy organization's use of collaboration as a tool to help advance specific public policy goals. Nonprofit organizations are an integral and influential part of the policy process, and the chapter provides a resource for executive directors interested in adopting collaboration as an advocacy and lobbying tool.

The chapter is divided into six sections. First, we begin with a discussion of research on collaboration in the nonprofit context. This discussion then transitions into a discussion of the barriers to nonprofit advocacy. Next, nonprofit collaborative activities, nonprofit advocacy and lobbying, and organizational characteristics leading to nonprofit advocacy are defined and explored. Fourth, the methodology introduces state nonprofit associations and their relevance to this study, in addition to the methods for data collection and analysis. Fifth, results of the analysis are discussed exploring the relationships between the likelihood to participate in collaborative activities when engaging in advocacy, organizational characteristics, and the perceived effectiveness of this tactic. We conclude by noting the contributions of the study to the larger body of nonprofit research and practitioners in the field.

Defining Collaboration from a Nonprofit Context

Nonprofit organizations are increasingly using collaboration as a tool to tackle complex problems (Guo & Acar, 2005; Morris, Gibson, Leavitt, & Jones, 2013). Catalysts for collaborative efforts include resource dependency, shared education, values, and coordinated strategic decision-making (Nicholson-Crotty, 2009). A significant amount of research exists on what motivates nonprofit organizations to engage in collaboration, including the benefits that can be gained at both the organizational and program levels (Leroux & Goerdel, 2009; Mulroy & Shay, 1998), as well as the multiple barriers these organizations face when entering into a collaboration (Snavely & Tracy, 2000). Empirical studies on trends of privatization, federalism, and contracting between the nonprofit and public sectors are plentiful, but research exploring nonprofit collaboration is less abundant. Of the studies on nonprofit collaboration that do exist, many focus on addressing the organizational motives to participate, defining the makeup of the collaboration, and explaining the purpose of the nonprofit collaboration.

However, there is still much to be discovered about the use and value of collaboration and how it relates to delivering information to the general public and policymakers. The possibility is explored in this chapter that collaboration could be helpful for increasing prevalence and efficacy of advocacy programs. First, an understanding of collaboration's many interpretations, motivations, and barriers is essential for practitioners and researchers exploring the impact of nonprofit organizations on public policy. It is necessary to understand the nuances of nonprofit collaboration in order to identify the potential value added to advocacy efforts.

Defining collaboration has proven to be an elusive task for researchers as such a definition must "encompass all observable forms and exclude[s] irrelevant issues" (Wood & Gray, 1991, p. 143). Furthermore, the diversity of types, participants, and benefits of collaboration prove defining the term to be a difficult endeavor. Collaboration can be defined along a number of axes, including degrees of resource-sharing, objectives of the collaboration, and degrees of formality.

For example, Selden et al. (2006) note that collaboration occurs when organizations share "resources, authority and rewards" and through "integrating staff, joint planning or joint budgeting" (p. 414). In a nonprofit collaboration, decision-making responsibilities and ownership of the outcomes will be shared (Guo & Acar, 2005). This sharing of financial responsibilities, staff time, and organizational and community level rewards will influence the implementation and results of the collaboration (Sowa, 2008).

Nonprofit collaboration is also defined by examining the objective of the collaboration, such as a particular program, problem, issue, or client that is being served or addressed (Selden et al., 2006). The activities undertaken by a collaboration can define a nonprofit collaboration, where organizations partake in client referral, information-sharing, strategizing on problems, and devising procedures for serving each other (Guo & Acar, 2005; Murray, 1998; Snavely & Tracy, 2000).

Another distinguishing characteristic of nonprofit collaboration is the degree of formality of the collaboration, which can be determined by institutional factors like mandating contracts and grants or by government order (Smith, 2007), as well as an organization's interdependence with other members of the collaborative alliance (Guo & Acar, 2005). Guo and Acar (2005) offer a typology of nonprofit collaboration based on level of formality that includes eight variations. Formal collaboration types include joint programs, parent subsidiaries, joint venture, and mergers; whereas informal variations include information-sharing, referral of clients, sharing of office space, and management service organizations (Guo & Acar, 2005). Resource sufficiency and institutional factors have been explored as driving forces of whether an organization is more likely to involve itself in a formal or informal collaboration (Guo & Acar, 2005). Guo and Acar (2005) found formal nonprofit collaboration most likely occurs when an organization is old, has a large budget, receives government funds but has few other revenue streams, has broad linkages, and is not in education or social services.

Many scholars argue that organizational relationships exist on a continuum varying from informal to multiple levels of formality, established by process functions and degree of resource-sharing (Selden et al., 2006; Sowa, 2008; McNamara, 2012). As Selden et al. (2006) explain, on one end of the continuum is cooperation, distinguished by having at its core personal relationships and informal arrangements that act as the cohesion between organizations. Coordination is further along the continuum, where organizations "make an effort to calibrate their actions" while maintaining independence; while at the other end of the spectrum exists service integration, where organizations work together to provide services to mutual clients (Selden et al., 2006, p. 414).

As indicated by this brief discussion of nonprofit collaboration, and as outlined in previous chapters of this book, collaboration is a difficult concept to define. Within the realm of nonprofit organizations, definitions of collaboration often center on program- or client-specific outcomes or on the formality of the collaboration. We shift our attention now from program-oriented definitions of nonprofit collaboration to an action-oriented approach of nonprofit collaboration—that of collaborative activities of nonprofit organizations for the purposes of advocacy and lobbying.

Barriers to Nonprofit Advocacy

Although the opportunity exists for nonprofits to engage in advocacy efforts, and there are clearly significant benefits, why is there still a tendency for some nonprofit organizations to avoid advocacy? It can be argued that the legal, resource, and institutional obstacles that exist can be too intimidating (Boris & Krehely, 2002).

There have been several attempts by the U.S. government to reduce the potential and power of nonprofit advocacy, most notably with the Istook Amendment in 1995. Understandably there is friction between the notion that nonprofit organizations are subsidized by tax dollars, especially 501(c)3 organizations with their additional privilege of donations being exempted to the donor, and their role in influencing public policy (Kimberlin, 2010). It is notably plausible considering that many nonprofits often have a narrow constituent base, and serve very specific interests, although designated appropriately as a type of service provider—such as for education, civic, or health purposes for example. The Istook Amendment would have prohibited receipt of federal funds, like grants, if the nonprofit spent more than 5% of its privately garnered funds on political activity (Bass, Arons, Guinane & Carter, 2007; Kimberlin, 2010). The amendment was ultimately defeated; however, its introduction has certainly brought increased attention to the issue.

Concerns about losing nonprofit status because of engaging in lobbying activities can be common among nonprofit executives. Many nonprofit executives have trouble linking advocacy efforts to their mission, which is of utmost importance in nonprofit organizations (Bass et al., 2007). Mission creep, mission drift and mission disobedience are all errors that are punishable with losing tax exemption status. Such a hurdle can be mitigated with increased manager innovation and knowledge of legal and organizational standards (Bass et al., 2007; Kimberlin, 2010).

Resource dependency theory helps to explain both propensities and barriers for nonprofit organizations to engage in advocacy efforts (Bass et al., 2007; Salamon, 1995). Nonprofit organizations receiving government funding see an opportunity to receive more funding if they advocate more. Those nonprofit organizations that receive government funding could also be more enamored of the democratic system where they are empowered to advocate for their own benefit. With such an understanding of the system and passion for participation, they could be more likely to engage in advocacy (Salamon, 1995).

Yet there has been conflicting research in recent years on the influence of funding on advocacy programs. Significant and extensive studies by researchers such as Bass et al. (2007) have found that the data can be inconsistent. Bass et al. (2007) and Chaves, Stephens, and Galaskiewicz (2004) found a negative relationship among the amount of funding received from government grants and an organization's advocacy participation, primarily due to fear of attracting negative attention and losing those grants. However, Bass et al. (2007) also found that the amount an organization engages in advocacy increases with the amount of government funding, possibly explained by the increased political capacity of large staffed and large budgeted organizations.

Conversely, Child and Grønbjerg (2007) would argue that funding sources are not an obstacle. The data from their 2007 profile of the Indiana nonprofit sector yielded that there is no statistically significant relationship between government funding and willingness to advocate. Furthering the variance, Schmid, Bar, and Nirel (2008) found that among nonprofits in Israel the source of funding does play a role, as government grants motivate an organization's conformity to policies, serving as an obstacle to advocacy. Although research on the role of funding sources and the types of advocacy nonprofits engage in is more limited, Mosley (2011) found that government funding leads healthcare service nonprofit providers to insider tactics, because of greater access to decision-makers and increased legitimacy due to the source of their funds. Such data would lend itself then to the notion that collaboration could be a potential mitigation tool when funding sources are inhibiting participation in advocacy, because the many partners would diversify and dilute the presence of any restricting agents.

Nonprofits also suffer from lack of institutional knowledge when deciding to engage in advocacy. Advocacy, and more specifically lobbying, requires interacting with a highly professionalized and experienced institution of public policy (Mosley, 2011). Engaging in advocacy requires an understanding of how laws are made at the local, state, and federal levels, as well as an understanding of how to influence people. This can be prohibitive and overwhelming if nonprofit advocates lack an understanding of how to write letters, form memos, galvanize constituents, organize press conferences, and build coalitions (Bass et al., 2007). Lack of such technical skills and training can be a serious impediment for nonprofit organizations engaging in advocacy.

Bureaucratization can also be an impediment, as increased structure and boundaries can decrease innovation in marginalized communities, and they will resort to more conventional approaches and avoid advocacy (Leroux & Goerdel, 2009). The lack of trained staff can lead some organizations to make use of their publics for advocacy efforts, however direct service organizations often are reluctant to use clients to advocate as they feel clients should be served, not utilized (Donaldson, 2008; Kimberlin, 2010).

Collaborating with public, private, and nonprofit sector organizations offers nonprofits a way to overcome these barriers. Thus, collaborative advocacy is an attractive option when nonprofit organizations want to lobby or advocate with the intent of influencing public policy.

Nonprofit Collaborative Advocacy

The nonprofit literature suggests a number of motivations for nonprofit advocacy of public policy issues. A wide variety of nonprofit organizations participate in advocacy efforts to accomplish legislative goals (Mulroy & Shay, 1998). Ferris (1998) and Reid (2000) note that nonprofit organizations advocate in the interest of influencing agenda-setting, policy design, implementation, and evaluation of public policies. Berry and Arons (2003) suggest nonprofit organizations advocate to pursue, defeat, or protect important social programs that benefit society. Child and Grønbjerg (2007) note nonprofit organizations advocate in the interest of supporting, changing, or preventing laws impacting the nonprofit sector. Finally, Nicholson-Crotty (2007) states nonprofit organizations advocate in the interest of building rapport with legislators. Motivation to take on the sometimes daunting but potentially rewarding objective of advocacy to achieve these goals is widespread and often made more inviting by the appeal of collaboration (Leroux & Goerdel, 2009).

Nonprofit organizations often adapt to—and challenge—changing political environments by collaborating with one another, even though they may differ in their resource base, geography, history, and social concerns of target populations (Mulroy & Shay, 1998; Reid, 2000). Connections within the political environment can enable nonprofit organizations to be better positioned for advancing their own political goals when the opportunity arises. Organizations that have collaborated on non-advocacy programs are likely to use those established network connections in future advocacy efforts. For example, health service nonprofit providers are often mandated by government to work with other public and nonprofit agencies to achieve program goals. It is these benefits awarded by collaboration that nonprofit organizations can make use of to mitigate the barriers to engaging in advocacy.

Nonprofit organizations that work and share resources with other organizations to influence public policy or the political environment are said to be engaging in collaborative advocacy. Collaborative advocacy includes any advocacy activity undertaken by multiple organizations in a planned and concerted manner. It is possible that collaborative advocacy can increase funds, knowledge, potential for program success, organizational profile, and organizational legitimacy through the sharing of resources. Organizations that might not otherwise be motivated to, or capable of, engaging in advocacy programs can find additional options to do so by collaborating with other partners, whether from the nonprofit sector, government agencies, or private business. The potential benefits to collaborative advocacy are increased efficiency, cost-effectiveness, new funding sources, and greater legitimacy (Takahashi & Smutny, 2002). However, the process can often be intimidating, keeping nonprofit organizations out of the advocacy arena. The potential challenges to collaborative advocacy are territorial issues, addressing differences, expanding communication, coping with tensions and power relations, maintaining accountability, identifying appropriate representation, and the time spent establishing and maintaining collaborations (Takahashi & Smutny, 2002).

Despite the growing practice of collaborative advocacy, very little empirical research focuses on barriers in the nonprofit context (Foss & Nielsen, 2012). Additionally, while the importance of collaboration among nonprofit organizations has been recognized in the nonprofit literature, studies examining the perceived effectiveness of collaborative advocacy have been aperiodic over the last two decades. Further, the theories that do exist in the literature habitually do not take into consideration the generalization of those theories to a broader context, which leads to predicting and testing at a level that does not correspond with the intention of the original theory (Foss & Nielsen, 2012).

While we want to stay away from such generalizations, we can say that on a broader scale, rather than seeing potential challenges to collaborative advocacy as barriers, research is framing them as "facilitating factors" (Israel, Schulz, Parker, & Becker, 1998). This viewpoint could be a good application for nonprofit collaborative advocacy. For example, one method of overcoming tensions, power relations, and maintaining accountability may be to develop working standards that promote open communication (Israel et al., 1998). As Gray (1989) states, "Collaboration operates on the premise that the assumptions disputants have about the other side and about the nature of the issues themselves are worth testing" (p. 13). Thus, any collaborative advocacy effort as a whole should be prepared to work through any perceived barriers to goal attainment in favor of the idea that casting aside any limited and preconceived notions could lead to a greater outcome than any of the collaborators envisioned. Because research linking organizational characteristics and the likelihood to participate in collaborative advocacy are limited (Miller-Stevens & Gable, 2012), we seek to explore this tactic to inform leaders of nonprofit organizations of the strengths and weaknesses of collaborative advocacy as a tool to disseminate information and influence public policy.

Advocacy Versus Lobbying

Before we can speak to the link between organizational characteristics and advocacy in nonprofit organizations, we must define two often-interchanged terms in the nonprofit literature: advocacy and lobbying. First, we address the definition of 'advocacy.' Advocacy is defined as:

> an attempt, having a greater than zero probability of success, by an individual or group, to influence another individual or group to make a decision that would not have been made otherwise and that concerns the welfare of interests of a third party who is in a less powerful status than the decision maker.
>
> (Sosin & Caulum, 1983, p. 13)

Advocacy includes any activity or tool used by an organization to inform the general public of its mission, program goals, or stance on a public policy issue.

In contrast, lobbying includes the use of direct or grassroots tactics targeted to influence an elected official or an elected official's staff members on a specific law. The Internal Revenue Service regulates nonprofit organizations to deter them from spending a "substantial part" of their overall budget on activities involving "carrying on propaganda, or otherwise attempting, to influence legislation" (Internal Revenue Service (IRS), Measuring Lobbying: Substantial Part Test, 2014).[1] Nonprofit organizations are allowed to spend portions of their budget on lobbying activities based on this substantial part test, but if they do not adhere to these IRS regulations they may lose their tax-exempt status. With looming penalties from the IRS like excise taxes and losing tax-exempt status, it is understandable that nonprofit organizations are cautious to engage in lobbying activities (Ruggiano & Taliaferro, 2012). However, there are many ways to engage in advocacy that do not involve the direct influence of legislation. For example, educational meetings and materials are considered advocacy, yet not considered lobbying—and therefore any spending on these types of activities does not threaten a nonprofit's tax-exempt status.

This study refers to both advocacy and lobbying within the broader context of tactics used to influence public policy. Although we do not believe the two words should be used interchangeably, we recognize that in much of the nonprofit literature the two words are used in tandem because lobbying is one subset of activities under the larger umbrella of advocacy. Thus, we turn to a discussion of nonprofit advocacy and the organizational characteristics that may influence a nonprofit organization to participate in lobbying or advocacy activities.

Organizational Characteristics and Nonprofit Advocacy

Organizational characteristics have also been addressed within the context of nonprofit advocacy. Results have conflicted as to whether larger staff and budget size have an impact on a nonprofit organization's decision to participate in advocacy activities (Child & Grønbjerg, 2007; McNutt & Boland, 1999; Rees, 1999). Other studies have found that more advanced technological equipment in an organization impacts participation in advocacy efforts (Child & Grønbjerg, 2007; McNutt & Boland, 1999), whereas organizational age does not (Rees, 1999). The size of a nonprofit organization, number of members, and operational budget are also found to have an impact on how often advocacy tactics are used (Mellinger & Kolomer, 2013; Rees, 1999). Organizational structure, learning, resource dependence, and resource competiveness are also found to contribute to nonprofit organizations' willingness to participate in advocacy activities (Leroux & Goerdel, 2009).

While these studies have highlighted the organizational characteristics that are attributed to participation in advocacy from a broader context, there is still much to be learned about a nonprofit organization's participation in collaboration for advocacy purposes. Overall, a variety of direct and indirect tactics are available to nonprofit organizations that choose to engage in advocacy activities, and collaboration is one of these tactics (Burstein, 1998; Mosley, 2011). Thus, it is the aim of this research to determine whether the use of collaboration in nonprofit advocacy can be determined by organizational characteristics, and whether this tactic is perceived as effective at influencing the public and policymakers.

Methodology

This study employs a mixed-methods approach including a survey and follow-up interviews. We explore state nonprofit associations that are members of the National Council of Nonprofits. At the time of this study, 40 state nonprofit associations were members of the National Council of Nonprofits with a collective membership of over 24,000 nonprofit organizations (National Council of Nonprofits (NCN), 2010). The National Council of Nonprofits represents its membership of state nonprofit associations on a national level, whereas state nonprofit associations represent their nonprofit members on a state or local level (NCN, 2014). State nonprofit associations reflect the parent organization's goal of "promoting the interests of the nonprofit community and ensuring a seat at the table on all policy initiatives that impact the nonprofit sector" and "actively participat[ing] in coalitions and public policy campaigns at the state and national levels" (NCN, 2014). The associations participate in advocacy activities to represent their membership on a diverse selection of policy and advocacy concerns at the national, state, and local levels including such issues as legislation on lobbying reform, the rights of nonprofit organizations to communicate and interact with elected or appointed officials, supporting tax incentives for charitable giving, seeking to influence regulatory activities of state and federal agencies that have a monitoring function over the nonprofit sector, or laws that regulate procurement issues of the nonprofit sector. Thus, state nonprofit associations are of particular interest to scholars and practitioners exploring collaboration and advocacy activities. It should be noted, however, that because state nonprofit associations are specifically designed to represent a group of organizations, the associations may be more inclined to engage in collaborative activities. This may be considered a limitation of the study because responses to the survey and interview questions may be biased.

Questions for the survey were adopted from three previously administered surveys related to interest group and nonprofit advocacy and lobbying, including McNutt and Boland's (1999) survey of social work associations' use of advocacy strategies, Berry and Arons's (2003) survey of nonprofit organizations' impacts on political participation, and Wilson's (1981) survey of interest groups' use of advocacy strategies in the federal policy arena. The survey instrument asked participants to report on organizational characteristics, including age of the organization, number of total paid staff and volunteers, number of paid staff and volunteers working on policy and advocacy activities, annual operating expense budget, and percentage of overall budget and time spent on policy activities, in addition to each associations' frequency of use and perceived effectiveness of 48 lobbying and advocacy tactics over the period of 2008–2009. This chapter focuses on organizational characteristics of the state nonprofit associations and questions related to frequency of use and perceived effectiveness of collaborative advocacy activities.

The survey was sent to 138 staff members identified by their rank, title, and position description as noted on each state nonprofit organization's website. Surveys were sent by mail and electronically to individuals identified as working on policy or advocacy issues for the organization with an average of three surveys sent to each association. Because most state nonprofit associations have a small paid staff ranging from three to 32 individuals, the number of participants in the study is limited. Forty-seven of the 138 distributed surveys were returned equaling a 34% response rate. The small number of completed surveys may be considered a limitation of the study, however 26 (65%) of the 40 state nonprofit associations are represented in the sample.

Descriptive statistics were run to determine similarities and differences between the organizational characteristics of the state nonprofit associations, to describe the prevalence of use of collaborative activities, and to determine the perceived effectiveness of this tactic. Survey data were also analyzed using chi-square statistics to determine relationships between the variables of organizational characteristics and use and perceived effectiveness of collaboration as an advocacy tactic. Statistical significance of the chi-square was determined using an alpha level of significance of 0.05, thus p-values below 0.05 were considered significant. Because the sample size is small, a median split was run to dichotomize the independent and dependent variables into categorical variables for chi-square bivariate analyses. This statistical approach is commonly used by social science researchers to simplify continuous variables (MacCallum, Zhang, Preacher, & Rucker, 2002).

Follow-up interviews were conducted to gain a more in-depth understanding of the organizational characteristics of the state nonprofit associations, the circumstances in which state nonprofit associations participate in collaboration for advocacy purposes, and the perceived effectiveness of their participation as an advocacy tactic. The interviews were semi-structured and conducted over the telephone. Each interview lasted approximately 20–40 minutes. Follow-up interviews asked participants to elaborate on the ways they used collaboration as an advocacy tactic, their perceived effectiveness of this tactic, whether their operational budget, organizational age, or number of employees have an impact on the strategies the organization chooses to use for lobbying and advocacy activities. Of the 47 individuals who responded to the survey, 13 agreed to participate in a follow-up interview representing 11 state nonprofit associations. The interviews were transcribed for template analysis following King's (2004) method for coding interviews.

Results

Unlike previous research exploring organizational characteristics and participation in nonprofit advocacy, the analyses did not reveal a significant relationship between participation in collaborative activities and age of an organization, number of total paid staff and volunteers, number of paid staff and volunteers working on policy activities, or percentage of overall budget spent on policy activities. However, a significant relationship was found between overall annual expense budget and participation in collaborative advocacy activities ($\chi^2 = 3.93$, $df = 1$, $N = 26$, $p = 0.047$), in which associations with annual expense budgets greater than $500,000 are more likely to participate in a collaboration with the goal to advocate to the general public and policymakers than those with budgets less than or equal to $500,000. These results are surprising in that, aside from annual budget size, organizational characteristics appear to have no impact on whether a state nonprofit association chooses to collaborate for advocacy purposes.

When comparing the 48 tactics listed in the survey, results show that joining coalitions or government relations committees (collaborative advocacy activities) is the second most frequently used lobbying and advocacy tactic of state nonprofit associations with a rating of often, but not ongoing.[2] As Table 10.1 indicates, all but one of the remaining lobbying and advocacy tactics are used sometimes but not often—or less—including tactics such as encouraging board members to contact policymakers, emailing legislators and their staff members, having personal meetings with legislators, or inviting legislators to speak at a public event. These results indicate a strong reliance on collaborative advocacy to disseminate information to the general public and lawmakers.

Results of the interviews indicate state nonprofit associations participate in both short- and long-term collaborations with other nonprofit and public-sector organizations. A short-term collaboration may be formed around a specific policy issue with a limited purpose. For example, one respondent explains her state nonprofit association collaborates with other nonprofit and public organizations to address short term funding issues in her respective state, such as HIV/AIDS or teen pregnancy programs, that are facing state budget cuts in a particular year. Another respondent provides an example of participating in short-term collaborations formed for the 2010 census. These collaborations attempt to educate other nonprofit organizations and the public on the importance of the 2010 census and how the census impacts policy issues in that particular state.

State nonprofit associations also participate in long-term collaborations formed to educate the public, nonprofit organizations, and elected officials on ongoing policy issues. For example, one state nonprofit association joined a coalition in 2003 that addresses fiscal and economic issues impacting the nonprofit sector. Because these fiscal and economic issues are not yet resolved, the coalition continues to exist to educate and advocate on behalf of the nonprofit sector's economic concerns. Another state nonprofit association participates in a collaboration focused on voter registration issues. The collaboration is ongoing and meets actively during election years, but only occasionally during non-election years.

Overall, results of the interviews indicate state nonprofit associations primarily participate in collaborative activities for the purposes of advocacy when a policy issue is impacting the nonprofit sector as a whole within that association's respective state, and in general the collaborations address non-partisan issues. The collaborations vary in size, and they may include business organizations or other advocacy groups that bring an element of expertise to the table.

Participants of the survey were also asked to report their perceived effectiveness of joining coalitions or government relations committees (collaborative advocacy activities) to influence the public and policymakers on policy issues. The tactic rates the fourth highest in perceived effectiveness when compared to the other 48 lobbying and advocacy strategies, after having personal meetings with legislators, inviting legislators to speak at a

Table 10.1 Twenty Most Frequently Used Tactics for Lobbying and Advocacy Purposes

Tactic	Frequency of Use[1]		Tactic	Frequency of Use[1]	
	Mean	SD		Mean	SD
1. Email members of your association	3.56	(0.68)	11. Contact legislators through written letters	2.34	(1.20)
2. Join coalitions or government relations committees of nonprofit organizations	3.10	(1.07)	12. Write press releases for major local newspaper (print or online)	2.29	(1.08)
3. Encourage board of directors to contact policymakers	2.89	(1.10)	13. Hire consultant or staff member to conduct media relations	2.27	(1.50)
4. Have personal meetings with legislators	2.74	(1.26)	14. Contact legislators by telephone	2.19	(1.21)
5. Contact staff members of legislators through email	2.73	(1.33)	15. Testify at legislative or administrative hearings	2.16	(1.50)
6. Contact legislators through email	2.66	(1.08)	16. Mail newsletters/pamphlets to members of your organization to encourage them to contact policymakers	2.05	(1.75)
7. Contact staff members of legislators by telephone	2.46	(1.35)	17. Create blogging website for community networking	2.03	(1.53)
8. Have personal meetings with staff of legislators	2.43	(1.22)	18. Contact other elected officials and/or their staff members by email	2.01	(1.10)
9. Develop community networks (Facebook or MySpace)	2.35	(1.48)	19. Have personal meetings with other elected officials and/or their staff	1.88	(1.25)
10. Invite legislators to speak at an event/public meeting sponsored by your organization	2.35	(1.25)	20. Invite other elected officials and/or their staff to speak at a public event/public meeting sponsored by your organization	1.79	(1.15)

Note
1 Scale of Frequency of Use: 4 = Ongoing; 3 = Often, but not ongoing; 2 = Sometimes, but not often; 1 = Infrequently; 0 = Never.

212 J. S. Machado et al.

public event sponsored by the association, and testifying at legislative or administrative hearings.

While the majority of interviewees remark that collaboration is an effective tactic, a number of concerns are addressed in the interviews. For example, one respondent remarks that coalitions "may have effectiveness reaching and influencing the [lobbyist, legislator, or public], but there may not be success at actually passing the bill." A second respondent notes concerns of partisanship. The majority of state nonprofit associations consider their organizations as general issue organizations, and they do not want to be viewed as partisan or focused on one issue over another. Concerns of partisanship may cause tension between members of a coalition when the members are deciding what role the group should take on when advocating for a policy issue. A third respondent expresses concern in defining roles within coalitions. In an illustration of the tension that can arise between collaborative members regarding role definitions, the respondent states members of the coalition must ask:

> What is going to be the duration of the [coalition] coming together ... what is the common ground that they can advocate for because many partners might have some differing positions on things, [and then] honing down to what we can all agree on and advance as a coalition, and [finally] what do we need to do individually in [the coalition].

One additional respondent expresses her frustration working in collaboration with other organizations by saying:

> Nonprofit organizations do not collaborate well together because they oftentimes do not understand what collaboration means and they think they are going to get infected by their neighbor's baggage. So, let's say I'm coming to the table with an agenda, but we only want to collaborate on one point of it. One organization may not be willing to collaborate with the other organization because they are not on the same page morally [or] ethically. They are always looking at the broader picture and they want to be perfect—there's a lack of pragmatism there. So policy coalitions are difficult and that makes working with policy coalitions very challenging and tedious—labor intensive— but it's essential because charities are not at the table early enough in the planning process [of public policies] to become an integral part of the planning. We are always an afterthought [of legislators].

Clearly there is an interesting paradox in state nonprofit associations' decisions to participate in collaborative advocacy activities. The tactic is commonly used and is perceived as effective, but there are no measures in place to determine the actual impacts of the tactic. Issues of effectiveness merit further discussion in future studies.

Discussion

This study seeks to explore the perceived effectiveness of nonpr⟨ oration as a lobbying and advocacy tactic. Findings suggest state associations are dedicated to their organizations' missions of pa⌐ᵤ.ᵢₚₐ.ᵢₙₕ in advocacy to further the nonprofit sector's policy agenda, and they often engage in both short- and long-term collaborative activities with other organizations to achieve those goals.

Interviews yielded that state nonprofit associations make decisions on whether to participate in short-term policy collaborations based on the duration of pressing advocacy issues. When a specific policy is targeted—whether for approval, defeat, or revision—short-term collaboration is often the tactic of choice. Advocacy efforts involving long-term collaboration are also used, although not as often, to address issues involving multiple policies that are concurrent, interrupted, or even lack a specific legislative agenda such as the previously noted coalitions formed on voter registration regulations. Such efforts are ongoing with no set time for dissolution.

Another factor impacting whether state nonprofit associations participate in collaborative advocacy is the size of the association's annual expense budget. State nonprofit associations with larger annual expense budgets tend to participate more frequently in collaborative activities. This finding is in line with Guo and Acar's (2005) assertion that nonprofit collaboration is most likely to occur when a nonprofit organization has a large budget. Surprisingly, the size of an association's annual expense budget is the only statistically significant organizational characteristic that impacts an association's decision to participate in a collaboration. A likely explanation for this relationship is that participation in collaborations with other organizations may require more dedicated resources than other advocacy tactics, and thus a larger budget would yield more flexibility in dedicating funding toward this type of activity. It is also plausible that organizations with larger budgets have higher profiles with more appeal to partnering organizations.

Clearly, state nonprofit associations participate in collaborations that engage in advocacy activities under a number of different circumstances. One driving factor for participation appears to be the missions of the associations and organizations. As noted in the interviews, the missions of the organizations involved in collaborative advocacy provide a common ground and purpose for the organizations to come together. This is especially true for nonprofit organizations with missions that emphasize advocacy activities. Policy issues also appear to impact the duration in which state nonprofit associations participate in collaborations. These findings lead to the conclusion that participation in collaboration for advocacy purposes may be predictable if the organization has a large annual expense budget, a strong mission dedicated to advocacy, and a policy environment that requires a call to action to defend or promote issues impacting the nonprofit sector.

The overwhelming majority of state nonprofit associations report there is some level of effectiveness achieved through joining collaborations of organizations to advocate or lobby for a policy issue. However, follow-up interviews reveal concerns with effectiveness of collaborating including obstacles to success such as clear objectives and partisanship problems within the collaboration. These obstacles could at the very least inhibit organizations from participation in collaborations. The first obstacle for effective collaboration to advocate is the issue of clear objectives. If the success of collaboration is measured only when policy issues are resolved, changed, or enacted, then organizations that have little success are likely discouraged from engaging in collaborations in the future. A second obstacle is that of partisanship. Many nonprofits wish to maintain their political independence to further their capacity to build diverse revenue sources and networks. However, collaboration for the purpose of advocacy may require addressing political figures to some degree, whether in person, by mail, or indirectly through representation.

Nonprofit organizations shy away from what is perceived as partisan collaboration. Finding a way to work together is a third obstacle nonprofit organizations face when determining whether to participate in collaborations that engage in advocacy activities. Nonprofit collaborations often encounter a variety of potentially difficult issues that go along with cooperative efforts including the need for shared values, clear and common goals, unified voice, and an equal distribution of workload. When there is an absence of the characteristics that enable cooperation, nonprofit organizations will shy away from taking on the ambitious challenge of participating in collaborations. Each of these obstacles support similar findings by Mosley (2011) and Bass et al. (2007) that nonprofit organizations may be willing to participate in collaborative advocacy, but their lack of institutional knowledge and understanding of proper communication with policymakers may be a deterrent to participation in this type of activity.

While this study focuses specifically on collaborations that engage in advocacy activities, the findings can be discussed within the larger body of literature on the relationship of organizational characteristics and participation in advocacy. The results support Rees's (1999) finding that organizational age does not impact whether a nonprofit organization chooses to advocate, and Child and Grønbjerg's (2007) finding that budget size does impact this decision. The follow-up interviews support nonprofit organizations' intentions for advocacy, as suggested by Reid (2000), in that state nonprofit associations enter into collaborations to advance the legislative agendas of nonprofit organizations. Further, the evidence supports Child and Grønbjerg's (2007) conclusion that nonprofit organizations share a vibrant relationship with the legislative arena and have much at stake in the forming of public policy. Regardless of the difficulties that it may accompany, state nonprofit associations perceive this tactic as an effective method for impacting the public and policymakers.

Whether nonprofit organizations are encouraged or discouraged to participate in advocacy efforts because of resource capacity or political environment, one thing is evident from the research discussed here—nonprofit organizations choose not to participate in advocacy efforts alone. This study offers two primary contributions to research on nonprofit collaboration, lobbying and advocacy. First, the research contributes to the dearth of literature on the growing influence of nonprofit umbrella associations and their influence in the policy arena. Second, implications of collaborative activities are illustrated for consideration by nonprofit leaders entering into these types of agreements for the purpose of advocacy. These observations are an especially valuable contribution for leaders in the nonprofit sector wishing to make an impact on policy issues through collaboration with other organizations.

Conclusion

Nonprofits are an essential part of service delivery, but they have difficult work to do to maintain their level of influence. Nonprofit advocacy can increase an organization's legitimacy, increase its profile, improve the operating environment of the organization, and improve the lives of an organization's clients. Collaboration is a useful tool for tackling complex problems such as those that often face nonprofits. If coupled together, advocacy and collaboration can be a powerful tool to promote improved client services and effective accomplishment of program- and organizational-level goals. The findings from this study provide insight for nonprofit leaders wishing to impact public policy by showing that not only is collaboration a commonly used and effectively perceived lobbying and advocacy tactic, but also a useful tool in supporting an organization's advocacy ambitions.

Notes

1 These regulations have created confusion among nonprofit organizations due to the ambiguity of the word 'substantial' and the government's reluctance to clarify the meaning of this word. However, in 1976 Congress passed the Lobby Law (updated in 1990) that established the 'h-elective' to clarify rules for lobbying by 501(c)3 charitable organizations. The h-elective declares that "many expenditures that have some relationship to public policy and legislative issues are not treated as lobbying and so are permitted without limit" (Smucker, 1991, p. 68). More importantly, the h-elective specifies that nonprofit organizations may spend up to a defined percentage of their budgets for lobbying without threatening their tax-exempt status. Nonprofit organizations opting for the h-elective can spend 20% of the first $500,000 of their budget on lobbying activities with a sliding scale that changes as organizations' expenditures increase (Internal Revenue Service, Measuring Lobbying Activity: Expenditure Test, 2014). These guidelines are known as the lobbying-expenditure test (Avner, 2002). While the h-elective appears optimal for nonprofit organizations participating in lobbying activities, only 2.4% of all 501(c)3 organizations have applied for the h-elective due to a lack of education and misinformation (Berry, 2007).

2 Similar to advocacy and lobbying, respondents interpreted coalitions and collaboration as one and the same. Thus, the words are used interchangeably throughout the discussion of the results.

References

Avner, M. (2002). *The lobbying and advocacy handbook for nonprofit organizations: Shaping public policy at the state and local level.* Saint Paul, MN: Wilder Foundation Publications.
Bass, G., Arons, D., Guinane, K., & Carter, M. (2007). *Seen but not heard: Strengthening nonprofit advocacy.* Washington, DC: The Aspen Institute.
Berry, J. M. (2007). Nonprofit organizations as interest groups: The political passivity. In A. Cigler & B. Loomis (Eds.), *Interest group politics* (7th ed.) (pp. 235–255). Washington, DC: Congressional Quarterly Press.
Berry, J. M., & Arons, D. (2003). *A voice for nonprofits.* Washington, DC: Brookings Institution Press.
Boris, E., & Krehely, J. (2002). Civic Participation and Advocacy. In L. Salamon (Ed.). *The state of nonprofit America* (pp. 299–330). Washington, DC: Brookings Institution Press.
Burstein, P. (1998). Interest organizations, political parties, and the study of democratic politics. In A. M. Costain & A. S. McFarland (Eds.), *Social movements and American political institutions* (pp. 39–58). Lanham, MD: Rowman & Littlefield.
Chaves, M., Stephens, L., & Galaskiewicz, J. (2004). Does government funding suppress nonprofits' political activity? *American Sociological Review, 69*(2), 292–316.
Child, C., & Grønbjerg, K. (2007). Nonprofit advocacy organizations: Their characteristics and activities. *Social Science Quarterly, 88*(1), 259–281.
Donaldson, L. (2008). Developing a progressive advocacy program within a human services agency. *Administration in Social Work, 32*(2), 25–47.
Ferris, J. M. (1998). The role of the nonprofit sector in a self-governing society: A view from the United States. *Voluntas: International Journal of Voluntary and Nonprofit Organizations, 9*(2), 137–151.
Foss, N. J., & Nielsen, B. B. (2012). Researching collaborative advantage: Some conceptual and multilevel issues. In H. G. Johnsen & R. Ennals (Eds.), *Creating collaborative advantage: Innovation and knowledge creation in regional economies* (pp. 185–198). Burlington, VT: Gower Publishing Company.
Gray, B. (1989). *Collaborating: Finding common ground for multiparty problems.* San Francisco, CA: Jossey-Bass.
Guo, C., & Acar, M. (2005). Understanding collaboration among nonprofit organizations: Combing resource dependency, institutional and network perspectives. *Nonprofit and Voluntary Sector Quarterly, 34*(3), 340–361.
Internal Revenue Service (IRS). (2014). Measuring lobbying: Substantial part test. Retrieved from www.irs.gov/Charities-&-Non-Profits/Measuring-Lobbying:-Substantial-Part-Test.
Israel, B. A., Schulz, A. J., Parker, E. A., & Becker, A. B. (1998). Review of community-based research: Assessing partnership approaches to improve public health. *Annual Review of Public Health, 19,* 173–202.
Kimberlin, S. (2010). Advocacy by nonprofits: Roles and practices of core advocacy organizations and direct service agencies. *Journal of Policy Practice, 9*(1), 164–182.
King, N. (2004). Using templates in the thematic analysis of text. In C. Cassell &

G. Symon (Eds.), *Essential guide to qualitative methods in organizational research* (pp. 256–270). Thousand Oaks, CA: Sage.

Leroux, K., & Goerdel, H. (2009). Political advocacy by nonprofit organizations. *Public Performance and Management Review, 32*(4), 514–536.

MacCallum, R., Zhang, S., Preacher, K., & Rucker, D. (2002). On the practice of dichotomization of quantitative variables. *Psychological Methods, 7*(1), 1940.

McNamara, M. (2012). Starting to untangle the web of cooperation, coordination, and collaboration: A framework for public managers. *International Journal of Public Administration, 35*(6), 389–401.

McNutt, J. G., & Boland, K. M. (1999). Electronic advocacy by nonprofit organizations in social welfare policy. *Nonprofit and Voluntary Sector Quarterly, 28*(4), 432–451.

Mellinger, M. S., & Kollmer, S. (2013). Legislative advocacy and human service nonprofits: What are we doing? *Journal of Policy Practice, 12*(2), 87–106.

Miller-Stevens, K., & Gable, M. (2012). Antecedents to nonprofit advocacy: Which is more important – Governance or organizational structure? *Journal for Nonprofit Management, 15*(1), 21–39.

Morris, J. C., Gibson, W. A., Leavitt, W. M., & Jones, S. C. (2013). *The case for grassroots collaboration.* Lanham, MD: Lexington Books.

Mosley, J. (2011). Institutionalization, privatization, and political opportunity: What tactical choices reveal about the policy advocacy of human service nonprofits. *Nonprofit and Voluntary Sector Quarterly, 40*(3), 435–457.

Mulroy, E., & Shay, S. (1998). Motivation and reward in nonprofit interorganizational collaboration in low-income neighborhoods. *Administration in Social Work, 22*(4), 1–17.

Murray, V. (1998). Interorganizational collaborations in the nonprofit sector. In J. M. Shafritz (Ed.), *International Encyclopedia of Public Policy and Administration* (Vol. 2) (pp. 1192–1196). Boulder, CO: Westview.

National Council of Nonprofits (NCN). (2010). *About Us.* Retrieved from www.councilofnonprofits.org/about-us.

National Council of Nonprofits (NCN). (2014). *Public Policy.* Retrieved from www.councilofnonprofits.org/index.php.

Nicholson-Crotty, J. (2007). Politics, policy, and the motivations for advocacy in nonprofit reproductive health and family planning providers. *Nonprofit and Voluntary Sector Quarterly, 36*(1), 5–21.

Nicholson-Crotty, J. (2009). The stages and strategies of advocacy among nonprofit reproductive health providers. *Nonprofit and Voluntary Sector Quarterly, 38*(6), 1044–1053.

Rees, S. (1999). Strategic choices for nonprofit advocates. *Nonprofit and Voluntary Quarterly, 28*(1), 65–73.

Reid, E. J. (Ed.). (2000). *Nonprofit advocacy and the policy process: Structuring the inquiry into advocacy.* Washington, DC: The Urban Institute.

Ruggiano, N., & Taliaferro, J. D. (2012). Resource dependency and agent theories: A framework for exploring nonprofit leaders' resistance to lobbying. *Journal of Policy Practice, 11*(4), 219–235.

Salamon, L. (1995). *Partners in public service: Government-nonprofit relations in the modern welfare state.* Baltimore, MD: Johns Hopkins University Press.

Salamon, L. (2002). The resilient sector: The state of nonprofit America. In L. Salamon (Ed.), *The state of nonprofit America* (pp. 3–61). Washington, DC: Brookings Institution Press.

Schmid, H., Bar, M., & Nirel, R. (2008). Advocacy activities in nonprofit human service organizations: Implications for policy. *Nonprofit and Voluntary Sector Quarterly, 37*(4), 581–602.

Selden, S. C., Sowa, J., & Sandfort, J. (2006). The impact of nonprofit collaboration in early child care and education on management and program outcomes. *Public Administration Review, 66*(3), 412–425.

Smith, C. (2007). Institutional determinants of collaboration: An empirical study of county open space protection. *Journal of Public Administration Research and Theory, 19*(1), 1–21.

Smucker, B. (1991). *The nonprofit lobbying guide.* San Francisco, CA: Jossey-Bass.

Snavely, K., & Tracy, M. (2000). Collaboration among rural nonprofit organizations. *Nonprofit Management and Leadership, 11*(2), 146–165.

Sosin, M., & Caulum, S. (1983). Advocacy: A conceptualization for social work practice. *Social Work, 28*(1), 12–17.

Sowa, J. E. (2008). Implementing inter-agency collaborations: Exploring variation in collaborative ventures in human service organizations. *Administration & Society, 40*(3), 298–323.

Sowa, J. E. (2009). The collaboration decision in nonprofit organizations. *Nonprofit and Voluntary Sector Quarterly, 38*(6), 1003–1025.

Takahashi, L. M., & Smutny, G. (2002). Collaborative windows and organizational governance: Exploring the formation and demise of social service partnerships. *Nonprofit and Voluntary Sector Quarterly, 31*(2), 165–185.

Wilson, G. K. (1981). *Interest groups in the United States.* New York, NY: Oxford University Press.

Wood, D., & Gray, B. (1991). Toward a comprehensive theory of collaboration. *Journal of Applied Behavioral Science, 27*(1), 139–162.

11 Collaborating for Accountability
Implications for the Judiciary

Amy M. McDowell

The judiciary is charged with providing means for peaceful resolution of disputes. Today, the judiciary is increasingly made aware of social problems that exist in the community through the disputes that it is called upon to address. A wide variety of social problems, such as homelessness, substance abuse, mistreatment of children and the elderly, environmental harms, and a myriad of financial claims (including failure to pay, foreclosure, tax evasion, misuse of funds, and fraud) are brought to the judiciary's attention through criminal as well as civil disputes (Lang, 2011). Often, the judiciary is in a position to identify trends that involve these problems within the community. For example, the judiciary may observe a dramatic increase in the number of foreclosure cases filed within a year, or in the number of petit and grand larceny charges brought against individuals that are homeless. This means that the judiciary is in a position to help quantify both the frequency and magnitude of community social problems as well as to use its authority to enforce judicial orders to craft potential resolutions in individual cases.

While the judiciary enjoys a uniquely authoritative position that enables it to address these social problems on a case-by-case basis, the judiciary alone is incapable of resolving these social problems. Without engaging in collaborative efforts with community and justice system stakeholders, the judiciary is only able to address these problems, quite literally, one case at a time. Yet the public, who elects the judiciary in many states, and elects those who appoint the judiciary in the remaining states, expects more (Rottman & Strickland, 2006). The public expects that the judiciary will not only provide a just outcome in each individual case that is brought before it, but will also create a body of case law that provides society with parameters to govern acceptable behavior as well as provide predictable consequences for violations that occur (Institute for Court Management, 2011). This creation of case law is the traditional way that the judiciary can contribute to resolution of social problems within the community on a larger scale. However, by actively collaborating with partners that also have an interest in these social problems, the judiciary is able to enhance its responsiveness to community needs on a grander scale. Through collaboration, the judiciary is able to more effectively contribute to a collective solution.

Examples of collaborative efforts involving the judiciary are on the rise. Use of problem-solving court dockets, such as mental health and substance abuse courts, routinely demonstrate how judiciaries collaborate with members of the executive and legislative branches, as well as private and nonprofit agencies to provide services to participants. The problem-solving court model, which adopts a holistic approach to help participants conquer underlying issues such as lack of employment, substance abuse, mental illness, and homelessness, is such a popular collaboration that new dockets, such as veterans' reentry courts, are being added across the country. Other collaborations, such as that between the judiciary and the executive branch to provide probation and parole services, are more familiar.

The purpose of this chapter is to partially fill a gap in the collaboration literature by exploring the role that the judiciary plays as a collaborative partner. To fulfill this purpose, collaborations between the judiciary and its justice system partners are examined through the lens of accountability.[1] We suggest that while the judiciary strives to meet public expectations, its capacity to address wicked social problems is limited. However, collaboration enables the judiciary to accomplish both objectives. By increasing its impact on wicked problems[2] through collaborative efforts, the judiciary also enhances its responsiveness to public expectations—all the while preserving the delicate system of checks and balances that exists between the three branches of government.

We propose that a desire to be responsive to community needs is one of the core reasons why the judiciary engages in collaboration. To make this case, we first review some brief but necessary background on the judicial branch. Next, the role of the judiciary within the collaboration literature is examined, followed by a discussion of reasons why the judiciary may be interested in collaboration. To make the necessary linkage to accountability, several constructs of accountability are shared, with emphasis on how these constructs support collaborations involving the judiciary. A framework to analyze three different types of collaboration involving the judiciary is then presented with illustrative examples. Finally, the work concludes with a discussion of two unique challenges that the judiciary faces when it chooses to engage in collaborative efforts—inter-branch funding and judicial impartiality.

Brief Background on the Judiciary

The terms 'judiciary' and 'court' are often used interchangeably, but there is an important distinction to be made. The term 'judiciary' is used throughout this work to refer to the third branch of government. In the United States, this could be the federal judicial branch or one of the 50 state judicial branches (Rottman & Strickland, 2006). The judicial branch is represented by and acts through an individual or body that has decision-making authority on its behalf. Depending on the structure of the judicial branch that is being observed, this may be the judiciary's supreme court, its chief justice, a judicial council, or its centralized administrative office (Rottman & Strickland, 2006).

In contrast, the term 'court' is used to reference a single organizational unit within the judiciary that is charged with resolution of disputes. Each judiciary has a number of courts that are arranged in a hierarchy, such as the superior or circuit court, the court of appeals and the Supreme Court (National Center for State Courts, 2010). Some courts are assigned to preside over cases at the community level (typically the superior or circuit court) whereas others have statewide jurisdiction and preside over cases that originate from any community within the state (the court of appeals and the Supreme Court) (National Center for State Courts, 2010). The court may have either trial jurisdiction (meaning the court presides over original cases that have not yet been heard) or appellate court jurisdiction (meaning the court is reviewing a case that has been previously tried for any errors that occurred in application of the law to the case) (Tobin, 1999). A court may also be characterized as having limited or general jurisdiction. A limited jurisdiction court only hears cases involving specific subject matter, for example, Denver, Colorado's water courts address matters involving water usage and rights, whereas in Virginia, the Juvenile and Domestic Relations District Courts hear cases involving individuals under the age of 18 or involving individuals who are related and/or cohabitate (National Center for State Courts, 2010). In contrast, a court with general jurisdiction may hear a broad range of case types (Tobin, 1999).

Each individual court has one or more judges and administrative responsibilities. In the smallest courts, there may only be one judge and one court administrator (who also performs other duties, such as judicial clerk or bailiff), or the judge may serve in both judicial and administrative roles (Tobin, 1997). In larger courts, there is often a professional court administrator or manager that handles the administrative operations of the court, or it may be directed by a judge that has leadership responsibilities (such as a chief or presiding judge) in addition to presiding over cases (Tobin, 1997). These larger courts often also have several functional units (e.g., the civil unit, the criminal unit, the juvenile unit, etc.) or have specialized dockets (e.g., the traffic docket, drug court, the civil docket, etc.) (Tobin, 1997).

Both the judiciary and individual courts may engage in collaboration. The most important point about the distinction between the two is that when the judiciary is an active participant in collaboration, the judiciary as a whole is represented, including all of the courts that fall under its authority. This is useful for a statewide approach to social problems. In comparison, when a court engages in collaboration, it does so only on its own behalf, and does not bind the judiciary or any other court. Courts may also engage in collaboration through the individual functional units described above. In other words, the court may choose to participate in a collaboration involving criminal case matters but not civil or juvenile case matters. This is particularly advantageous when there is a local or regional issue of concern that is the subject of the collaboration.

The Role of the Judiciary in the Collaboration Literature

Writing in Federalist #78 in support of the separation of powers, Alexander Hamilton famously described the judiciary as "the least dangerous" branch of government (as cited in Quinn, 1993, p. 163). To support this position, Hamilton proclaims that:

> [t]he executive not only dispenses the honors, but holds the sword of the community. The legislature not only commands the purse, but prescribes the rules by which the duties and rights of every citizen are to be regulated. The judiciary, on the contrary, has no influence over either the sword or the purse; no direction either of the strength or of the wealth of the society; and can take no active resolution whatever. It may truly be said to have neither force nor will, but merely judgment; and must ultimately depend upon the aid of the executive arm even for the efficacy of its judgments.
>
> (As cited in Quinn, 1993, pp. 162–163)

Hamilton's description suggests that the judiciary is a necessary but relatively powerless component of the three-branch system of checks and balances. The judiciary is characterized as passive; a neutral arbiter incapable of taking action even to enforce its own judgments. By so judging the judiciary, Hamilton makes a mistake that is reflected throughout the contemporary literature on collaboration—he discounts the power of the judiciary.

A survey of literature on collaboration reveals that while the executive and legislative branches are frequently discussed, the judiciary is largely omitted. For example, Bardach and Lesser (1996) suggest specific roles in collaboration for the legislature and the executive, but notably exclude the judiciary (pp. 220–221). Admirably, Ansell and Gash (2007) make an attempt to include the judiciary, stating that "our intention is to include public institutions such as bureaucracies, courts, legislatures, and other governmental bodies at the local, state, or federal level" (p. 545). However, they are unable to do so because, despite a study of 137 cases, "the typical public institution among [the] cases is, in fact, an executive branch agency" (p. 545).

When the judiciary is mentioned in the collaboration literature, it is often viewed in its traditional role as neutral decision-maker. Bingham and O'Leary (2011) consider the judiciary within the context of modern collaborative management. Using separation of powers as the foundation for their analysis, the authors take a strict view of the role of the judiciary, suggesting that the judiciary "does not initiate action" (Bingham & O'Leary, 2011, p. S79). They further characterize the role of the judiciary as "acquiesce[ing] in actions on which the other two branches agree" (Bingham & O'Leary, 2011, p. S80). As such, the role of the judiciary is passive—to review administrative actions once a controversy occurs (Bingham & O'Leary, 2011).

This is also the view adopted by Forrer, Key, Newcomer, and Boyer (2010), who note that the judiciary "places a check on 'arbitrary and capricious' behavior[s] of agencies and their officials" (p. 478). While this is a logical and widely espoused view of the judiciary, it is also shortsighted. We suggest that, just like the other branches of government, the judiciary is a powerful collaborative partner for social change.

Reasons to Collaborate

There is a mystique about the judiciary for those that are unfamiliar with it that leads to the incorrect assumption that the judiciary has some special motivation for engaging in collaboration. However, the reasons that motivate the judiciary to collaborate include the same reasons that the legislative and executive branches choose to do so. For example, in the current economy, sharing of resources is a necessity (Hall, 2009). With lean staffing structures, the opportunity to identify interdependencies and to reduce duplicative services due to fragmentation while simultaneously increasing capacity for services are worthwhile goals, especially when public funds are at issue (Hall & Suskin, 2010). Additionally, the judiciary has long realized that its mission cannot be accomplished in a vacuum. For example, courts may convict criminals, but partnerships with law enforcement agencies to apprehend suspects and with correctional facilities to detain convicted criminals are a necessary outgrowth of the judiciary's responsibility to preside over criminal cases.

The judiciary has grown accustomed to providing necessary services to respond to wicked problems, especially problems that have become social crises, such as foreclosures, homelessness, child welfare, and substance abuse. A series of problem-solving courts that address local community problems, such as housing, substance abuse, inadequate parenting skills, and mental health needs, have taken hold across the country as a direct result of courts' ability to observe trends in litigation and to respond to local community needs (Reinkensmeyer & Murray, 2012; Mundell & Jefferson, 2012). Most recently, veterans' reentry courts have been created to assist veterans returning from war who do not have the necessary resources or community support and thus struggle with the effects of post-traumatic stress disorder, substance abuse, or financial stress, among other challenges (Russell, 2009).

The literature suggests a wide variety of reasons why organizations may engage in collaboration that equally apply to the judiciary. Page (2004, p. 591) indicates that collaboration allows sharing of critical information and resources. One example involves mental health courts which have valuable information in their case files about the type and frequency of mental health related illnesses in the community (Waters, Cheesman, Gibson, & Dazevedo, 2010). By sharing this information, the judiciary can partner with community agencies and nonprofits to identify appropriate resources available to assist individuals who suffer from mental illness.

Similarly, McNamara (2012, p. 389) suggests that organizations that collaborate do so to increase their capacity to address problems, to identify interdependencies, and to reduce fragmented services. The judiciary is a powerful partner to increase capacity to address problems both because of its ability to use the force of law to support collaborative efforts and because the judiciary enjoys a higher level of public trust and confidence than the other branches of government (American Bar Association, 1999; Rottman, 2005). By partnering with the judiciary, fragmentation of services may be lessened; opportunities exist to enhance both pre- and post-trial services that community actors may already provide but fail to coordinate among the service providers. Such opportunities often uncover interdependencies that were previously overlooked.

Bingham and O'Leary's (2011) work posits a desire to improve services coupled with a recognition that the challenge is bigger than a single organization as incentives for collaboration. This characterization is clearly applicable to the judiciary. Over time, the judiciary has become responsible for matters that move beyond the resolution of disputes. Enforcing judgments, ordering reparations, overseeing drug and alcohol screens, and similar activities, step outside the strict boundary of deciding cases (Clarke, 2013). Yet, the judiciary has become a natural partner in collaborations to address complex social problems because communities often become aware of an increase in incidents of homelessness, crime, or domestic violence as a result of increases in court cases filed involving these issues. Just as the judiciary is unable to resolve such issues in the community on its own, neither are existing community partners.

Bardach and Lesser (1996) suggest that collaboration is motivated by a desire for effectiveness; that collaboration gives power to those closest to the problem and its potential solutions. Community solutions to social problems can be addressed more effectively when the judiciary is involved; the judiciary has the authority to order individuals to participate in specific community programs that aim to address the underlying causes of problems. Similarly, the judiciary can rely upon other agencies to intervene in ways that it cannot due to limitations on its authority.

Gray (1985) argues that collaboration arises out of crisis, and is a reaction to "indivisible problems" that are not owned by a single organization (p. 912). This is likely in part a reflection of Rittel and Webber's (1973) famous description of "wicked problems," which captures the complexity of public policy issues (p. 160). Issues commonly reach crisis level once legal action is taken to bring the matter before the judiciary. An example of a collaborative response arising out of crisis was development of a foreclosure pilot program in Miami, Florida, to address the backlog of greater than 83,000 foreclosures (Castellanos, 2012).

This list is not exhaustive as there are likely other reasons that induce and support collaboration efforts. Yet, there remains an important element missing from among these reasons to collaborate. This reason is accountability. The idea is partially reflected in Bardach and Lesser's (1996) suggestion that collaboration is motivated by a desire for effectiveness. It also incorporates Page's (2004, p. 592) perspective that collaborative partners seek to be responsive to stakeholder demands. However, neither of these perspectives fully encompasses accountability as a reason to collaborate. The literature addresses how to maintain accountability within a collaboration, but does not appear to consider accountability as a reason to engage in collaboration at the outset. We propose that accountability in the form of desire to be responsive to community needs as a reason to engage in collaboration is a central driver of collaboration for the judiciary that is worthy of examination.

Constructs of Accountability

For purposes of examining the role of accountability in the judiciary, three constructs of accountability are referenced from the applicable literature. First is Bardach and Lesser's (1996) dyadic typology. The authors suggest that there are two different types of accountability: (1) accountability to; and (2) accountability for (Bardach & Lesser, 1996, p. 197). Accountability to addresses *to whom* the organization must be responsive, whereas accountability for addresses *for what* the organization is responsible. Because the judiciary is a branch of government, it is accountable to the public. Accountability for is often described as 'justice,' an indistinct concept that references the judiciary's obligation to provide neutral and impartial decisions to resolve disputes. Accountability for represents the judiciary's mission, whereas accountability to requires the judiciary to respond to a diverse group of stakeholders, i.e., the public. This requires balancing competing demands as recognized by Forrer et al. (2010); two examples are: (1) ensuring accessibility of court services to the public while maintaining impartiality; and (2) timely processing of criminal cases while also accommodating other case types.

A second construct of accountability applicable to collaboration with the judiciary is found in O'Toole's (1997) work. O'Toole identifies three values that reflect the U.S. conception of democracy (1997, p. 448). These values are: (1) responsibility for effecting the public interest; (2) responsiveness to public preferences; and (3) enhancement of political deliberation, civility, and trust (O'Toole, 1997, p. 448). All three of these values are applicable to the judiciary. A famous essay by Roscoe Pound (1906) suggests that public dissatisfaction with the courts exists for a variety of reasons that reflect the judicial system's inability to carry out the public's interest and the judiciary's perceived lack of responsiveness to public preferences. Pound's work was viewed as an early call for court reform, and has served as a standard against which the judiciary may measure the extent to which it is responsive to the public. The third value espoused in O'Toole's (1997) framework of democratic accountability is reflected in the work of the judiciary. In fact, it goes to the very heart of the judiciary's existence as both a peaceful and trusted mechanism to resolve disputes.

Studies have demonstrated that the public has a relatively strong level of trust and confidence in the judiciary, an important component of accountability for the judiciary (American Bar Association, 1999; Rottman, 2005).

A third construct of accountability that is referenced throughout the literature arises from the performance measurement movement. This accountability perspective is accountability for results and is also embraced by the judiciary. Page (2004) suggests that this type of accountability focuses on measuring outcomes, and involves something deeper than oversight or reporting. Rittel and Webber (1973) also discuss accountability for results, describing its focus as outputs. This accountability framework is important to the judiciary because there is a focus on outcomes in the judiciary's administration. Performance measures, such as CourTools and the High Performance Court Framework, have gained popularity as mechanisms to gauge the performance of individual courts, and, by extension, the judiciary (National Center for State Courts, 2005; Ostrom, Hanson, & Burke, 2012).

While measures of productivity are important, such as the number of cases closed versus number of cases filed, the public is interested in outcomes. Examples of outcomes reported by courts include the number of drug court graduates, the number of individuals incarcerated, and the number of children adopted. Part of the focus on outcomes is because the public demands results. The difficulty for the judiciary is that outcomes directly relate to complex social issues that are not controlled merely by the judiciary's actions. Instead, a variety of causes and factors interact to create a single outcome in each case. Thus the judiciary, while being held accountable for outcomes, is not fully in control of the precursors that lead to those outcomes.

The common theme in each of these three theories of accountability vis-à-vis the judiciary is that the judiciary constantly seeks ways to increase its accountability to the public for tough social problems that cross court dockets. Collaboration offers one mechanism for the judiciary to achieve this goal. While the judiciary may not be in a position to directly address wicked social problems, it is able to increase its accountability by being responsive to litigation trends and local community needs through collaborative efforts. For example, being poised to sound the alarm to local public officials that foreclosure filings are on the rise in the community provides an opportunity to collaborate to proactively address community needs (Castellanos, 2012). One option is to strategically deploy social services to provide targeted support to families in foreclosure, thereby avoiding other potential negative outcomes, such as homelessness, that are often associated with foreclosures. Such opportunities provide value to the community by encouraging a comprehensive approach to wicked problems. Because collaboration offers a mechanism to demonstrate increased accountability to the public, it is viewed by the judiciary as not only an opportunity but a necessity. In short, accountability is a core reason that motivates judiciaries to collaborate.

Three Types of Collaborations

Within the judicial environment, there are three types of collaborations: (1) within branch; (2) between branch; and (3) external branch collaborations. This typology is only possible when a definition of collaboration is adopted that permits inclusion of non-state actors. Scholars that espouse a more restrictive definition of collaboration, such as Ansell and Gash (2007), would reject this typology. We suggest this typology because the states' judiciaries offer numerous examples that provide support for each type of collaboration, suggesting that collaborations are undertaken based on situational needs (see Table 11.1).

Within Branch Collaboration

The first type of collaboration examined is within branch collaboration. This type of collaboration refers to arrangements between state supreme courts, offices of court administration, presiding judges, trial judges, trial court administrators, and court personnel to resolve specific judicial branch challenges (Mundell & Jefferson, 2012). The key to this type of collaboration is that it brings together subject matter experts from various roles and geographic locations within the branch to address a shared problem.

A classic example from the judicial literature is collaborative efforts to unify, a process by which state judiciaries undertake efforts to create "operational coherence" through centralized policymaking (Tobin, 1999). The goal is to speak with one voice on major policies and operations throughout the judicial branch, from trial courts to the state supreme court, and among all administrative units (Durham & Becker, 2012). Unification can be undertaken in specific areas, such as administration and budgeting, or in provision of specific services, such as IT or human

Table 11.1 Three Types of Collaborations Within the Judicial Environment

Within Branch	*Between Branch*	*External Branch*
Brings together experts from various roles and geographic locations within the judicial branch to address a shared problem within the judiciary	Brings together representatives from the executive and/or legislative branches with the judicial branch to address a common objective or goal that would be unobtainable if the judiciary acted independently	Brings together representatives from the executive and/or legislative branches along with nonprofit and/or for-profit organizations with the judicial branch to address a common objective or goal that would be unobtainable if the judiciary acted in concert with the executive or legislative branches or independently

resources support (Tobin, 1999). Because unification initiatives must take into consideration needs of courts throughout the state, including trial and appellate courts, as well as limited and general jurisdiction courts, these types of initiatives are well suited for collaboration.

The theory underlying unification seeks to assure uniform provision of services. Take the idea of a uniform case management system, a common technology project among the courts, as an example. Such a system can provide a "standardized statewide solution to address the automation of certain trial court functions and the availability of a digital case file" across the state (Velez, 2012, p. 8). The case management system is used across court units for various purposes by all of the state's trial courts; yet it must also allow for needs at the appellate court level. Judges and their clerks access records for case information, whereas the clerk's office accesses it to upload necessary information and documents. Pre- and post-trial services access the system to identify community services that are available to the parties, and post-trial services access the system to record and ensure compliance with court orders. Other court units access the records for various administrative purposes, such as to track the use of alternative dispute resolution mechanisms, compliance with deadlines like compulsory discovery, and payment of fines and fees. Finally, because cases can be appealed from the trial court, the digital case file provides the information necessary to process and hear a case by the state's appellate court(s).

In Florida, such a project is currently underway. The Trial Court Integrated Management Solution project incorporates representatives from various positions within the state judiciary to collaborate on the need for and the required components of the system (Velez, 2012). The effort brings together individuals with information, expertise, and skills necessary to create a product that automates records management across the state. Specifically, this collaboration uses "case-specific workgroups" to bring together "judges, case managers, and subject matter experts" (Velez, 2012, p. 12) to examine issues related to each case type, i.e., criminal cases, civil cases, family cases, etc. Participants include representatives from the Supreme Court, the Office of the State Courts Administrator, the Clerks of Court, and four standing court committees that focus on issues of trial court performance and accountability, statistics and workload, families and children in the courts, and technology (Velez, 2012).

Within branch collaboration that brings together individuals with knowledge of the needs and processes from all of the hierarchical levels of court administration is critical to ensure that the uniform system meets each stakeholder's needs. It is further complicated by the reality that prior to adoption of a uniform process, each court within the state may have its own system and administrative policies for gathering and accessing case information depending on local caseload, resources, and preferences. Bringing together geographically disperse representatives is thus also crucial. Failure to identify and involve all of the judiciary's stakeholders— from each of the state's various courts and court types and its centralized administrative offices—in a collaborative effort could lead to great expense and loss of time. Ultimately, the system developed would likely be inefficient and, in the worst case scenario, unusable.

No one portion of the judiciary owns the case management system or the potential solution to sharing of case information. If the system fails to meet the judiciary's needs, there is a direct impact on the judiciary's accountability to the public—specifically, the judiciary's ability to meet the public's demands for efficient and effective trial court services, and by extension, to hear case appeals. While none of the individual stakeholders with the judiciary own the solution to the case management problem, each would be impacted by a negative outcome. In other words, this is a shared problem to which within branch collaboration offers a potential solution that the individual stakeholders, or the judiciary, would not otherwise likely obtain.

Between Branch Collaboration

The second type of collaboration is between branch collaboration. This refers to collaborations that occur between the executive and judicial branches, the legislative and judicial branches, or all three branches of government to address issues of common interest. For example, it is not uncommon for a state judiciary to partner with the executive branch to provide probation and parole services, creating an executive body to oversee provision of services with representatives from both branches (Tobin, 1999). Likewise, the legislature may seek input from the courts, such as case statistics, when making funding and other policy decisions (Tobin, 1999). For example, a popular problem-solving court model, the mental health docket, has much information that is of value, including data on recidivism rates, cost of treatment, frequency of compliance with treatment, and number and type of participating facilities (Waters et al., 2010). Such information informs legislative policymaking.

An example of between branch collaboration was created in Missouri to address juvenile delinquency. The executive branch's Division of Youth Services, the judiciary, and the legislature collaborated to create diversion programs to address juvenile justice needs in the community, an issue of mutual interest across the three government branches (Wilson, 2013). Collaboration members include both the executive agency's advisory board and representatives from the judiciary (Wilson, 2013). Local court personnel collaborate directly with agency service coordinators to address cases (Wilson, 2013). The collaborative has enjoyed a "sustained ... commitment" from the legislature to support its efforts, eliminating unnecessary roadblocks to collaboration (Wilson, 2013, pp. 5–6). A key benefit of the Missouri collaborative is that relationships and communications between the branches have improved not only in the area of juvenile justice, but in other areas as well (Wilson, 2013).

In this case, each branch of government contributes a unique resource that allows the collaboration to craft a mutual solution to a shared community problem—an increase in juvenile delinquency. The executive branch con-tributes subject matter expertise provided by its Division of Youth Services employees; the legislature offers both funding and public political support for the collaboration; and the judiciary maintains personal jurisdiction over the juveniles who are brought into the juvenile justice system, creating an oppor-tunity for the judiciary to order juveniles to participate in a variety of treat-ment and diversion programs identified by members of the collaborative. By combining the unique resources that each branch commands, the state of Missouri is able to share information and resources more effectively. This in turn leads to identification of existing interdependencies and overlap in service areas, and prevents duplication of efforts. The combined effort of the three branches enhances government capacity to address the rise of juvenile delinquency incidents in a coordinated fashion, drawing on each branch's strengths. As demonstrated, the key to this type of collaboration is the com-bined efforts of representatives from two or more branches of state govern-ment to accomplish an objective or goal that would be unobtainable if the judiciary acted independently.

External Branch Collaboration

The third type of collaboration is external branch collaboration. It involves collaboration by the judiciary with the executive and/or legislative branches along with nonprofit and/or for-profit organizations. This type of collabo-ration is a common approach to address a variety of community-based social concerns ranging from mental health to drug addiction to child welfare. For example, some judiciaries have empowered the courts to create specialty or problem-solving courts, such as mental health courts, to bring together the judiciary and private service providers to meet the needs of citizens (Lang, 2011). The key to this type of collaboration is that non-governmental entities join the collaboration to accomplish goals that are viewed as otherwise unobtainable if the judiciary acted alone or in concert with the executive or legislative branches.

In the case of mental health courts, individuals who are charged with criminal offenses that have underlying mental health causes may opt to participate in mental health court in lieu of criminal court proceedings. The goal of a mental health court is to take a comprehensive approach, rather than incarcerating an individual in jail or prison as punishment for behaviors that are motivated by mental health issues. Mental health courts also acknowledge that services to address underlying mental health issues are often not available to individuals who are incarcerated, and that incarceration may exacerbate poor mental health (Denckla & Berman, 2001). Adopting a holistic approach, mental health courts take advantage of a pool of community resources and stakeholders to facil-itate resolution of criminal charges, to rehabilitate the accused, and to treat underlying mental health concerns to prevent recidivism (Denckla & Berman, 2001).

Another popular example of external branch collaboration is efforts to increase public civic education. One such effort, the South Carolina iCivics program, has received national recognition for its outreach efforts (Press Release, n.d.). The program seeks to educate students on civics issues using an interactive, online format and encourages students to share their knowledge with adult family and caregivers. Drawing upon the iCivics program created by former Supreme Court Justice Sandra Day O'Connor, members of the judiciary collaborate with members of school districts, iCivics national coordinators, the South Carolina Defense Trial Attorneys' Association, and the South Carolina Bar to increase civics awareness among schoolchildren (Press Release, n.d.). The collaboration has led to distribution of "Justice Case Files" (graphic novels that highlight court proceedings) in over 65 public schools, opportunities for students to attend oral arguments at the South Carolina Supreme Court, live streaming of cases from the South Carolina Supreme Court to classrooms, and a program for social studies teachers to "learn how to bring law to life for their students" (Press Release, n.d.).

The South Carolina collaborative has raised public awareness of the importance that civics plays in education because it involves so many different types of stakeholders, representing each of the government's branches as well as nonprofit interests. Many of the stakeholders are prominent public figures, which further heightens awareness (Press Release, n.d.). Additionally, because the stakeholders represent different areas of focus (education, public outreach, public service, and the pursuit of justice), combining their resources reinforces the collaborative's message in multiple environments (e.g., in both South Carolina's classrooms and its courtrooms). The collaborative has taken advantage of multiple sources to engage its audience, such as the Internet, course curriculum and teaching resources, and one-of-a-kind in-person experiences (Press Release, n.d.). Together, the collaborative's members have increased their capacity to address a pervasive matter of public concern that utilizes each member's unique strengths and resources. Although the members are likely to compete for priority over one another for financial and nonfinancial support of their core missions, their shared vision of a public that is civically engaged has led to a productive collaboration.

Challenges to Collaboration

The judiciary experiences many of the same challenges that other organizations that engage in collaboration encounter. However, there are also challenges that are unique to the judiciary's environment. Two challenges in particular impact the judiciary's collaborative efforts; they are inter-branch funding and judicial impartiality.

Inter-Branch Funding

Judiciaries are not revenue-generating entities. This means that judiciaries must rely solely upon an external entity for funding (Tobin, 1999). Despite the common misperception, payment of fines and fees to the court does not offset the judiciary's operating expenses or enhance its bottom line (Tobin, 1999). Rather, funds are collected on behalf of the state which chooses how funds are used; often funds are used to support other executive or legislative branch initiatives and the judiciary does not benefit (Rottman & Strickland, 2006).

Depending on the state, judiciaries receive funding either from the legislature or the executive branch (Rottman and Strickland, 2006). Often, funding has restricted uses, such as requirements that specific line items be used for particular purposes (Rottman & Strickland, 2006). During the budget cycle, the judiciary must also account for its use of funding to the funder (Rottman & Strickland, 2006). This arrangement means that the judiciary is prohibited from implementing additional means to increase its funds, such as charging new fees or increasing the amounts of existing fees for service. Nor may the judiciary dictate how collected funding is used. Thus, if the funder does not permit or approve of a collaborative effort, the judiciary may not be able to participate in a collaboration as a matter of practicality despite the fact that it has the necessary authority to engage in collaborative efforts as an independent branch of government. Even if the funder does not explicitly prohibit funding for a collaborative initiative, insufficient funding may prevent participation. Conversely, because judiciaries are reliant upon the other branches for funding, they may feel pressure to join a collaborative effort as a condition of funding or to counteract indirect threats to sources of funding.

This raises a related challenge. Because the judiciary is funded by the other government branches, the misperception persists that the judiciary partially derives its authority from these other branches (Tobin, 1999). Thus, the judiciary may not appear to be completely autonomous when participating in a collaboration even though it is a co-equal of the executive and the legislature. As a result, potential collaborative partners may be disinclined to partner with the judiciary or may mistakenly presume that the judiciary is acting with the approval of the executive or legislative branch—even when the judiciary is expressly acting against such preferences.

The funding conundrum is one that is specific to the judiciary. The judiciary enjoys all of the rights and responsibilities given to it by the Constitution as an independent branch of government, yet it has no money of its own to fund its constitutionally mandated responsibilities (Tobin, 1999). In modern times, the number and associated expenses of those mandated activities has continued to grow, leaving the judiciary with little, if any, discretionary funding to support voluntary initiatives, such as collaboration (Tobin, 1999). Even if a collaborative effort may support the judiciary's mandated functions, unique funding structures may prevent the judiciary's participation.

Judicial Impartiality

The other significant challenge faced by the judiciary arises from the concept of judicial impartiality. The judiciary is the so-called least dangerous branch of government because it is designed to be the neutral arbiter. Members of the judiciary (i.e., judges) are meant to be impartial and free from bias, prejudgment, and conflict of interest in the eyes of the public (American Bar Association, 2008). However, maintaining this status means that members of the judiciary are prohibited from or restricted in their participation in a wide variety of activities (American Bar Association, 2008). Likewise, individuals that represent the third branch of government (even those who are not judges) must be cautious because their actions are a direct reflection upon the judiciary. The judiciary is prohibited from making public policy, for example. The irony is that many issues for which judiciaries would find participation in a collaboration desirable directly impact public policy.

Another limitation is that judges and individuals who work for the judiciary may not comment on ongoing cases (American Bar Association, 2008). Judges must also refrain from giving the impression that they hold a particular opinion about a case that is currently on their docket or may be assigned to their docket for trial (American Bar Association, 2008).

These limitations mean that participation by the judiciary in a collaborative must be carefully delimited. This does not, however, make participation in a collaborative by the judiciary impossible. To the contrary, judiciaries throughout the nation have partnered with local community groups and service providers to make a difference in their communities. They do so by avoiding any comment on cases currently on the court's docket and by limiting the types of activities in which they participate. For example, judicial codes of ethics provide guidance as to the types of activities that judges may undertake in support of policy change (American Bar Association, 2008). Many permit a judge to give a public lecture or to teach, for instance. The judiciary may also provide support by assigning representatives who are not judges to the collaborative, thus avoiding potential violations of the judicial code of ethics.

The impact of these challenges is that while judiciaries may participate in collaborations, they do so subject to unique challenges and limitations that can make their participation quite complex. To be a successfully contributing member of a collaborative, judiciaries must carefully craft the type of support they will provide to the collaboration, as well as their manner of participation. The judiciary would be wise to identify specific constraints at the outset of the collaboration so as to avoid unnecessary complications that may arise.

Conclusion

Many of the elements of collaboration parsed in the literature apply equally to collaborative arrangements that involve the judiciary. On the other hand, the judiciary's unique role as the third branch of government also holds important implications—and limitations—for collaborations that include the judiciary or its constituent courts. Yet, the collaborative literature is nearly silent with regard to these issues, and, in particular,

234 A. M. McDowell

with respect to the judiciary's participation as a potential partner in collaboration (Bardach & Lesser, 1996; Ansell & Gash, 2007; Bingham & O'Leary, 2011). We have sought to partially address this gap in the literature by examining the judiciary's participation in collaborative efforts viewed through the lens of accountability.

One important contribution to the literature is demonstration that the judiciary regularly participates in collaborative efforts to address complex social problems (Lang, 2011). It is increasingly important to address the judiciary's role as a collaborative partner as collaborations that involve the judiciary, such as problem-solving courts, are on the rise. An implication for future collaborations is that the judiciary can be a powerful contributor as a member of a collaboration. A second implication is that collaboration partners need to understand and respect the unique limitations that the judiciary must adhere to when participating in a collaboration. This may require considerable flexibility from other collaboration partners, and some may find that the price is too high to justify their participation. In this case, the collaboration should carefully consider what the judiciary brings to the collaborative, and whether the collaborative's goals may best be pursued without the judiciary's involvement. Similarly, before joining the collaborative, the judiciary must consider what risks its participation may raise and whether the constraints of judicial impartiality prohibit the judiciary's participation (American Bar Association, 2008).

Another contribution to the collaboration literature is the observation that accountability is a particularly important construct for the judiciary that offers a powerful incentive for collaboration with both justice system partners and other entities. This incentive may be even more powerful for the judiciary than for other collaboration partners. It is a theme that is of central interest to the judiciary, as the judiciary seeks ways to increase its transparency and responsiveness to community needs. It also represents a distinct advantage that the judiciary holds over the other branches of government, as research suggests that the judiciary is viewed more favorably by the public than the executive and legislative branches (American Bar Association, 1999; Rottman, 2005). Thus, this work expands upon the existing treatment of accountability in the collaboration literature by suggesting that the desire to increase accountability may be a powerful consideration for engaging in collaboration.

Finally, a three-part typology is offered to examine the collaborative efforts of the judiciary, with illustrative examples. These examples demonstrate how the judiciary collaborates in three distinctive environments to enhance its mission to resolve disputes (Mundell & Jefferson, 2012; Durham & Becker, 2012; Velez, 2012; Wilson, 2013; Denckla & Berman, 2001; Waters et al., 2010). The broader implication is that each type of collaboration offers a specific advantage(s) depending on the social problem under scrutiny and the judiciary's goals. In many cases, the type of collaboration will be dictated by the scope of the problem and identification of the partners necessary to craft a solution in response. For example, systemic issues within the judiciary are best suited for within branch collaboration; public concerns that benefit from executive or legislative involvement are effectively addressed using between branch collaboration; and wicked problems that require a more inclusive group of stakeholders, such as community nonprofit organizations or members of the public, are appropriate for external branch collaboration.

In conclusion, further reflection upon Hamilton's characterization of the judiciary as the "least dangerous" of the government branches suggests that the judiciary is particularly well suited to address some of society's most wicked problems using collaborative efforts (as cited in Quinn, 1993). Indeed, the judiciary frequently aims to do exactly that—driven largely by its desire to increase its responsiveness to the community—while fulfilling its mission to resolve disputes.

Notes

1 It is important to note that accountability in the judicial context varies from traditional academic notions of accountability. While both elected and appointed members of the judiciary have limited accountability to either voters or an appointing authority, judiciaries across the United States have undertaken efforts to increase their responsiveness to the public through use of performance measures and transparency. This chapter argues that judiciaries also use collaboration as a tool to enhance their responsiveness to community needs.
2 As defined by Rittel and Webber to capture the complexity of public policy issues (1973, p. 160).

References

American Bar Association. (1999). *Perceptions of the U.S. justice system*. Chicago, IL: Author.
American Bar Association. (2008). *Model code of judicial conduct*. Chicago, IL. Author.
Ansell, C., & Gash, A. (2007). Collaborative government in theory and practice. *Journal of Public Administration Research and Theory, 18*, 543–571. doi: 10.1093/jopart/mum032
Bardach, E., & Lesser, C. (1996). Accountability in human services collaborative: For what? And to whom? *Journal of Public Administration Research and Theory, 6*(2), 197–224.
Bingham, L. B., & O'Leary, R. (2011). Federalist no. 51: Is the past relevant to today's collaborative public management? *Public Administration Review, 71*(s1), S78–S82.
Castellanos, M. (2012). *Assessing the foreclosure pilot program in Miami, Florida*. (Court Project Phase Paper, ICM Fellows Program).
Clarke, T. (2013). *Triage protocols for litigant portals: A coordinated strategy between courts and service providers*. Williamsburg, VA: National Center for State Courts.
Denckla, D., & Berman, G. (2001). *Rethinking the revolving door: A look at mental illness in the courts*. New York, NY: Center for Court Innovation.
Durham, C. M., & Becker, D. J. (2012). *A case for court governance principles*. Boston, MA: Harvard Kennedy School of Government.

Forrer, J., Key, J. E., Newcomer, K. E., & Boyer, E. (2010). Public-private partner-ships and the public accountability question. *Public Administration Review*, 70(3), 475–484.

Gray, B. (1985). Conditions facilitating interorganizational collaboration. *Human Relations*, 38(10), 911–936. doi: 10.1177/001872678503801001

Hall, D. J. (2009). How state courts are weathering the economic storm. In C. Flango, A. McDowell, C. Campbell, & N. Kauder (Eds.), *Future trends in state courts 2009* (pp. 1–4). Williamsburg, VA: National Center for State Courts.

Hall, D. J., & Suskin, L. (2010). Reengineering lessons from the field. In C. Flango, A. McDowell, C. Campbell, & N. Kauder (Eds.), *Future trends in state courts 2010* (pp. 36–41). Williamsburg, VA: National Center for State Courts.

Institute for Court Management. (2011). *Purposes and responsibilities of courts.* Williamsburg, VA: National Center for State Courts.

Lang, J. (2011). *What is a community court? How the model is being adopted across the United States.* New York, NY: Center for Court Innovation.

McNamara, M. (2012). Starting to untangle the web of cooperation, coordination, and collaboration: A framework for public managers. *International Journal of Public Administration*, 35(6), 389–401. doi: 10.1080/01900692.2012.65527

Mundell, B. R., & Jefferson, W. B. (2012). *Herding lions: Shared leadership of state trial courts.* Boston, MA: Harvard Kennedy School of Government.

National Center for State Courts. (2005). *CourTools.* Williamsburg, VA: Author.

National Center for State Courts. (2010). *Court statistics project.* Williamsburg, VA: Author.

Ostrom, B. J., Hanson R. A., & Burke, K. (2012). Becoming a high performance court. *The Court Manager*, 26(4), 35–43.

O'Toole, L. J., Jr. (1997). The implications for democracy in a networked bureau-cratic world. *Journal of Public Administration Research and Theory*, 7(3), 443–459.

Page, S. (2004). Measuring accountability for results in interagency collaboratives. *Public Administration Review*, 64(5), 591–606.

Pound, R. (1906). *The causes of public dissatisfaction with the administration of justice.* Chicago, IL: American Judicature Society.

Press Release. (n.d.). *S.C. chief justice receives award for civics-education work.* Columbia, SC: South Carolina Judicial Department.

Quinn, F. (Ed.). (1993). *The federalist papers reader.* Washington, DC: Seven Locks Press.

Reinkensmeyer, M. W., & Murray, J. S. (2012). Court-community connections: Strategies for effective collaboration. In C. Flango, A. McDowell, D. Saunders, N. Sydow, C. Campbell, & N. Kauder (Eds.), *Future trends in state courts 2012* (pp. 28–33). Williamsburg, VA: National Center for State Courts.

Rittel, H. W., & Webber, M. M. (1973). Dilemmas in a general theory of planning. *Policy Sciences*, 4, 155–169.

Rottman, D. B. (2005). What Californians think about their courts. *California Courts Review*, 6–9.

Rottman, D. B., & Strickland, S. M. (2006). *State court organization, 2004.* Wash-ington, DC: U.S. Department of Justice, Bureau of Justice Statistics.

Russell, R. T., (2009). Veterans treatment courts developing throughout the nation. In C. Flango, A. McDowell, C. Campell, & N. Kauder (Eds.), *Future trends in state courts 2009* (pp. 130–133). Williamsburg, VA: National Center for State Courts.

Tobin, R. W. (1997). *An overview of court administration in the United States.* Williamsburg, VA: National Center for State Courts.

Tobin, R. W. (1999). *Creating the judicial branch: The unfinished reform.* Williamsburg, VA: National Center for State Courts.

Velez, K. (2012). *The trial court integrated management solution (TIMS) project for the Florida state courts system* (Court Project Phase Paper, ICM Fellows Program).

Waters, N. L., Cheesman, F. L., Gibson, S. A., & Dazevedo, I. (2010). *Mental health court performance measures: Implementation & user's guide.* Williamsburg, VA: National Center for State Courts.

Wilson, J. B. (2013). *Cross-branch collaboration: What can we learn from the collaboration between courts and the division of youth services in Missouri?* Boston, MA: Harvard Kennedy School of Government.

12 Social Capital, Collective Action, and Collaboration

Deniz Leuenberger and Christine Reed

Introduction

The formation and sustainability of collaborative governance requires organizational actors to overcome the collective action problem, defined as the tendency to exploit common-pool resources in the absence of norms and rules developed by actors to govern the use of natural resources. Collaboration is a term referring to a process of "diverse stakeholders working together to resolve shared dilemmas" (Heikkila & Gerlak, 2005, p. 583). It is related to a second generation of collective action theories challenging earlier assumptions that resolution of the collective action dilemma requires top-down regulation. That research addresses the question of social motivation and the importance of trust and trustworthiness—key elements of social capital (Ahn & Ostrom, 2008.) Our purpose in this chapter is to examine social capital theory in the context of common pool resource (CPR) institutions dealing with the management of natural resources.

According to Pierre Bourdieu, there are three types of capital: economic, cultural, and social (Bourdieu, 1986). Social capital is value based on networks and relationships, and allows informal cooperation and collaboration (Bourdieu 1986); and cooperation among groups with strong social networks that allows stakeholders to work toward a common goal (Raymond, 2006; Morris, Gibson, Leavitt, & Jones, 2013). Social capital is similar to trust and reciprocity in CPR institutions in the sense that it is tied to preexisting social networks, and in that it encourages and supports repeated engagement between institutional members. Collective action becomes a necessary component of any situation in which the tasks are of a significant size and require individuals to commit resources toward an outcome, while at the same time struggling with the temptation to break apart and tackle individual interests (Ostrom, 2005). Public actions, whether in government or nonprofit agencies, or as part of voluntary community management, are dependent on trust built through ongoing, repeated, and successful interactions. Each successful engagement creates social capital and provides a foundation for future participation, negotiation, and exchange.

Participants in the action can be NGOs, governments, or private organizations, with social capital leading to specialization, task division, and role definition around specific shared outcomes (Ostrom, 2005). For both larger scale networks with diverse participants and smaller networks whose members are less homogeneous, efficiency is increased as partners focus on components of collective action for which they are specialized and trust their partners to complete the remainder of tasks to benefit the whole. Social capital allows partners to trust each other enough to focus on individual organizational assets and to share them with the network for mutual benefit, instead of attempting to reach their goals by completing the entire series of tasks associated with success.

Social capital, in the form of norms and rules of behavior on how individuals interact with one another to achieve shared goals, is especially valuable to the governance of nonprofit and public organizations and community-based systems (Ostrom, 1992). These norms and rules provide collective action guidelines for new and old actors; and formal and informal rules establish parameters for longer term engagement. With specialized roles, the rules and parameters of engagement become even more important for effective decision-making and positive outcomes. Systems with higher levels of social capital not only are more efficient, but also are more flexible and adaptable to changes in the community. This resiliency allows them to tackle more complex problems that may require longer term planning and commitment by participants. Moving beyond individual relationships, social capital held between organizations can lead to commitments that move beyond the terms of individual leaders.

Public administration's interest in social capital and its role in collective action are tied to participation in decision-making. As participants work together to negotiate solutions to complex problems, their ability to depend on good will during the process is at the foundation of working together to solve the challenges of natural resource management. Social capital allows members of a community or larger scale collective action situation to invest in the process now because of an awareness of past and possible future outcomes. Building social capital requires documentation of successes and failures, and of the degree to which individual members are meeting their responsibilities. This history, whether formally or informally maintained, reduces information asymmetry for the group and increases awareness of actions that work or do not work in the short run and the long run.

The major research question addressed in this chapter is how social capital works to help overcome the collective action dilemma and foster collaboration. This chapter provides case studies that trace the role of social capital through two environment-focused systems, the Regional Greenhouse Gas Initiative and the Platte River Recovery Implementation Program. The two examples demonstrate the importance of accumulated social capital in creating effective decision-making mechanisms for common pool resource management.

Social Capital and Collaboration in Civil Society

Social capital is central to civil society because communities, voluntary organizations, government, and business must collaborate to achieve shared goals. Renegotiation of social contracts between stakeholders, investment in social capital, and an understanding that problems require collaboration strengthen civil society and improve outcomes (O'Connell, 1999). By contributing resources to the shared goals of the network, which may include time, money, and human resources, the organization invests in building trust with network members. In order for this investment to build social capital, the resources must be made available consistently and over the long run, without an appearance of a particular participant benefitting disproportionately from the relationship. As individual stakeholders become dissatisfied with the rules and/or practices of the system, change may take place, but the solidarity built by social capital allows the group to remain cohesive through the change (O'Connell, 1999). The crafting and recrafting of institutions must involve stakeholders and is an ongoing process (Ostrom, 1992).

Participation based on social capital becomes critical, because excluded stakeholders may filter and ignore governmental and formal rules and also create and enforce their own (Gibson, McKean, & Ostrom, 2000). Exclusion of individuals from the decision-making process, whether voluntary or involuntary, means that they do not have the ability to define the norms of collective action. Nonparticipation means not taking part in the action and not taking part in the decision-making that leads to action; however because problem-solving is tied to incentives, and increased participation can result in more effective solutions as well as increased access to rewards, individuals have a great deal of motivation to remain a part of the collective action situation (Ostrom, 1990). In such systems, shared resources are monitored and infractions are reported and punished as stakeholders pursue their own short-term and long-term interests (Ostrom, 1990).

When collective action is based on social networks and trustworthiness of participants, social motivations are enhanced and policymaking becomes "an on-going, continuously changing public dialogue among citizens, organized interests and policy makers" and is more equitable and participatory (Williams & Matheney, 1995; Weaver, Rock, & Kusterer, 1997). Success of the collaborative venture depends on the active participation of individual stakeholders (Ostrom, 1992). Collaborative action, in turn, depends on social capital that has been accumulated based on a history of mutual trust and available for investment in collective action to solve future challenges. Like other forms of capital, economic and human, social capital adds value to the final outcome.

Social Capital and Decision-Making

The value of social capital in reducing the costs of decision-making is also important to consider in collective action. Decisions about allocation of common pool resources by collective actors can be reached through majority rule or through unanimity (Buchanan & Tullock, 1962; Buchanan & Musgrave, 1999). Each of these decision-making tools offers cost advantages and disadvantages depending on the nature of the goods and services provided. Especially for goods and services that are routinely provided and for which there is little history of controversy in the decision-making process, unanimity may be costly in that a few outlier stakeholders can extend the time and money required for decision-making.

On the other hand, for publicly provided goods and services that could have significant negative impacts on a few members and for which there is the potential of legal overturning of decisions, majority rule may be more costly in the long run and the network would be better off seeking a solution to which all parties agree. In that case, the generalized set of rules, including those based on social capital with its associated norms of trust and reciprocity, limits the exploitation that results from majority rule models (Buchanan & Musgrave, 1999).

Social capital reduces opportunistic activity by individual actors. There is greater buy-in for the framework and structure around which decisions are made (Brennan & Buchanan, 1980). Additionally, rent-seeking behavior is minimized and the value of membership in the collective is increased (Buchanan & Musgrave, 1999). Social capital reduces the costs of decision-making and related action at the individual and group levels. This is critical in that all opportunistic activities produce short-term costs for others, and potentially long-term costs for everyone involved (Ostrom, 1992).

In groups with social capital to draw on, repeated interactions establish patterns of decision-making and solidify the decision-making process, reducing the number of decisions to be made. Fewer decisions lead to lower costs because actors are focusing on long-term goals instead of on short-term interests and because actors only negotiate on issues in which they have higher stakes and allow lower stake decisions to be driven by established processes and policies (Buchanan & Tullock, 1962).

The number of individuals and the associated costs of decision-making also play a part (Buchanan & Tullock, 1962). These costs are affected by homogeneity of the group and the size of the commons (Buchanan & Musgrave, 1999; Buchanan & Tullock, 1962). The more alike the value choices of the group, the less costly the decision-making process. Collective action, in order to be more efficient, should be organized in small rather than large networks due to problems of decision-making related to size and centralization (Buchanan & Tullock, 1962: Ostrom, 1992).

The costs of decision-making are at their lowest when the collective is small and homogeneous; and publicly provided goods are most efficiently provided in small, homogeneous coalitions with some predefined rules as to decision-making. Social capital is more likely to develop in small communities, because individuals come to collective action arrangements with previously established relationships. It is especially important, however, when the group does not have shared goals and has to address environmental issues or resource allocation issues. When stakeholders have competing interests, and when the scale of collective action increases, it may be more difficult to build and then draw upon social capital. Networks and trustworthiness allow participants to focus on the long-run instead of the short-run gains of exit, as discussed in the next section.

Social Capital, Exit, Voice, and Loyalty

'Exit' and 'voice' are terms that are important in understanding and building social capital and sustaining collective action. Social capital in this case provides a stable resource from which participants can draw to repair interpersonal or system problems instead of exiting the system when such problems occur. Again, long-run interests outweigh short-run temptations to exit the collective action situation. Hirschman (1970) believes that economists and scholars as a whole have paid little attention to repairing lapses in economic functioning and efficiency. Instead they attribute these lapses to competition, which in turn serves to eliminate inefficient players from the economic field.

Hirschman (1970) states that the lack of interest in repairing relationships is influenced by the assumptions that actors are fully and undeviatingly rational and that recovery from a lapse is not necessary in a competitive market. When social and political networks are evaluated as if they are markets, the potential of social capital to reinforce norms of mutual trust and reciprocity and to sanction participants is overlooked.

Hirschman (1970) introduces the concepts of 'exit' and 'voice' as a means of recuperating social relationships in collective action situations. Exit is a private action, and is economic in nature (Hirschman, 1970, 1993). Voice is the option of expressing dissatisfaction directly to the leaders of the offending organization or agency (Hirschman, 1970). It is likely to require group action and is more costly in regards to time and effort than is exit (Hirschman, 1993). Voice is political in nature and allows participants to delay the exit mechanism in pursuit of larger goals (Hirschman, 1970). Thus the voice option depends on the availability of social capital.

Exit is the primary option presented in economics, but it provides only two options: to leave or to stay. Voice is a critical alternative because of its graduated nature, as it can vary in intensity based on the problem and the importance to the participant (Hirschman, 1970). Voice is seen as an alternative to exit, in that exit eliminates the strongest, most vocal participants first who are often the most influential leaders and may offer meaningful solutions to collective action problems (Hirschman, 1970, 1993). Keeping the most influential participants requires social capital based on networks, trustworthiness, and mechanisms to punish exploitation in a trust situation (Ahn & Ostrom, 2008).

Individuals can use voice to build commitment and guide decisions that increase social capital resources. In organizations with social capital, exit and voice are balanced with loyalty wherein participants forgo radical actions in the short run because they see collective action as having longer term values. Loyalty is the decision to remain within the group, even when the individual is dissatisfied with a component of the network's plan or its actions.

Because the relationship of network members is built on repeated interactions from which the outcomes have been beneficial to them and social capital has been stored, individuals can draw on this reserve when the outcomes are not in their favor in the short run. Social capital mitigates the possibility of exit in the short run in favor of perceived benefits in the long run, thus providing greater stability to the group.

Social Capital Collective Action and Common Pool Resources

Systems which use common pool resources benefit from rules based on community norms that preserve these resources. Common pool resources are rival, in that they diminish in their value to individual users with the addition of users, and are non-excludable in that users cannot be kept from using the system through physical or legal barriers. Common pool resources are often publicly provided but are not pure public goods by the economic definition.

Public goods, by this definition, are non-rival and non-excludable, meaning that the addition of users does not diminish their value in use. Because government and markets are unable to successfully regulate complex natural resource systems that cross jurisdictional and functional boundaries, institutions which successfully manage them through collective action are especially valuable in public administration (Ostrom, 1990). Publicly provided goods, more of which are common-pool resources than pure public goods, require systems for collective action inside and outside of formal governmental networks, regulations, and actions.

According to Ostrom (1990), the characteristics of common pool resource institutions which are long-enduring include clearly defined boundaries, a match between local values, expectations, and norms and rules for appropriation and provision, collective choice arrangements, monitoring, graduated sanctions, conflict resolution methods, and recognition of the right to organize. There are both benefits and costs to common pool resource distribution systems. One benefit is sharing of transaction activities and their costs in the provision of goods (Ostrom, 1992). Communities can also benefit from sharing priority resources or goods as common pool resources that are inefficient to maintain privately. Examples are police or fire response systems that are necessary to maintain continuously and to access periodically, but because of their high cost if maintained privately are more effectively and efficiently provided as CPRs.

The risks of sharing common pool resources include free-riding, rent-seeking, and corruption (Ostrom, 1992). Opportunistic activities have

244   D. Leuenberger and C. Reed

short-term costs for those who are non-opportunistic, and long-run costs can impact all actors (Ostrom, 1992). Like other discussions of social capital and collective action in this chapter, there is an emphasis on balancing benefits in the short run and in the long run.

One potential problem of sustainable systems, however, is that incentives for new development override motivators for the maintenance of existing systems (Ostrom, Schroeder, & Wynne, 1993). Successful common pool resource institutions rely on existing stocks of social capital in order to sustain commitment to collective goals. Incentives normally powerful in keeping the group together may not be powerful enough to maintain the system, and outside intervention may be required in addition to networks and trustworthiness (Ahn & Ostrom, 2008). In these cases, the presence of government regulations, sanctions, and incentives may provide enough motivation to sustain collective action, because the costs of exit are higher than the cost of participation for collective members.

Applications of Social Capital and Collective Action

The following case studies illustrate the importance of social capital in overcoming two significant collective action dilemmas: first, the role of long-established relationships in providing a foundation for regional climate change and energy management by member states in New England; and second, the development of norms and rules developed by actors to govern the use of water and land along the Platte River in central Nebraska for the protection of endangered and threatened bird species.

The Regional Greenhouse Gas Initiative

An application of larger scale management of common pool resources with government intervention is the Regional Greenhouse Gas Initiative (RGGI). RGGI is the first mandatory market-based carbon dioxide emissions reduction program in the United States. The market-based emissions auction and trading system allows electric utilities to exchange the right to emit carbon dioxide, and revenues from the trade provide energy development resources for renewable, low-carbon emitting energy sources. The goals of RGGI are to reduce carbon dioxide emissions by 10% by 2018 and to use cap and trade revenues to build economic and environmental resources tied to green energy in the Northeastern United States.

The system is an 'auction only' system, which means it gives no preferences to existing users, and allows each of the partner states to auction their allocation of certificates. States are then charged with creating individual investment plans for the proceeds, including managing regressive impacts on electricity users from increased prices. Regressive impacts of the system include higher energy costs and the burden on lower income households, because the cost of energy and related increases is a larger portion of income.

The long-established relationships among member states increase the positive impacts of energy conservation on climate change and reduce pollution impacts. An increase in membership by states in RGGI creates mutual gains, as well as positive externalities for the region. Positive gains for environmental issues, such as climate change, require building relationships outside of arbitrarily established political boundaries and application at the scale of the bioregion. This means that positive impacts may require drawing on shared interests between individual states and tackling problems at a higher level.

In New England partnerships on a number of area initiatives ranging from transportation to energy management have depended on social capital built over generations as regional problems are solved. States are voluntary actors and draw on social capital built over time to solidify their long-run investments in the RGGI system. Political, social, and economic similarities also serve to solidify relationships and expand the likelihood of success.

Social Capital and Collaboration in Civil Society: RGGI

Cap-and-trade approaches set a maximum level of aggregate emissions within a system, assign rights to emit through a licensing process, and allow individual firms or organizations to trade those licenses (Tietenberg, 2006). The cap-and-trade approach uses both economic incentives and social capital to maximize outcomes. There are positive economic incentives for states and community partners to participate in RGGI, including additional resources for environment-focused nonprofit organizations and for charitable organizations providing energy assistance or home energy management programs. States themselves derive direct financial resources from the system and have control over distribution of these resources. The management of the common pool resources aligned to RGGI's mission and the distribution of resources depend on social capital and established organizational relationships.

Air quality and climate change management are common pool resource outcomes of collective action in the RGGI system. If an auction mechanism is adopted, producers initially bear the cost of negative externalities when they purchase a license and then pass these costs on to consumers. Models of license distribution in cap-and-trade systems include distribution free of charge (a subsidy), sale at a fixed price, and sale through auction (Hufbauer, Charnovitz, & Kim, 2009). Emissions trading is seen as a flexible option relative to regulatory models of carbon emissions management because reduction can occur from a variety of system components within a single firm and because firms can obtain the reduction from an another firm (Tietenberg, 2006).

Recent applications of cap-and-trade programs in the United States include RGGI and the Western Climate Initiative (WCI) (Raymond, 2010). In both cases, state governments work with each other and with private and public institutions to manage carbon dioxide emissions through macro- and micro-level changes. Participation in the initiative is mandatory for electric utilities, but voluntary for organizations working with emissions management and education at the household level and for organizations providing aid programs that redistribute resources to low-income families for heating and home energy efficiency renovations. The voluntary nature of civil society member participation draws directly on social capital previously established between private and public organizations in the system.

Social Capital and Decision-Making: RGGI

In comparing early and recent cap-and-trade programs in the Unites States, several differences emerge. Older principles of cap-and-trade processes discouraged the assignment of private rights to public resources, saw initial allocations as having little value to environmental advocates, supported allocation privileges for current and past users, and distrusted auction models (Raymond, 2010). More recent approaches to cap-and-trade maximize the role of the market in carbon emissions management through "explicit and transferable" assignment of property rights (Tietenberg, 2006). Specific changes to the cap-and-trade system include integration of seasonality of emissions, balancing of cost reduction and environmental benefit, and aggregation and limiting of emissions so as to allow new entrants into the system (Tietenberg, 2006). The RGGI system incorporates many of these more recent changes to the principles of cap-and-trade options.

RGGI contributes to the management of the commons around global climate change and carbon emissions management by providing market mechanisms and the structural/legal foundation for the system at the regional level. Although a mandated system for utilities, it is a voluntary process for states. It begins to manage emissions by establishing boundaries, rules, and monitoring within the energy sector, while also providing infrastructural development resources. Because the rules and mandates are designed in partnership with the energy industry and partner states, the major actors are, in effect, bounding their own common pool resource system.

Social capital is critical in the voluntary nature of participation, and it is also critical in the stakeholders' ability to create meaningful decision-making rules. An alternative would be to treat the system as a "club" or "a voluntary group deriving mutual benefit from sharing one or more of the following: production costs, the members' characteristics, or a good characterized by excludable benefits" (Sandler & Tschirhart, 1980).

Social Capital, Exit, Voice, and Loyalty: RGGI

In the RGGI system it is important to understand the role of exit, voice, and loyalty. As discussed earlier, state participation in RGGI is voluntary and is completely dependent on loyalty to the initiative. This loyalty may be built on shared vision and mission, on positive perceptions of the political and social value of participation, and on accumulation of social capital from repeated interactions between states over the long run. Additionally, exit may be too expensive an option, with the economic and social benefits of participation outweighing costs of membership. The voice option also has intense value, with a demonstrated value in decision-making wherein participants may opt in, instead of out, simply because of the desire to remain vocal and active in the decision-making.

Interestingly, New Jersey left the collaborative in 2011, using the exit option discussed earlier. Estimates are that New Jersey would have gained over $100 million in the auction process while reducing emissions and pollution in the state. In 2014, there were intense discussions about re-entry into RGGI, although at the writing of this chapter New Jersey continued to operate outside of the RGGI system. The use of exit in this particular case is especially interesting given the activeness of the voice option in the RGGI system, especially in the design of revenue distribution methods and in the choice of resource recipients.

Although the revenue collection process is uniform across states, individual states have the option to distribute revenues as they choose. It will be important to continue to watch developments in the exit of New Jersey from the RGGI system, because they run contrary to expectations that are based on the accumulated social capital built between member states between 2005 and 2011; and because the voice option in the exit, voice, and loyalty approach would suggest that voice would be the preferred option to exit. It is possible that the long-run outcome will be re-entry into the collective action system based on these characteristics.

The Platte River Recovery Implementation Program

The Platte River Recovery Implementation Program (PRRIP) began on January 1, 2007 following more than 10 years of negotiation among the governors of Nebraska, Colorado, and Wyoming, and the U.S. Department of Interior, as well as stakeholders representing water users and environmental organizations. The trigger event was a jeopardy biological opinion issued by the U.S. Fish and Wildlife Service (FWS) under the Endangered Species Act regarding impacts of federally funded water diversion and storage projects on listed bird species: the whooping crane, interior least tern, and piping plover. The FWS also designated a stretch of the Platte River in central Nebraska as critical habitat. The FWS withdrew its jeopardy opinion, allowing existing water development projects to proceed in exchange for an agreement to meet an overall objective reducing deficits to target flows by 130,000 to 150,000 acre feet per year and to purchase 10,000 acres of land to restore nesting and roosting sites in the critical habitat area.

A Governance Committee (GC), staffed by the Headwaters Corporation (HWC), has decision-making authority for all aspects of the PRRIP. Many other ecosystem restoration programs are only advisory to federal agencies. The GC is a stand-alone entity that manages a large common pool resource. As Freeman (2010, p. 408) put it in his epic history of the PRRIP:

> This has been a tale of how powerful rival self-seeking water providers—historically defensive of their settled regimes—were mobilized to transcend prisoners' dilemma dynamics on issue after issue to forge a new state-federal system of water commons governance that has promised to slow and eventually reverse habitat degradation and thereby overcome the tragedy of the commons on a segment of the central Platte River.

Averting a tragedy of the commons caused by individual exploitation of surface and groundwater happened because the FWS exchanged regulatory certainty for defined contributions of money, water, and land. The solution to the collective action (prisoners') dilemma was a self-governing common-pool resource institution rather than top-down regulation by the FWS. Although the agency is represented on the GC, and has the ultimate say whether the Program is in compliance with the ESA, federal officials have played a more nuanced role than as enforcer.

The FWS has held back from taking a hard line on implementation, allowing states, water users, and environmental organizations represented on the GC to develop a socially sustainable process for resolving differences in approaches to managing the Platte River. The continued existence of the Program is due to the conviction among many GC members that the alternative—individual project consultations under the ESA—could be much worse (Reed et al., 2012). Nevertheless, social capital has played an important role in ways suggested in the introduction to this chapter.

Social Capital and Collaboration in Civil Society: PRRIP

Organizations invest in building social capital in a number of ways, by contributing time, money, and human resources toward shared goals. As Ostrom (1992) argued, sustaining a common pool resource institution is a continuous process. It follows that trust and reciprocity depend on a consistent infusion of resources, as well as a belief among participants that no one is benefitting disproportionately from the arrangement. Another important aspect of social capital is inclusion of organizations with an important stake in the outcome, and access to the benefits of collective action. Finally, collective action based on social networks and trustworthiness leads to dialogues among representatives of organizations with diverse interests, perspectives, and ideas.

The PRRIP illustrates the importance of building social capital. The initial water contributions for the first, 13-year, increment of the Program were distributed proportionally among the three states: An Environmental

Account of storable inflows to Lake McConaughy in the northwestern 'panhandle' corner of Nebraska is expected to yield an average of 36,000 acre feet per year (AFY). Wyoming's plan is to use the Pathfinder Dam and Reservoir modification project to yield about 34,000 AFY. Colorado's Tamarack Plan I should contribute about 10,000 AFY near the state line with Nebraska (Freeman, 2010). The difference between this total of 80,000 AFY and the objective of 130,000–150,000 is 50,000 to 70,000 AFY. The Program is now in the process of designing projects to meet specific milestones, primarily through water 'retiming' rather than purchasing or leasing irrigated farmland. Taking land out of agricultural production would harm the Nebraska economy.

The trust and reciprocity that developed as a result of these initial negotiations have sustained recent efforts. One of the fears of water users was that the PRRIP would remove irrigated land from agricultural production. Instead, the Program has funded a major project to capture water in excess of 'target flows' or monthly flows based on a model hydrograph—typically occurring from November to February—then store and release portions of that water when needed for migrating, nesting, and roosting bird species, encompassing the period from mid-March to mid-November. The benefits to the participants are twofold: regulatory certainty and assurances that the Program will seek all possible ways to meet its responsibilities without relying on 'buy and dry' strategies that would harm the agricultural economy.

Social capital has been the source of a continuous and inclusive dialogue among GC members and the HWC staff. Nowhere is its importance more evident than in the Adaptive Management process; its design is based on 10 'Big Questions' about the effects of critical habitat restoration on the three listed bird species. The GC reached consensus on these questions with input from HWC staff and the Independent Scientific Advisory Committee (ISAC); however, there are two competing visions for managing the Platte River reflected in the Big Questions. The first seeks to restore the natural flow regime of the river, including in-channel nesting and roosting habitat. The second seeks to use primarily mechanical means to widen the river channel and build off-channel sites for nesting and fledging terns and plover (Reed, Campbell, George, Leuenberger, & McCarty, 2014).

The initial results are inconclusive, and subject to interpretation; however, the importance of social capital is evident in the willingness of the GC to allow both strategies to play out over time using adaptive management experiments and monitoring the response of listed species. Dialogue at quarterly GC meetings respects the need to maintain a separation between the science and policy implications of adaptive management. Nevertheless, the stakes are high, and it remains to be seen whether the existing stock of social capital will sustain further discussions and, ultimately, a consensus on next steps for managing the Platte River.

The key may be the stance of the FWS: will officials insist on a more expansive water objective as a condition for approving a second program increment in 2019? Or will substantial doubt about the meaning of adaptive management data lead the FWS and other members of the GC to agree to extend the first increment until a different vision for managing the Platte River emerges from the process?

Social Capital and Decision-Making: PRRIP

Social capital can reduce the costs of decision-making in a collective action situation, because by definition it reduces the likelihood of opportunistic behavior by participants. In addition, social capital leads to established patterns of decision-making that can reduce the time involved and the number of decisions to be made. It may also allow members to focus on more long-term goals, because they trust that collective action will meet their short-term needs.

Social capital is more likely to develop in smaller networks, because relationships are more likely to form there than in large, complex organizations. Smaller networks, in turn, can make decision-making less costly because the governing body is less dependent on subcommittees and specialized staff to handle scientific and technical issues, or large advisory committees that require time and energy to coordinate. On the other hand, social capital also allows participants to trust one another to divide up the tasks involved in implementing a complex program.

The organization of the PRRIP reflects many of these principles. The GC has established a pattern of meeting quarterly, rotating locations among the three states. Meetings start early afternoon on Tuesday and adjourn by noon the next day. This schedule allows GC members to fly or drive in and out and meet within a two-day time frame. Dinner is 'on your own,' and members use that occasion to continue discussions from the meeting or to re-establish social ties.

Because the GC has been meeting since 2007, and because the turnover of members has been quite low, the stock of social capital accumulated over the years has allowed members to discuss potentially divisive matters in a civil, mutually respectful manner. The relatively small size of the GC, considering the scope of the Program and the complexity of the issues, lowers the cost of decision-making.

The role of the HWC staff is critical to increasing the efficiency of decision-making, because of their expertise in hydrology, biology, biosystems engineering, land acquisition, and natural resources management. Staff members support several committees, and there is a GC liaison as well as staff from member organizations on the water advisory, land advisory, and technical advisory committees.

A pattern of decision-making has evolved over time in which agenda items are first discussed within the advisory committees then brought to the GC for final discussion and approval. Decisions are by consensus; if there are any objections to a motion, the chair refers the matter back to the advisory committee (Reed et al., 2012). While decision-making is costly in terms of staff specialists and the time involved in referring issues to advisory committees, the overall size and complexity of the PRRIP is modest compared to the Florida Everglades and California Bay-Delta (CALFED) ecosystem recovery programs.

Social Capital, Exit, Voice, and Loyalty: PRRIP

The option to exit from the Program is always present; however, participants have chosen voice as their preferred option. As stated earlier, voice is political in nature and allows participants to delay the exit mechanism in the pursuit of larger goals. The voice option depends on availability of social capital, as does loyalty—the third option. In the case of the PRRIP, GC members have clearly opted for voice and loyalty over exit.

The prospect of individual ESA consultations may have been the major reason why GC members originally avoided exiting from the PRRIP. As time goes on, however, the FWS has begun to play a different role, reluctant to wield the ESA 'hammer,' and more inclined to search with others on the GC for solutions that rely on some degree of mechanical intervention because of irreversible changes in surface water flows, sediment balance, and channel width. This more nuanced role reinforces the benefit of voice and loyalty options for other GC members.

Social Capital, Collective Action, and Common Pool Resources

As discussed in the introduction to this chapter, successful common pool resource institutions rely on existing stocks of social capital in order to sustain commitment to collective goals. One problem identified by Ostrom et al. (1993) is that incentives for new development may override motivations for maintaining existing arrangements. Social capital is one resource that may help to resist development pressures.

It is often assumed that local arrangements are more likely to develop social capital than state-federal programs, like the PRRIP. It is just as likely, though, to see local collective action derailed in small communities because of a comparative lack of financial capital needed to withstand development pressures. The loss of family farms to corporate agriculture is just one example. State contributions plus federal appropriations through the U.S. Bureau of Reclamation for the PRRIP create the financial capacity to balance pressures for water development against the habitat needs of listed bird species.

Whether outside intervention in the form of public regulations, incentives, and sanctions help to sustain collective action is a question for future research. It would be ironic if government intervention were found to be necessary to sustain local collective action, however, because much of Ostrom's research concluded that local self-governance was not only possible but also desirable. In the case of the PRRIP, the ESA has undoubtedly countered the political influence of the agricultural economy that is heavily dependent on irrigation.

In addition, a 2004 Nebraska law requires integrated management plans to balance supply and use of groundwater with a hydrological connection to surface water, such as the Platte River. Both the PRRIP and the integrated water management planning process have brought together participants with little previous experience in working together, including surface and groundwater users. Overcoming the collective action problem when it means crossing surface and groundwater, as well as jurisdictional, boundaries requires that the benefits of collective action in this new context outweigh the costs for all participants: local irrigation districts, groundwater users, as well as government agencies.

Conclusion

The examples of RGGI and PRRIP provide evidence that there is a need for additional research on collective action networks for environmental resources management, especially for those that are common pool resources. While evidence as to the value of such networks at the smaller scale has been documented by Ostrom and others, there is little direct evidence of the effectiveness of such systems at the larger scale in achieving complex goals. As environmental issues often require resolution at the scale of ecological systems and bioregions, instead of politically or socially established boundaries such as states, partnerships built on social capital are critical.

It is still unclear in the examples provided whether there will truly be positive environmental impacts in the long run, even when stakeholders appear to be communicating and engaging in decision-making. When at this scale action decisions are necessary, it is possible that the degree of social capital banked may not be enough to resolve the most difficult of problems. This may especially be true as the system moves beyond planning to action or when action steps move from simpler, easier to achieve goals to more complex, resource-intensive, or politically divisive goals.

Collective action founded on social capital resources provides a means of managing scarce common pool resources in complex public administration arenas. While the strengths of collective action include increased opportunity for stakeholder participation, improved long-term decision-making, and alternatives to strong government regulation and intervention, there are also some challenges as well. Challenges include:

1   potentially high costs of institutional negotiation, which may reduce investment in action steps in lieu of investment in the decision-making process;
2   limited data on long-term outcomes, especially for larger and non-homogenous systems;
3   uncertainty as to the degree of necessary government involvement in larger scale systems;
4   unclear and competing action steps for short-term and long-term goal achievement in all collective action networks.

Some research has been completed on the role of social capital in decision-making for positive environmental change where common pool resources are involved. Ostrom's work has provided a great deal of insight into smaller systems, and provides a baseline for understanding more complex systems. Exploration of more complex systems and data collection that looks at systems over the long run will add a great deal to our understanding of applications in social capital, collective action, and collaboration.

References

Ahn, T., & Ostrom, E. (2008). Social capital and collective action. In D. Castiglione, J. Van Deth, & G. Wolleb (Eds.), *The handbook of social capital* (pp. 70–100). New York, NY: Oxford University Press.

Bourdieu, P. (1986). The forms of capital. In J. Richardson (Ed.), *Handbook of theory and research for the sociology of education* (pp. 241–258). New York, NY: Greenwood Press.

Brennan, G., & Buchanan, J. M. (1980). *The power to tax: Analytical foundations of a fiscal constitution.* New York, NY: Cambridge University Press.

Buchanan, J. M., & Musgrave, R. A. (1999). *Public finance and public choice: Two contrasting visions of the state.* Cambridge, MA: MIT Press.

Buchanan, J. M., & Tullock, G. (1962). *The calculus of consent: Logical foundations of constitutional democracy.* Ann Arbor, MI: The University of Michigan Press.

Freeman, D. (2010). *Implementing the Endangered Species Act on the Platte Basin water commons.* Boulder, CO: University Press of Colorado.

Gibson, C., McKean, M., & Ostrom, E. (2000). *People and forests: Communities, institutions, and governance.* Boston, MA: MIT Press.

Heikkila, T., & Gerlak, A. (2005). The formation of large-scale collaborative resource management institutions: Clarifying the roles of stakeholders, science and institutions. *The Policy Studies Journal, 33,* 583–612.

Hirschman, A. O. (1970). *Exit, voice, and loyalty: Responses to decline in firms, organizations, and states.* Cambridge, MA: Harvard University Press.

Hirschman, A. O. (1993). Exit, voice, and the fate of the German Democratic Republic: An essay in conceptual history. *World Politics, 45,* 173–202.

Hufbauer, G. C., Charnovitz, S., & Kim, J. (2009). Global warming and the world trading system. Washington, DC: Peterson Institute for International Economics.

Morris, J., Gibson, W., Leavitt, W., & Jones, S. (2013). *The case for grassroots collaboration.* Lanham, MD: Lexington Books.

O'Connell, B. (1999). *Civil society: The underpinnings of American democracy.* Hanover, NH: University Press of New England.

Ostrom, E. (1990). *Governing the commons: The evolution of institutions for collective action.* London, England: Cambridge University Press.

Ostrom, E. (1992). *Crafting institutions for self-governing irrigation systems.* San Francisco, CA: Institute for Contemporary Studies.

Ostrom, E. (2005). *Understanding institutional diversity.* Princeton, NJ, and Oxford, England: Princeton University Press.

Ostrom, E., Schroder, L., & Wynne, S. (1993). *Institutional incentives and sustainable development: Infrastructure policies in perspective.* Cambridge, MA: Westview Press.

Raymond, L. (2006). Cooperation without trust: Overcoming collective action barriers to endangered species protection. *The Policy Studies Journal, 34*, 37–57.

Raymond, L. (2010). The emerging revolution in emissions trading policy. In B. G. Rabe (Ed.), *Greenhouse governance: Addressing climate change in America* (pp. 101–126). Washington, DC: Brookings Institute Press.

Reed, C., Bartle, J., Aiken, D., George, M., Leuenberger, D., & Campbell, A. (2012). *The potential of collaborative governance: The Platte River Recovery Implementation Program.* Lincoln, NE: Robert J. Daugherty Water for Food Institute.

Reed, C., Campbell, A., George, M., Leuenberger, D., & McCarty, J. (2014). Social capital in large-scale environmental collaboration: the case of the Platte River Recovery Implementation Program. *Water Policy, 17*(3), 472–483.

Sandler, T., & Tschirhart, J. T. (1980). The economic theory of clubs: An evaluative survey. *Journal of Economic Literature, 17*, 1481–1521.

Tietenberg, T. H. (2006). *Emissions trading principles and practice* (2nd ed.). Washington, DC: Resources for the Future.

Weaver, J. H., Rock, M. T., & Kusterer, K. (1997). *Achieving broad-based sustainable development: Governance, environment, and growth with equity.* West Hartford, CT: Kumarian Press.

Williams, B. A., & Matheny, A. R. (1995). *Democracy, dialogue, and environmental disputes: The contested languages of social regulation.* New Haven, CT: Yale University Press.

13 Exploring Interagency Collaboration in the National Security Domain

A Distinct Form of Collaboration?

Brian Martinez[1]

Introduction

This research investigates interagency collaboration concepts and practices in the context of a national security setting. Interagency collaboration practices exist side by side with traditional hierarchical organizational structures and practices. The Government Accountability Office (GAO) defines interagency collaboration as "any joint activity that is intended to produce more public value than could be produced when the agencies act alone" (Steinhardt, 2005, p. 4). Interagency collaboration enables governmental responses to complex missions and tasks associated with intractable national-level problems. Interagency organizations require collaborative mechanisms to improve partnerships with other organizations. GAO defines collaborative mechanisms as arrangements or applications that facilitate the implementation of collaboration goals (Mihm, 2012). These mechanisms are thought to support practices that can enhance and sustain interagency collaboration efforts (Steinhardt, 2005).

A review of the academic and practitioner literature precedes investigation into an exemplar for interagency collaboration. This analysis responds to questions about whether interagency collaboration is a viable structural counterpart to purely hierarchical organizations, particularly as a means to resolve intractable national-level problems. The principal research question asks: what organizational mechanisms support interagency collaboration practices? A related question asks how interagency collaboration is differentiated from other forms of collaboration. Assuming collaboration practices are a requirement for operating in the interagency environment, do mechanisms better facilitate collaborative capacity to resolve national-level problems? This chapter explores interagency collaboration in the context of the national security domain, an arena in which collaboration has become an important element of interorganizational activity. We will examine this activity by analyzing several exemplar cases to illustrate the foundational concepts of interagency collaboration.

Four primary activities comprise the chapter. First, a review of concepts begins the process to differentiate and specify interagency collaboration. In particular, mandated collaboration differentiates interagency collaboration from other forms of collaboration. Next, a list of interagency collaboration mechanisms is explored. Third, an exemplar of interagency collaboration from the national security domain is found to support conceptual interagency mechanisms. Intractable and complex problems may be nowhere more evident than in the national security domain concerned with the defense, foreign relations, and protection of national interests. Last, recommendations for future research focus on improving understanding relationships between interagency collaboration mechanisms and interagency effectiveness.

Interagency Collaboration in the Scholarly and Program Evaluation Literature

Interagency Collaboration Concepts in the Scholarly Literature

Defining interagency collaboration as a distinct form of collaboration is unresolved in the scholarly and practitioner literatures (Agranoff, 2012; Steinhardt, 2005). There is agreement that wicked problems are the basis for partnerships between agencies (Bardach, 1998; McGuire, 2006; O'Toole & Meier, 2003). The literature provides instructive characteristics and features for interagency collaboration. First, interagency collaboration is an organizing concept for agency responses to big and complex problems (Ansell & Gash, 2008; Gray, 1989; Rainey, 2009). Second, the purpose of interagency collaborations is to resolve "nettlesome" problems (Agranoff, 2006, p. 59; Bin, 2008; Kaiser, 2011; Mandell & Keast, 2008). Third, problem-solving in the interagency domain is a complex process involving many actors, and factors.

Interagency collaboration is an evolving phenomenon. The concept of institution differentiates between public institutions and private or nongovernmental (e.g., not-for-profit) organizations. Two key factors help explain the emergence of interagency as a principally institutional form of collaboration. First, the perceived rise in interagency practices in the federal government is attributed to governmental expansion at all levels (Agranoff, 2012). Second, the expansion or growth of government is described as a response to hyperpluralism. The concept of hyperpluralism characterizes increasing demands upon government from an increasing number of stakeholders. The picture created by hyperpluralism is one of poor system reliability because the system is overloaded with requests and underserved by resources.

In short, interagency collaboration is thought to be a response to system overloads. Some scholars even believe that the nature of hyperpluralism is redefining federalism (Kettl, 2002). This means that government must operate more interdependently and with more partners. The federalist model refers back to traditional hierarchical structures of government and governing. If institutions no longer meet their missions going it alone, then new and revised administrative and management practices are needed to respond to demands placed upon federal programs, and to the complexity inherent in these new relationships (Agranoff, 2012; McGuire, Agranoff, & Silvia, 2010). Where these relationships begin and end, and to what end are important questions.

The challenge to define concepts and practices in interagency collaboration is illustrated by the difficulties to define the boundaries of wicked problems. Boundary definition can be thought of as administrative processes to understand specifics about the problem, responses, authorities, and required expertise. Domain concepts assume a set of actions to align stakeholder efforts and resources with what must be done, by the right organizations, and to achieve desired effects or outcomes (Trist, 1983).

In interagency domains outcomes to national-level problems require planning and organizing through interinstitutional, multi-jurisdictional, and multisector means. An example helps to underscore the importance of specifying the interagency domain. Conceptualizing collaboration as a state process, interagency activity can be an instrument of the government to seek strategic objectives to create or maintain order through national security (Kaiser, 2011). Interagency collaborations can be directed towards the development of solutions to intractable policy problems at the federal level. Margerum (2008) proposes a typology of collaboration based on institutional theories and levels of decision-making that are believed to be prerequisites for policy implementation. In Margerum's view, collaboration requires understanding of organizational history, technical complexity, power dynamics, membership size, and resources. The structure of interagency collaborations considers such factors.

Collaboration structure relates to planning and other requirements for commitment and expertise. Gray (1989) cites Whetten and Bozeman's (1984) taxonomy and identifies three kinds of organizational alliances (structures): "federations, councils, and coalitions" (p. 21) with federations being the most organized. Foster and Meinhard (2002) recommend that size, age, and other organizational factors can influence roles, participation, and level of influence in the collaborative process. The authors conceive that larger organizations are more likely to collaborate in interagency domains because they have more resources than smaller organizations (Foster & Meinhard, 2002).

Government reports cited in the scholarly literature describe types of interagency activities to distinguish between collaboration as a broad concept, and other types of activities and organizational arrangements (Agranoff, 2006, 2012; Bardach, 1998; Gray, 1989; Hardy, Phillips, & Lawrence, 2003; Margerum, 2008; McGuire et al., 2010). The Congressional Research Service (CRS) identified a list of six interagency arrangements that parallel the academic literature (Kaiser, 2011). The CRS list begins with collaboration based on organizational parity. Second, a lead agent characterizes coordinating activities. Third, mergers rely upon combining the resources of multiple agencies. Fourth, integration is the nonpermanent transfer of resources from one agency to another for a specific project or task. Fifth, networks require the participation of multiple levels of government that can include federal, state, local, tribal, and even foreign countries. Last, partnerships are comprised of not-for-profit organizations, for-profit companies and firms, government-sponsored enterprises, and government-chartered corporations. Interagency practices that support these structural forms align with basic collaboration concepts.

Collaboration concepts for interdependence and networks are particularly important to interagency collaborative practices. The practice of agencies working together to solve common problems is a form of interdependence (Gray, 1989). The path to interdependence, as has been discussed throughout the book, is paved by an inability of any one organization to resolve a big and complex problem (alone). Interagency collaboration dynamics require different leader behaviors to implement and manage interdependence with other organizations. "The tools of leadership upon which effective managers of single agencies rely tend to be especially difficult to deploy in collaboratives" (Page, 2003, p. 315). Horizontally structured networks are characteristic of interagency collaborations (Agranoff, 2012). In practice, interdependence is born from interagency network structure. The addition of private organizations and nongovernmental third-party organizations to the problem process creates a complex network to achieve common goals (Agranoff, 2006, 2007; McGuire et al., 2010). Understanding the limits to organizational power and reach requires different leader and organizational approaches in the networked and cross-sector interagency collaboration environment (Agranoff, 2006, 2012; Bardach, 1998; Gray, 1989).

Two examples of what happens in organizations during interagency collaborations adds further dimension. First, collaborating partners normally cleave to their primary missions while participating in the network. Challenges may appear to reconcile collaborative network practices with hierarchically organized bureaucracies (Agranoff, 2006, 2012; Ansell & Gash, 2008; Bardach, 1998; Kaiser, 2011; Mandell & Keast, 2008; McGuire et al., 2010). Second, power (to make decisions, to expend resources, etc.) within the collaboration is contingent upon many participant factors. Power dynamics extend to the inner workings of the collaboration as well. Interorganizational theory posits that power dependence is a necessary characteristic of collaboration as a regulating force within networks (Agranoff, 2012). Strategic management theory borrows from theories of change, economic theory, and networks to explain collaboration as a resource that uses power-sharing to achieve common goals (Bryson, Berry, & Kaifeng, 2010).

Differences between hierarchically structured organizational decision-making and collaborative decision-making are confirmed by the conceptual literature. Page (2003) believes that public managers must understand the implications of shared power and authority to manage across organizational lines. Decision-making and implementation of strategies for collaborations requires managers to use participatory, inclusive processes (Page, 2003, p. 336).

National-level problems require complex command and control relationships to enable decision-making at the most appropriate level, indicating a need for "interoperable management" (Agranoff, 2012, p. 122). The dynamic nature of certain interagency collaboration tasks necessitates flexible decision-making that can be consensus based or shared. Agranoff (2012) cites GAO's defining characteristics for interoperable management as goals, planning, operating principles, operational information, role differentiation, communication, and operating systems to achieve coordinated responses (Jenkins, 2004). Conceptually, interoperable management is a tool to reconcile environmental complexity.

Planning is one of the functions embedded in the requirement for interoperable management and is informed by operations manuals and program information (Agranoff, 2012). Planning and other capacities have to transform to respond dynamically to interagency wicked problems. Response mechanisms must be reconciled with practices and constraints embedded in more traditional organizational hierarchical structure and culture (Mandell & Keast, 2008; McNamara, 2012; Vangen & Huxham, 2011).

Interagency Collaboration in the Government Evaluation and Practitioner Literature

GAO defines interagency collaboration in the government evaluation literature as "any joint activity by two or more organizations that is intended to produce more public value than could be produced when the organizations act alone" (Steinhardt, 2005, p. 6). The Government Accountability Office confirms the evolving nature of interagency collaboration as "activities that others have variously defined as cooperation, coordination, integration, or networking ... because there are no commonly accepted definitions of these terms and we are unable to make definitive distinctions between these different types of interagency activities" (as cited in Steinhardt, 2005, pp. 6–7). The Congressional Research Service noted that GAO's broad definitions led to the discovery of hundreds of collaborative activities among federal agencies (Kaiser, 2011).

Three goals are posited in the practitioner literature to differentiate interagency collaboration from other forms of collaboration: unity of effort through complementary organizational activities; second, a comprehensive approach to problem identification, definition, and solutions; and lastly, support to agency missions (Pendleton, 2010a). At the federal level, interorganizational partnerships are formed through interagency and cross-sector organizational practices (Mihm, 2014). GAO claims that interagency domains and collaborations can be categorized according to responses to emergencies and nonemergency problems (Mihm, 2014). The relative immaturity of interagency collaboration concepts is demonstrated by the absence of accepted definitions in the practitioner literature to clearly define task forces, working groups, councils, and committees (Mihm, 2012). However, GAO contends that interagency groups are the most commonly occurring organizational form of collaboration (Mihm, 2014). GAO's recommendations to implement practices in collaborative groups are based on how interagency task forces, working groups, councils, and committees defined outcomes, measured performance and ensured accountability, established leadership approaches, and used resources (Mihm, 2014, p. 2).

Similar to scholarly concepts that define a collaboration continuum of cooperation, coordination, and collaboration (Mandell & Keast, 2008; McNamara, 2012), the previous section listed six organizational collaborative arrangements including collaborating, coordinating, merging, integrating, networking, and partnering (Kaiser, 2011). Congressional researchers report that overlap and hybridization within different types of activities and arrangements in a single effort is not uncommon (Kaiser, 2011). Interagency organizational complexity adds degrees of difficulty to understanding the propositions and mechanisms for collaboration (Steinhardt, 2005).

The extant literature documents the perception that collaboration as human endeavor is built on trust. Practitioners identify individual participation as an interpersonal issue. An executive director of the Chief Human Capital Officers Council states, "We have different people every time working on council initiatives.... People are more willing to play ... if they are members of a community" (Bonner, 2013, p. 31).

The practitioner literature discusses the risks of interdependence, noting that risk is an inherent part of interagency collaborations given complexities that exist in the federal government. In particular, Bonner (2013) notes that collaboration participants must balance between tasks and relationships. Bonner defines tasks as charter and goals ... and contrasts these with relationships as "evolving connections between members" (Bonner, 2013, p. 30). Addressing the risks of interdependence, "many agencies are embracing meta-leadership skills and capabilities so that they can develop leaders who understand and can work in these complex and ambiguous endeavors" (Bonner, 2013, p. 32).

GAO recommends four key practice areas to strengthen interagency collaboration: (1) develop overarching strategies; (2) create collaborative organizations; (3) develop a well-trained workforce; and (4) improve information-sharing (Pendleton, 2010b, p. 2). GAO also identified key practices to help federal agencies enhance and sustain collaborative effort. GAO's recommended interagency collaborative practices include: articulating common outcomes, establishing mutually reinforcing or joint strategies, monitoring and reporting results, and reinforcing agency and individual accountability (Steinhardt, 2005, pp. 4–5). Alternatively, a simple framework to evaluate collaboration progress monitors initiation and membership, how the work gets done, and transition and closure (Bonner, 2013). Drawing from traditional public program evaluation, requirements for accountability are a typical feature of interagency collaboration mandates (Stanton, 2008).

Drivers of Interagency Collaboration Practices

Mandated Collaboration

The interagency literature defines a formal (mandated) collaborative arrangement as an authorization in the form of public law, executive order, administrative directive, or memorandum of agreement (Kaiser, 2011). Policy and legal mandates provide involuntary motivations for organizations to address complex problems through interorganizational means (Moynihan et al., 2011; Vangen & Huxham, 2011). Interagency collaboration can be explained by the proposition that the more persistent and complex the national-level problem, the more that hierarchically organized agencies require new structures, concepts, and practices to generate responses (Cone, 2013; Dubik, 2009; Kaiser, 2011; Mihm, 2000; Steinhardt, 2005). "In addition to diverse motives for participation, partnerships reflect varying degrees of capacity and involvement when policy requirements initiate their development and/or expansion" (Ivery, 2008, p. 56). In short, collaboration across agencies requires a re-evaluation of top-down management practices.

Understanding the effects of mandates on collaborations is another important consideration. Mandated collaboration can be identified by documents and initiatives that are national in scope and are intended to address issues that require participation from multiple federal agencies and other levels of government and sectors (Mihm, 2012). Interagency collaborations retain elements of discretionary participation and horizontal relationships (Kaiser, 2011). Therefore, mandated forms of interagency organizing still require negotiation over rules, structures, and governing relationships. Thomson, Perry, and Miller's (2009) dimensions, for example, invite questions about the constraints and context of policy-mandated collaborations. In policy-mandated collaborations, are social capital (i.e., mutuality and norms) more or less consequential than the structural dimensions (i.e., governance and administration), or agency (i.e., organizational autonomy) dimensions?

Funding authorizations formalized through the federal budgeting process further differentiate interagency collaboration in the federal sector. Shared behaviors enable agencies to overcome problems associated with budgetary austerity and political uncertainty (Thomson et al., 2009). However, various complex federal budgeting and funding mechanisms govern interagency missions. For example, the purpose statute (31 U.S.C. 1301(a)) prohibits federal officials from using appropriated funds for purposes other than those intended by Congress.

Governmental structure is an important aspect of mandated collaboration. Presidential and congressional leadership can mandate interagency collaboration activities. The proposition that leadership mandates to reform government practices lead to better (or worse) outcomes deserves ongoing consideration from scholars and practitioners (Light, 2008). Examples of mandated collaboration in the national security domain specify accountability to Congress as a feature of policy directives. In one example from the national security domain, in 2008 Congress directed the Secretary of Defense to submit a plan to improve and reform the Department of Defense's (DOD) participation in and contribution to the interagency coordination process on national security issues (Congress, 2008a). In 2009, Congress gave authority to the Secretaries of Defense and State and the Administrator of U.S. Agency for International Development (USAID) to jointly establish an advisory panel to advise, review, and make recommendations on ways to improve coordination (Congress, 2008b). In 2010, Congress required the Secretary of Defense to describe the details of how the Department would coordinate across joint, service, interagency, and coalition activities (Congress, 2009). Supporting these mandates, the GAO asserts the "need for change to improve interagency collaboration on national security matters" (Pendleton, 2010b, p. 2).

The Interagency Environment

The practitioner and scholarly literature chronicles a similar account of contemporary developments, attributing devolution (e.g., contracting-out and third-party service providing), rapid technological change, and competition for scarce resources to explain developments in interagency behavior (Agranoff, 2012; Kettl, 2002; Pendleton, 2010b; Thomson et al., 2009). An understanding of the effects of policy mandates on organizational mission is important to understanding interagency collaboration as a distinct form of collaboration. According to scholars and field experts, the drivers of interagency collaboration include many environmental factors that can affect nongovernmental, public, and private organizations. Policies can be a catalyst for new organizational forms to meet legal requirements levied upon organizations. However, "whether collaborations are mandated or constrained by government, nation-wide policies and local priorities alike will have an effect on the goals of the collaboration and the processes by which they are to be achieved" (Vangen & Huxham, 2011, p. 544).

Despite structural incompatibility with traditional hierarchy, practitioners believe that new interorganizational practices will enable governmental responses to complex problems. "Two-thirds of federal executives believe interagency collaboration is 'critical' to solving geopolitical issues—and will increase mission effectiveness—but ... clearer directives on partnerships must be put in place" (Booz Allen Hamilton, Inc., 2010, p. 1). Partnerships for wicked problems in war and terrorism underscore the need for interagency practices to resolve geopolitical issues.

War and terrorism contributed to interagency wicked problems and created urgent needs for data analysis of complex national security issues

(Heikkila & Gerlak, 2005; Kettl, 2000, 2002). Threat responses required new technologies to meet security demands in the aftermath of 9/11 (Kettl, 2002). These tasks do not fall to a single agency. The era of the so-called unblinking eye saw rapid developments in digital data information processing (*The Economist*, 2012). Satellites and drones were used to gain multiagency advantage in difficult to monitor porous national borders in the war on terror and the war on drugs. Information-sharing between partners is at the heart of planning and organizing for wicked problems in the national security domain.

The drivers of interagency action are abundant and include a diverse set of explicit and implicit mandates. Policy mandates for agency and cross-agency goals can impact interorganizational (i.e., interagency) responses to changing world events. Law and statute governing interagency relationships can have unique limitations on collaboration alternatives. Scholarly findings confirm that the federal sector continues to interact with the private sector and quasi-governmental organizations in ad hoc and persistent fashion, to meet growing demands for various security services (Kettl, 2000, 2002). In the age of sequestration, austerity, and budget uncertainty, agencies face deep resource constraints while their core missions remain unchanged; this is driving them to work together (Bonner, 2013, p. 30). The next section explores a list of mechanisms that are thought to facilitate interagency collaboration practices. The mechanisms were developed from over seven years of GAO study to enable interagency collaboration activities. The need for a framework of mechanisms to enable collaboration imperatives implies that policy mandates by themselves may be insufficient to accomplish policy outcomes.

Applying GAO Collaboration Mechanisms to Interagency Collaborative Behavior

This section explores a list of mechanisms developed by the GAO, and reported by Mihm (2012) in GAO report 12–1022, *Key Considerations for Implementing Interagency Collaborative Mechanisms*. The list is a tool to evaluate collaboration potential at the organization level. The mechanisms are intended to support organizational practices that facilitate interagency collaboration.

Interagency mechanisms for collaboration are defined in the evaluation literature "as any arrangement or application that can facilitate collaboration between agencies" (Mihm, 2012, p. 4). Organizational mechanisms for collaboration encompass an array of organizational capacities including: strategy, organizing for collaboration, leadership, personnel, organizational agreements, joint program efforts, communities of practice, and collaboration technologies (Mihm, 2012). Conceptually, collaboration mechanisms serve many purposes. They are believed to be the foundation for enabling organizational factors like trust and leadership, and for establishing practices between organizations that make collaboration efforts more durable and lasting (Mihm, 2012). Collaboration initiatives are developed to resolve wicked problems. The application of organizational collaboration mechanisms to interagency practices could facilitate (wicked) problem resolution.

Between 2011 and 2012, GAO developed a list of 12 mechanisms to define interagency capacity to facilitate collaboration (Mihm, 2012). GAO developed the list of collaboration mechanisms informed by literature reviews of scholarly and practitioner work, and through interviews with scholarly and practitioner experts (e.g., Robert Agranoff, Eugene Bardach, and representatives from the National Academy of Public Administration) (Mihm, 2012). The list of mechanisms benefitted from over 300 previous evaluations and findings in 36 GAO reports published between 2005 and 2011 (Mihm, 2012). The evaluation included interagency activities in international affairs, defense, and homeland security and others (Mihm, 2000; Pendleton, 2010a, 2010b, 2010c; Scott, 2011; St. Laurent & Williams-Bridgers, 2009; Steinhardt, 2005, 2010). The list of mechanisms is listed next. Next, the mechanisms are applied to an exemplar of inter-agency collaboration in the national security domain, namely humanitarian assistance. GAO's 12 mechanisms are reported in GAO (12–1022) and follow in their original order with brief definitions.

1 Presidential assistants and advisors. This mechanism advocates the need for a Presidential appointee in the Executive Office of the President to focus on momentous issues.
2 Collaboration structures within the Executive Office of the President. Task forces, councils, commissions, committees, or working groups administer consequential but temporary support for interagency issues.
3 National strategies and initiatives. This mechanism formalizes issues in a document or an initiative that cuts across many agencies or levels of government. National-level and organizational strategy should be linked where possible. Issues that cut across organizational boundaries should be addressed in strategic documentation and organizational plans.
4 Interagency groups. This mechanism formalizes the leadership for task forces, working groups, councils, and committees through either agency-level leadership (e.g., agency department heads) or component- and program-level staff.
5 Designation of leadership. This mechanism designates the lead and supporting relationships to further establish accountability. Accountability for lead and support roles and responsibilities includes organization-level designation and acknowledgement by collaborating organizations. Organizational responsibilities may include various administrative functions for facilities, on-site personnel management, and other logistics and operational requirements to fulfill collaboration needs within and across organizational operations. Strategic management of intractable problems should assign responsibility inside

organizations and within the collaboration for various outputs and outcomes.

6   Geographic-based office/co-location. An office may be maintained to facilitate collaboration effort between organizations located in a geographic region. Personnel can also be co-located in one facility.

7   Positions and temporary transfers of personnel. Personnel administration for collaborations should be accomplished deliberately by participating organizations. Assignments to task forces, working groups, councils, and committees, etc. should include defined responsibilities and establish accountability for collaboration at the individual level. GAO identifies three types of positions. First, personnel that work between agencies fill collaborator positions. Second, in liaison positions personnel are temporarily assigned to another agency. Lastly, personnel details permit work to be performed for another agency by personnel who remain assigned to their parent organizations.

8   Specially created interagency offices. These offices have authority and resources to navigate a policy area that spans numerous agencies.

9   Interagency agreements and memorandum of understanding. Agreements may be needed to document a myriad of special organizational arrangements to support collaboration goals.

10   Joint program efforts. At the heart of organizational-level collaboration, GAO identifies three joint program efforts (Mihm, 2012). First, joint budgeting and funding processes establish resources to be used by more than one agency. Second, joint exercising and training leverages resources to prepare organizations to respond together. Interdependence during emergencies at home and abroad spawned a multitude of requirements for interagency and interorganizational training coordination (Morris, Morris, & Jones, 2007). Third, joint development of policies, procedures, and programs requires agreeements and arrangements that are mutually supporting across interagency collaborative effort. Joint development of policies, procedures, and programs is viewed as a prerequisite to joint operational efforts. The intended result is synchronization and interoperability gains across collaborating organizations.

11   Conferences and communities of practice. These forums are required to discuss common problems, to exchange information, and to develop agreements on future actions. Forums may be used to monitor collaboration performance, and determine evaluation and reporting requirements.

12   Collaboration technologies. Technologies for information-sharing such as databases, web chat, web portals, and specialized networks can enable face-to-face and virtual communications between disparately located collaboration partners.

Analyzing Organizational Capacity in the National Security Domain Through the GAO Collaboration Mechanisms

A National Security Interagency Exemplar: Humanitarian Assistance

This section examines a specific example of a complex, wicked problem in the national security domain, namely humanitarian assistance. The following section explores the alignment of practices documented in GAO reports for U.S. government humanitarian assistance with GAO's proposed list of mechanisms. The humanitarian assistance exemplar was drawn from various GAO reports on interagency efforts in national security (GAO 10–801, GAO 10–962, GAO 10–822t). Humanitarian assistance is the aid and action intended to "save lives, alleviate suffering and maintain and protect human dignity during and in the aftermath of man-made crises and natural disasters, as well as to prevent and strengthen preparedness for occurrences" (Global Humanitarian Assistance, 2014, Definition section, para. 1). The GAO reports contain details of interagency collaboration between U.S. government agencies, international partners, and nongovernmental and private organizations in the aftermath of earthquakes that shook Haiti in January 2010 (Pendleton, 2010c). The reports also chronicle periodic humanitarian assistance in Central America during Operation Continuing Promise (Pendleton, 2010c). An exact one-for-one comparison of collaboration mechanisms to interagency practices is not practical conceptually. However, the analysis demonstrates how the mechanisms impacted interagency collaboration practices. The analysis also exposes linkages between factors such as trust that support collaboration practices.

Presidential advisors are mechanisms for collaboration in humanitarian and other interagency initiatives. The National Security staff in the Executive Office of the President includes the Secretary of Defense, the Chairman of the Joint Chiefs of Staff, and the Attorney General and other key members. Advisors to the President play critical roles during emergencies. The Government Accountability Office (GAO) and the Congressional Research Service (CRS) indirectly support intent by Executive leadership to understand the challenges and opportunities of interagency initiatives. Although GAO and the CRS work for Congress, the President appoints the head of GAO, the Comptroller General of the United States, to a 15-year term from a slate of Congressionally proposed candidates. Any of the many offices in the Executive Office of the President can and do serve as advisors to the President, especially during times of emergency like the Haiti earthquakes. Given the military's role during the Haiti response, the Chairman of the Joint Chiefs ostensibly fulfilled reporting responsibilities to the President and other leaders in the aftermath of the humanitarian crisis.

Shared awareness of the security environment establishes a basis for strategic interagency mechanisms. As a collaboration mechanism, the

United States National Security Strategy responded to geographically localized problems by developing goals for interagency and international partner collaboration capacity and capabilities (Obama, 2010). Military organizations have regional responsibilities to address "challenges such as corruption, crime, transnational terrorism, natural disasters, and poverty that impact the security and stability of the region" (Pendleton, 2010c, p. 1). In the same year as the Haiti disaster, in testimony to the Subcommittee on National Security and Foreign Affairs, House of Representatives, the GAO outlined the security environment, with participation by the Department of State and the U.S. Agency for International Development (USAID) and other agencies characterizing "a wide-range of challenges (e.g., terrorism, illicit trafficking, organized crime) that are often exacerbated by conditions of poverty and profound cultural and demographic tensions" (Pendleton, 2010a, p. 1). In the 2010 National Security Strategy a "Whole-of-Government Approach" (p. 14) is cited to "update, balance, and integrate all of the tools of American power" (p. 14) to work with allies and partners. Haiti disaster responders exemplify a "whole-of-government approach" (p. 24) counting 10 interagency partners to develop strategic plans, improve information-sharing and develop compatible policies (Pendleton, 2010c).

Establishing lead and support relationships contribute to mechanisms and practices for delivery of emergency services. Humanitarian assistance operations in the Caribbean region required persistent collaboration between Department of State, U.S. Agency for International Development, Department of Homeland Security, Department of Justice, and the Office of the Director of National Intelligence (Pendleton, 2010c). During the Haiti relief effort the U.S. military performed lead and support roles with interagency partners and nongovernmental organizations (Pendleton, 2010c).

Specific legal mandates reinforce relationships between interagency missions and policy originated collaboration. Pendleton (2010c, p. 7) notes that the 2008 DOD Guidance for Employment of the Force required a test case for U.S. Southern Command "to seek broader involvement from other departments in drafting theater campaign and contingency plans". Given U.S. Southern Command's responsibilities for the geographic region that includes the Caribbean, these plans would be tested by the Haiti response.

Collaboration goals were enhanced by factors of trust, open dialogue, and transparency with partners in the specific domain space (Pendleton, 2010c). These factors contributed to identifying and filling leadership positions by interagency and public-private sector organizations involved in various humanitarian assistance efforts (Pendleton, 2010c). Interagency and nongovernmental partnering increased mission capacity through volunteers for primary interagency missions during the 2009 Continuing Promise humanitarian assistance mission (Pendleton, 2010c). During the Continuing Promise mission, U.S. Public Health Service officers filled 49 medical, engineering, and environmental health positions, while nongovernmental organizations filled 97 medical positions that could not be filled by the military. The addition of nongovernmental medical personnel enabled the interagency mission to increase "medical services by a reported 25 percent more primary care patient treatments, 50 percent more surgical procedures, 33 percent more optometry and eyeglasses services, and 25 percent more outpatient care" (Pendleton, 2010c, p. 13).

Individual positions and organizational structure serve as mechanisms for working with collaboration partners. Top interagency leadership at U.S. Southern Command directed a reorientation away from a Napoleonic (numbered) structure to identify organizational units, and toward a structure associated with interagency goals (Pendleton, 2010c). This orientation resulted in collaborative practices that were not transferrable to the operational emergency response environment during the Haiti disaster relief operations, as the organization was no longer organized for hierarchically arranged command and control relationships required for effective emergency responses (Pendleton, 2010c). Unclear leadership roles and goals are examples of incomplete interagency collaboration mechanisms. In contrast, GAO reports the number of NGOs (nongovernmental organizations including not-for-profit) participating in the Latin American/Caribbean interagency mission rose from 3 in 2007 to 20 in 2009, attributing the rise to the development of an interagency unit designed to work with public and private stakeholders in the domain (Pendleton, 2010c).

Agreements and memoranda of understanding with collaboration stakeholders are effective mechanisms to support collaboration goals. The development of a Public-Private Cooperation Division at U.S. Southern Command as a regional interagency organization was dedicated to engaging the public and private sectors. In one example, the office negotiated details and agreements to work with the largest NGO in South America— Food for the Poor (Pendleton, 2010c). Humanitarian assistance operations to relieve the stresses of poverty and illness abroad increasingly include responses from public-private organizations and nongovernmental organizations. Interagency partnering with Food for the Poor resulted in enhanced collaboration in the form of recurring and more robust humanitarian assistance efforts in South America (Pendleton, 2010c).

Three joint program efforts offered mechanisms for practices at the organizational level of collaboration: budgeting and funding, exercising and training, and policies, procedures, and programs (Mihm, 2012). First, joint budgeting and funding among interagency partners contributed to operations, research, and development for interagency requirements (Pendleton, 2010c). Second, medical and engineering services delivered during Operation Continuing Promise combined service delivery with joint exercises and training. The interagency goal is to provide humanitarian assistance in combination with training for U.S. military and international partner medical personnel and engineers (Pendleton, 2010b, pp. 12–13). Last, the whole-of-government approach was cited as an example of joint development of policies, procedures, and programs. In a report to Congress, GAO noted the need to implement policies and strategies to monitor interagency progress, reporting that collaboration is enabled by improved integration through "coordinated planning and policymaking for deliberate and inclusive interagency process" (Pendleton, 2010b, p. 14). The absence of clear policy can inhibit or prevent collaboration activities in the security domain. In 2010 there was no policy to inform interagency and other collaboration partners on how to collaborate with U.S. Southern Command. Policy and procedures (e.g., to share information) between collaborating organizations during exercises, training, and real-world operations are required to enable collaboration outcomes (Pendleton, 2010c).

As a separate mechanism, GAO documented the importance of information-sharing during exercises and operations, stressing the importance and role of conferences with interagency partners to share expertise (Pendleton, 2010c). As documented by the GAO reports on humanitarian assistance, successful collaborations gain competitive advantage through resource-sharing, including personnel, certain assets, authorities, and intelligence information (Pendleton, 2010c).

Research Findings

The analysis explored a framework of collaboration mechanisms to understand the relationship between factors that support interagency collaboration practices, and between mechanisms that facilitate practices. The list of mechanisms proposed by GAO implies that successful interagency organizations must develop a diverse set of management and leadership capabilities, with foundations in public administration, interorganizational studies, network management, policy, and strategic management. The analysis of mechanisms and the humanitarian assistance exemplar demonstrate the difficulties and challenges of implementing effective interagency collaboration practices. Comparatively, the challenges and failings noted exemplify scholarly and practitioner perspectives documented in the literature.

Pressures to resolve complex problems, limited resources, and complex organizational environments characterize intractable interagency problems. The federal sector struggles with a catalog of wicked interagency problems. At face value, an apparently continuous cycle of national security activity requires interagency collaboration between the Department of Defense, State Department, the international development agency, Homeland Security, and other agencies. As the interagency community reflects back upon a decade of war and threats at home and abroad, yesterday's threats become the historic building blocks to tackle a new generation of interagency wicked problems. The absence of an overarching theoretical framework for interagency collaboration leaves practitioners to choose from a potpourri of extant theories and practices to determine, rather independently, approaches and processes to address collaboration mandates.

Policy-mandated collaboration is differentiated from other forms of collaboration by a lack of voluntary organizational and individual behaviors to initiate participation. Innovative practices to engender collaboration outcomes at the organizational level may be stifled by narrow, unfunded policy objectives. The absence of overarching and mutually reinforcing strategies among collaborating organizations will continue to challenge the development of meaningful measures for collaboration activity.

The complex federal resource management structure is another distinct feature of interagency collaboration. Policy and program mandates may be insufficient to support broad collaboration objectives as mandates do not typically consider an exhaustive list of organizational requirements needed to accomplish policy objectives. Measurements for efficiency and effectiveness have proven insufficient to monitor and measure progress towards complex policy outputs and outcomes. The Office of Management and Budget (OMB) recognizes that program information alone insufficiently evaluates collaboration outcomes (Agranoff, 2006). The area of budgeting and funding deserves further research and coverage to understand the opportunities inherent in joint effort. Legal, cultural, and trust issues may impair interagency creativity and innovation to enhance collaboration practices.

Interagency responsiveness in the national security domain requires further recognition of and definitions for interoperable management concepts and practices. The development of interoperable management concepts adds dimension to the collaboration literature and further distinguishes interagency from other collaboration forms. Collaboration activities in the national security domain are dependent upon interoperability between partner organizations. Information-sharing between interagency and other partners to support interactivity is a wicked problem in and of itself. Interoperability management is therefore an output of interagency collaboration (Agranoff, 2012).

Scholars and practitioners acknowledge the likelihood that interagency managers will default to traditional organizational structure in parallel with new organizational apparatuses (Pendleton, 2009; U.S. Department of Homeland Security, 2015). Organizations must achieve new flexibilities to accommodate and balance interagency collaboration goals with core mission requirements. Hierarchical and collaborative structures must be flexible enough to invite and accommodate participation by nongovernmental and international partners.

Research Recommendations

A research agenda is required to maintain focus on recent interagency experience in the national security domain. Interagency organizational histories provide context to study and understand a range of interagency behaviors. After 11 years of prosecuting two wars, collaboration and collaboration-like practices are common in DOD and other interagency organizations (Kettl, 2002; McGuire et al., 2010). DOD and State Department personnel practiced collaborative behaviors learned during a decade of warfare, and that required multinational, multiagency, and nongovernmental partnerships to address 'wicked problems' associated with expansive nation-building and security responsibilities not seen since World War II.

Meaningful measures for interagency and partner activity in the security domain should be developed. In particular, GAO's work to define organizational mechanisms should be continued to facilitate developments in interagency collaboration. Concepts and definitions for interagency collaboration in the national security domain must achieve meaningful distinctions between the range of interagency behaviors that include cooperative, coordinative, and collaborative interactions. Organizational and environmental context is needed to explain how collaboration phenomenon can remedy complex problems (Bardach, 1998; Clarke & Fuller, 2010; Margerum, 2008; McNamara, 2012; Stanton, 2008; Steinhardt, 2005).

Conclusion

Gray (1989) describes organizational collaborations as a vehicle for action learning where organizations undergo evolutionary and significant changes in response to their environments. Gray suggests that systems and their environments are interdependent to the extent that as one changes it creates a need for change in the other (1989). Collaboration as a change management tool holds much promise for agencies to deliver increased effectiveness in an adaptive and challenging security environment. Continued improvements in interagency collaboration concepts and practices are needed to respond to national security threats that are "unconventional, diffuse, and ambiguous … that arise from multiple sources" (Pendleton, 2010c, p. 1). In the national security domain, collaboration mechanisms may enable peace and security that can be shared with partner nations. Understanding the boundaries of interagency interdependence requires real-world participation in largely unmapped organizational and theoretical terrain. Understanding the features and limitations of interagency interdependence provides a path toward innovation in the federal sector.

This research illustrates the need for a framework to evaluate interagency collaboration capacity that is flexible enough to accommodate a broad range of real-world contexts. By definition, interagency collaboration is a call for interorganizational responses to rapid changes in world events; i.e., to interpret changing truths (Patton, 2002). The necessity for capacities to respond to change represents distinct truths about the interagency environment, and notably the national security domain. The evaluation literature documented a set of defined practices as a means to identify and define ideal organizational relationships (i.e., boundaries). The promise of interagency collaboration as means is to bring resolution as ends to new and recurring national-level problems and challenges.

Note

1 The views presented in this chapter are those of the author and do not necessarily represent the views of DOD or its components.

References

Agranoff, R. (2006). Inside collaborative networks: Ten lessons for public managers. *Public Administration Review*, 66(Special Issue), 56–65.

Agranoff, R. (2007). *Managing within networks: Adding value to public organizations*. Washington, DC: Georgetown University Press.

Agranoff, R. (2012). *Collaborating to manage: A primer for the public sector*. Washington, DC: Georgetown University Press.

Ansell, C., & Gash, A. (2008). Collaborative governance in theory and practice. *Journal of Public Administration Research and Theory*, 18(4), 543–571.

Bardach, E. (1998). *Getting agencies to work together: The practice and theory of managerial craftsmanship*. Washington, DC: Brookings Institution.

Bin, C. (2008). Assessing interorganizational networks for public service delivery: A process-perceived effectiveness framework. *Public Performance & Management Review*, 31(3), 348–363.

Bonner, P. (2013). Balancing task with relationship to create interagency collaboration. *The Public Manager*, 42(2), 30.

Booz Allen Hamilton, Inc. (2010). New study shows interagency collaboration critical to "smart power" but barriers to integration persist—federal executives see range of benefits from smart power (press release).

Bryson, J. M., Berry, F. S., & Kaifeng, Y. (2010). The state of public strategic management research: a selective literature review and set of future directions. *American Review of Public Administration*, 40(5), 495–521.

Clarke, A., & Fuller, M. (2010). Collaborative strategic management: Strategy formulation and implementation by multi-organizational cross-sector social partnerships. *Journal of Business Ethics*, 94, 85–101.

Cone, R. W. (2013). Building the new culture of training. *Military Review*, 93(1), 11–16.

Congress. (2008a). *Duncan Hunter National Defense Authorization Act for Fiscal Year 2009*. (Pub. L. No. 110–417). Washington, DC: U.S. Government Printing Office.

Congress. (2008b). *National Defense Authorization Act for Fiscal Year 2008*. (Pub. L. No. 110–181). Washington, DC: U.S. Government Printing Office.

Congress. (2009). *National Defense Authorization Act for Fiscal Year 2010*. (Pub. L. No. 111–84). Washington, DC: U.S. Government Printing Office.

Dubik, J. M. (2009). Learning at the speed of war. *Army*, 59(4), 2.

Foster, M., & Meinhard, A. (2002). A regression model explaining predisposition to collaborate. *Nonprofit and Voluntary Sector Quarterly*, 31(4), 16.

Global Humanitarian Assistance. (2014). *Defining humanitarian assistance*. Retrieved from www.globalhumanitarianassistance.org/data-guides/defining-humanitarian-aid.

Gray, B. (1989). *Collaborating: Finding common ground for multiparty problems*. San Francisco, CA: Jossey-Bass.

Hardy, C., Phillips, N., & Lawrence, T. B. (2003). Resources, knowledge and influence: The organizational effects of interorganizational collaboration. *Journal of Management Studies*, 40(2), 321–347.

Heikkila, T., & Gerlak, A. K. (2005). The formation of large-scale collaborative resource management institutions: Clarifying the roles of stakeholders, science, and institutions. *The Policy Studies Journal, 33*(4), 583–612.

Ivery, J. A. (2008). Policy mandated collaboration. *Journal of Sociology & Social Welfare, 35*(4), 53–70.

Jenkins, W. O., Jr. (2004). *Federal leadership and intergovernmental cooperation required to achieve first responder interoperable communications (Report to Congressional Committees).* (GAO-04–963T). Washington, DC: U.S. General Accounting Office.

Kaiser, F. M. (2011). *Interagency collaborative arrangements and activities: Types, rationales, considerations* (Report No. 7–5700 R41803). Washington, DC: Congressional Research Service.

Kettl, D. F. (2000). *The global public management revolution.* Washington, DC: Brookings Institution Press.

Kettl, D. F. (2002). *The transformation of governance, public administration for 21st century America.* Baltimore, MD: The Johns Hopkins University Press.

Light, P. C. (2008). A government ill executed: The depletion of the federal service. *Public Administration Review,* (May/June), 413–419.

McGuire, M. (2006). Collaborative public management: Assessing what we know and how we know it. *Public Administration Review, 66,* 33–43. doi: 10.1111/j.1540–6210.2006.00664.x

McGuire, M., Agranoff, R., & Silvia, C. (2010). Collaborative public administration [Special issue]. *Public Administration Review, 66*(s1), 33–43.

McNamara, M. (2012). Starting to untangle the web of cooperation, coordination, and collaboration: A framework for public managers. *International Journal of Public Administration, 35,* 389–401. doi: 10.1080/01900692.2012.655527

Mandell, M. P., & Keast, R. (2008). Evaluating the effectiveness of interorganizational relations through networks. *Public Management Review, 10*(6), 715–731. doi: 10.1080/14719030802423079

Margerum, R. D. (2008). A typology of collaboration efforts in environmental management. *Environmental Management,* (41), 487–500. doi: 10.1007/s00267–008–9067–9

Mihm, J. (2000). *Managing for results: Barriers to interagency coordination.* (GAO/GGD-00–106). Washington, DC: U.S. Government Accountability Office.

Mihm, J. (2012). *Managing for results: Key considerations for implementing interagency collaborative mechanisms.* (GAO-12–1022). Washington, DC: U.S. Government Accountability Office.

Mihm, J. (2014). *Managing for results: Implementation approaches used to enhance collaboration in interagency groups.* (GAO 14–220). Washington, DC: U.S. Government Accountability Office.

Morris, J. C., Morris, E. D., & Jones, D. M. (2007). Reaching for the philosopher's stone: Contingent coordination and the military's response to hurricane Katrina. *Public Administration Review, 67*(s1), 94–106.

Moynihan, D. P., Fernandez, S., Kim, S., LeRoux, K. M., Piotrowski, S. J., Wright, B. E., et al. (2011). Performance regimes amidst governance complexity. *Journal of Public Administration Research & Theory, 21*(s1), 141–155.

Obama, B. (2010). *National security strategy.* Washington, DC: White House.

O'Toole, L. J., Jr., & Meier, K. J. (2003, August). *Managing upward, downward, and outward: Networks, hierarchical relationships and performance.* Paper presented at the annual meeting of the American Political Science Association, Philadelphia, PA.

Page, S. (2003). Entrepreneurial strategies for managing interagency collaboration. *Journal of Public Administration Research and Theory*, 13(3), 30. doi: 10.1093/jopart/mug026

Patton, M. Q. (2002). *Qualitative research and evaluation methods.* Thousand Oaks, CA: Sage.

Pendleton, J. (2009). *Defense management actions needed to address stakeholder concerns, improve interagency collaboration, and determine full costs associated with the U.S. Africa command.* (GAO 09–181). Washington, DC: U.S. Government Accountability Office. Retrieved from http://purl.access.gpo.gov/GPO/LPS113398.

Pendleton, J. (2010a). *Interagency collaboration practices and challenges at DOD's Southern and Africa commands.* (GAO 10–962T). Washington, DC: U.S. Government Accountability Office.

Pendleton, J. (2010b). *Key challenges and solutions to strengthen interagency collaboration.* (GAO-10–822T). Washington, DC: U.S. Government Accountability Office.

Pendleton, J. (2010c). *U.S. southern command demonstrates interagency collaboration, but its Haiti disaster response revealed challenges conducting a large military operation.* (GAO 10–801). Washington, DC: U.S. Government Accountability Office.

Rainey, H. G. (2009). *Understanding and managing public organizations* (4th ed.). San Francisco, CA: Jossey-Bass.

Scott, G. A. (2011). *Veterans' education benefits: Enhanced guidance and collaboration could improve administration of the post-9/11 GI Bill program.* (GAO 11–356R). Washington, DC: U.S. Government Accountability Office.

St. Laurent, J. A., & Williams-Bridgers, J. L. (2009). *Interagency collaboration: Key issues for Congressional oversight of national security strategies, organizations, workforce, and information sharing (Report to Congressional Committees).* (GAO 09–904SP). Washington, DC: U.S. Government Accountability Office.

Stanton, T. (2008). *Improving collaboration by federal agencies: An essential priority for the next administration.* Washington, DC: National Academy of Public Administration.

Steinhardt, B. (2005). *Results-oriented government: Practices that can help enhance and sustain collaboration among federal agencies.* (GAO-06–15). Washington, DC: U.S. Government Accountability Office.

Steinhardt, B. (2010). *An overview of professional development activities intended to improve interagency collaboration.* (GAO 11–108). Washington, DC: U.S. Government Accountability Office.

The Economist. (2012). Difference engine: Unblinking eye in the sky. Retrieved from www.economist.com/blogs/babbage/2012/01/civilian-drones.

Thomson, A. M., Perry, J. L., & Miller, T. K. (2009). Conceptualizing and measuring collaboration. *Journal of Public Administration Research and Theory*, 19(1), 23–56.

Trist, E. L. (1983). Referent organizations and the development of interorganizational domains. *Human Relations*, 36(3), 22.

U.S. Department of Homeland Security. (2015, January 27). *DHS history.* Retrieved from www.dhs.gov/history.

Vangen, S., & Huxham, C. (2011). The tangled web: Unraveling the principle of common goals in collaborations. *Journal of Public Administration Research & Theory*, 22(4), 731–760.

Whetten, D. A., & Bozeman, B. (1984). *Policy coordination and interorganizational relations: Some guidelines for sharing power.* Paper presented at the Conference on Shared Power, Humphrey Institute and School of Management, University of Minnesota.

14 Future Trends in Collaboration Research

Katrina Miller-Stevens and John C. Morris

Introduction

The first chapter of this book presents the argument that 30 years of work in the area of collaboration have produced a number of perspectives explaining the concept in addition to many unanswered questions in collaboration research. Thus, our goal in this book is to provide a more thorough understanding of the theoretical and practical implications of collaboration and the state of knowledge in the field. To accomplish this task, the book began by addressing definitional aspects of collaboration, then exploring theoretical advancements of the field, concluding with examples of the practical applications of the concept. We provide a collection of ideas that we believe will challenge the reader, as well as help the reader synthesize many ideas and discussions in the dynamic study of collaboration.

At the beginning of the book, we note five overarching themes that have been identified to help provide clarity on the topic, each of which has been woven throughout the book. The five overarching themes include (1) definitional clarity is a challenge; (2) collaboration is constantly evolving; (3) collaboration can be understood as both organizational process and structure; (4) not all collaboration is equal; and (5) interdisciplinary approaches to collaboration are fruitful. This closing chapter begins with a review of each theme and examples of its presence throughout the book. The chapter ends with a discussion of unanswered questions and future trends in collaboration research.

Revisiting the Themes in this Book

One of the most important contributions of this book is to help academics, students, and practitioners sort through the dynamic body of literature defining collaboration. The first theme noted in this book is that the *definitional clarity of collaboration* is complex and no universal definition exists. We dedicate an entire chapter to address this issue, but the theme is prominent in the introduction of every chapter of the book. In our quest for a solid definition of collaboration, we run into even more dimensions and intricacies that muddle our search.

In our chapter dedicated to the definitional issue, Mayer and Kenter (Chapter 3) identify nine elements they consider to be critical to defining collaboration. Drawing from an expansive review of the literature, they note that most definitions of collaboration include the elements of communication, consensus decision-making, diverse stakeholders, goals, leadership, shared resources, shared vision, social capital, and trust. While these elements appear in many definitions of collaboration within this book, the elements are missing from others. What most of the definitions have in common is the foundational link to Gray's (1985, 1989) initial work in collaboration that acknowledged a need to study the processes and operational aspects of parties working together to solve problems.

The search for a definition is also confounded by the use of 'collaboration' as an adjective, rather than a noun. Machado, Miller-Stevens, and Joannou Menefee (Chapter 10) refer to collaborative advocacy, while Leuenberger and Reed (Chapter 12) discuss collaborative governance. McNamara (Chapter 6) adopts a descriptive use of the word 'collaboration' by exploring collaborative public management, the collaborative convener, and the collaborative entrepreneur. These chapters identify specific activities within civil society that are conducted in a collaborative manner.

From this brief overview, and as illustrated in the chapters in this book, our second theme is clear that *collaboration is constantly evolving*. Williams's (Chapter 2) work on the theoretical development of collaboration thoroughly addresses the conceptual changes of collaboration and the frameworks and typologies that have emerged to explain the varying interpretations of this concept. His chapter concludes by offering four observations that help us understand why the field is constantly evolving, and why there is no solid definition of collaboration. First, emergent behavior in collaborative processes makes theoretical generalizability and conceptual operationalization of this concept challenging. Second, frameworks and typologies capture different relationships between collaboration input, process, and output variables. Third, the frameworks and typologies are not generalizable to different contexts and situations. Finally, the distinction of typologies and frameworks explaining collaboration, cooperation, or coordination is not always clear. Thus, the field of collaboration is constantly evolving to help identify missing elements of existing frameworks and typologies, and to create frameworks and typologies to apply to new contexts.

As part of the effort to sort through frameworks and typologies of collaboration, our third theme emerges that *collaboration can be understood as both organizational process and structure*. Much of the literature on collaboration addresses the processes between organizations within a collaboration, most often as the process related to inputs (in the form of resources) and methods used to achieve the outputs (in the form of tasks accomplished or decisions made) of the collaboration. Many of the chapters in this book discuss collaboration from the organizational process perspective. For example, Joannou Menefee (Chapter 7) explores the role of conflict in the collaborative process. Her work addresses the notion that parties in a collaboration have a common goal, but they may not agree on the path to goal achievement. McNamara (Chapter 6) discusses the role of the collaborative entrepreneur as the person tasked with developing relationships between actors in the collaboration, relevant stakeholders, and the external environment.

Aside from the process perspective, the structure of a collaboration is also a dominant theme in the book. It is generally agreed upon that collaboration occurs in an interorganizational environment where relationships form between two or more organizations. The specific forms of interactions between actors—or what these collaborations look like—differs depending on the context of the research. For some, the focus is on a specific domain such as Martinez (Chapter 13) who provides a discussion of the structure of collaborations in the national security domain. In a similar manner, McDowell (Chapter 11) explores the role that the judiciary plays as a collaborative partner. She proposes three types of collaboration that occur in the judiciary including within branch, between branch, and external branch collaboration.

Two of the chapters in the book offer new models to explore both organizational processes and structure of collaboration. Williams, Merriman, and Morris (Chapter 9) suggest a new perspective on collaboration through life-cycle models found in the organizational theory literature. The authors propose a revised life-cycle model for collaboration that includes six discrete phases a collaboration moves through including issue, assembly and structure, productivity, rejuvenation, decline, and dissipation. Miller-Stevens, Henley, and Diaz-Kope (Chapter 8) also present a new model to view dimensions of collaborative federalism from a governance perspective. Their model illustrates collaborative relationships between federal, state, and local government agencies with organizations in the nonprofit and public sectors, and how elements of collaborative governance impact these relationships.

The fourth theme found throughout the book is that *not all collaboration is equal*. Numerous chapters in the book refer to previous literature that classifies different forms of collaboration along a continuum, most often referring to the continuum of cooperation–coordination–collaboration. Williams (Chapter 2) addresses the theoretical development of this continuum, among other continuums, and helps the reader untangle the intermingled meanings of these concepts. In a related vein of research, McNamara (Chapter 4) deciphers the differences between mandated and voluntary collaboration by exploring what procedural, structural, or managerial differences exist between the two types of collaboration. In this effort, McNamara expands an existing model to include and operationalize mandated and voluntary collaboration on the continuum of cooperation–coordination–mandated collaboration–voluntary collaboration.

Finally, the last theme carried throughout this book is that *interdisciplinary approaches to collaboration are fruitful*. While much of the literature on collaboration is driven from the perspectives of public administration and policy, this book expands this body of literature by incorporating approaches from different fields of knowledge to help explain collaboration. Examples of this theme are plentiful throughout the book and provide a wide range of perspectives. For example, Grasse and Ward (Chapter 5) relate the field of biology to explain networks and collaboration, while also incorporating literature from the nonprofit sector. Miller-Stevens, Henley, and Diaz-Kope (Chapter 8), Machado, Miller-Stevens, and Joannou Menefee (Chapter 10) and Leuenberger and Reed (Chapter 12) also incorporate concepts from nonprofit and civil society literatures into their chapters. McDowell (Chapter 11) combines ideas from legal and judiciary perspectives into her discussion of collaboration, while Williams, Merriman, and Morris (Chapter 9) adapt organizational theory concepts to ideas of collaboration.

As illustrated, the five themes presented in Chapter 1 of this book thread their way throughout the volume. We acknowledge, however, that many other themes exist that were not included in our list of five. Our purpose in identifying the five themes is to add some clarity and structure to the discussion of collaboration, and we hope this approach has been useful to the reader. While the purpose of this volume is to expand the state of knowledge in the area of collaboration, we also hope the reader will finish this book with a list of questions for future research. To begin this discussion, we offer a few suggestions of our own for future research in this area.

The Unanswered Questions: Future Trends in Collaboration Research

The chapters in this volume have raised as many questions as they have attempted to answer. If we are correct that the study of collaboration is an evolving field of inquiry that is still (more or less) in its infancy, then the preponderance of unanswered questions should be neither surprising nor worrisome. The underlying purpose of this volume is to identify the 'cutting edge' of collaboration research, but such efforts have two equally important purposes: to understand the state of knowledge in a knowledge arena, but also to understand the future of that knowledge arena. We thus conclude this project by delineating some specific questions and streams of inquiry in collaboration research that are ripe for further action by scholars in the field.

Why Does Collaboration Fail?

Much has been written in the past 30 years about how to succeed at collaborative energies. Efforts at theory-building have focused almost entirely on the conditions for successful collaboration, as well as how to detect 'success' in collaborative settings. Notably missing from the literature, however, are efforts to understand why collaboration fails. Empirically, not all collaborations are successful, yet we have little guidance to help us understand the underlying causes for failure. On one hand, we may be tempted to suggest that collaborations fail because they fail to meet some precondition necessary at the formation of the interaction. However, given the definitional uncertainty present in this arena, there is little guidance provided to understand which preconditions are critical for success. We may also be tempted to conclude that flaws in the process of collaboration can lead to failure, but which elements of collaboration process are critical for success? Is an inability to reach initial agreement about goals sufficient cause for failure?

A more basic issue concerns the very definition of 'success.' Is 'success' defined by outputs from the process, such as agreements, or tangible, positive changes in the nature of the problem to which collaboration is applied (see Mandarano, 2008)? Or, as Morris, Gibson, Leavitt, and Jones (2013) suggest, is 'success' better defined as a successful process for its own sake? In other words, if collaborative efforts beget further collaborative efforts, can claims of success be substantiated?

One may also consider whether collaborations may reach a natural end point, as suggested by the life-cycle chapter in this volume. The study of collaboration is new enough that we do not yet have access to longitudinal studies of collaboration, so the notion of a life cycle of collaboration is largely speculative at this point. However, if one accepts the premise that collaboration is a form of organization, then it seems reasonable to assume that collaborations are subject to the same forces as other forms of organization. It is also possible (although somewhat unlikely) that the problem for which the collaboration was formed is no longer either relevant or important enough to warrant large-scale effort.

We suggest that all of these factors may be possible. However, lacking a sufficiently robust theoretical framework through which to address this question is a significant barrier to progress on this question.

Do We Need a Single Definition of Collaboration?

In the first chapter of this book, we raised the question of the importance of a single working definition of collaboration, as well as the consequences for the lack of a single definition. Although Chapter 3 addresses the issue of definition, the careful reader will note that none of the chapters in this volume (including Chapter 3) offer a single, unambiguous definition of the term. While some may view this condition as a weakness (see Wood & Gray, 1991), we prefer to interpret this as evidence of the need for additional research and debate among scholars in the field.

Furthermore, if we are correct in our observation that there is more than one 'flavor' of collaboration, it may well be the case that no single definition, or set of characteristics, can adequately capture the richness of the range of interactions subsumed under the banner of 'collaboration.' The distinction between 'voluntary' and 'mandated' collaboration illustrates this point: if we accept that both types of interaction exist, then any definition of 'collaboration' must necessarily exclude statements about the entry of participants into the interaction. An alternative might be to develop a single, broad definition of collaboration, and then work to develop definitions for each identified subtype of interaction. We suggest that such an ideal is very much a future state, but one that scholars in the field should consider.

An alternative possibility worthy of exploration is that the definition of collaboration depends largely on the underlying ontological, epistemological, or methodological approach adopted by the observer. If one conceives of collaborations as a naturalistic phenomenon, for example, it may be that the operative definition of 'collaboration' is different than one who conceives of collaboration in a rational, positivistic manner. Most efforts to define collaboration, including those in this volume, tend to treat the collaboration literature in a holistic manner, but it is reasonable to suggest that a nuanced categorization of the literature may reveal more agreement within categories than is evident when viewing the literature in its entirety.[1] It remains the subject of future research to determine whether such differences exist.

Are Existing Typologies of Collaboration Adequate?

Related to the question of definition is the issue of the utility of existing typologies of collaboration. Based on the work in this volume, we may reasonably conclude that collaboration is not a monolithic concept, but rather a form of interaction that is highly variable and dependent upon the setting in which it is found. While many scholars have offered typologies of collaboration (along with other forms of interaction), there is insufficient empirical evidence at this point to confirm or disconfirm the utility of these typologies. The lack of empirical evidence gathered through replication studies leaves us no alternative but to rely largely on intuition and anecdotal evidence. From a methodological point of view, the overwhelming preponderance of the extant literature reports case study data, each with its own framework, assumptions, and methodological protocol. The same critique can thus be applied to the collaboration literature as was applied to the first generation of implementation literature by Goggin, Bowman, Lester, and O'Toole (1990): that the literature is "atheoretical, case-specific, and noncumulative" (p. 13). To combat this state of affairs it is critical that existing typologies be applied and evaluated in alternative settings to determine whether the typologies have merit. The nature of the work may well lend itself to case study methodologies, but the lack of replication limits the theoretical (and practical) utility of these typologies.

We suggest that the current academic environment places a great deal of emphasis on the development of new theory, at the expense of replication. To the extent this is true, the incentives and rewards (publications, grants, etc.) are skewed to those whose work is somehow different than the extant work. We believe a more productive path is to combine deductive and inductive approaches to empirical research, with the explicit goal to confirm or disconfirm existing typologies. A study could begin by testing an existing typology or framework (deductive), and a determination made about the utility of that framework. If the framework is confirmed, we have further evidence to support the framework. If the framework is disconfirmed, either in part or in whole, then the researcher might offer an alternative formulation based on the data from that effort. This inductive effort would seek to modify the existing framework based on the new data, with the explicit goal of reporting both successes and failures based on the original framework.

What Motivates People (and Organizations) to Collaborate?

The underlying motivations for collaboration are not well understood by scholars. The extant literature generally describes collaboration as a voluntary process, which suggests that motivations are important. However, if we are correct that collaboration can be either voluntary or mandated (in the case of public organizations), then motivation assumes a different role in collaboration theory, depending on the nature of the incentive present. There will also be a difference between individual (or personal) motivation and organizational motivation. While there is a broad literature that discusses both personal- and organizational-level motivation, the collaboration literature has yet to embrace this issue.

What Kinds of Problems is Collaboration Best Suited to Solve?

Much of the collaboration literature presumes that collaboration is employed to address "wicked problems" (see Rittel & Webber, 1973)—problems so large and complex that they defy solutions, and that cannot be solved by just one organization (Gray, 1989; Morris et al., 2013). This point of view is so pervasive in the literature that the existence of such a problem is taken almost as a necessary precondition to collaboration.

One policy arena in which a great deal of collaboration research has been conducted is that of watershed management. There is a burgeoning body of work that suggests collaboration is not only appropriate to address watershed management problems, but that collaboration can be exceptionally successful in this arena (Leach, 2006; Margerum, 2008; Morris et al., 2013). Watershed management problems often span multiple political jurisdictions over a large area, and collaboration seems to be a means to bring disparate actors into a process to address watershed issues. Collaboration has also been applied to many other arenas, including transportation (Ergun, Kuyzu, & Savelsbergh, 2007), social services (Bronstein, 2003; Graham & Barter, 1999), wildlife management (Reed, 2015) education (Lawson, 2004), and emergency management (Simo & Bies, 2007; Waugh & Streib, 2006). In spite of this range of policy arenas and problems, we have little in the way of guidance to suggest the conditions under which collaboration is appropriate. There is a clear need for better theory to understand the nature of the problems for which collaboration is best suited. Is there an ideal (or a minimum) 'size' of problem? Are there limits on the number of stakeholders that can be accommodated in a collaborative effort? Is there a geographic limitation on the appropriateness of collaboration, as suggested by Morris et al. (2013)? Although the literature contains many recommendations, these statements are largely atheoretical, limited in application, and thus of little use to guide future research or practice.

As noted earlier in this chapter, the extant literature on collaboration leans heavily on case study methods, which in turn limits the generalizability of the results reported in that literature. A concomitant feature of the literature is the rather remarkable array of settings in which collaborative activity has been studied. At first glance, the casual observer may conclude that collaboration works nearly everywhere, as most published research reports on cases of successful collaboration. A closer inspection of the literature reveals that, while the range of settings is indeed wide, it is not deep—that is, we do not find replication studies in different policy arenas. Without additional cases to examine, we can say little about any single policy arena.[2] Additional work is needed to determine whether there are any patterns present within different arenas.

Can Public Agencies 'Manage' Collaboration?

One of the enduring debates in the collaboration literature revolves around the question of whether collaboration can be 'managed' in the same sense that a public organization can be managed. Theorists such as Agranoff and McGuire (2003), Mattessich, Murray-Close, and Monsey (2001), and Weber and Khademian (2008) argue that there is an implicit set of skills and techniques available to managers that allow for the effective management of collaboration. Other scholars such as Leach (2006) and Ansell and Gash (2007) suggest that the skills required to make collaboration work are fundamentally different than those required for traditional agency-based public management.

Underlying these efforts is a premise that requires additional conceptualization and debate. If a network-based model of collaboration is operative, then participation in the interaction is necessarily voluntary. Most network-based work related to voluntary collaboration defines the interaction as willing participation between equals. While some "convener" role must exist to provide a focal point for the interaction (see McNamara & Morris, 2012), the lack of barriers to entry into the interaction, coupled with a requirement for participative decision-making (Beierle, 1999; Kathi & Cooper, 2007; Morris et al., 2013) raise reasonable questions about the degree to which the term 'management' can apply to collaborative interactions. Conversely, if one assumes that participants can be mandated to collaborate (see Chapter 4), then the underlying premises of collaboration are necessarily altered. Because a mandate is, in effect, an authoritative order in the Weberian sense, more traditional conceptions of public management may be more suited to collaboration.

The question of collaborative management is especially relevant in the case of what Moore and Koontz (2003) refer to as "mixed" collaboration forms—collaboration that includes actors in the form of both agencies and citizens. While traditional management processes and values are well understood by agency participants, citizen participants may chafe under a set of practices best suited for an environment in which legal-rational authority empowers participants according to rank. Moreover, requirements for process and adherence to rules (see Kaufman, 1977) for accountability might be viewed as inefficient, constraining, and counterproductive. In short, goal-oriented individuals and a process-driven environment may make 'management' of collaborative activities problematic. Additional work is needed to better define the role of 'management' in collaborative settings, and to develop both models and useful advice to practitioners for how to reconcile a need for management (and public accountability) in a setting that encourages rampant egalitarianism.

How Can Scholars Better Translate Collaboration Theory into Practice?

At the heart of the scholarly literature in collaboration is a general desire to link collaboration theory to collaboration practice. As noted elsewhere in this chapter, much of the work to date has been grounded in case study approaches, roughly evenly split between deductive approaches (e.g., Bryson, Crosby, & Stone, 2006; Morris et al., 2013; Sabatier et al., 2005), and inductive approaches (e.g., Koontz & Thomas, 2006; Nyerges, Jankowski, Tuthill, & Ramsey, 2006; Raededke, Nilon, & Rikoon, 2001). Other scholars speak directly to the link between theory and practice. Ansell and Gash (2007) provide a framework to discern the important variables in successful collaboration, an undertaking similar to that of Mattessich et al. in 2001. The goal of this work is to provide actionable information to aid practitioners in the formation and operation of collaborative efforts.

In our judgment, collaboration is an arena in which there remains a communication gap between practitioners and theorists. As Gray (1989) notes, practitioners have a desire to work together to solve problems, whether they make the choice willingly or whether they "fail" (Bryson et al., 2006) into collaboration. Our own research into collaboration leads us to conclude that many practitioners are drawn to the idea of collaboration, but have little idea about how to carry out a collaborative effort (Morris et al., 2013). This is not to suggest that collaboration designed and implemented by practitioners cannot be successful, but rather that success may be more a question of luck than careful deliberation and planning. The kinds of questions raised in our discussion are critical not only to efforts to understand collaboration in a conceptual sense, but to efforts to translate the theoretical strides into ideas, lessons, and cautionary tales that will allow for successful collaboration in practice.

Conclusion

The last 30 years has seen a rather remarkable leap in our knowledge about the kinds of interactions possible to address wicked problems, particularly the interaction referred to as 'collaboration.' While we know much about collaboration, there is much yet to learn. In spite of the growth in our knowledge, we have done little as a discipline to address Wood and Gray's (1991) observation concerning the definition of collaboration. If 'collaboration' is indeed one type of interaction along a continuum of interactions (and we suggest that it is), then we must be better able to separate 'collaboration' from its neighbors. Until we are better able to define the unique characteristics of collaboration, we will be limited in our ability as researchers to develop generalizable theory, or provide useful guidance to practitioners to aid their efforts to ameliorate their 'wicked problems.'

In spite of this limitation, we also suggest that the future of collaboration research is bright—there are still many unanswered questions, and much to be learned. As is clear in this volume, these unanswered questions are capturing the attention of a new generation of scholars, and they bring both an enthusiasm for the endeavor and the ability to rest on the shoulders of the previous generation of scholars. The past 30 years of research has produced a solid foundation of knowledge on which to build. As public resources continue to decline, traditional approaches to address public problems will become less useful, and alternative approaches such as collaboration will be more important. The ability to muster resources and work together across traditional sectoral boundaries will be an important component to future governance, and the knowledge of how to both understand these imperatives and how to make them work in practice is the challenge for the next generation of scholars. If the work in this volume is any indication, the future is in good hands. Or, as Pat McDonald (1986) of the band Timbuk3 wrote, "The future's so bright, I gotta wear shades."

Notes

1 We are indebted to Andrew Williams for helping to crystallize this point.
2 An exception to this may be the area of watershed management; a large (and growing) body of work that examines this arena is available. While a full examination of this case is beyond the scope of this chapter, we contend that the existing body of work is consistent enough to suggest that watershed management may be well suited to collaborative efforts. However, we must also note that many of the other limitations noted in this chapter also exist in this arena—a lack of definitive theory, clear definitions, and a general reliance on case study findings.

References

Agranoff, R., & Mcguire, M. (2003). Collaborative public management: New strategies for local governments. Washington, DC: Georgetown Press.

Ansell, C., & Gash, A. (2007). Collaborative governance in theory and practice. Journal of Public Administration Research and Theory, 18, 543–571.

Beierle, T. C. (1999). Using social goals to evaluation public participation in environmental decisions. Policy Studies Review, 16(3/4), 75–103.

Bronstein, L. R. (2003). A model for interdisciplinary collaboration. Social Work, 48(3), 297–306.

Bryson, J., Crosby, B., & Stone, M. (2006). The design and implementation of cross-sector collaborations: Propositions from the literature. Public Administration Review, 66, 44–53.

Ergun, O., Kuyzu, G., & Savelsbergh, M. (2007). Reducing truckload transportation costs through collaboration. Transportation Science, 41(2), 206–221.

Goggin, M., Bowman, A. O., Lester, J. P., & O'Toole, L. J., Jr. (1990). Implementation theory and practice: Toward a third generation. Glenview, IL: Scott, Foresman/Little, Brown Higher Education.

Graham, J. R., & Barter, K. (1999). Collaboration: A social work practice method. Families in Society: The Journal of Contemporary Social Services, 80(1), 6–13.

Gray, B. (1985). Conditions facilitating interorganizational collaboration. Human Relations, 38(10), 911–936.

Gray, B. (1989). Collaborating: Finding common ground for multiparty problems. San Francisco, CA: Jossey-Bass.

Kathi, P. C., & Cooper, T. L. (2007). Connecting neighborhood councils and city agencies: Trust building through the learning and design forum process. Journal of Public Affairs Education, 13(3/4), 617–630.

Kaufman, H. (1977). Red tape, its origins, uses, and abuses. Washington, DC: Brookings Institution Press.

Koontz, T., & Thomas, C. (2006). What do we know and need to know about the environmental outcomes of collaborative management? Public Administrative Review, 66(Special Issue), 111–121.

Lawson, H. A. (2004). The logic of collaboration in education and the human services. Journal of Interprofessional Care, 18(3), 225–237.

Leach, W. (2006). Collaborative public management and democracy: Evidence from western watershed partnerships. Public Administrative Review, 66(Special Issue), 100–110.

McDonald, P. (1986). The future's so bright, I gotta wear shades. Title track from the album Greetings from Timbuk3, I.R.S. Records. Retrieved from http://en.wikipedia.org/wiki/The_Future%27s_So_Bright,_I_Gotta_Wear_Shades.

McNamara, M. W., & Morris, J. C. (2012). More than a one-trick pony: Exploring the contours of a multi-sector convener. Journal for Nonprofit Management, 15(1), 84–103.

Mandarano, L. (2008). Evaluating collaborative environmental planning outputs and outcomes: Restoring and protecting habitat and the New York-New Jersey harbor estuary program. Journal of Planning and Education Research, 27, 456–468.

Margerum, R. D. (2008). A typology of collaboration efforts in environmental management. Environmental Management, 41(4), 487–500.

Mattessich, P. W., Murray-Close, M., & Monsey, B. R. (2001). Collaboration: What makes it work (2nd ed.). St. Paul, MN: Fieldstone Alliance.

Moore, E., & Koontz, T. (2003). A typology of collaborative watershed groups: Citizen-based, agency-based and mixed partnerships. *Society and Natural Resources, 16*, 451–460.

Morris, J. C., Gibson, W. A., Leavitt, W. M., & Jones, S. C. (2013). *The case for grassroots collaboration: Social capital and ecosystem restoration at the local level.* Lanham, MD: Lexington.

Nyerges, T., Jankowski, P., Tuthill, D., & Ramsey, K. (2006). Collaborative water resource decision support: Results of a field experiment. *Annals of the Association of American Geographers, 96*(4), 699–725.

Raededke, A., Nilon, C., & Rikoon, S. (2001). Factors affecting landowner participation in ecosystem management: A case study in south-central Missouri. *Wildlife Society Bulletin, 29*(1), 195–206.

Reed, C. (2015). *Saving the Pryor Mountain mustang: A legacy of local and federal cooperation.* Reno, NV: University of Nevada Press.

Rittel, H. W. J., and Webber, M. (1973). Dilemmas in a general theory of planning. *Policy Sciences, 4*, 155–169.

Sabatier, P. A., Focht, W., Lubell, M., Trachtenberg, Z., Vedlitz, A., & Matlock, M. (2005). *Swimming upstream: Collaborative approaches to watershed management.* Cambridge, MA: MIT Press.

Simo, G., & Bies, A. L. (2007). The role of nonprofits in disaster response: An expanded model of cross-sector collaboration. *Public Administration Review, 67*(s1), 125–142.

Waugh, W. L., & Streib, G. (2006). Collaboration and leadership for effective emergency management. *Public Administration Review, 66*(s1), 131–140.

Weber, E., & Khademian, A. (2008). Wicked problems, knowledge challenges, and collaborative capacity builders in network settings. *Public Administration Review, 68*(2), 334–349.

Wood, D., & Gray, B. (1991). Toward a comprehensive theory of collaboration. *Journal of Applied Behavioral Science, 27*(2), 139–162.

Index

Page numbers in *italics* denote tables, those in **bold** denote figures.

PG 89-115
PG 199-218

Made in the USA
Columbia, SC
09 August 2022